FEMALE SOLDIERS —
COMBATANTS OR NONCOMBATANTS?

FEMALE SOLDIERS — COMBATANTS OR NONCOMBATANTS?

Historical and Contemporary Perspectives

Edited by Nancy Loring Goldman

CONTRIBUTIONS IN WOMEN'S STUDIES, NUMBER 33

 GREENWOOD PRESS
WESTPORT, CONNECTICUT • LONDON, ENGLAND

Library of Congress Cataloging in Publication Data
Main entry under title:

Female soldiers—combatants or noncombatants?

    (Contributions in women's studies, ISSN 0147-104X ; no. 33)
    Bibliography: p.
    Includes index.
    1. Women soldiers—Addresses, essays, lectures.
    2. Combat—Addresses, essays, lectures. I. Goldman, Nancy L. II. Series.
UB416.F45   355.1'088042   81-13318
ISBN 0-313-23117-6 (lib. bdg.)   AACR2

Library of Congress Catalog Card Number: 81-13318
ISBN: 0-313-23117-6
ISSN: 0147-104X

First published in 1982

Greenwood Press
A division of Congressional Information Service, Inc.
88 Post Road West
Westport, Connecticut 06881

Printed in the United States of America

10 9 8 7 6 5 4 3 2 1

To the Fellows of the Inter-University Seminar
on Armed Forces and Society

CONTENTS

TABLES

FOREWORD

Shall women be involved in combat? That is, shall women be integrated into military assault units in the contemporary U.S. military establishment? This is an emotionally charged issue that raises complex questions about military organization.

Female Soldiers—Combatants or Noncombatants? is a valuable contribution to this debate. It examines in depth numerous case studies that probe historically and analytically for countries in Europe, Africa, and Asia the record of the use of women in the military and their combat performance. The findings make fascinating reading for the student of military organization and military operations. These cases also present the issues policymakers concerned with women in combat have to confront.

But the question of women in combat itself needs to be clarified; this volume makes a pointed contribution to identifying two different meanings of the term. First, in many nations' armed forces there has been an increase in the use of women in military organizations. These women perform essentially noncombat and combat-support tasks. They engage in traditional, female tasks in the health field, communications and in administration. Recently, some have been employed in traditional male assignments, as, for example, mechanics and military police. Society and its political leaders think of these women as engaged in noncombat or combat-support roles, but there is an important sense in which these women are in combat. In the event of hostilities they are located in combat zones and will be exposed to the lethal consequences of enemy military action. Although they are located in combat zones, they are restricted in their ability and opportunity to perform combat roles.

The second meaning of women in combat involves the selection, training, and preparation of women in order to participate as combat personnel in military assault units—ground, air, and naval. Assault units carry the war to the enemy and produce either victory or defeat. In the course of battle, assault units may take up defensive positions; and, in fact, with the growth of a deterrent strategy defensive positions proliferate. But the crucial criterion is that assault units both inflict casualties and are subject to casualties. When this volume analyzes the historical record of women in combat, it is not limited solely to the first meaning of combat but is also concerned with the second meaning. If the first meaning creates controversy, then the second raises deeply disruptive political issues.

The importance of this study rests in the careful collection and analysis of the documentary data both on the expansion of the combat support roles of women and on the direct use of women in combat units. Both historically and geographically the scope of the study is immense; the case studies focus on the period since the American and French revolutions and on a broad sampling of industrialized and developing nations.

We live in a time in which social scientists emphasize the importance of so-called thought-out decisions and the development of explicit policies. They may be correct in pointing out that in the contemporary period it has become more and more important to formulate a precise policy concerning the utilization of women in the military. In the past, according to my reading of this research, the expansion of the role of women in the armed forces came slowly and came more as a result of the immediate pressure of military circumstances and less as the result of deliberate decisions. This is not to overlook the importance of ideological and cultural factors as barriers to the mobilization of women into the armed forces and especially into combat units. To a considerable extent, the increasing use of women as support personnel came slowly in military units because women were thought of as a personnel pool that could replace men. Then, men could assume combat and front-line duties. But as this process of replacement has been pressed women have become exposed extensively to the dangers of enemy firepower. In any future conventional war in central Europe, women can certainly be expected to be subjected to extensive enemy fire. I speak not of civilian casualties but of support personnel in uniform. In the United States and other highly industrialized nations with complex weapons and massive logistical systems, under conditions of conventional hostilities the distinction between combat support and actual involvement in combat becomes vague.

The historical analysis of women in active combat, highlights the difference between the mobilization of women in the past and the current dilemmas that policymakers face. In the past, the few cases of the mobilization of women into combat units were not so much the result of premeditation as the result of the sheer presence of circumstances. Women were armed when the homeland was invaded or when survival of a sociopolitical movement was at stake. Under conditions of relatively simple military organization and simple weapons, it was possible rapidly and directly to mobilize women into basic combat units. After the crisis, the pattern generally was to release women from such units. In the contemporary setting in the highly industrialized nations using women in combat units means to recruit special categories of women, to train them and to deploy them effectively; doing so means creating and implementing an overt policy. At the time of this study the leaders of the highly industrial-ized nations have not made such a decision and the issue has not emerged in most developing nations.

Comparative analysis of national case studies is a new frontier in social research. This book extends the strategy of such analysis of societal change to the role of women in the military and thereby makes a note-worthy contribution to the study of military organization.

Morris Janowitz

ACKNOWLEDGMENTS

The editor wishes to acknowledge her profound gratitude to the Ford Foundation and the United States Army Research Institute for the Behavioral and Social Sciences, which funded the project; to Towson State University Foundation, Towson, Maryland, which administered it; to the chairman of its Sociology Department, Professor Irwin Goldberg, who managed it; and to the officers and members of the Inter-University Seminar on Armed Forces and Society, and particularly its chairman for the past twenty years, Professor Morris Janowitz, whose encouragement and counsel have been indispensable in preparing this book. She also appreciates the help she has received from Professor Richard Stites, Georgetown University, and the contribution of all of the participants of the symposium on women in the armed forces to the success of this book.

ABBREVIATIONS

AA	Anti-aircraft Command (Great Britain)
AAA	Anti-aircraft Artillery (United States)
ACLU	American Civil Liberties Union (United States)
AFŽ	Anti-Fascist Front of Women (Yugoslavia)
ALN	Army of National Liberation (Algeria)
ATA	Air Transport Auxiliary (Great Britain)
ATS	Auxiliary Territorial Services (Great Britain)
AVNOJ	Anti-Fascist Council of the People's Liberation of Yugoslavia
CHEN	Chail Nashim (Women's Army Corps) (Israel)
CNO	Chief of Naval Operations (United States)
CNR	Civilian Nursing Reserve (Great Britain)
CPY	Yugoslav Communist Party
CS	Combat support (United States)
CSS	Combat service support (United States)
DACOWITS	Defense Advisory Committee on Women in the Services
DLK	Danmarks Lottekrops (Denmark)
DOSAAF	Volunteer Society for the Support of Army, Navy, and Air Force (Russia)
ELAS	National Republican Liberation Army (Greece)
ERA	Equal Rights Amendment (United States)
ES	Emergency Service (Great Britain)
FANY	First Aid Nursing Yeomanry (Great Britain)
FLN	National Liberation Movement (Algeria)
FMF	Fleet Marine Force (United States)
FRG	Federal Republic of Germany
GSVAD	General Service, Voluntary Aid Despatchment (Great Britain)
GVN	Government of Vietnam based in Saigon
HIM	Home Guard (Israel)
HISH	Field Forces (Israel)
ICP	Indochinese Communist party (Vietnam)
IDF	Israel Defense Forces

IRA	Irish Republican Army
JSDF	Japanese Self-Defense Forces
KFK	Kvindeligt Flyvekorps (Women's Air Force Home Guard) Denmark
KMK	Kvindeligt Marinekorps (Women's Naval Home Guard) Denmark
MOS	Military Occupational Specialities (United States)
MTS	Motor Transport Service (Great Britain)
NATO	North Atlantic Treaty Organization
NCO	Noncommissioned officer
NLF	National Front for the Liberation of South Vietnam
NOB	National Liberation Struggle (Yugoslavia)
NOP	National Liberation Movement (Yugoslavia)
NOV	National Liberation Army (Yugoslavia)
NSD	National Service Department, Women's Branch (Great Britain)
NSDAP	National Socialist German Worker's Party
NVA	*Nationalen Volksarmee* (German Democratic Republic's "National 'Peoples' Army")
OCFLN	Civilian Organization of the National Liberation Front (Algeria)
OSS	Office of Strategic Services
PAVN	People's Army of Vietnam
PLA	Vietnamese People's Liberation Army
PLAF	People's Liberation Armed Forces (Vietnam)
POW	Prisoner of War
QAIMNS	Queen Alexandra's Imperial Military Nursing Service (Great Britain)
QMAAC	Queen Mary's Auxiliary Army Corps (Great Britain)
RAFNS	Royal Air Force Nursing Service (Great Britain)
ROTC	Reserve Officers' Training Corps (United States)
SKOJ	Youth League (Yugoslavia)
SPAR	U.S. Coast Guard Women's Reserve (*"Semper Partus"* or "Always Ready")
TDF	Territorial Defense Forces (Yugoslavia)
TFNS	Territorial Forces Nursing Service (Great Britain)
UDR	Ulster Defence Regiment (Great Britain)
USAAF	U.S. Army Air Force
USMCR	U.S. Marine Corps Reserves
VAD	Voluntary Aid Despatchment (Great Britain)
VMRO	Macedonian Revolutionary Organization (Yugoslavia)
WAAC	Women's Auxiliary Army Corps (Great Britain and United States before it was changed to WAC)

WAAF	Women's Auxiliary Air Force (Great Britain)
WAC	Women's Army Corps (United States, first established as WAAC)
WASP	Women Airforce Service Pilots (United States)
WAVES	Women Accepted for Voluntary Emergency Service (United States)
WCC	Women's Convoy Corps (Great Britain)
WEC	Women's Emergency Corps (Great Britain)
WL	Women's Legion (Great Britain)
WLMTS	Women's Legion Motor Transport Section (Great Britain)
WRAC	Women's Royal Army Corps (Great Britain)
WRAF	Women's Royal Air Force (Great Britain)
WRNS	Women's Royal Navy Service (Great Britain)
WSTC	Women's Signallers' Territorial Corps (Great Britain)
WUDR	Women of the Ulster Defence Regiment (Great Britain)
WVR	Women's Volunteer Reserve (Great Britain)
YPA	Yugoslav People's Army

FEMALE SOLDIERS —
COMBATANTS OR NONCOMBATANTS?

INTRODUCTION

Female Soldiers—Combatants or Noncombatants? is the fruit of an international symposium on the role of women in the armed forces, sponsored by the Inter-University Seminar on Armed Forces and Society and held at the University of Chicago in October 1980. The symposium was conducted in conjunction with the Twentieth Annual Conference on Armed Forces and Society. Participants from the United States and a half dozen foreign countries presented their findings, which were then critiqued and discussed. The unusual interest that the symposium elicited at the conference was striking evidence that the issue of women in the armed forces has come of age—in academic and military circles as well as for the general public. The papers that are most relevant to the issue and most representative of the variety of national experiences are reproduced in this volume. Although the broader context of women in the armed services is treated in all the papers, the principle focus is on the history of and the present-day experience of women in the armed services and on the prospects of women serving in wartime combat.

A decade ago such a focus would have been premature, if not out of the question, in most discussions either of the future of women or the future of war. At present it is unquestionably a burning issue and the idea of opening combat specialties to women in the U.S. armed forces has become one of central concern to the U.S. military and the U.S. government. During the past decade the United States has witnessed a dramatic increase in the utilization of women in its armed forces, and this trend is expected to continue well into the 1980s. With this augmentation of female personnel and with social pressure for equal employment opportunity for women, the armed forces have opened almost all military job categories and military occupational specialties (MOS) to women. Those remaining closed to them are direct combat specialties, such as service on combat vessels and aircraft and in combat branches, such as infantry and armor. It is over these residual exclusions that the controversy rages.

What has been the policy of other nations and of our own in the past on the issue of women at war? What is the present situation and the likely pattern of development? These are the principle questions addressed by the papers that follow. Part I presents examples from the historical and

3

contemporary experience of Great Britain, Germany, revolutionary Russia and the USSR, Yugoslavia, Vietnam, Algeria, and Israel. Part II examines the current status of women in Greece, Japan, Denmark, and Sweden, nations that have had little if any experience with women in the armed forces in their past and are closely linked to the United States in diplomatic and security relations. Part III brings the controversy directly to the U.S. soil with a background paper that sets the problem, a sharp argument against the use of women in combat, and an equally pointed defense of women's right to choose a combat function within the armed services.

The topic of women in military combat deals with fundamental issues of national survival in revolution and in war. It deals with deeply held and emotionally laden values and sentiments. It would be an overstatement to assert that social analysis will produce a single explanation of the patterns and trends in the utilization of women in military combat. It would be an even greater overstatement to say there is a central uniformity in these patterns and trends, although there have been important commonalities and uniformities.

One can even make an argument that with the breakdown of traditional military institutions, the role of women in combat became a widespread problematic issue, either as part of national revolutionary movements or in more conventional military hostilities. The transformation of society from a peasant-based system to a more urban and technologically based nation state has meant that the issue of women in the military has had to be faced informally and responded to with explicit policies. Although women had at times been in military combat in the premodern period, women in combat first became a salient issue with the advent of the industrial and French revolutions. This occurred because of the ideological goals in the search for social equality in those periods and because the complex military organizations that came after the industrial revolution had greater potential for utilizing women.

In attempting to integrate the findings of historical case studies of women in combat, it is clear that we are dealing with two persistent and comprehensive dimensions: (1) the process of institutionalization, which incorporates the increasing division of labor and the emergence of complex, modern, large-scale bureaucratic institutions; and (2) the cultural norms and values that are reflected in religious, ethical, and political goals. There are extensive commonalities in the institutions of the nation state as they make increased use of technology and science, but, as comparative studies of societies show, cultural values are varied and persistent and the impact of social change is powerful and enduring. These dimensions affect the use of women in combat.

Our research indicates that over the last two centuries powerful barriers to the utilization of women in combat have existed worldwide. This restriction is a major concern in the history of women in combat. Women have had an essentially protected social position even in societies that are becoming "modern." As a result of cultural values and women's "special" place, the restriction on their deployment in combat has been particularly comprehensive. Using the theoretical format of comparative analysis of societal change, we are not only dealing with cultural and normative values but also with institutional barriers to their military mobilization. Military institutions that make use of women must of necessity be more complex in their organization. This must be kept in mind in assessing the conditions under which women are utilized in combat or combat-type roles.

Our historical case studies permit two types of observations from the perspective of comparative analysis of societal change: the actual use of women in combat through World War II and the contemporary issues of women in the post-World War II deterrent forces. Women have been effectively utilized in combat during revolutionary settings when the society is undergoing fundamental social and political changes. Communist revolutions of our century are good cases in point. Likewise, women have been effectively utilized in combat when the society has been invaded, so that the military uniform or the bearing of arms does not increase the danger that women face; such involvement by women occurs especially when the very existence of the society is at stake and when women are extensively molested and raped by the invader (the Soviet and Yugoslavian defenses in World War II are examples).

Clearly the cultural factor is important both in national revolutions and in defense of the national homeland. Utilization of women in combat over the last two centuries has been seen only in a minority of cases. One can also assert that the stronger the emphasis on ideology of social equality, the greater the potential for utilization of women in military combat. But with the exception of the Soviet and Yugoslavian cases in World War II and Israel in its war of independence—and these cases should not be overstated—the utilization of women in combat during the last two centuries has not been extensive. Whether it can be, will be, or should be in the future is something the reader may ponder after reading this book.

The Goldman and Stites paper, "Great Britain and the World Wars," illustrates a number of themes that are also prominent in the experiences of other nations at war recounted in this volume. One of these was the extreme reluctance of British society to allow any significant numbers of women in any significant role until such a national emergency of great magnitude was perceived as the manpower shortfall announced in the middle of World War II. Another is how problems of social or sexual integration related to those of military integration, specifically how efforts to "militarize" or defeminize female troops in external ways (uniforms, ranks, titles) in order to allay the public fear of sexual intermixing ran up against the military establishment's reluctance to grant women any of the traditional trimmings and trappings of the military life. A third is the steady growth of military jobs for women connected with the changing technology of war. And finally, the fundamental shift in the problem of women in the British military from one of sexual tension and public concern to one of professional status and opportunity. British women, with rare and isolated exceptions, did not bear arms or serve in combat or aboard most combat conveyances (ships, planes, armor) in the world wars and have yet to serve in combat on active duty. One of the main arguments in favor of combat training for women in Britain, as in many other countries, has been their vulnerability as unarmed soldiers in close-to-combat situations and localities. The force of this argument had recently been recognized by Parliament and in 1981, women of those British armed services, under certain conditions, have been given weapons and training in how to use them. As in the United States, the recent growth of women's participation in the armed forces has been partly connected with the most recent phase of the feminist, or women's rights, movement.

Germany, in contrast to England and other countries, did not respond to massive manpower shortfalls by resorting to the use of women in large numbers. In both world wars and now in 1981 a profound historical and cultural hostility to the use of women for military purposes has shaped the West German decision-making process. Jeff Tuten's "Germany and the World Wars" shows how this national value has been a constant factor of German life even when, as during World War II, the country was desperately in need of troops of every sort. Women were used as auxiliaries in World War I, chiefly in communications. When the Nazis came to power the deepest wells of sexual conservatism resurfaced and created a tension between the ideology and the national need. The ideology was retained, women were utilized (in small numbers), and the contradiction was masked by such means as indirect conscription from civilian service (the "Duty Year") through nursing into auxiliary and support services (especially antiaircraft) and by maintaining the fiction that women attached to the service were strictly civilian. Only at the end, as the nightmare of defeat loomed large over the fatherland, did the authorities plan a women's combat battalion and mixed partisan units. These plans did not see the light of day. The German pattern has been to resist the presence of women in the armed forces in anything but a marginal, preferably civilian, capacity. The principle was reaffirmed in 1956 when the Federal Republic constituted its new armed forces. Even today fewer than 30 percent of the civilian employees of the army are female. But as in many other places, demographic pressures have reopened the debate and have made likely the future growth in the use of women in the armed forces. If we can judge from the past (it is not always possible to do so), the Germans will be among the major resisters to the notion of women armed and trained for combat.

The case of pre- and postrevolutionary Russia, almost unstudied until the late 1970s, is of enormous importance on three counts. In the first place this nation is perceived by many in the United States and Western Europe as the most probable adversary in a future war. Second, its utilization of women in combat during both of the world wars is the single major example of the large-scale use of women in combat in regular international war. And finally, since it also presents a striking example of the use of women in what is variously called revolutionary war, war of liberation, or partisan action (in the Russian revolutionary movement, in the Civil War of 1918–1920, and in the occupied Soviet Union of World War II), it has become a model for insurgent movements of liberation around the world, particularly the third world. Griesse and Stites in "Russia: Revolution and War" show conclusively how Soviet society has differed from the other examples in this book on almost every major issue. Soviet women have been: directly engaged in combat with arms of every sort, in separate units as well as mixed units deployed in combat (on the ground and in the air), used in support troops in massive numbers and used for political and ideological mobilization, even, depicted as a warrior, and as a media figure. They have also suffered many casualties. Public debate over the use of women in the military has been almost completely absent. In spite of this stark difference from other societies discussed here, the Soviets have nonetheless exhibited their own brand of conservatism; the presence of women at the front was resisted in all three of the wars described by Griesse and Stites; commanders had to "relearn" the values of women personnel; resentment and ridicule continued to stalk Soviet women soldiers in all services even at their most dedicated and heroic moments; and women were demobilized from the service after the Second World War and have continued to be absent up to the early 1980s— although the training of Soviet girls indicates that they could if needed repeat their performances of 1914, 1918, and 1941.

The Soviet experience, because of its richness and variety, highlights the importance of an understudied but crucial aspect of women in arms in the twentieth century: women's role in irregular, or partisan, warfare. The history of occupied Europe in World War II proved, particularly in places like Italy, France, Yugoslavia, Poland, and the Soviet Union, both the special value of women in resistance movements, and their ability to withstand the trauma of combat danger (a point that George Quester makes later on in the volume on U.S. women in espionage work). Irregular warfare is not just a matter of forest bands, concealment of wireless sets, sexual infiltration, terror, and sabotage—all functions carried out spectacularly by women. In the Soviet model and in many subsequent anticolonial wars and wars of independence or national liberation, it is also the political, agitational, cultural, and educational work of women that is so striking, novel, and effective. In Yugoslavia, China, Vietnam, Cuba, Mozambique, and other places, women have been used during irregular warfare not only as combat fighters and disorganizers, but also as teachers, spreaders of propaganda and literacy, emancipators, fighters against religion, and so on. As policymakers debate the problematics of using their own women in combat for future conventional wars, they must not lose sight of the fact that so-called third world, brushfire, and revolutionary wars are likely to enlist—without much prior debate—a large number of very effective women, whether Communists, Nationalists, or indigenous radicals.

Barbara Jancar's "Yugoslavia: War of Resistance" illustrates both the possible dimensions of women's combat and political roles in resistance wars and the ambiguous relationship of such participation to overall equality of women in the military and in society. Yugoslavia's bitter war of resistance against the alien occupiers and the indigenous Fascists is a perfect example of the Soviet model of revolutionary war, later renamed "all-peoples' war" by the Chinese, whose experience was somewhat similar in 1937–1950. Yugoslavia has a long tradition of female fighters. They first fought in the early nineteenth century against the Ottoman Turks. In the war of resistance large numbers of women were involved and they had a high performance record; women in the National Liberation Army had an even higher mortality rate than men; and they had an outstanding role in politicizing, educating, mobilizing, and administering the liberated areas. All of this activity was performed under the official Communist and AVNOJ (Anti-Fascist Council of the National Liberation of Yugoslavia) slogans of equality of women. But Jancar's paper also shows clearly that even maximum participation in quantity and quality in a combat war situation does not guarantee equality in the service, in other walks of life, or in the postwar society. She points out the persistent conservatism that resulted in stark inequalities in numbers, decision-making powers, rank, type of activity, and everything else connected with the fighting; the lingering sexism or use of females for personal purposes; and the willingness of the military to use women for the most dangerous missions in the emergency of a desperate struggle and then to demobilize them after the emergency is over. This is a particularly clear-cut example of a phenomenon that was almost universal in twentieth-century military utilization of women. At present the regular forces of Yugoslavia have few or no women, although they are prominent in the local territorial reserves, the militia. Young girls, as in Soviet Russia still, receive military medical training in the event of future invasion.

The case of Vietnamese women presents obvious parallels with those of the two other Communist countries, Russia and Yugoslavia: the social myth of a "people's war," active guerrilla warfare, female martyrs, schools of mobilization and training for women, the use of sexual contact as a weapon, and so on. There are novelties as well, as William Duiker shows in his "Vietnam: War of Insurgency." One of these is the interesting use of women (of the Viet Cong) to propagandize women of the other side (South Vietnam), in this case to project the message of exploitation and the evils of the "poisonous weeds" of American bourgeois culture in Saigon. Another, during the French and the American phases of the "liberation" war, was the mass march of women for political and disorganizational purposes in the urban areas, a mode of activity that won the participants the name "long-haired army." Another still was the relatively high rank of many women in the Viet Cong and in the Peoples' Liberation Armed Forces of the North; at one point 40 percent of regimental commanders and the deputy commander of the entire army were women. On the other hand, we see again that massive participation of women in the war, Hanoi waitresses and peasant wives in rice paddies with rifles at the ready, and terms such as "long-haired army" did not add up to large-scale regular participation of women in combat per se, as it did in Russia and Yugoslavia. Even in the South, where irregular war flourished, women were used mostly to carry supplies, thus earning them from a foreign observer the sobriquet "the water buffalo of the revolution." And as Duiker tells us, even in artillery batteries, women were expected to carry shells, clean the guns, and bring refreshments to the male gunners. Such modernized Confucian slogans describing women's roles as "the five goods" and "the three responsibilities" in the end meant that women were expected to give their full weight to the war effort and also perform their traditional roles in the family, in the fields, and in the factories.

Djamila Amrane's paper "Algeria: Anticolonial War" shows yet another side of the role of women in struggles that are becoming increasingly common in our time. As in the case of Russia, Yugoslavia, and Vietnam, we see a milieu of poverty and rural backwardness, a cruel war with a foe regarded as an alien occupier (in this case the long-established French *colons*), and an enthusiastic participation of young women and girls, with similar violence, retribution, and suffering. The milieu in Algeria was fundamentally different from that in the previous examples. Here we have no Communist party leading the resistance movement and waving, among other things, the banner of women's liberation. Instead we have a Muslim society which placed its stamp even upon the radical National Liberation Movement (FLN). Women's role in this movement more closely resembles the activities of women in early modern wars and occupations than of modern and modernizing ones: provision of food and lodging, minor espionage, liaison, concealment and movement of arms (bullets hidden among noodles in a basket), medical aid, and so on. Only 2 percent of the women engaged in terror-related activities like the planting of bombs, not always done for killing. The trial, condemnation to the guillotine, and pardoning of a handful of these women gave rise to a legend about Algerian women in combat during this war. There was no such thing, the author tells us. Although the life of even cooks and medics in the Algerian *maquis* was harrowing and fraught with danger, it was nothing like the combat life of women in Yugoslav, Russian, Chinese, and other Communist revolutionary wars. Furthermore, their role was in no way connected to a program or promise of equality or liberation, except of liberation from the hated French.

In her paper "Israel: The Longest War" Anne Bloom cites the following words of Aviva Cantor Zuckoff: "If we go through the Bible and legends carefully we see that whenever Jewish survival is at stake, Jewish women are called upon to be strong and aggressive. When the crisis is over, it's back to patriarchy." This could serve as a fitting epigram not only for the story of Israeli women in the military but also for those of many other societies treated in this volume. Bloom's account of Jewish-Palestinian-Israeli women on active service from the first migrations of eighty years ago through the pioneer-defense, the anti-British struggle, and the independence war of 1948–1949 is full of rich detail depicting the drama, complexity, and, in some ways, uniqueness of the Jewish-Israeli struggles and of women's role in them. In the earlier fighting they served as scouts, spies, liaison agents, and fighters, the battle against the British in certain aspects resembling the Algerian fight against the French. In the 1948 war, women emerged as full-scale soldiers in combat and near-combat roles, as teachers and administrators, and as morale builders. In their scope of activity, Israeli women were much closer to their Yugoslav and Russian counterparts than to the Algerian women rebels in that the ideology of most Zionists contained a strong element of women's equality. But when the new permanent Israeli Defense Forces were created in 1949, women were excluded from combat roles altogether. Since then women have had a low profile in the military, in spite of the expectation that many would serve again in a much broader range of activity if war should be visited upon the state of Israel. This is a further illustration of the neglected fact that there is no necessary correlation between the level of women's participation in a given war and the place of women in their nation's army in peacetime.

The experience of women at war ought to caution scholars, soldiers, citizens, and policymakers against making flat assertions or invoking supposedly immutable truths about the nature of women, of warfare, and of the relationship between the two. But certainly a few generalizations are possible at this point. One is the extreme variation in the use of women in combat, depending upon historical and cultural traditions, prevailing ideo-logical or religious systems, and the concrete circumstances of the war in question. Political and military decisions to put women into combat have almost always been made by men. The decisions have often been *ad hoc,* with ample variations among services and branches, and with great reluc-tance and ambivalence. Preference in almost every example has been to put women toward the "tail" and not the "tooth," to use current American terminology. When the line between support and combat has been crossed and women have been permitted to fight or even recruited for fighting, it has been in a situation perceived as desperate and always in the context of occupation or invasion of one's native land by outsiders. The cases of Russia, Yugoslavia, Vietnam, Algeria, Israel, and many others not dis-cussed in this volume speak eloquently to this point. The only time the Germans came even close to creating combat units for women was at the very end of World War II, when their country was invaded on all sides amid a disastrous nightmare of national disintegration. How well did women fight when they fought is a question posed again and again in this book. Answers vary from case to case—and no one can ever measure the *effectiveness* of a particular fighting element in a wholly scientific way. But perceptions are recorded and can be reported: commanders every-where have praised the performance of their own women in combat when it occurred, however much they would have preferred to have fighting men instead of fighting women. The main negative critique of women's combat prowess, recorded by German soldiers in Russia, arose out of infantry combat situations.

How did the experience affect women who engaged in combat? And how did the public respond? As to the first, it appears that once women entered the service in support capacity and saw how the military worked, some of them aspired to more active roles in the fighting, out of various motives of ambition, patriotism, self-expression, hatred of the enemy, and a mixture of all these. The evidence presented here does not allow a clear statement about either the extent of motivation or the number of women so motivated, since the overwhelming majority of women in all the cases remained in noncombatant support roles. When allowed to form female combat units, women seem to have developed a special kind of group psychology of mutual support, very different in content, but similar in function, to "male bonding." Those in integrated units struggled against discrimination to the best of their ability and largely overcame prejudices by proving their worth in battle or in support. The presence of female individuals or female units does not seem to have threatened the sense of male bonding that Jeff Tuten talks about in his argument against the use of women in combat. If one thing can be said without any qualification whatsoever, it is that women never achieved equality in or out of the service during or after the wars as a result of their role in combat. Historical forgetfulness and ingratitude appear in almost every instance treated in these pages. As to public response to women in combat, the following observations can be made: the sexual issue has declined perceptibly; the argument that it is "barbarous" to expose women to fire is also declining due to the technology of war; and in nations with the highest participation (USSR), public debate has been almost nonexistent. At a more general level, it ought to be pointed out that the concept of totalitarianism is of almost no use in studying the use of women in war, witness the contrasting cases of Britain, Nazi Germany, and Stalinist Russia.

In Part II four papers deal with nations that have not had important historical experience with women in the armed forces: Greece and Denmark, both NATO countries; Japan, which has a special military relationship to the United States; and Sweden, a neutral nation. When comparing these societies in terms of their utilization of women in the military and comparing them to the countries in Part I with historical wartime experience, it is very difficult to discern a clear pattern. Greece and Japan, countries of profound traditions of patriarchy and hostility to women's equality contrast sharply with each other in recent years in their attitudes towards women in service: both operate at low levels of utilization, but the Japanese have displayed a cautious willingness to allow women into the service in a variety of roles and once there to accept them and to respect them, whereas the Greek males have shown great difficulty in accepting women into a military environment in spite of the official decision to do so. Since the papers do not address the same issues, it is more useful to discuss them together around the points where they do intersect rather than to summarize each of them. Prior to 1980, Sweden, a neutral nation, had employed women for civilian defense rather than for military service. In 1980, however, women were admitted to the Swedish air force as officers; plans to admit women into the army and air force are also underway. Most officer positions are to be open to them. Denmark, like Sweden has a tradition of greater equality of the sexes than found in the other societies in question; and its relatively accepting and rational use of women, taken together with the contrasting examples, seems to indicate that the use of women in the armed forces is often a mirror of what women do and are permitted to do in civilian society. For example, if one seeks the reason for the differences between the halfheartedness, inefficiency, and resentful acceptance pattern of Greek women and the opposite situation in Denmark, and Sweden, one ought not question directives but rather look into the national environment of these two very different societies.

All these countries—as well as most of those in Part I—deny women a combat role. On the other hand, some of them offer basic training in weapons. Sweden also plans to do so. This is another example of the difficulty of trying to define in a rigid way training for a combat role. Marksmanship and familiarization with small arms, widely offered to and even demanded of women soldiers nowadays, does not mean that women are expected to use these weapons; it certainly does not mean that the use of them in combat is intended. The purpose, as variously defined, is to make them more like soldiers, to introduce them to the essence of military life (firing a gun), and to enable them to protect themselves in the event that their support roles in wartime are enveloped by combat. A vivid example of misunderstanding on this issue is the myth of the Israeli parachute women. It is popularly believed that Israeli women have fought as paratroopers and will fight in future wars in this capacity. The truth is that, after their exclusion from combat with the creation of the Israel Defense Forces, women have not fought except in a fortuitous and incidental way. They do serve as parachute women, but this simply means that they fold the parachutes that the men will wear in airborne operations. They wear a special uniform, insignia, and beret, make a very martial impression, and are held in high regard. But they do not fly or make jumps. These and other Israeli women receive basic training with the automatic rifle or submachine gun and would be able to wield it if, in extreme circumstance, they had to do so. Since in parades, they bear these weapons, the popular image is one of large forces of female machine gunners. Because in some Western societies, Britain for example, the issue of weapons training was long tied to *training for combat* and *use in combat*, the two have been falsely linked. This is not, however, to deny any link: if women are trained in the use of weapons, there is likely to be less resistance in time of war, or certain kinds of wars, to their using them.

If we combine our knowledge of the wartime experiences in Part I and the peacetime experiences in Part II, we see at once that predictability in matters of women in combat is a very risky business indeed. Past participation in combat, as in the USSR and Yugoslavia, has not meant present combat roles and does not seem to indicate future ones—except in the event of foreign invasion. Marginal or zero participation in past combat, as in Britain and the United States, has not prevented considerable ferment, policy debate, and even action in bringing women closer to combat training and combat readiness in these countries. Every society is subject to a fluctuating combination of forces and circumstances, domestic and foreign. These include: disappearance of the draft; decline in male enlistments; demographic shortfalls; a vigorous women's movement; egalitarian notions concerning the need to distribute equitably the duties, liabilities, and privileges of citizenship; the growth of technology and the change of the ''tooth-to-tail'' ratio in the direction of the ''tail''; security perceptions; and so on.

One thing that emerges from all the papers, if only by their muteness on the subject, is that women have never (in anything more than minuscule numbers) been in combat overseas or outside the boundaries of their countries. With the minor exception of some female Soviet aviators and armored personnel who fought their way through Eastern Europe into Germany, this had been the case everywhere. Women are drawn into combat, when at all, only when their native land is menaced by occupying forces. But even if this were to happen again in many other places around the globe, the evidence seems to suggest that once the foe is ejected, the women will not remain a permanent feature of the combat services in combat roles. In the unpleasant exercise of projecting who might fight whom in what kind of war, one would be hard put to imagine the deployment for combat of Japanese women in China or North Korea; Greek women in Turkey or Cyprus; or Danish women in East Germany or Estonia.

One more observation is needed—on public debate. The nature of that debate has changed: it is nowadays more serious and more scientific, though flashes of emotion break out from time to time. The papers in this volume make the reader privy to some of these debates—in the chancery of the prime minister of Japan, in statistical bureaus of Copenhagen, in the Israeli Knesset, on the pages of U.S. newspapers and in the manpower offices of the Department of Defense, and in Bundeswehr circles—everywhere in fact where a free press and relatively easy access to government decision makers prevail. The Soviet Union, whose major postures on troop utilization are shrouded in secrecy, is an obvious exception. The scope of the debate is widening with each passing year with the awakening interest of the media and the proliferation of polls in and out of the armed services. Women in combat, for better or for worse, is becoming a people's issue.

The third part of this volume focuses on the U.S. military—its past experience with women in the services as well as the debate of the 1980s on allowing women to serve in combat. George Quester's paper, ''The Problem,'' takes us briefly through the history of the American experience with women in the armed forces from World War I to the present. The pattern is a familiar one: limited use in both major world wars as noncombatant auxiliaries or in separate units such as nursing, minimal integration, inferior status, a slight upgrading of women's services during the Second World War, and demobilization after both wars. Two important points emerge: the effect of a lack of a perception of genuine manpower shortage on the utilization of women; and the relatively successful use of females in the espionage and intelligence operations of World War II, which showed them capable of handling fear, stress, interrogation, and sexual overtones connected with their work. The big increase in the interest of women in the military—and vice versa—occurred in the 1970s as a combination of factors: the diminishing birthrate, the elimination of the draft and the creation of an all-volunteer force as a result of the trauma of Vietnam, and the surge of a vigorous movement towards women's equality in our society. The author carefully assesses these developments and comments on the changing cast of public opinion on the issue of women in the service and the possibility of women entering combat. Vivid illustrations from the mass media of the 1940s, contrasted with the matter-of-fact tone of present-day discussions, show that the issue of women and the military has risen above the earlier tittering triviality and is now treated seriously by most parties concerned. Recent press coverage of female training units certainly bears this out.

Jeff Tuten's "The Argument Against Female Combatants" is blunt and vigorously stated. After indicating a sharp line that he sees dividing military from civilian approaches to the problem, he outlines in detail the nature of past participation of American women in war and peace, showing how they have moved from roles in combat service support to combat support and how many of them now serve on the verge of a combat role, particularly at the divisional level. Tuten frames his argument around military effectiveness—the desire to win wars—and not around issues of social justice. Within this frame, he argues the physical, psychological, and social inadequacy of women for combat, freely invoking historical examples as he does so. By physiological inadequacy he means upper-body weakness, relative lack of stamina, endurance, speed, and coordination. By psychological inadequacy he means relative lack of aggressiveness, namely, the urge to kill, and lack of evidence that women could withstand the grinding fear and stress of actual battlefield combat. And by social inadequacy he means the damage that the presence of women in combat could do to male bonding, the atavistic urge for men in combat to create a kind of masculine warrior ethic. Certain basic assumptions in Tuten's argument will surely excite interest if not controversy. One is the stress on the physical nature of combat and the ultimate decisiveness of close-in fighting, flowing from the doctrine that ultimately the infantry wins wars. Another is the assertion that historically women's presence in combat has been infinitesimal, and when found, wholly ineffective. Some of the papers have told a somewhat different story. Tuten concludes that the inclusion of women in combat roles in the U.S. armed forces could spell disaster for our national security.

Mady Segal, in "The Argument for Female Combatants," takes on Tuten's thesis and adds a number of counterarguments to the debate.

Segal argues from a wide variety of vantage points. In the name of logic, she discounts the physiological arguments by stating that not all women are weaker than all men, that males have emotional cycles comparable to the menstrual mood, that not all women get pregnant or have child-care problems, and that much of modern warfare is technological, not hand-to-hand combat with full field pack and rifle. In the name of epistemology, she answers the concern about stress and fear by saying that there is no evidence either way. In the name of analogy, she reminds readers that antiquated arguments against black men serving in combat resemble those used against women. In the name of morality, she insists that social justice is an American national objective that must be considered alongside military preparedness. And in the name of practicality she warns that exclusion of women from combat on principle could lead to their widespread exclusion from other areas of military life where they are considered essential. This last resembles the rationale of Admiral Zumwalt, discussed in Quester's paper, to the effect that the presence of women in certain roles and in large numbers is a national security requirement (this particular example goes against the simplistic assumption of some that those who favor women in the service tend to be doves and their opponents hawks). Segal adduces other arguments for the inclusion of women combatants in the armed services; the most significant aspect of her paper is her assertion that if women are not assigned to combat now, the issue will continue to arise and eventually the decision will be made in favor of women in combat. Combat as a mode of self-defense, often invoked in the European cases, is not present in Segal's chapter.

A gradual expansion in the utilization of women in the peacetime forces has taken place since World War II. Women have entered combat support and combat-related units and have even had specialized combat assignments. The military has been affected by the greater societal influences. It has responded to trends in employment in civilian society, which have been duplicated in the military, and by institutional issues, including the shortage of personnel in the all-volunteer forces. The increased reliance on technology has led to an expansion of the military roles that women are defined as capable of performing (the structure of an advanced industrial society creates pressure for employment equality of the sexes). As a result, in the last decade, the question of women in combat has been broadened from a military issue to a sociopolitical question. The institutional dimensions are subtle, complex, and important. The line between combat and noncombat becomes more and more difficult to draw. Moreover, women in combat support roles become highly vulnerable to potential attack. Cultural aspects, however, remain dominant. The resistance to full equality for women in society—civil or military—is powerful. This is especially the case in combat. In fact the issue of women in combat supplies a test of the logic of full equality. A clearcut resolution of the issue of women in combat cannot emerge during a period of prolonged tension under the Soviet/U.S. strategy of deterrence. The scope of women's roles in the military continues to grow, but with sharp limitations. The important conclusions from the case study material seem to indicate that the ambiguities and tensions in the position of women in civilian society will be mirrored by similar distinctions in the military establishment. Women are involved in classes of combat roles, reflecting the drive toward equality, but will they be restricted from effective participation in ground combat assault units? Students of advanced industrial society point out that technology and science do not eliminate societal ambiguities and tensions. The role of women in combat is a pointed case.

PART I | THE EXPERIENCE OF WAR

1 | GREAT BRITAIN AND THE WORLD WARS

Nancy Loring Goldman and
Richard Stites

When examining British women's service in wartime, one is struck by a number of contrasts. The first is how much has changed since the early 1900s; the second, how little some things have changed. Britain was not a military society in the nineteenth century. It had seen no major wars since the time of Napoleon. Its empire was won by small contingents of soldiers, propelled around the globe by a magnificent fleet; it was held together by active commerce, the cooptation of natives into military operations, and superb organization. Although the navy and the colonial service possessed a kind of national mystique, the armed forces as such, especially the army, enjoyed no status comparable, for example, to that in continental kingdoms such as Prussia, Germany, and Russia. Women, when thought of at all in connection with the military, were seen as colonial wives, adornments of officers' societies, and, although rarely before 1881, as nurses. The image of Florence Nightingale of the Crimean War in English fantasy, fiction, and film was a misleading one. She and her nurses remained in Turkey, far from the field of action, while Russian nurses (whose role is almost unknown to historians) served directly on the battlefields in the Crimean Peninsula.[1] On the other hand, Nightingale so gripped the imagination of the Victorians that a women's nursing service became permanent after 1881. A generation later it spawned new units bearing a variety of designations: QAIMNS in 1902, TFNS in 1906, WCC in 1907, and FANY in 1907 (see Table 1.1). The major shift in women's roles took place in World War I from purely nursing into other support functions.

Sponsored by the U.S. Army Research Institute for the Behavioral and Social Sciences. The views and conclusions in this document are those of the author and do not necessarily represent those of the sponsor or the U.S. Government.

Table 1.1
Abbreviations of British Military Organizations cited in Chapter 1

AA	Anti-aircraft Command (Ack-Ack), 1938 (Members of ATS employed in AA in 1941)
ATA	Air Transport Auxiliary, 1939
ATS	Auxiliary Territorial Services, 1938 (successor to WAAC-QMAAC)
ES	Emergency Service, 1936
FANY	First Aid Nursing Yeomanry, 1907
GSVAD	General Service, Voluntary Aid Despatchment, 1917
MTS	Motor Transport Service, 1938 (Those members of FANY which were absorbed by ATS)
NSD	National Service Department, Women's Branch, 1915
QAIMNS	Queen Alexandra's Imperial Military Nursing Service, 1902
QMAAC	Queen Mary's Auxiliary Army Corps, 1918
RAFNS	Royal Air Force Nursing Service, 1918
TFNS	Territorial Forces Nursing Service, 1906
VAD	Voluntary Aid Despatchment, 1909
WAAC	Women's Auxiliary Army Corps, 1917
WCC	Women's Convoy Corps, 1907
WEC	Women's Emergency Corps, 1914
WL	Women's Legion, 1915 (Officially recognized 1916)
WLMTS	Women's Legion Motor Transport Section, 1916
WRAC	Women's Royal Army Corps, 1949
WRAF	Women's Royal Air Force, 1918 (Renamed WAAF, Women's Auxiliary Air Force, in World War II)
WRNS	Women's Royal Navy Service, 1917
WSTC	Women's Signallers' Territorial Corps, 1914
WUDR	Women of the Ulster Defence Regiment, 1975

In the 1980s, thirty-five years after Britain's last major war, women are now a legitimate and proper source of personnel in the permanent armed forces. They have their own units and commanders; they wear the uniform, salute, live in barracks, and obey women officers. Their function as nurses has broadened from 1900 into a wide range of technical jobs. Their self-image is no longer the sweetly pious one of angels of mercy administering to the flower of British manhood for the sacred cause of Britain, with quasireligious costumes, nomenclature, and ethos. The new image is a far more matter of fact one of economic (and partly social) opportunity. Service for women has become a job, rather than an exalted mission. The haloes of female heroism have given way to wrinkles of concern over pay scales, promotion schedules, and mobility. From another perspective, however, women are still seen as distinctly ancillary elements in the British armed services, not only by some military authorities who resist further integration and utilization, but also by public opinion, and by some of the women themselves. Beyond this persistent image is the reality that women are still confined to "support" functions—many of a sophisticated nature to be sure, but outside armed combat and direct fighting roles, and often of a domestic, logistical, or clerical kind. In some ways, military society resembles civilian society in Britain, but civilian society of a generation back.

The sources concerning British women in the armed forces include numerous official documents, particularly debates in the House of Commons and army and other service statements. These are supplemented by polls and opinion samplings. We thus know a good deal about what the government and certain sectors of the public have thought about female participation in service over the years. We know much less about how women felt and even acted in the two world wars because the existing corpus of personal memoirs and biographies of military women themselves have not yet been systematically researched and interpreted.

In comparing the British references to the Soviets', the nation we have chosen for comparison, we see almost the opposite situation. The literature on Soviet women in the wars bulges with reference to personal experience from memoirs, newspaper interviews, cameo closeups of women at the front, and so on. Much of this is pious in tone and sometimes overly ideological or patrioteering. These materials nevertheless give us unmistakable impressions of the heroism, ardor, agony, and toughness of Soviet women who fought in the revolutionary and international wars of this century. On the other hand, official Soviet sources of military history are almost mute on details of the decision-making process, of the actual numbers and roles and social background of the women, and many other things we would like to know. Independent public opinion surveys are nonexistent in the Soviet Union; and the human drama of conflict, integration, adjustment, sexual tensions, and all the rest must be projected, extrapolated, and often conjectured from the fragmentary data we have. All in all, what one British writer says about his own case, that "the historical development of the non-medical services is remarkably poorly documented,"[2] applies with equal vigor to the Soviet Union. Until serious and extensive historical monographs appear on this still novel subject of study, we must be content with preliminary summaries such as this.

What of the relationship of political culture to the utilization of women? Since women in Britain have their own services and theirs is a democratic, or free, society, different from the Soviet Union on both counts, one might be tempted to correlate democracy, women's own aspirations, and the incidence of women's participation. The relationship is infinitely more complicated than that. British women have the vote now, had it at the time of World War II, and were (in the form of the suffragist and suffragette movements) vociferously pushing for it at the time of the first war. But their participation was hardly just a reflection of this. Women dropped their feminist militancy in 1914 and promised to support the war effort. They did so, but pretty much in the way they were told to do by the War Office and other organs of authority. Women did not shape the nature of their participation in any significant way except to say that they were willing and ready to help. Ironically, the most independent units were those made up largely of upper-class women who could purchase their own uniforms, emblems, and vehicles (FANY). Since then, British women have lobbied successfully for further participation, but their possession of the vote does not seem to have been used to further any women's military cause. In the Soviet Union women's economic experience, educational level, technical skills, the regime's determination to use women in any capacity they could, and the relative absence of a belief in the delicacy or fragility of women determined the kind of massive and direct role that they played in the war of 1941. Women were mobilized but used in a severely limited way in democratic Britain; mobilized and heavily used in nondemocratic Soviet Union; and hardly mobilized or used at all in another nondemocratic society, Nazi Germany.

WORLD WAR I

Scope of Activity

Even a brief glance at the nomenclature and the dates of formation of the units for women in the World War I period (see Table 1.1) indicates clearly that their formation was unplanned and that there were considerable overlap and intersection of organizations and an abundant lack of agreement and clarity about roles of women in war. This confusion was in keeping both with the British tradition of policymaking and with the ambiguous, even tense, status of women at that time. It also reflected service rivalries and traditions of various services and combat arms (there were for example at least seven units in this list that explicitly dealt with nursing duties). The formation dates of the units closest to combat, mostly 1917 and 1918, also show the great reluctance of the military to use women for anything more than a support force. The laborious unfolding of the story of how, and under what difficulties and discussions these units emerged, has been related elsewhere. The first units were purely civilians in the service of the military, as opposed to the later pure auxiliaries. The

WEC was formed in 1914 to serve as a clearing house for women who wished to engage in war work; the WVR, like the American USO of later times, ran canteens for servicemen but dressed and drilled in a military manner; the WSTC organized women radio personnel to replace signallers on the home front. The first paid volunteer unit was the Women's Legion, largely cooks and drivers for the army.[3]

Nursing, as in other lands, provided the transitional wedge for women to move from civilian medicine to combat battlefield nursing. It was a difficult transition. Early nurses associated with the British army were either from the Red Cross or of private, local, or religious provenance. A unit of Scottish nurses, for example, was not permitted in the British zones and so they went to Macedonia on the Serbian front, served in all medical roles, and moved in battlefield conditions. British Red Cross nurses in Belgium were rejected by their own army but worked for the Belgians and the French. The British nurse, Edith Cavell, who was executed by the Germans for espionage, had been serving in Belgium since before the war. At home the numbers of nurses in the two prewar nursing services associated with the military, the QAIMNS and the TFNS, totaled only about twenty-six hundred; by 1918 the number had grown to over eighteen thousand. VAD and FANY, Red Cross affiliates also from before the war, blossomed and eventually were deployed abroad; the former largely lower-class women were paid by the army, the latter, a more elite (formerly private) unit of lady ambulance drivers and nurses with a taste for adventure. By the war's end, separate women's units had their own nursing elements as well. The other major auxiliary work that was near combat was transport, mostly driving: the Motor Transport Section of the Women's Legion (about one thousand drivers) was notorious for its independent-minded and self-sufficient women members.[4]

The creation of units of military women, that is women who were paid, controlled, and uniformed by the armed services (in contrast to the civilians and volunteers and to the nurses who were somewhat in between), was a tortuous process. In 1915 the NSD was created with a women's branch to facilitate recruitment and placement of women into war industry and auxiliary military roles. There was much resistance by civilian and military men to involving women beyond this for both historical and social reasons. But there were factors working in the other direction as well: persistent demand to serve by women's groups, the presence of nurses already in all three services, and the need for women's services to replace men without going through trade union problems. Halfway through the war, in May 1916 after brutal losses of men at the front, the War Office went through a conscription crisis, at one point considering the drafting of fifty-year-old men. By early 1917 the army was ready to use women to replace soldiers going to the front and the WAAC was formed in January and February. About twelve thousand women were sent to rear echelons (the Line of Communications) in France, and about fourteen thousand served in England. The first to go abroad were fourteen cooks from the WL. In April conscription of women was discussed, but it was never implemented. At the end of the year, the WRNS was formed to support the Royal Navy on shore duty only; and early in 1918, with the separate formation of the Royal Air Force, the WRAF was established. About eighty thousand women served in these three branches by the end of hostilities in November 1918. Thus during World War I women served in three basic capacities: as civilian, paid or voluntary, in various support functions; in women's military units (auxiliaries), WAAC, WRNS, and WRAF; and as nurses.[5]

Problems of Integration

Wars are in many ways like revolutions: they set up problems and conditions that radically alter the previous status of certain elements in society. In terms of both the social-sexual mores of Edwardian England and the country's venerable and rigid service traditions, the presence of women in the military represented revolutionary behavior. The two major levels of integration of women into the services were social and institutional. The first had to do almost entirely with gender roles and problems. Many officers resented the presence of women in war on general principle: "conservative Englishmen deem them a nuisance," as one observer put it concisely.[6] Many soldiers, as often happens, emulated their superiors in their contempt for women. Other enlisted personnel had more concrete reasons for hating the women who came to replace them. For example, cooks from the WL replaced males who were then sent to the front; the men then jammed the burners of the stoves, and one is reported to have told the women that they were sending men to their deaths.[7]

Sexual anxiety loomed large in the opposition of some elements of British society to the appearance of women in the military, in whatever capacity. How much actual sexual contact took place is, of course, impossible to say. The pregnancy rate among the WAACs was three per thousand, lower than the civilian rate. But the fact remained that middle-class women, sheltered at home, mingled not only with men but also with women of lower-class backgrounds who were considered, with some justification, to have more "open" moral standards and wider experience with men. "They are mostly girls of a class that knows few restrictions, who, with the exception of those previously in domestic service, have always had what they call their 'evenings' when they roamed the street or went to the cinemas with their 'boys,'" wrote a contemporary observer in 1919.[8] The intermix of classes posed a menace to social values as much as did the proximity of the sexes. Added to this was the widely known "virile" image of the Tommy, who, like the doughboy, the *poilu,* and the *frontovik* in other lands, was projected in barracks culture and in popular media as brave and tough and a great lover. Rumors began to spread at once about immoral behavior in the services: high pregnancy rates, drinking and fraternization with men, the army as an organized brothel system (reinforced by still fresh images of camp followers and 19th-century attempts to organize and inspect prostitutes for service in navy towns). Mothers were concerned about their daughters being stationed far from home and free of parental supervision, working in the company of the military who were thought to be sexually starved.

The authorities took some interesting measures to arrest or diminish these rumors.[9] Strict rules of movement, dress, and comportment were widely publicized. The female uniforms were partly defeminized (for example, removing the breast pocket, which was thought to emphasize excessively the bust).[10] The salute and other military symbols were introduced for women in order to reduce the external sex differences. The classical relation of rich–man–poor–girl in British class-ridden society was prevented from being reenacted in the service by extending the prohibition of fraternization of officers and men to officers and women of the ranks. On the other hand, organized, supervised, and very proper, activities involving both sexes were encouraged and touted as the norm; indeed, many marriages arose out of wartime experience. Most effective of all, the government constantly publicized the wholesomeness of the military milieu and refuted the recurring rumors. The records of the Ministry of Labour and other organs concerned with image and rumor-quashing must make some fascinating reading for present-day military authorities faced with similar problems. The capstone of government policy was having Queen Mary assume the honorific title of Commandant-in-Chief of the corps and having it renamed after her (QMAAC) in April 1918.[11] After this, according to some sources, the rumors perceptibly subsided. Who, after all, would dare to sully an organization under so august a patronage?

Institutional integration—how "military" would the women's military organizations become—overlapped in some ways with the problem of sexual integration. The male military decision makers who pushed for greater integration seem to have done so for two main reasons: to diminish the visible sexual differences and thus allay the rumors; and, in the words of an Adjutant-General's office statement of April 1917, "to secure the continuity of labour and control of women."[12] Those who opposed the trend were less articulate but almost as effective. Women were uniformed, billeted, and paid by the military and were sent abroad, and thus were more "military" than VAD or WL or other civilian formations. But commanders successfully resisted identical uniforms and insignia and discouraged the female use of the salute. Women enrolled instead of enlisting, had no ranks and titles equivalent to those of the males, and had officials instead of officers. These officials were called controllers and administrators or, for NCO levels, forewomen. In fact, the status of military women was wholly, and no doubt deliberately, ambiguous: they were taken into the army but recruited by the Ministry of Labour and by women's organizations; depending upon the offense and the location, they were subjected to different disciplinary codes; and they were described simultaneously as having military designation but as civilian employees. Since most women in these units were grateful for even partial integration (the units were created very late in the war), there seems to have been little resistance to the ambiguity among the recruits themselves, although much discussion among the organizers and the authorities. The tension remained unresolved: treating the women like females meant invoking the "sexual problem"; treating them like soldiers meant treading on the traditional preserve of the male gender.

Observations

The three major attitudinal perspectives on the question of female service in the war were public opinion (the most elusive), military opinion, and feminist opinion. The military was perfectly happy to have the *services* of women (particularly in war work), but not enthralled with having women *in service*. Public opinion was more fluid and complex. Aside from moral concerns, there was a clear undercurrent of generalized opposition to the expansion of women's visibility (some of this surely inherited from the backlash against the military suffragettes, who had employed physical violence in the years immediately preceding the war).[13] "We in England," wrote F. T. Jesse, "grew so tired in the early days of the war, of the fancy uniforms that burst upon women. Every other girl one met hed an attack of khakiitis, was spotted as the pard with badges, and striped as the zebra." By the end of the war, the seriousness of women, their uniformity and organizational strictness, and official patronage had somewhat eroded this hostility. The participation of women in war, again in Jesse's words, "had become regular, ordered, disciplined and worthy of respect."[14] Feminists, while ceasing their militant agitation of recent years and pouring their energies into the war effort, did so in the hope that this would serve their cause. It did. Many women engaged in war service for feminist reasons: to show their worth, their special skills, and their organizational ability. Such work helped also to erode some lingering resistance to "work" among women of certain social strata. The war industries helped expand enormously the industrial roles of the female half of the population. And, at the end of the war, women did get the vote.

What impact did women's participation have on the armed services?

About eighty thousand British women served in the military units (see note 5, p. 42). This was greater than the number of Russian women in the same war (1914–1917) and about the same as Russian women in the civil war (1918–1920). But in both these Russian wars, women served in direct combat; in the civil war they served in a wide variety of military and political roles. British women in the WAAC were restricted; their functions were organized into clerical, transportation, quartermaster, and communications categories. The WRAF had a similar organization of functions. Women in all services did not fly, travel aboard ships, or fire weapons. On the other hand, women were killed and wounded by shellfire and in raids from aircraft, and they were cited for valor on a few occasions for their conduct in perilous situations. But their worth must be judged on their performance of the limited support functions that they were assigned; and these they carried out efficiently. Their camps were self-contained and enmeshed in a strict regimen of order, discipline, and rigid morality. Leaders were women of the upper class (the two major WAAC commanders were the daughter of an officer of a good family with organizational experience and a physician of similar social origin). Thus the women's military community emulated both the male military sphere and British society as a whole in terms of its class-education division of labor. The result, according to contemporary accounts, was good management, high morale, and effective performance.[15] Although British women did not yet serve ''as'' armed forces, they moved from a position of serving exclusively ''for'' to serving ''with'' those forces.

All the military units of women were dissolved in the few years after the armistice of 1919; some WRAF personnel served with occupation troops in Germany for a while. The volunteers—FANY, the WLMTS, and VAD—were kept intact, since their existence had predated the war. Interorganizational rivalry, plus the apparent lack of any major incentive to increase women's military role between the wars, prevented these somewhat related bodies from unifying. With the growing diplomatic crises of the late 1930s—German rearmament, the Italian invasion of Ethiopia, the Spanish civil war, and the rest—a new organization, the Emergency Service, was formed in 1936. This was in effect a women's reserve officers training corps, which became the training echelon for the revived services after 1939. In 1938, the year of the Munich crisis, WL and VAD were merged, with FANY retaining a separate but attached status. Its strength was about 16,000 enlisted- and 914 officer-level women. In the same year, ATS was organized to unify and coordinate the previous functions of ES; WAAC-QMAAC and WRAF were subsumed under ATS (the WRAF was later detached, and ATS became the successor of WAAC only).[16] When Hitler invaded Poland in September 1939, a new stage in the history of British military women began.

WORLD WAR II

Scope of Activity

As might be expected, the scope of women's participation in World War II was much greater than in the first war. The civilian groups such as FANY and MTS still retained their basically independent and upper-class tone (FANY women wore silk stockings, for example; titled women tended to gravitate to MTS), but a few of the FANY branched out into more spectacular and romantic roles as saboteurs and spies in occupied France.[17] The various nursing units also increased in size and, because of the higher technological level of this war, were more exposed to danger from various kinds of enemy fire. The RAFNS had 21,300 nurses as compared to 130 in the earlier war.[18] The biggest change, however, came in the redefinition and vast expansion of the three military women's units: ATS, WRAF, and WRNS. In April 1941 (two and a half years after hostility began) ATS and WRAF were given "complete military status," at least on paper. In December 1941, after much debate, conscription was introduced in the face of critical manpower shortages. It became effective in early 1942. By September 1943 over 450,000 women were in service (9.39 percent of the armed forces). Volunteers always greatly outnumbered conscripts during the war. Twenty-two recruitment centers were set up nationwide and two officer training centers for women at Edinburgh and Windsor. Commissions were for the first time given to women, and women were brought under regular military disciplinary law. (See Table 1.2 for figures).[19]

This later version of WAAC was initially called WADS—a designation which the women opposed for obvious semantic reasons (cotton wadding was a traditional means of menstrual stoppage; female soldiers at drill had been described as "waddling"). It was renamed ATS in 1938. It was the first, the largest, and the least popular of the military units among women volunteers. The 200,000 or so women serving in 1943 were in at least eighty different military specialties ("trades" in British; MOS in American terminology). In the skilled division were about 3,000 clerical personnel, 9,000 technical, 3,000 communications, and 4,000 cooks; in the nonskilled categories were, among others, 30,000 orderlies and 15,000 drivers. Approximately 57,000 ATS used in AA (air defense or antiaircraft) work were in fire control, searchlight operations, targeting, hit confirmation, and other aspects of AA operations. A typical battery had 189 men and 299 women, with the men doing all the firing and the women most of the accompanying functions. Thus the most combat-oriented segment of the largest military unit for women did not fire guns but worked on subsidiary operations.[20]

The most popular branches were WAAF (the new name of WRAF),

Table 1.2

Number and Percent of Women Utilized by the Armed Forces of Great Britain:
1939-1945 (by service and year)

DATE	NO. WRNS	% NAVY	NO. ATS	% ARMY	NO. WAAF	% AIR FORCE	TOTAL IN 3 SER-VICES	% IN SER-VICES
Dec. 1939	3,400	1.56	23,900	2.08	8,800	3.93	36,100	2.27
Dec. 1940	10,000	2.92	36,400	1.72	20,500	4.01	66,900	2.26
Dec. 1941	21,600	4.59	85,100	3.51	98,400	10.80	205,100	5.39
Dec. 1942	39,300	6.49	180,700	6.58	166,000	15.06	386,000	8.67
Mar. 1943	45,000	6.87	195,300	6.92	180,100	15.96	420,400	9.13
June 1943	53,300	7.47	210,300	7.29	181,600	15.81	445,200	9.38
Sept. 1943	60,400	7.84	212,500	7.35	180,300	15.51	453,200	9.39
Dec. 1943	64,800	7.89	207,500	7.19	176,800	15.04	449,100	9.19
Mar. 1944	68,600	8.20	206,200	7.14	175,700	14.94	450,500	9.20
Dec. 1944	73,400	8.60	196,400	6.64	166,200	14.44	436,000	8.79
June 1945	72,000	8.42	190,800	6.13	153,000	13.87	415,800	8.20

SOURCE: Great Britain Central Statistical Office (1951: Table 10).

number one, and the WRNS. The WAAF had fifty-seven different specialties in transport, mechanics, repair, communications, code work, parachute repair, cooking, photography, and radar, among others. Women also dominated the operation of air defense barrage balloons on British soil. But they did not fly. Ironically, women of the civilian ATA served as pilots (100 of the 800 were women), flew transport missions, and were shot down (women were 15 of the 173 killed in action). The glamour of the air force, the legendary reputation of RAF fliers, the conditions of work, and the fact that WAAF was designated as having military status must have accounted for the great popularity of WAAF among women. Navy was second in popularity among volunteers, but navy women were even more remote from combat than WAAFs. WRNS women lacked military status; about one-third of them lived at home and commuted to their work as drivers, clerks, housekeepers, and communication and technical specialists, just like females in the civilian economy. Few ever served aboard ship.[21]

Problems of Integration

Opinion surveys that were more extensive than those of the 1914 war indicated that both civilian and military men still opposed women in service as a general rule. A sampling of ATS women themselves questioned during the war indicated that they thought they had a poor image among the public.[22] Some of the opposition in the military was to the relatively high level of absenteeism and wastage, of women resigning at will at various stages of their training. There was no way to enforce desertion laws against women, even though they were recruited by the draft. The sexual question also asserted itself. In the first place pregnancy was a bigger problem than in World War I, although the rate was still lower than among unmarried civilian women of a comparable age group (21.8 per 1,000). (Single women between the ages of twenty and thirty were eligible for the draft.) In ATS it was 15.4 per 1,000 at the first counting, but jumped to double that figure in 1943; and these figures were higher than comparable ones of World War I. The apparently larger number of women who were asserting their sexual freedom were given "paragraph elevens," a compassionate discharge. It was generally agreed that army life was no place for a pregnant woman, married or not. The problems of transporting pregnant women, of detecting pregnancy early, and the still rather rigid perceptions of pregnant women in visible positions all conspired to make the army very careful to screen out pregnant women as soon as possible.[23]

Since the pregnancy rate was higher than in World War I, perhaps there was good reason for traditional mothers to fear for their daughters' virtue. Parental concern continued to be a public relations issue for the high command. In the AA, for example, the army experimented with mixed batteries composed of young women and middle-aged men (these did not work for reasons of generational not sexual tensions). Members of Parliament, on the other hand, seemed to be more alive to the perils of women being corrupted on "the wilder shores of love," that is, for instance, in overseas commands among non-British peoples. "There are dangers," warned a House of Commons speaker, "not dangers of the battlefield, but where the moral standards do not perhaps compare favorably with those of this country."[24] But when the war ended, the authorities favored very much the idea of sending British service women to Germany in order to diminish the incidence of fraternization with local German females—a distinctly manipulative device.[25]

There was a higher level of institutional integration of women in the armed forces in World War II, but not much higher. The minimal increase over World War I was not because integration did not work well where it was tried, but because the commanders kept it in check. For example, women were commissioned as officers, not officials. Recruitment bodies used intelligence tests and even personal references in some outfits. Women tended to flow into the branch that they preferred. Reports were issued from time to time that the valor of women under fire boosted male morale; and the morale of women, according to a few impressionistic observations, was higher in the zones nearest combat. In the most common ''combat'' situation, the AA batteries, teams of both sexes worked very well (especially after young women were teamed up with men their own age). The Ministry of Information reported that ''Far from resenting the ATS the men in the mixed batteries show a very real pride in the girls' work and are the first to defend them against their critics.''[26]

On the other hand, women did not mix well in some situations; radar crews was a case in point, although there is no precise evidence to explain why. More important, women were paid unequally to men, and, in spite of the ''military'' designation, they remained separate in all important ways, as in World War I. The major reason for this segregation (in addition to the still widespread opposition to the whole phenomenon) was the strict adherence to the definition of women soldiers, sailors, and airwomen as ''noncombatant.'' Added to this was the familiar problem of all detailed units, namely that women often came under dual and overlapping jurisdiction which occasionally created friction between the women's command structure and the men's.

Observations

When comparing British women's participation in World War II with that of World War I, the growth seems impressive indeed, both in numbers (see Table 1.3) and range of specialties (although the proliferation of technical occupational terms tends to obscure some basic similarities between 1914 and 1939 military roles). Another way to look at the problem is to compare it with female participation in the Soviet Union in the same war. In both cases, the regime wanted to stress economic utilization of women, although the Soviets were far in advance due to massive industrialization drives of the 1930s. Both resisted bringing women into war, but both succumbed to perceptions of manpower needs and introduced forms of conscription (in Britain two years after the war began in 1939; in the Soviet Union, informally, soon after June 22, 1941). The Soviets had a much larger contingent of female university and technical school graduates. Compulsory assignment of British women to overseas theaters was paralleled by Soviet disbursement of women to all major geographical

Table 1.3

**Women in WAAC, World War I, and in ATS, World War II
(by number and year)**

DATE	NO. WAAC	DATE	NO. ATS
Aug. 1917	2,377	Dec. 1939	23,900
Sept.	3,095		
Oct.	5,240		
Nov.	16,228		
Dec.	20,198		
Jan. 1918	22,470	Dec. 1940	36,400
Mar.	33,026		
Apr.	35,553		
May	33,471		
June	35,230		
July	36,260		
Aug.	37,147		
Sept.	38,463		
Oct.	39,733		
Nov.	40,850		
Dec.	39,742		
Jan. 1919	37,993	Dec. 1941	85,100[1]
Feb.	35,632		
Mar.	32,208	Dec. 1942	180,700[2]
Apr.	29,740	Dec. 1943	207,500
May	27,129	Dec. 1944	196,400

SOURCES: War Office (1920, p. 206); Central Statistical Office (1951, p. 9).
   1. April 21, 1941: New Military status for WAAF and ATS announced. June 19, 1941: ATS and WAAF granted new military status by Army Council Instruction. Dec. 4, 1941: National Service (No. 2) Act passed making women liable for conscription.
   2. April 23, 1942: First recruits called up under conscription.

fronts in the huge state. We have little data on what motivated British women to go to war, but the heavy Soviet motif of hatred and vengeance against alien occupiers was certainly missing. The main organizational difference was that the British formed all-female branches—ATS, WAAF, and WRNS. The Soviets had no counterparts to these; women served either in small all-female units or were intermixed, depending on the situation. Soviet women also had more prewar preparation for service in a number of paramilitary organizations that were popular among women and stressed military virtues.

The British debate about combat status for women shows how ambivalent the military and the civilian authorities were on this issue. Given the new military technology of World War II, it was clear that many noncombatant functions of the earlier war were very close to the combat situation and exposed to danger. The existence of long-range guns that could reach rear support elements and hospitals was often invoked by those who thought that being in service was almost equivalent to being in combat (although, logically, one could have argued that the development of the long-range bomber and later the V-2 rockets made all civilians "combatant" in the sense of exposure to fire). Referring to AA service, a member of Parliament, Edith Summerskill, said "Surely, nobody here thinks for one moment that the Germans will treat women on gun sites as noncombatants."[27] The government, in any case, adhered to the "noncombatant" definition. Women were not to bear arms, serve in assault units, in front-line battle, aboard ships, in tanks, or in fighting planes. By this definition, then, women were not eligible to receive combat decorations, although they were granted other military honors. The casualty figures for the three services were as follows: 624 killed, 98 missing, 744 wounded, and 20 captured (of which 751 were ATS, 611 WAAF, and 124 WRNS).[28] Soviet women, by comparison, fired every weapon, served in almost every type of unit and combat situation (as snipers, riflewomen machine-gunners, tankers, mortarwomen, pilots, bombardiers, navigators, artillerists, and the like). Tens of thousands served as partisans in the Ukrainian and Belorussian forests, while only a handful of British women were dropped in eastern France to serve in the Maquis resistance movement there. The Russian *partizanka* (partisan) became a wartime media figure. There was nothing on the British scene comparable to this.

A vivid way of contrasting the numbers and impact of British and Soviet women at war is in the AA services. The British women were called "Gunner Girls," but did not fire the guns; they worked in mixed crews with males doing the actual firing. Soviet women were said to have replaced over 300,000 men in these occupations and as gunners. Females dominated many AA positions in Moscow, Leningrad, and other major cities, had their own officers, and worked most often in all-women units.

Soviet sources liked to depict their women warriors as brave and martial—the sexual element was almost always downplayed, except to invoke wifely or maternal virtues. No public discussion of morals or of pregnancy problems were held as in Britain. British sexual vagrancy was not severely punished; Soviet soldiers who violated the segregation orders and impregnated a female soldier could be put in prison for ten years. There was initial hostility in both armed forces to women; and in both cases apparently the feeling eroded, at least partially, as women became more visible and useful. But the Soviets had a much more fluid deployment of women in small units and interspersed in male units. British women almost always served under their own officers and the British officer was reputed to be reluctant to order or discipline a female subordinate. Soviet male officers do not seem to have had such problems. This difference reflected the individual natures of the two societies. In Russia women were already familiar not only as workers and professionals but also as fighters in the revolutionary movement and in the civil war of 1918–1920. Nevertheless, in spite of the muteness of Soviet materials, there are sufficient hints in the literature that the Soviets also had their problems of integration.

Comparison of numbers deployed do not tell very much because the Soviet figures are so flat and vague. About a million women are said to have fought in the war, about 800,000 of them in the armed forces (the rest presumably as partisans). This compares to the peak British figure of about 450,000, halfway through the war. Thus British women constituted 9 to 10 percent of the total armed forces as compared to 8 percent for Russian women. But of these, a half million are described as "serving at the front" in the Soviet Union, an obviously broad definition of front-line activity. The British equivalent was minuscule, which is hardly surprising or even very revealing. The British women had no revolutionary tradition of female participation on a large scale, no mobilization organs to press women into service in mass numbers, and no presence of foreign and brutal invaders on their own soil.

THE PEACETIME SERVICES

The climate of military opinion in 1945 was different from that of 1918. No rosy dawn of goodwill and permanent peace brightened the postwar landscape as it had seemed to do after World War I. Demobilization was necessary, of course, but the War Department had decided to retain a women's element in the peacetime army; it had shown its worth. It took three years to construct the legislation and pass it through the Parliament. In the meantime, a small nucleus of women remained in the ATS and some of the other units. In February 1949 the Women's Royal Army Corps, a direct revival of ATS, was established. Jobs were few in the postwar years and the operation was very modest, a situation that enabled slow and stable growth. Since then the history of WRAC has been one of slow expansion of jobs and of numbers and the gradual raising of status, particularly for officers. Each decade has seen the debate between budget trimmers and those who wish to expand the service. The women's movement of the 1960s and 1970s clearly had an influence in raising the public awareness of women; grim unemployment figures have also sent many girls and young women into the services in search of a career. WAAF, renamed WRAF, was revived under the same bill; the navy, clinging to its own traditions of separateness established the WRNS, Women's Royal Navy Service.[29]

The WRAC is the biggest of the women's services (sixty-five hundred as compared to fifty-four hundred in the WAAF and thirty-nine hundred in the WRNS), based on estimates for 1981,[30] and therefore best illustrates the realities and problems of everyday military life for women in the 1980s. It retains its administrative autonomy with parallel organization, which is financially costly but valuable in giving women command experience. The director-WRAC is a brigadier, still the highest rank a woman can achieve. Women officers serve in many advisory functions at various high echelons in the army. There were only nine hundred officers, as of January 1980. Their examinations for promotion are the same as for men. Women officers tend to have slightly better school records than men, but they still cannot attend the highest level of the military educational establishment, the Royal College for Defence Studies, although they have penetrated most others. Women officers serve in all-male units in a variety of capacities, often specialized (welfare, counseling), as well as commanding women's units. Since 1974, enlisted women have had the choice of inspecting the actual job opportunities and requesting a particular job *before* being inducted, a reform that has helped in recruitment and reduced wastage and job turbulence. The WRAC trades in 1977 were:

Administrative Assistant
Analyst (Special Intelligence)
Artificer (Instrument)
Artificer (Telecommunications)
Bandswoman
Combat Radioman
Clerk
Clerk (Assistant Programmer)
Clerk (Royal Army Pay Corps)
Clerk (Shorthand Writer)
Communication Centre Operator
Cooks (Two groups)
Data Telegraphist
Driver
Experimental Assistant (Gunnery)
Hairdresser
Kennelmaid
Medical Orderly
Mess Caterer
Mess Steward
Movement Operator
Military Policewoman—Provost
Military Policewoman (Special Investigation Branch)
Operator (Electronic Warfare)
Operator Intelligence and Security
Postal and Courier Operator
Physical Training Instructor
Radio Telegraphist
Radar Operator (Light Air Defence)
Rider/Groom
Stewardess
Storewoman (Royal Army Ordnance Corps)
Switchboard Operator
Technical Clerk[31]

WRAC women are required to live on base. There are a few independent all-female units (headquarters companies in London and in Germany performing paper functions); most are in integrated units. Disciplining of women soldiers is still done only by women officers. Roles are widening all the time, but not very dramatically or rapidly. Women are still primarily engaged in domestic, clerical, driving, and other menial work, but some get into the military police or even intelligence roles. The closest women have come to a wartime situation is in Northern Ireland. About six hundred women serve in the Ulster Defence Regiment (UDR) in communications, road duty, and border patrols (all unarmed). The women of the UDR, called "greenfinches" because of their high-pitched voices on the radio, are interesting for at least two major reasons. In the first place, they are the closest thing to women in combat. Ironically, one of the reasons for the formation of the WUDR, the name of their unit, is that female terrorists of the Irish Republican Army (IRA) and other groups were being utilized to conceal weapons and explosives in their garments. Women of the UDR were recruited locally to search females, to set up road checks, to accompany night patrols, to operate radios, and to man operations rooms. In a way, it is one of the rare examples of using women in a military situation against other women. The other interesting aspect of the Greenfinches is that they were recruited locally and put directly into a British regiment, instead of being detailed from the WRAC. This is the first case of complete integration of males and females in a British military unit. Commentators are already pointing to it as a possible model for future units along the road to complete male-female integration of the armed forces.[32]

The most fascinating sociological research on women and the British armed forces is the surveys of background, motivation, and personality conducted among selected volunteers. Two recent studies show a large proportion of women to be: consciously committed to and not casual about enlistment; often connected to the military through family; aged sixteen to twenty when making the decision to join; and of lower-class or working-class families with rarely more than a high school education, seeing the army as a "second chance" for schooling. Culturally, the sample appears to be nonintellectual, not joiners of local or teenage activity groups, with passive leisure habits (TV watching, disco, cheap fiction, pop music) rather than creative ones. Traditionally feminine and somewhat authoritarian (in conformity with an English working-class background), the young women appear to have low hopes for success or fulfillment in their own hometowns or locales and thus view the service as a broadening and enriching milieu (1) with sufficient structure to deal with insecurity; (2) with sufficient variety to prompt a hope for association and perhaps adventure; and (3) with sufficient texture to provide a kind of surrogate family or community which they seem to feel missing at home. Students of social processes and systems might well see the impact of the new army upon English society, particularly upon lower-class females, to be at least as important a human question as the impact of women upon the army. It also seems to show that the army draws those who have not much better to do in their own milieu.[33]

The problems of women adjusting to a peacetime military career—and of the army adjusting to women—are many and complex. In a mid-1970s survey of women's complaints and problems, many respondents felt that the basic training phase was too severe, too restrictive of movement and behavior, and also "unreal" in terms of their future activity. When asked about job preference, the responses seemed to point to driver, "phys-ed" instructor, and military police as the high status jobs; to clerk and domestic chores as the low status; and to cooking as something in between (requiring a skill and perhaps relating to role perception for the future). Responses indicated that excessive social distance and aloofness between female officers and enlisted women was not seen as a major problem, which may indicate that "newer" institutions may be open to a more democratic kind of ethos, or even—although this is very speculative—that there might exist a kind of female democratic style (there is at least a hint of it in the Soviet wartime experience of one female unit). Most women in the service are young: in this sampling, 50 percent were twenty years old or younger; 36 percent twenty to twenty-four; the officers only a little older on the average. This also might account for a somewhat looser and less castelike relationship between officers and nonofficers than existed formerly.[34]

Respondents indicated in general that greater satisfaction in the military was directly related to greater job opportunities. But the average service term for a female was 2.55 years as compared to 4.90 for the male. There exists a kind of vicious circle, similar to that of any civilian society. Employers (in this case the military) are reluctant to offer more kinds of and better jobs for a group that will use its training and then leave. Women leave because of the perceived limitations on job opportunity, movement, promotion, flexibility, and the rest. Some observers have suggested that the lack of a sufficient number of role models (specifically, female career officers and senior enlisted personnel) accounts for the high turnover (or job turbulence, as it is called). But this itself is part of the vicious circle. Most women separate from service (more than half) at the end of their enlistment period ("engagement" in British); 21.8 percent do so voluntarily after getting married. Marriage is still difficult to combine with a military career for a woman. "At the moment," one English recruit in the sample commented, "the Army is not a career for *women*, it is a career for *spinsters*." The majority of servicewomen want what men want: good jobs, rapid promotion, chance for travel or mobility (or to choose place of service, including at home), and flexibility. Those who perceive these goals as not sufficiently available tend to resign after their initial enlistment, and so the army has become a kind of stopping-off place for many women, one from which they have no doubt gained much. But the army must pay the bill for the constant training and retraining. It wishes to attract and keep women and get a suitable return on its investment in them. But it is also faced with a dilemma: if it offers jobs and promotions at the desired rate, women will be competing with men even more than now and in a more visible way. One of the best ideas for alleviating the problem of married soldiers is to offer more flexibility, for example, by posting spouses together or giving the woman an unpaid leave until she can be posted with her husband. No one has yet produced a solution for the problem of pregnant servicewomen; they are still forced to terminate service after pregnancy becomes known.[35]

What is the future likely to hold? We can only judge by the kinds of debates that are currently engaging the minds of military authorities of both sexes. Chief among these are the following: updating and reassessing (and perhaps renaming) the services; the recent providing of self-defense weapons training for women (which might lead to conventional combat training); pilot training for the WAAF; higher or equalized pay for women (this would be difficult to defend given the special status and the greater freedom and safety of women in the services);[36] a wider range of jobs and ranks (perhaps beyond brigadier, currently the senior rank for women); coeducation at all officer's training institutions and military educational institutions (for example, the Royal Military Academy at Sandhurst, the best-known officer training academy); and liability of women to military discipline from male officers (the reverse is already possible). One thing that emerges from all these suggestions and debates is that British writers on the subject are very much aware of what is being done in other societies, particularly in the United States, which is seen not only as the major ally, but also as a model that might be emulated at least in some respects. Brigadier Eileen Nolan, former commander of the WRAC, commented on total integration, which some people have suggested, by saying that "the road towards complete integration [must be] taken slowly, steadily and firmly. Only then can we be completely sure that women will take their full part in the army of the future."[37]

The issues that seem to generate the most heat are combat training and combat roles for women in the future.[38] At one end of the spectrum are those, called "militants" or "amazons" by their opponents, who invoke the current American model for combat training and the historical Israeli model for combat roles. They are accused by their critics of being inspired by exaggerated notions of women's liberation and total equality. (Parenthetically, it should be noted, however, that in 1964 the U.S. Congress did pass the Civil Rights Act, which prohibits discrimination in employment on the basis of sex. The United States, which does not have an Equal Rights Amendment to the U.S. Constitution, has greater roles for women in the military than Britain, which has the Sex Discrimination Act, but restricts its women to noncombatant jobs.) Arguments against this position range from those who say that women cannot perform in combat to those who say that women in Britain do not want to perform in combat. Given the experience of Soviet, Yugoslav, and Israeli women, among others, the first argument is weak indeed. The second, however, seems to have great force. Those who have spoken out on the issue in interviews and conference speeches seem to oppose combat for women, and this certainly seems to be the majority opinion among women in the service, not to mention British society at large. But like almost everything else involved with the role of women today, this is subject to change—and change at perhaps a faster pace than most people expect. The expanding numbers of women in the service mean the increasing exposure to battle of some sort in a future war; with this comes the need for some sort of defensive weapons training; and from this—given the difficulty in the heat of combat to distinguish offensive from defensive action—the escalation of women into combat operations. On another note, some authorites suggest that since international law does not identify women *ipso facto* as noncombatant, in the future women, even those in truly noncombat jobs, might be labeled and treated as combatants.[39]

Two different but related social problems have, therefore, emerged in British society since 1914: one, the problem of integrating women into a wartime situation which the British faced in 1914 and in 1939; the other, the gradual and permanent introduction of women into a military society (the peacetime services). Concerning wartime experience, it is clear that the role of women in the services was limited but useful—how useful is impossible to say. In combat their impact was virtually nonexistent. This may change in any future war. If peacetime problems of integration are solved, then one can at least expect greater and better participation of women in the various support services because of the permanent existence of cadres and recruits. Integration problems arose in both wars but were never approached systematically; problems were dealt with on an *ad hoc* basis in the midst of very grave disasters; it could hardly have been otherwise. Nowadays, in tranquil times, the army—and women themselves—are freer to experiment, to plan, to assemble data, to analyze and discuss, and to try to correct major difficulties in the man-woman relationship in the army. The biggest discernible shift seems to have been away from sexual fears and into economic aspirations and family complexities. In other words, the "woman question" in the British armed forces is resembling more and more the "woman question" in society at large. Both the civilian and the military social planners and opinion makers are confronting the problem of the ambit of women's roles, the nature of her mobility and equality, and the complexities that family life introduces into the bigger problem. No one as yet seems close to any definitive solution; but the answers—as well as the questions asked—seem to get more realistic with each passing year.

NOTES

1. J. S. Curtiss, "Russian Sisters of Mercy in the Crimea, 1855–1856," *Slavic Review* (March 1966): 84–100.

2. G. Glaister, "Servicewomen in the British Army" (Unpublished paper, Royal Military College of Science, No. 2 1977), (p. 19). Prepared for Gwyn Harries-Jenkins Research Project, "The Role of Women in Armed Forces. CMRI Panel." ERO Grant #DAERO 77-G-092.

3. The literature on volunteer and war work is large: see Great Britain, Parliament, *Parliamentary Papers (Commons),* Session February 4, 1919 to December 23, 1919, vol. 31 (Reports, vol. 24) Cmd. 167 ("Report of the Great Britain War Cabinet on Women in Industry . . . "); Helen Fraser, *Women and War Work* (New York: G. Arnold Shaw, 1918); Edward Bell, "British Women's Emergency Corps," *Survey* (October 1914): 64; Edith Abbott, "The War and Women's Work in England," *Journal of Political Economy* (July 1917): 641–78; N. H. Webster, *Britain's Call to Arms: An Appeal to our Women* (London: Rees, 1914). For a sample of contemporary rhetoric: see H. M. Usborne, *Women's Work in War Time: A Handbook of Employments* (London: T. Werher Laurie, 1917); and "Women's Work in the War" in *History of the War* (London: *The Times,* 1915).

4. For nursing in wartime see: Violetta Thurstan, *Field Hospital and Flying Column* (London: G. P. Putnam, 1915); "Women Doctors' Wonderful Work Amid War's Horrors," *Literary Digest* (February 1918): 40–41; Elizabeth Haldane, *The British Nurse in Peace and War* (London: J. Murray, 1923); Sister Martin Nicholson, *My Experience on Three Fronts* (London: Allen and Unwin, 1916); E. B. Knocker, "Dr. Hector Munro's Ambulance Corps; Diary Pevsye, September 1914–January 1915" (Unpublished manuscript at the Imperial War Museum); Baroness T'Serclaes and Mairi Chisholm, *The Cellar House of Pevsye* (London: A. & C. Black, 1917); St. Clair Stobart, *The Flaming Sword in Serbia and Elsewhere* (New York: Doran, 1916); "The First World War Papers of Nurse E. Bertram at the Scottish Women's Hospital" (Unpublished manuscript at the Imperial War Museum); "Miss Cavell's Execution," *Review of Reviews* (December 1916) 659–60. The figures are from Great Britain, War Office *Statistics of the Military Effort of the British Empire During the Great War 1914–1920* (London: His Majesty's Stationery Office, 1922), hereafter cited as War Office, *Statistics* (1922).

5. Data on units; debates, and figures may be found in: War Office, *Statistics* (1922); Public Record Office, War Office Files 162 (31, 33, 34, 42, 60, 65 and Adjutant General's papers); see also Great Britain, Air Historical Branch, 1917–1918, (File Air 1) WRAF General File, 1917–1918. Books and articles include Barbara McLaren, *Women of the War* (London: Hodder and Stoughton, 1917); Pauline Gower, *Women with Wings* (London: J. Long, 1938); H. M. Cowper, *A Short History of Queen Mary's Army Auxiliary Corps* (London: Women's Royal Army Corps Assoc., 1967); J. H. Leslie, *An Historical Roll with Portraits of Those Women of the British Empire to Whom the Military Medal has Been Awarded During the War* (Sheffield: W. C. Leng, 1919–1920); "British Women in War Service" *Current History Magazine* (May 1917) 351–52; F. Tennyson Jesse, *The Sword of Deborah: First-Hand Impressions of the British Women's Army in France* (London: Heinemann, 1918) [one of the major accounts]; George Patulo, "The

Tommy WAACS,'' *Saturday Evening Post* (December 1917) 6–7; and H. A. Jones, *The War in the Air* (Oxford: Clarendon, 1937).

6. Arthur Gleason, *Golden Lads* (New York: Century, 1916), pp. 72–74.

7. For other antiwomen episodes, see Patulo, "Tommy WAACS," p. 6.

8. Jesse, *The Sword of Deborah*, p. 53.

9. See the discussion in War Office, File 162 (42).

10. Molly Izzard, *A Heroine in Her Time: A Life of Dame Helen Gwynne-Vaughan 1879–1967* (London: Macmillan, 1969), p. 351.

11. War Office, *Statistics* (1922), p. 205.

12. War Office File 162 (34), April 10, 1917.

13. Two fine treatments of the relationship between society and women at war are: Arthur Marwick, *The Deluge: A Study of British Society and the First World War* (London: Bodley Head, 1965); and idem, *Women at War 1914–1918* (London: Fontana, 1977), the best concise history of the problem.

14. Jesse, *The Sword of Deborah*, p. 8.

15. Eileen Nolan, "Management of Women in the British Army" (Unpublished manuscript, 1978, pp. 1–2). Prepared for Gwyn Harries-Jenkins Research Project, "The Role of Women in Armed Forces. CMRI Panel." ERO Grant #DAERO 77-G-092.

16. Great Britain, Parliament, *Parliamentary Debates,* November 1941 to November 1942, p. 4; Shelford Bidwell, *The Women's Royal Army Corps* (London: Leo Cooper, 1977), p. 51.

17. Russel Braddon, *Nancy Wake* (London: Cassell, 1956) (the account of a general's wife who joined FANY and underwent combat and espionage training and was active in combat activities with the Maquis).

18. D. Collett Wadge, ed., *Women in Uniform* (London: S. Low, Marston, 1947), p. 29. For various treatments of the general role of women and of nurses and support work by women see: Irene Ward, *FANY Invicta* (London: Hutchinson, 1955); Peggy Scott, *British Women in War* (London: Hutchinson, 1940); J. B. Priestley, *British Women go to War* (London: Collins, 1943); Yvonne Macdonald, *Red Tape Notwithstanding* (London: Hutchinson, 1941); Bessy Myers, *Captured* (London, New York: D. Appleton Century, 1942); British Information Services, *Women's War Work in Britain* (New York: British Information Services, 1943); John Drummond, *Blue for a Girl* (London: W. H. Allen, 1960); Eileen Bigland, *Story of the WRNS* (London: Nicholson and Watson, 1946).

19. General works on women in the armed services include: Russell Birdwell, *Women in Battle Dress* (New York: Fine Editions, 1942); Mary Anderson, *British Women at War* (London: J. Murray and Pilot Press, 1941); Phylis Bently, "British Women in the Forces," *Britain* (January 1943): 9–15; Elizabeth Ewing, *Women in Uniform* (London: Batsford, 1975).

20. For accounts of ATS, see: Helen Gwynne-Vaughan, *Service with the Army* (London: Hutchinson, 1942); Anthony Cotterell, *She Walks in Battledress* (London: Christophers, 1942); Eileen Bigland, *Britain's Other Army: The Story of the ATS* (London: Nicholson and Watson, 1946); Sylvia Norman, "Camp with the ATS," *Spectator* (August 1939): 212–13; Federick Pile, *Ack-Ack* (London: George Harrap, 1949) [by the air defense commander]; Muriel Barker, "Freddie Pile's Popsies" (Unpublished manuscript, 1972, London: Imperial War Museum).

21. Contemporary accounts are too numerous to cite. For postwar treatments see, among many others: Mary Settle, *All the Brave Promises* (New York: Delacorte, 1966); Alison King, *Golden Wings* (London: Pearson, 1956) [about the ATA]; S. E. Knapp, *New Wings for Women* (Oxford: Crowell, 1946); Edith Baker, *WAAF Adventure* (London: Lonsdale, 1948).

22. Great Britain, Ministry of Information, "The Social Survey of ATS" (Unpublished typed report, London, Imperial War Museum).

23. Figures: Parliament, November 1941 to November 1942, p. 231. Commentary: Settle, *All the Brave Promises,* p. 63.

24. Great Britain, Parliament, *Parliamentary Debates (Commons),* 5th Series, vol. 407, p. 858. For additional debates in Parliament vis-à-vis women in the service see identical titles for the following years: 1941, vol. 370, pp. 1699–1700; 1943, vol. 389, pp. 598–99; 1943, vol. 391, pp. 2111–2201; 1944, vol. 396, pp. 157–58; 1944, vol. 397, pp. 1320–21; 1944, vol. 398, p. 1227; 1944, vol. 406, pp. 1957–64; and 1945, vol. 407, pp. 841–906.

25. Ibid., 1945, vol. 407, p. 862.

26. Great Britain, Ministry of Information, *Roof over Britain: The Official Story of Britain's Anti-Aircraft Defences 1939–1943* (London: His Majesty's Stationery Office, 1943), p. 59. See also Pile, *Ack-Ack,* and Hugh O'Connor, "Women Man the Guns," *American Magazine* (October 1941): 14–15, 73.

27. Quotation: Parliament, 1943, vol. 391, p. 2114. See also ibid., 1944, vol. 398, p. 1227; and 1945, vol. 407, p. 842; Bidwell, *Women's Royal Army Corps,* p. 74; and Pile *Ack-Ack,* pp. 189–94.

28. Great Britain, Central Statistical Office, *Statistical Digest of the War* (London: His Majesty's Stationery Office, 1951), p. 13.

29. A brief account of the reemergence of the services is in Bidwell, *Women's Royal Army Corps,* pp. 135–41.

30. *Defence in the 1980s: Statement on the Defence Estimates,* 1980, vol. II, *Defence Statistics* (London, 1980), Cmnd. 7826-II, p. 31. In January 1980, 15,800 women represented 4.9 percent of the armed forces in Britain.

31. On military trades and other information: Bidwell, *Women's Royal Army Corps,* pp. 138–40; Glaister, "Servicewomen"; Nolan, "Management."

32. "Women of the UDR," *British Army Review* (December 1975); 30–32. WRACs have also served in the force sent to Zimbabwe, Rhodesia, in early 1980. *Defence in the 1980s,* I, Cmd. 7826-I, p. 61.

33. The samples were taken in 1969 and 1975–1976. See Glaister, "Servicewomen," pp. 9–11.

34. Glaister, "Servicewomen," pp. 12–14.

35. Glaister, "Servicewomen," pp. 14–19 (quotation, p. 19). Ethnic problems are not mentioned in the sources, although there are black women in the service.

36. Equal pay for both sexes was introduced in 1975 except for the extra increment (the "X factor"), given men in light of their additional burdens.

37. Nolan, "Management," p. 14; "Women in the United Kingdom Forces: Annex N to Minutes of 1977 Conference Dated 11 November 1977" (Unpublished typed manuscript); and Charles Owen, ed., *The Future of Women in the Armed Services* (March 1978), pp. 3–14 reports on a seminar given at the Royal United Services Institute for Defence Studies (RUSI) on June 23, 1977. For a discussion

of women and combat, and integration versus equality for women in the British services, see also N. B. Thomas, "Women in Armed Forces," in *Royal United Services Institute for Defence Studies* (September 1981), pp. 54–61.

38. In December 1980 the defence secretary announced that compulsory training in the use of pistols, rifles, and automatic guns would be introduced shortly for WRAC members. Army women with "genuine objections" would be exempted. WRAF women would have the option of such training; but those of the WRNS would not. It was stressed that this was strictly for personal and base defense and not a move toward bearing of arms or combat roles for women. *Daily Telegraph* (December 3, 1980).

39. *Lifesplan Arts* (Undated Sunday supplement 1977), a description of training conditions and some of the debates and opinions; *The Future of Women in the Armed Services;* and *Women in the United Kingdom Forces,* p. 2.

2 | GERMANY AND THE WORLD WARS

Jeff M. Tuten

INTRODUCTION

Julius Caesar chronicled the manner of warfare of numerous Germanic tribes during 57 to 51 B.C.[1] From that time to the present, there is no record of German women being employed in actual combat operations. Indeed, the Germans have been consistently ultraconservative in their employment of women in paramilitary* roles, as well. This conservatism is reflected by the fact that it was only in 1975 that the first woman ever was accepted into the *Bundeswehr* with full military status.[2] This paper examines the history of the paramilitary employment of women in the twentieth century in an attempt to explain the basis of recent German practice and to predict that of the future.

TWENTIETH CENTURY BACKGROUND

Trevor Depuy has chronicled the rebirth of German Military excellence in his book, *A Genius For War*.[3] In the course of this rebuilding, a strong bias in favor of manning the officer corps with members of the German nobility was maintained. During the last half of the nineteenth century and the first half of the twentieth, the royal Prussian army, in particular, and the royal Bavarian, Saxon, and Württemberg armies were molded by men who adhered to the *Junker* ethic,[4] which extolled the honor and glory of war and, parenthetically, exclusively reserved warfare for men. During

---

Sponsored by the U.S. Army Research Institute for the Behavioral and Social Sciences. The views and conclusions contained in this document are those of the author and do not necessarily represent those of the sponsor of the U.S. Government.
* Editor's note. The term *paramilitary* is used because German female military personnel were not granted military status and were considered civilians. British women in the various military auxiliaries by comparison were considered military personnel.

the same period, Germany's European neighbors were turning to a less traditional model, which reflected increasing democratization.[5]

The period 1850 to 1914 appears to have been one of slow but steady progress in the expansion of women's rights in France, the United Kingdom, the United States, and Germany.[6] The sex roles did not vary greatly among the Western industrialized nations on the eve of the Great War. None of those nations' armies included women.

WORLD WAR I

Neither the Germans nor their adversaries foresaw the scope, intensity, or duration of World War I. Earlier European wars of the latter half of the nineteenth century had been characterized by extensive maneuver followed by decisive victory in set piece engagements, which led to early cessation of hostilities. Victory was, in turn, followed by the imposition of limited demands on the defeated state. Demands on the civil economy tended to be slight both because the wars were concluded quickly and because the large materiel and munitions expenditure rates made possible by advances in weaponry had not yet been experienced. Indeed the German's Schlieffen Plan, which opened the war, was well designed to produce a quick victory. Except for a failure of nerve on the part of its executors, it probably would have done so.[7]

There was to be no quick and glorious war, concluded before the home economies were disturbed. Instead, Germany and Austria on the one hand and France, the United Kingdom, Russia, and Italy on the other hand found themselves locked in a long and enormously expensive war of manpower and materiel attrition. It was precisely the type of war Germany could not afford to fight. Germany had no populous and productive overseas possessions from which to draw manpower and resources, but France and the United Kingdom did. In any case, the British navy controlled the seas. Thus, Germany was forced to make large demands upon its industrial work force. Moreover, this came at a time when the males in the work force were being conscripted in ever-increasing numbers to replace the losses sustained in a protracted, two-front war.

Women were increasingly drawn into the German industrial work force but not in numbers sufficient to offset the numbers and skills of the men conscripted for the imperial army. By 1916 the manpower situation caused Field Marshal Hindenburg to ask the government to enact mandatory labor service laws that would cover women as well as men.[8] This proposal was distinctly unpalatable to Chancellor Bethman-Hollweg and the *Reichstag*. The measure was opposed by the male trade unions as well as the majority of women's organizations. Thus, instead of a forced labor law that included women, Hindenburg got the *Vaterlandisches Hilfsdienstge-*

setz (National Auxiliary Service Act) of December 5, 1916. This law subjected males between seventeen and sixty years of age to compulsory labor, but excluded women from its provisions.

When it became clear that legislative measures to increase the number of female workers in war industry would fail, the German War Office established Women's Work Centers *(Frauenarbeitstellen)* to recruit and distribute female workers to war industries. Seidler reports that, at the end of the war, approximately 700,000 women were at work in the armaments industries under the Work Centers' auspices.[9] Continuing manpower shortages caused the German General Staff to undertake more radical measures in the spring of 1917. Through appeals in the German press, women were asked to accept paid jobs in the army rear-area support establishment and, thus, relieve soldiers for the front. To the considerable surprise of its managers, the *Etappenhelferinnen* (Rear-Area Women's Auxiliary) program proved to be quite popular. Several hundred women were hired and employed in rear-area garrisons as laborers in supply and ammunition depots, in veterinary hospitals, in various related positions, and as clerical workers in military staff offices. Most of these women were drawn from the working class.

The *Etappenhelferinnen* were quartered in separate billets. They did not wear uniforms or have a rank structure. They were never considered to be *in* the army, but were civilian women employed *by* the army. The question of arms training or other military training was never even considered. Nevertheless, they did perform tasks previously performed by soldiers.

These successes encouraged the General Staff to start a parallel but more highly structured program to train female volunteers to replace army signal corps soldiers in rear-area and zone-of-the-interior telecommunications functions. The first volunteers began training in May 1918. At the time of the armistice the following November, approximately 500 women were in communications training or had completed it and were awaiting assignment. Because the armistice intervened, none of these members of the Women's Signal Corps *(Weibliches Nachrichtenkorps)* were actually deployed. As with the Rear-Area Auxiliaries, arms training was not considered. The women were viewed as employed by, but not in, the army.

The largest group of women to provide support to the imperial army were the approximately 100,000 nurses who served both within Germany and in rear areas in France and Belgium and in other theaters. The United States and Great Britain had accorded military status to their nurses following the American Civil War and Crimean War, respectively.[10] In World War I the Germans adhered to the more traditional pattern of employing civilian nurses who served without military status. About 90 percent were provided by the German Red Cross and the rest were nursing sisters from religious orders.

We can begin to discern a pattern. The Germans of the Great War era were reluctant to employ women in war-related activities. When that employment became necessary due to severe manpower shortages, they were careful to employ, not enlist, women. "Soldiering" remained the province of the German male. Women might serve but never soldier.

THE WEIMAR PERIOD

The end of World War I ushered in a decade of gradual economic recovery. During this period women in the industrialized countries enjoyed steady, if not spectacular, gains in economic and social status. Enfranchisement of all German women over twenty years of age quickly followed the removal of the kaiser in 1918. In 1929 6.7 percent of the German National Assembly *(Reichstag)* were female.[11] (In the same year, fifteen female members constituted 2.1 percent of the British House of Commons and 1.1 percent of the House of Representatives.) Women who had left their homes to serve the Fatherland by working in industry in many cases retained their jobs after the war and the independence the jobs conveyed. But this improvement in women's status was not universally applauded. It ran counter to traditional German values embodied in the old Imperial Civil Code, which still had the force of law. Similar suspicion and discomfort was being experienced by the more conservative elements throughout Western Europe as well as in the United States.

During the Weimar period perhaps the most vociferous opponent of women's increasing emancipation was the growing National Socialist German Worker's party (NSDAP or the Nazi party). The Nazis, led by Adolf Hitler, constructed their own model of what a German woman should be. This image derived from a rather strange mix of nostalgia for the mythic past and Hitler's fanatic racial beliefs. Highly simplified, the position was that the so-called Aryan race was all important and its expansion and growth was of paramount importance. Because women were the "mothers of the *Volk*," their central role was that of motherhood and homemaking. Man's world was the state, woman's was the home. Men were the warriors, women were the producers of warriors.

The Nazi view of a woman's role was proclaimed loudly and repeatedly both before and after their assumption of power (the *Machtubernahme* or Nazi party) in 1933. Their position was strengthened as a result of the worldwide depression of the 1930s. With millions of German men jobless, the Nazis called for a return of women to the home so that men might work. The party was particularly desirous of rooting out *Doppelverdienern,* female workers who were married to working men, thus needlessly displacing men. As for unmarried women, they were encouraged to get married and quit their jobs and bear "Aryan" children. These views were never translated systematically into fully enforced policies even after the Nazi rise to power. Nevertheless, the underlying beliefs were deeply held, and they strongly influenced German policy until the fall of the Third Reich.

PREWAR GERMANY UNDER THE NATIONAL SOCIALISTS

In 1931 the *Reichstag* enacted a voluntary labor service law. In May and June 1935 the Nazi-controlled *Reichstag* passed two important laws. First came the Compulsory Military Service Act, which specifically empowered conscription of males for military service.[12] Its general section called on all German men and women to serve in case of war.[13] Thus, in theory at least, authority to conscript women for military service existed from 1935 until the end of the Third Reich.

In June 1935 the National Labor Service Law *(Reichsarbeitdienstege- setz)* was passed.[14] This law made all German youth liable for a compulsory six-month term of labor service (later increased to one year of service). German men were conscripted quickly into this labor-service program. Labor service for women, however, was made voluntary and remained so until 1939.[15] Even then, and despite Germany's pressing need for labor later in the war years, the total number of young women serving at one time never exceeded 150,000.

In 1931 Germany was suffering from unemployment.[16] By 1936 Germany was employed fully and suffering the initial effects of a labor shortage. The Nazis thus were placed in an awkward position. They either had to change their ideological position on the role of women or accept a severe labor shortage. When war came, the problem became more severe.

WORLD WAR II

On the eve of World War II the various elements of the German armed forces occupied military garrisons throughout Germany. A substantial number of male and female civilian personnel were employed by the units in garrison, particularly the higher level headquarters and supply units. When mobilized and deployed, the formations were required to replace their civilian employees with soldiers. Deployment of civilian personnel with the field army was specifically prohibited.[17] The prohibition applied both to troop units and staff and supply echelons. At the start of the war approximately 140,000 women were employed by the German army alone. Of these, about one-third were clerical workers and the remainder were unskilled laborers.[18]

Initially, there was neither plan nor intention to employ civilians with the deployed forces of the field army. However, the quick victories of

1939 and 1940 left the *Wehrmacht* with large occupation, administrative, and logistic tasks in the occupied, annexed, and allied countries across Europe. It quickly became apparent that the static nature of these organizations and their distance from active combat theaters made the resumption of the employment of women possible. For menial labor, local civilians were hired. For staff, clerical and administrative work, the dictates of security ruled out the use of local nationals.

After the fall of France, a considerable number of German females began to appear in field army units, even though their presence there was not authorized. Wives, girlfriends, and assorted female relatives and acquaintances arrived at an alarming rate on the army's heels. This caused the command authorities in France hastily to develop and promulgate regulations restricting and regulating the employment of civilians. At the same time, it caused the resurrection of the World War I women's auxiliary concept.

THE WOMEN'S AUXILIARY SERVICES

The Army

At the start of the war the Army Signal Corps numbered 128,000 soldiers. By 1943 that number had grown to 220,000. Many were assigned to telephone and teletype exchanges. The capability of women to perform these duties did not escape army manpower authorities. Indeed, garrison telephone switchboards and teletype centrals in Germany for years had been populated by female employees. In their early efforts to free soldiers for combat assignments, the army naturally turned to the concept of the Women's Signal Auxiliary, which had been created but not employed in 1918. Although no prewar plans had been made to do so, the *Nachrichtenhelferinnen* was reactivated in late 1940. Apparently the idea of transferring civilian communications employees from the replacement army was considered first but rejected because they were needed there, and many were married and tied to their homes. Additionally, younger women were considered more suitable for foreign service.

In any case, the army turned to the German Red Cross for its womanpower needs. This was possible because in 1938 Hermann Göring, in his position as commissioner for the Four-Year Plan, had issued a decree requiring that all single women work one "Duty Year" *(Pflichtjahr)*.[19] Only after they had done their Duty Year did single German women become eligible for employment of their choice. The Duty Year employment had to be as an agriculture worker or house worker. Nurses' aides, kindergarten teachers, and welfare workers had two-year terms. The prospect of heavy farm labor or menial house work made the other options very attractive, particularly that of nursing. Thus, in 1940, the Red Cross had a considerable surplus of female nurses' aides serving their two-year *Pflichtjahr*.

The Army High Command approached the German Red Cross which agreed to transfer suitable women from its nurses' aide reserves to the army for communications training and assignment to the army's Signal Auxiliary. The Red Cross furnished the initial contingent and almost all the subsequent Signal Auxiliaries.[20] Note that most of these women had volunteered for the Red Cross in order to satisfy their Duty Year requirement. They were subsequently transferred to the army and assigned paramilitary duties. Thus, in effect, they were conscripted indirectly. However, the Signal Auxiliary service was popular and most nurses' aides volunteered.

The women selected had to meet stiff medical, moral, and security standards. All were between ages eighteen and twenty-four. The army reserved the right to reject anyone found unsuitable. After selection and preliminary training and indoctrination at local military district headquarters, they went to the Women's Signal Auxiliary School at Giessen, where they lived in barracks while training as telephone switchboard, telegraph, or radio operators. The Giessen Signal School acted as the central headquarters and depot for all army Signal Auxiliaries.

The problem of outfitting the women with uniforms was solved simply. The standard gray Red Cross women's uniform was isssued. The Red Cross badges were replaced with the army's national emblem worn embroidered in silver on the right breast of overcoat, jacket, and blouse. The standard army field cap was substituted for the nurse's cap. A gold lightning flash was worn on the left sleeve and was the distinctive emblem of the Women's Signal Auxiliary.

By agreement of the army and the Red Cross, pay scales and living conditions were held as close as possible to those applying to Red Cross nurses serving military hospitals.

The Signal Auxiliaries had a rank structure equivalent to that of the Army, as follows.

Signal Auxiliary	U.S. Army Equivalent (Approximate)
Nachrichtenvorhelferin	Recruit
Nachrichtenhaupthelferin	Private
Nachrichtenoberhelferin	Private First Class
Nachrichtenunterfueherin	Sergeant
Nachrichtenstabsfueherin	Sergeant First Class
Nachrichtenhauptfueherin	Master Sergeant
Nachrichtenoberfuerherin	Lieutenant

Special badges of rank were worn on the sleeve. The ranks did not, however, correspond to those of the official military. (The German army private was a *"gefreiter,"* not an *"oberhelferin."*) The Signal Auxiliary ranks conferred limited supervisory authority over other auxiliaries only and no command authority.

Women's Signal Auxiliaries were always employed in closed groups, never mixed with soldiers performing similar duties. Regulations also required that they work in groups of not fewer than five under female supervisors. They were billeted together. When serving in occupied territories, they were forbidden to leave their quarters except in pairs or in larger groups. Medical care was provided by military doctors. Seidler reports that duty time lost due to sickness was substantially higher than for men.[21] However, one army source reports sickness among the Signal Auxiliaries as rare.[22]

Organized in the late 1940s, the number of army Signal Auxiliaries serving with the field army reached eight thousand in 1942 and stabilized at that number for the remainder of the war. They served in all countries in which the German army was stationed, from Greece to Finland. (They were restricted, however, from those areas in Russia in which partisan activity was high.)

Shortly after the formation of the Signal Auxiliary, the Staff Auxiliary was organized. Personnel were recruited from the ranks of civilian employees of the replacement army garrisons in Germany. (Thus, *ad hoc* recruitment of sweethearts was prevented.) Assignment was for not fewer than one or more than two years. Married women could not serve in the same territory in which their husbands served. The minimum age was nineteen. All were subjected to rigorous medical examinations and security checks.

Uniforms similar to those of the Signal Auxiliary were provided. Post exchange privileges were authorized as was military medical treatment. Annual home leave was provided. Staff Auxiliaries were billeted together and employed together in groups of not fewer than five. About one-third of the higher staff clerical jobs in occupied Western Europe were filled in this way by German women. Although authority existed to require such service abroad under the National Service Decree, it proved unnecessary to make involuntary assignments as ample volunteers were forthcoming. Approximately 12,500 Staff Auxiliaries were serving in all foreign territories by the end of 1942, and this number remained fairly constant for the remainder of the war.

Air Force Auxiliaries

The *Luftwaffe* was the most intensive employer of women, and women in the German air force came closest to performing combat service. The *Luftwaffe* began the war with a large number of female civilian employees.

They were particularly numerous in the communications elements and in the ranks of aircraft spotters and in weather stations.

The German conquest of Europe was followed by a requirement to defend the new territories from air attack. This produced a very large manpower bill at a time when men were in increasingly short supply. Like the army, the air force turned to women, organizing the Air Force Women's Auxiliary *(Luftwaffenhelferinnen)*. They were raised, trained, and managed along lines similar to the army auxiliaries. The majority were employed in clerical and communications duties, but a substantial number were assigned to duties that bordered on being indirect combat positions.

Specifically, large numbers of the Air Force Auxiliaries served as *Flakwaffenhelferinnen* (Antiaircraft Auxiliaries). In this service, they were assigned to searchlight batteries, barrage balloon batteries, and radar batteries. There they replaced soldiers, generally on a three-for-two basis. By the end of the war, 350 searchlight batteries were manned by women's auxiliaries. Each battery had forty-four *Helferinnen*. They lived a rigorous outdoor life. Others, later in the war, were trained as aircraft mechanics and assigned to air force bases throughout Germany. By the end of 1941 there were 35,000 *Luftwaffenhelferinnen*, and that number exceeded 100,000 by 1945. It is clear that these women were critical to the functioning of the German air force in World War II.

Navy and Other Auxiliaries

The German navy organized and employed approximately twenty-thousand Navy Auxiliaries in clerical and communications duties. The *Waffen SS* organized its own *SS Helferinnen*. Strength was maintained at about five thousand.

Military Status

The Germans were extremely careful throughout the war to maintain the essential nonmilitary status of the various service auxiliary organizations. Women's auxiliaries were neither trained in the use of arms nor were they allowed, under any conditions, to use them. Early in the war, the Germans had captured well over 100,000 Russian female soldiers who held full combatant status. This apparently horrified the Germans, who referred to the Soviet female soldiers as *Flintenweib,* a pejorative which translates to "musketwomen" in English. The *Helferinnen* were cautioned constantly against letting themselves become such musketwomen. In 1943 the Armed Forces High Command published an order specifically for auxiliaries directing their conduct if capture was imminent and if captured.[23] Its first two clauses strongly cautioned against using firearms even as a last resort.

The Germans did not consider their female auxiliaries to be soldiers.

They consistently described them as "civilians serving with the Armed Forces." In all cases, they carefully preserved this legal relationship. (It is interesting to note, however, that the order that forbade use of arms to prevent capture is, in all other respects, almost identical to the standing order for soldiers upon capture. For instance, captured auxiliaries were allowed to give only name, rank, serial number, and date and place of birth.)

Official differences notwithstanding, the distinction between the *Helferinnen* and the military women of other armies appears to have been technical at best. The auxiliaries of the German armed forces were, in fact, performing duties which were performed by women auxiliaries in the U.S. Army. Moreover, they were in uniform, subject to military discipline and to the military justice system.

Götterdämmerung

By late 1943 the tide had turned against the Third Reich. Even the millions of forced labor workers from throughout Europe and the prisoners of war could not satisfy the manpower demands of the German war economy. At the same time, battle losses had to be replaced. Manpower planners began to turn to more radical schemes to substitute women for both soldiers and male workers. At each step, however, Nazi ideological resistance prevented the direct conscription of women. Moreover, both Hitler and Göring remained opposed to the employment of women in more military, less feminine positions. Late in 1944 Hitler did agree to allow somewhat wider employment of female auxiliaries, but prohibitions against conscription or use of arms were continued.

In February 1945 all the women's auxiliary organizations were amalgamated into the Armed Services Women's Auxiliary Corps *(Wehrmachthelferinnenkorp)*. Concurrently, auxiliaries began to perform additional, more labor-oriented tasks, such as truck driving. At the same time, the total number increased substantially.

Late in 1944 the "People's Army" *(Volksturm)* had been organized with the mission of last-ditch defense of Germany. In March 1945 Hitler reluctantly acceded to requests by Martin Bormann and Heinrich Himmler and authorized the creation of a women's combat battalion on a trial basis. Subsequently, the *Werwolf* plan called for a guerrilla organization to be composed of both men and women. Neither the women's battalion of the *Volksturm* nor the *Werwolf* guerrilla groups were organized before the collapse of the Third Reich. Thus, no German women served in combat in World War II.

Inevitably, large numbers of women's auxiliaries were captured at the end of the war. Those captured by the Western Allies appear to have been treated as prisoners of war. With the exception of some of the *SS Helfer-*

innen, they were interned briefly in Prisoner of War (POW) camps and then released. Some of the *SS Helferinnen* auxiliaries were held for up to two years pending investigation of their wartime activities. In almost all cases where capture was by the Western Allies, treatment of the women appears to have been proper and humane. Fate was much less kind to those captured in the East. Many reportedly were abused, or executed, or both. Many others spent years in Eastern bloc labor camps. The horror stories told of them still circulate in Germany today. They no doubt influenced current German views on women in the military.

THE POSTWAR ERA

From 1945 until 1956 there were no West German military forces. The creation of the Federal Republic of Germany (FRG) returned sovereignty to the West Germans. In May 1956 the armed forces of the FRG *(Bundeswehr)* were organized. The creation of the *Bundeswehr* was preceded by prolonged, detailed, and frequently heated debate in the FRG Parliament *(Bundestag)*. While there was much controversy, total agreement was reached on the subject of the composition of the force; the *Bundeswehr* would be all male. A conscious, and unanimous, decision was made *not* to emulate the British or American practice of admitting women to the armed forces. Moreover, the framers of the FRG's constitution *(Grundgesetz)* reinforced the decision by including Article 12(a) which states that women " . . . may not under any circumstances render service involving the use of arms."

There were provisions, however, for female civilian employees, as there had been in prewar years. Women are now employed by the armed services throughout West Germany in considerable numbers. The Government White Paper on FRG armed forces published, in September 1979, reports that in that year 180,093 civilian workers were employed by various elements of the *Bundeswehr.*[24] Military units directly employed 83,000; the Federal Territorial Armed Forces Administration employed 71,500; 19,700 were in the armaments sector; and the remainder were in various schools and in the Federal Ministry of Defense. Of the total, 28 percent were women.

For twenty years after its creation, the question of allowing women to enter the *Bundeswehr* as soldiers lay dormant. The issue surfaced in 1975 due to medical officer recruiting and retention problems. The FRG draft was sufficient to bring in short-tour physicians. By 1975, however, consistent problems of retaining medical staff had eroded the career medical establishment to levels considered by officials to be dangerously low. Career military doctors who did remain were aging, and few younger physicians were available to replace them. Various incentives had failed to improve the situation. It was against this backdrop that the *Bundestag* acted, after prolonged debate, in 1975 to admit the first women to full membership in the *Bundeswehr*. The program was limited to female medical doctors. The first five were admitted in October 1975.

The issue of arming the female physicians was particularly difficult and was resolved only after heated public debate. In the end, it was decided to finesse the problem. Under international law, medical officers are non-combatants but are permitted to use weapons to defend their patients or themselves. The FRG Ministry of Defense requires male medical officers to defend their patients, if necessary, and therefore, all male medical officers are armed and given weapons training. Female medical officers are permitted, but not required, to defend themselves or their patients. Thus, female medical officers are offered pistols and training in their use, but are not required to take either. The question may very well remain academic because female medical officers are restricted from serving in forward-area field hospitals as well as aboard naval combatant vessels.

The first admission of female officer physicians came in 1975. At the end of 1979, there were forty-seven commissioned female medical officers in the *Bundeswehr*. From this number, one can see that, although the military sex barrier has been breached, no substantial penetration has been made. There apparently is no intention to militarize the nursing services. The Germans have had good service from their nonmilitary Red Cross and other nurses in two world wars. They apparently see no need for change.

East Germany

The postwar history of military practice in East Germany has, of course, been quite different than West Germany's. The earliest postwar military organizations in East Germany were the Factory Battle Groups *(Betrieb-skampfgruppen)*, which were organized in 1953. Both men and women were included and all were trained in the use of infantry small arms.

There was considerable propaganda during the formation of the German Democratic Republic's "National Peoples' Army" *(Nationalen Volksar-mee—NVA)* about its enlistment of women and their full equality with men in the NVA. Actual performance has been much less dramatic. The East Germans require premilitary training of all youth and provide it both in the schools and through official youth organizations such as the Socialist party's *Freie Deutsche Jugend* ("Free German Youth"). Small-arms training is provided to both males and females.

Women are allowed to volunteer for the NVA. The number of spaces open to women is small, and they are restricted to rear-area, higher staff positions. None serves in combat units. Nevertheless, women are given rigorous basic training and are trained in marksmanship. They wear the NVA uniform and are *in* the army, not merely employed by it. The precise number of female soldiers is not known but is thought not to exceed six thousand. It seems clear that the East Germans have gone much further than their FRG counterparts in admitting women into the military. It is equally clear from the numbers of women actually admitted and the combat unit restrictions that the basic German conservatism regarding female soldiers lingers on.

PROSPECTS FOR THE FUTURE

The preceding pages have outlined the historic refusal of the Germans to employ their women fully as combat soldiers. Indeed, they have consistently refused to admit them to membership in the military profession even with a combat exclusion. Only recently has this taboo been overcome. It is now likely that the demographic situation may further erode German conservatism on this issue. The annual draft-eligible pool of eighteen-year-old males is declining steadily in both East and West Germany. In West Germany the number of qualified and available draft-age males in 1988 will be substantially less than the total needed to maintain the *Bundeswehr* at its authorized and treaty-commitment level for that year. Thereafter, the shortfall will continue to worsen until the end of the century. In 1990 a male conscript shortfall of 50,000 is expected. By 1999 the annual male draftee yield will number 150,000 against an annual requirement of 250,000.[25]

It is, of course, impossible retroactively to change the birthrates of the 1960s. The Germans will, therefore, shortly be faced with very difficult military recruitment decisions, and debate on solutions has already begun in West Germany. Measures being discussed range from drafting foreign aliens working in Germany to accepting a smaller force. Other concepts include the increase in draftee tour lengths from the current fifteen months to twenty-four months or the employment of more civilians to offset the soldier shortfall. Naturally, the possibility of turning to women also is being discussed. In the end, a combination of these possible solutions is most likely. In the United States failure to attract sufficient male volunteers has forced the U.S. Army to turn increasingly to women. Consequently, both the absolute number and the female percentage of the total army has steadily risen since the demise of the draft. In West Germany the coming male manpower shortfall is likely to produce the same solution, but the path will be substantially more difficult because of the conservative aspect of German military institutions.

Nevertheless, the looming male manpower shortage is so large that it seems almost inevitable that the West Germans will, in the end, turn to women to maintain *Bundeswehr* strength. The East Germans will probably increase the currently small female contingent of the NVA. At the same time, the likelihood of the employment of female soldiers in combat operations by either Germany is quite remote. The most probable action will be a continuation of the World War II practice wherein women were, with some exceptions, employed in more traditional roles.

NOTES

1. Julius Caesar, *The Battle for Gaul,* trans. Anne and Peter Wiseman (Boston, Mass.: David R. Godine, 1980).

2. Franz W. Seidler, *Frauen zu den Waffen—Marketenderinnen, Helferinnen Soldatinnen (Women to Arms: Sutlers, Volunteers, Female Soldiers)* (Koblenz/Bonn: Wehr & Wissen, 1978), p. 395.

3. T. N. Dupuy, *A Genius for War, The German Army and General Staff, 1807–1945* (Englewood Cliffs, N.J.: Prentice-Hall, 1977).

4. Detlef Bald, "The German Officer Corps: Caste or Class?" in *Armed Forces and Society* 5, no. 4 (Summer 1979): 642–47.

5. Ibid.

6. Jill Stephenson, *Women in Nazi Society* (New York: Harper and Row, Barnes and Noble, 1975), pp. 13–17.

7. Dupuy, *A Genius for War,* p. 140.

8. Seidler, *Frauen,* pp. 25–26.

9. Ibid, p. 26.

10. Nancy Goldman, "The Utilization of Women in the Armed Forces of Industrialized Countries," *Sociological Symposium* (Spring 1977): 3.

11. Stephenson, *Women,* p. 3.

12. Seidler, *Frauen,* p. 44.

13. Ibid. The specific clause, contained in the opening section of the act, reads, "In addition to military service every male and female German will be liable to compulsory service in any other form for the Fatherland in time of war."

14. Leila Rupp, *Mobilizing Women for War: German and American Propaganda, 1939–1945* (Princeton, N.J.: Princeton University Press, 1978), pp. 80–81.

15. Ibid.

16. Stephenson, *Women,* pp. 103–5.

17. General Major Hellmuth Reinhardt, "Personnel and Administration Project 28, Part VI: German Women in War Service During World War II," trans. and ed. H. Heitman, HQS, European Command, Historical Division (MS #P-027 Koenigstein, May 16, 1949), pp. 51–52.

18. Ursula von Gersdorff, *Frauen im Kriegsdienst, 1914–1945 (Women in War Service, 1914–1945)* (Deutsche Verlag-Anstalt, 1969), p. 74.

19. Rupp, *Mobilizing Women,* pp. 81–82.

20. Reinhardt, "Personnel and Administration Project 28," pp. 134–35.

21. Seidler, *Frauen,* p. 113.

22. Reinhardt, "Personnel and Administration Project 28," pp. 146–47.

23. Seidler, *Frauen,* p. 170.

24. White Paper, "The Security of the Federal Republic of Germany and the Development of the Federal Armed Forces," (Bonn: Ministry of Defense, September 1979), p. 243.

25. Ibid., p. 226.

3 | RUSSIA: REVOLUTION AND WAR

Anne Eliot Griesse and
Richard Stites

War and revolution are two of the major motifs of Russian history in this century. One cannot really be understood without the other, so closely is Russia's present military condition linked with its past wars and its social transformation caused by the revolution. The female population has been involved in both. Women participated sporadically and minimally in Russia's nineteenth-century wars, as peasant partisans against the French in 1812 and as nurses since the Crimean War, and steadily and importantly in the Russian revolutionary tradition from the 1870s through the civil war.[1] As almost everywhere else in Europe, women played no real role in war until 1914. Then they appeared in a variety of roles and in the context of three separate historical episodes. In World War I, until the fall of the monarchy in February 1917, they entered individually as volunteers and fought in combat; during the eight months of the provisional government that succeeded the monarchy in 1917, they served in regularly constituted women's battalions; then after the Communist revolution of October 25, 1917, they fought against counterrevolutionaries in the civil war (1918–1920). Twenty years of peace and the virtual absence of women (1920–1941) followed until their massive involvement in World War II, called by the Soviets the Great Patriotic War, (1941–1945), and then again demobilization. In the course of the last sixty years or so of Soviet power, the Communists have developed a political, economic, and military style that makes their utilization of women dramatically different from that found among the Western, democratic, industrial states.

Sponsored by the U.S. Army Research Institute for the Behavioral and Social Sciences. The views and conclusions contained in this document are those of the author and do not necessarily represent those of the sponsor or the U.S. Government.

Women's role in the revolutionary struggle against the tsarist regime, although numerically small—several thousand at the most—had great symbolic and psychological significance. Radical males of the 1860s had made a cult of sexual equality, and women were invited to join the movement as equal partners, even though men usually made operational and tactical decisions. When the struggle took on momentum in the 1870s, women conducted propaganda, maintained conspiratorial apartments, kept secrets when interrogated, performed espionage work, smuggled inflammatory literature and weapons beneath their skirts, and handled explosives. Many engaged directly in violence. Vera Zasulich inaugurated the so-called era of terror in 1878 by shooting a prison official; Sofya Perovskaya (the daughter of a general) led the assault team that assassinated Tsar Alexander II in 1881, for which she was hanged. Many others, largely of the educated upper classes, and often the daughters of military officers joined the movement.[2]

Most radical parties endorsed the full equality of the sexes and when one of them, the Bolsheviks (the militant branch of Russian Marxism), came to power in 1917, it proclaimed full emancipation of women and invited women to assume their rightful role in defending the regime and in joining the political and economic processes connected with building socialism. Alexandra Kollontai became a government minister and an active propagandist during the civil war. In that position Kollontai, the daughter of a general, former wife of a colonel, and later wife of the Bolshevik naval commissar, seemed to symbolize the new roles of women. When Stalin consolidated his power in the early 1930s, much of the early Bolshevik feminism was muted and women were subjected to the manipulative style of the new Soviet order with its focus on mobilization and coercion rather than on liberation. But both the facts and the myths of women's emancipation in Soviet Russia still remained very much alive in the popular mind.

The history of Russian and Soviet women in military roles is still in its infancy. Only in the last decade have serious non-Soviet works begun to appear on any aspect of women's history in Russia.[3] The military sphere of Russia's past is particularly difficult for Western scholars to enter because the sensitivity of the Soviet regime leads it to deny them access to the necessary archives. Therefore, Western treatments of the subject must rely on the less than satisfactory printed sources and Soviet monographs on the subject. The former are hard to get in the quantities needed to build up a full and rich picture. Furthermore, even those readily available tend to be personal reminiscences and contemporary press reports, which are impressionistic, vague, pious, overdramatized and informed by the spirit of one-sided wartime propaganda. This fault is shared by the sources of other nations, to be sure, but it was especially acute in the reticent and tendentious press of the Stalin years. The best monographic work done since the war is that of Vera Semenovna Murmantseva, a political officer in World War II and a competent military historian.[4] Unfortunately her work is marred by vagueness of numbers, distribution, rank, and other key items to scholars. She also skirts some of the interesting issues of sexual and institutional integration, and her accounts are riddled with pieties. Other Soviet writers are even less satisfactory in these respects. In visits to Russia since 1967 Stites has tried to fill in some of the gaps with information and impressions gained in talking to scores of women veterans of World War II about their wartime experiences and feelings and about current modes of training and service for women.

WORLD WAR I

Scope of Activity

The women of the upper classes, the educated, and the feminists generally supported World War I. So did a number of Socialist women. Many radical Socialist women and urban factory hands did not; and it was their rioting that ushered in the Russian Revolution of February 1917. Feminists launched a war of words urging women to support the nation in return for which they would get the vote. Aristocratic women opened bandage points and hospital trains for their favorite regiments. Women workers poured into the factories, making up about half of the industrial labor force by 1917. A network of volunteer effort and charity was created by public-spirited citizens, and women were drawn into this also.[5]

Women entered the services and even went into combat, but in a peculiar and irregular way. As far as is known, the government did not even consider the issue of women in uniform, except for nursing which had a tradition since 1855. As early as 1915 Russian and Western press stories began telling of female soldiers sometimes disguised as men in infantry units and serving in combat. The response of the government was ambivalent: the practice was never legalized under the tsar, but some women were actually decorated for valor. Some were well-born; most seem to have been of the working class. A group of Moscow schoolgirls, in their midteens, said they wanted to "see the war and ourselves kill Germans."[6] Enemy troops were astonished and terrified when they encountered Russian women in uniform. Eighteen-year-old Mariya Golubyova had this to say about her feelings toward taking human life: "I had no sensation except to rid my country of an enemy. There was no sentimentality. We were trying to kill them and they were trying to kill us—that is all. Any Russian girl or any American girl in the same position would have the same feeling."[7]

The most famous woman combat soldier was Mariya Bochkareva, the daughter of a former serf. "My country called me," she wrote later, "and an irresistible force from within pulled me."[8] Personal motivations (including social or marital woes), patriotism, plus the army's lax attitude seem to have been the dominant factors in bringing women into a combat role. Bochkareva carried a gun, but she specialized in dragging wounded soldiers from under enemy fire. When the revolution erupted in early 1917, the army became honeycombed with elected committees that produced military democracy and desertion on a mass scale. Disgusted with the performance of male soldiers, Bochkareva received permission from the new provisional government to organize a women's shock battalion, or "Battalion of Death" to stiffen the back of the army and to shame deserting men. It was certainly the first instance in modern history in which women were used in all-female fighting units as models of military valor and performance in order to check desertion and fraternization with the enemy. About two thousand women volunteered in May when the unit was formed; but Bochkareva's harsh and rigid mode of discipline reduced this number to about three hundred. Socialist and other antiwar elements ridiculed the women's battalion; feminists, government officials, and prowar elements applauded it. The visiting British feminist, Emmeline Pankhurst, praised the unit and attended its farewell service. Bochkareva's women's battalion saw action on the Russian western front in June 1917. Many were killed in action; and when mass desertion again set in some of the male soldiers assaulted and killed a number of women soldiers. The unit was disbanded by its commander at the end of the summer. Similar outfits appeared in Moscow, Odessa, Ekaterinodar, and Perm, but only the last and Bochkareva's unit saw action. Eventually a women's military union was formed and a congress was held; but the October Revolution of the Bolsheviks, pledged to immediate peace, put an end to it.[9]

The final act of the women's military movement of the world war came on October 25, 1917, when a detachment of a Petrograd women's battalion helped defend the provisional government against the Bolsheviks' storming of the Winter Palace. On the other side of the barricades were Bolshevik women who had joined the proletarian paramilitary units known as Red Guards, shock troops of the Bolshevik revolution. When the civil war between Reds and Whites (anti-Bolsheviks) began, the skills of Bolshevik women were utilized on a grander scale: feeding, sanitary services, building fortifications, and digging trenches in beleaguered cities as well as propaganda, psychological warfare, espionage, guerrilla action, and conventional combat. All this was encouraged and coordinated by the Bolshevik (renamed Communist) regime itself, with the special aid of the Women's Section (Zhenotdel) of the Communist party. Nurses were trained in large numbers for this war, as for previous wars. The main difference was that Red Army nurses received rifle training and political indoctrination, and some of them became political commissars in army hospitals. Women fought in regular combat on every front (geographically, this was the most dispersed land war in history since the Mongols), from Siberia to the Crimea, from the Baltic to Central Asia. They served as riflewomen, armored train commanders, gunners, and demolition troops. Most were integrated, but some served in small all-female units of three hundred or so. Women partisans, scouts, and spies played a special role in combat, subversion, and intelligence gathering, often fraternizing with foreign interventionist troops to undermine their sense of purpose. Most important, women served in the *politotdel,* the agency of political propaganda, an area in which the Communists far outshone their White enemies. The agitation department of this operation was headed by a woman veteran revolutionary Vera Kasparova.[10]

Problems of Integration

It is instructive to discuss World War I and the civil war together precisely because of the vast difference between them. One was an international war against Germany and the other Central Powers, fought in the traditional ways; the other an internal political war between successful revolutionaries and unsuccessful counterrevolutionaries. Problems of integration were apparently never discussed in tsarist military circles. The appearance of women in certain units was fortuitous and unplanned, and the main policy seems to have been one of turning official eyes the other way. The easiest way to "integrate" for some women and in some units was simply to pose as men, which some were able to do for a remarkably long time before being discovered. When they were discovered, some were dismissed but others were kept on because of the impression they had already made in the guise of males. Like many other things in Russian history, this episode is redolent of antique fairy tales (or of Hollywood movie scripts). There is no record of how decisions were made. Those who joined in groups, like the high school runaways from Moscow, were allowed to keep together for mutual moral support; individual enlistees lived among the men. If the men treated them as comrades in arms, it was not due to egalitarian ideology, but rather to peasant ethos (the vast majority of soldiers were peasants) in which women had always been seen as doing hard physical labor. Bochkareva's battalion movement introduced the notion of separate units, with short-haired, sexless looking women, bivouacked and trained apart from males. Bochkareva was severely hostile to male-female contact on two counts: one sexual, the other a fear of infection by Bolshevik antiwar agitation. At one point, she actually bayoneted a female soldier in the act of fornication.

When we turn to the civil war, we see an entirely different political culture emerging, one which, for example, proclaimed the complete equality of the sexes. Little was done about realizing this equality, however, aside from legislation, proclamations, and the demanding of work and service from both sexes. The *Zhenotdel* set out consciously to introduce women into every aspect of military life and work. Prominent Bolshevik women paraded their determination to be accepted as equals in the struggle. Posters exalted the male-female team as the unit of struggle and liberation in contrast to the pastels of tearful sisters of mercy that had been the stock in trade of previous wartime propaganda. Men were expected, officially, to accept women in combat as a matter of course, without sexist resistance or pious welcome speeches. The reality, of course, did not always match the slogans and the aspirations of the regime. In the new Red Army, proletarian elements tended to be more sympathetic to women's participation; but the army also contained masses of peasants whose world outlook had hardly been penetrated by Communist ideals. A prominent Bolshevik woman herself recalls how she had to assert her right to operate as a purely military person and not as a woman (a commander contemptuously explained that he had no sidesaddle for her). Yet this same woman was notorious for her violence and even cruelty in action. Less prominent women must have fared even worse, but Soviet sources (almost the only ones available) tend to minimize this.

Most women served individually in male units. Large all-women units (auxiliary as in Britain, or combat as with the women's battalions) did not catch on. The largest female units were company size semiindependent detachments, such as the Communist Women's Combat Detachment or the Communist Women's Special Purpose Detachment, the latter employed in police, security, combat, and execution missions. At least one assault company of female infantry served in the Polish War of 1920. Integration was apparently easier in the partisan units that roamed the Urals, Siberia, and the Ukraine. According to the faint impressions we have from *belles lettres,* the men and women of forest, horse, and saber worked in a more flexible and socially democratic milieu than that of the regular forces. Love and sex were not abolished by any means in such units, and Soviet public opinion—at least official public opinion—was hardly concerned about such matters. Another interesting feature of the man-woman relation in the war was the role of women as teachers of men. The Whites did not use women for propaganda, but the Reds used them widely as well as using ethnic groups, such as Jews, and artistic figures. It is impossible to say how the men in the ranks reacted to the spectacle of a matter-of-fact Bolshevik woman regaling them with Marxist revolutionary slogans from the flat-car of a propaganda train; but it certainly showed that the Bolsheviks were trying with every resource at their disposal to reach the hearts and minds of the masses.

Observations

The only estimate of the total of women who fought in the battalions in World War I is five thousand.[11] To this one must add no more than one thousand individual and small group volunteers in the period before the battalions (1914–May 1917). Approximately eighty thousand women fought in the civil war, but this figure includes medical personnel. There are really no reliable comparative figures. In the tsarist period numbers were small but functions were many; even women aviators were used, the Russian air arm having been established with a handful of biplanes around 1910. In Bochkareva's time the numbers blossomed, all-female units predominated, and the function was largely unit combat (machine-gun companies and communications units were also involved with the battalion movement). In the civil war these two styles were combined and expanded. Little is known of the social origin of women soldiers of the World War I period, although lower classes seem to have predominated in all three periods. In the civil war, the ranks were mostly factory workers; the officers educated women and professional revolutionaries with underground experience. Women in the civil war held middle rather than low or high ranks, staff rather than line positions; in spite of the visibility in combat, most of them served in support functions. Perhaps the most remarkable thing about the World War I experience is the method by which women entered the armed forces and the stated purpose of the women's battalions—to shame the men. In the civil war labor conscription fell on members of both sexes and set the atmosphere for "the nation at war" mentality that was to be invoked in World War II.

One could hardly find a starker comparison to Britain's wartime experience with women. Once again, we see that the determining forces were political and geopolitical as well as ideological and social. There were no debates in the Russian Duma (parliament) about utilization of women. The front was so vast and mobile (from Riga to the Carpathians to the Black Sea), the situation so desperate, and the scene so chaotic that resistance to the presence of women was perhaps considered not worthy of the time required. Fears of sexual contact in Russia were less acute then in Britain (for example, dressing and undressing in front of another sex was by no means uncommon among the Russian lower classes). Russia was seen as being invaded, with its very existence menaced, in both 1914 and 1918; voluntary patriotism in the first instance and ideological mobilization in the second did the rest.

Zhenotdel, founded in 1919, was in a way analogous to the British Women's Emergency Corps: both served as clearing houses for women who wished to enter war industries and volunteer work. Neither had much power or many resources; but the WEC was more like a private club while *Zhenotdel,* a party organ, was more an instrument of the state (the government in Soviet Russia being almost coterminous with the top party leadership). In one respect there was near identity: when hostilities were over, women in both societies were eased out of the service. British upper-class women returned to their families and hobbies, working-class women to their mills; and all Russian women returned to the fearsome task of reconstruction and laying the foundations of socialism.

What happened to Soviet women between the wars? For one thing, they—along with all Soviets—went through the triple trauma of forced collectivization, rapid industrialization, and the blood purge of Stalin in the 1930s. One of the byproducts of massive industrialization, urbaniza-tion, and forced social mobility was the recruitment of women in unpre-cedented numbers into the ranks of industry. Hundred of thousands were brought into the economy and given a technical education. Certain profes-sions, such as medicine, became feminized. Women, although still bur-dened with home and family concerns, moved steadily into middle and sometimes high levels of industry, science, engineering, and technical work. Huge reserves of technical talent among women were present when war began in 1941. Women also participated in paramilitary activities. Sport and gun clubs offered sharpshooter training, and young women joined Osoaviakhim (Society for the Furthering of Defense, Aviation, and Chemical Warfare), founded in 1927. This group accounted for the few thousand women who had military training at the onset of war. It gave paramilitary exercises, coordinated mass calisthenics, and trained air raid wardens, drivers, parachutists, machine gunners, snipers, and technical workers. It was, in the words of the American scholar Merle Fainsod, ''a significant factor in making the Soviet population both machine-minded and war-minded.''[12] Along with the still officially held doctrine of equality of the sexes, however, arose a kind of conservative reaction in the Stalinist thirties to *actual* equality of the sexes and especially to sexual freedom, such as acceptance of abortion. Pronatalist, sexist, and suspicious of spontaneity, Stalinism assured that the Soviet high command would have a deeply ambivalent attitude to the participation of women in the next war.[13]

WORLD WAR II

Scope of Activity

When the Germans invaded in June 1941, the initial response of the government in regard to women was to stress the already growing theme of separation of functions: men to the front and women to replace them at the bench and on the farm. This was the major public theme in the early months of war. In the years 1932 to 1937, 87 percent of the newly employed had been women and they made up 40 percent of the industrial labor force.

In Leningrad, 24,000 of the 76,000 engineers were women. The regime wanted to utilize these skills in rear-area work. Women were also permitted into such heavy and dangerous occupations as mining. By 1942, 60 percent of the defense industry workers were women. Those not directly employed were mobilized into building fortifications and digging trenches. Only a handful of women (no figures are available) were estimated to have been in the service when the war broke out. These remained in service, but there was military and civilian resistance to augmenting their numbers during the first year. There were a few volunteers in 1941, but they were usually channeled into support, not combat, roles.[14]

By 1942 the manpower losses were so enormous that the policy of resistance gave way to outright mobilization. Most of this was done by Komsomol units (that is, Young Communists); eventually all childless women not engaged in war work were eligible to be called up for service. Grief and loss of loved ones seemed to account for the motivation of some and the regime also geared its propaganda machine to the exploiting of German atrocities, particularly against women and children.[15]

By 1943 Soviet women had entered all the services and assumed all the roles that they would take until the war's end: in infantry, antiaircraft defense, armor, artillery, transportation, communications, air, nursing, and partisan warfare (participation in the navy was minuscule and is almost undocumented). The Komsomol schools trained about a quarter of a million young women in weapons as mortarwomen, heavy machine gunners, light machine gunners, automatic riflewomen, snipers, and riflewomen. A Central Sniper Training Center for Women was established in May 1943. Every few months it turned out about 150 skilled shooters: by the end of the war these had killed 11,280 enemy troops. Snipers performed well and kept their own so-called kill-books, but they seemed to have trouble throwing grenades (there are many cases of self-inflicted grenade deaths among women—not all heroic) and climbing trees. According to Soviet sources, Nona Solovei killed an entire German company in twenty-five days, a remarkable achievement. The First Separate Women's Reserve Rifle Regiment, formed in February 1942, was another infantry training outfit that produced 5,200 women soldiers.[16]

Antiaircraft became virtually a feminized military specialty, with its own female officers and its hundreds of thousands of AA women. Unlike their British counterparts, they also fired the guns. How good were they? According to one German pilot, a veteran of the African campaign, they were very good indeed. "I would rather fly ten times over the skies of Tobruk than to pass once through the fire of Russian flak sent up by female gunners."[17] "Armor dislikes the weak," said one Soviet writer on military affairs.[18] Yet women served as tankers in all capacities. Mariya Oktyabrskaya, after her tanker husband perished in the fighting, purchased her own tank, named it "Front-line Female Comrade," and drove into battle to be killed herself near Vitebsk in 1944. Women served in the auto transport service (accounting for 75 percent of its personnel); and the Komsomol trained fifty thousand women communications workers.[19]

In the air, women were less numerous, but very visible and dramatic. Women fliers who had trained in Osoviakhim, air clubs, and civil aviation in the 1930s were on hand to serve when the war began. One of these, Marina Raskova, heroine of a spectacular all-female flight to the Soviet Far East, received letters from female aviators asking to enlist. As a member of the Supreme Soviet, she was able to put her request before the Ministry of Defense which granted her permission to form three women's combat aviation regiments. Under her direction, the 122 Air Group was formed near Saratov on the Volga, far from German lines, as a training unit. It eventually graduated about six hundred pilots who served in the three women's regiments. The 586th Interceptor Regiment, flying in Yaks (Yakovlev fighters), flew missions against German Stuka bombers and the Messerschmidt fighter convoys on all fronts and downed thirty-eight enemy planes (their own losses are not given). The 587th Short-Range Bomber Regiment was a tactical unit that strafed and bombed enemy positions and small supply depots; its range of combat was also great— from Stalingrad to East Prussia. The most famous of the three was the 588th Night Bomber Regiment, which started in the northern Caucasus with sporadic night bombing raids in light canvas biplanes and ended up in Poland flying as many as three hundred sorties a night! It is the only one for which we have figures: 4,376 members, of which 237 officers, 862 Noncommissioned Officers (NCO), 1,125 enlisted, and 2,117 "volunteers" (an undefined category). Individual female pilots served in male units as well. The composite picture suggested by the sources—even when allowing for piousness and hyperbole—is one of several thousand dedicated and brave women risking their lives daily and nightly and having a tactical, if not strategic, significance out of proportion to their numbers. It was another vindication of the Soviet program of technical education for women since 1930.[20]

Medical personnel deserve to be treated along with combat personnel because of their huge numbers, the presence of female doctors as well as nurses and orderlies, and the conditions under which they served. Women constituted: 43 percent of military surgeons (with postmedical school specialized training), 41 percent of front-line doctors (with six years of medical school), 43 percent of *feldshers* (medics) (with four years of paramedical training), 100 percent of nurses, and 40 percent of *sanitarkas* (aides and orderlies). They ran and staffed sanitation trains which brought medicine, beds, showers, and delousing equipment to the front and served and ran bandage points, medical stations, and base hospitals. Women were exceptionally visible in military medicine although less so than in civilian medicine where they dominated the profession numerically, not administratively. Medical courses were set up all over the Soviet Union, even in the factories. Medical women were also combatants and bore arms. Dr. Sofya Klitinova carried twenty Red Army men out from under enemy fire; nurse Zinaida Usnolobova-Marchenko performed a similar feat and was wounded so severely herself that she lost both arms and legs at the age of twenty-three. Elena Kovalchuk led an infantry assault after the male unit commander had been wounded. The line between medicine and combat almost disappeared near the front lines; women fought, carried arms, and died in action. From 1968 through 1981 Stites has talked informally to scores of Soviet women doctors and nurses in Russia who served in World War II. The most striking thing about their reminiscences and observations was their toughness, their matter-of-fact descriptions of hair-raising experience, and their near unanimous assurance that all women and all Soviet people would fight if there were another major war on Soviet territory.[21]

Figures for partisans in general and partisan women in particular come in widely divergent estimates. The best and most cautious figure seems to be that given by Murmantseva: 26,707 women out of the 287,453 partisans operating in January 1944.[22] This figure does not account for the tremendous fluidity and localism of the partisan movement that, by its very nature, drew in and then released thousands of men and women depending upon the geography of the front and rear at any given moment. In the forests of Belorussia, the scene of greatest partisan density, women made up 16 percent (about seven thousand) of the irregular forces. Women entered this mode of warfare almost at once. In June 1941 Stalin himself invited women to join the partisans; in July Marshal Budënny, who had seen many women fight in the civil war, urged men and women in the occupied areas to "join guerrilla detachments. Create new ones. Annihilate German troops, exterminate them like mad dogs. Derail trains. Disrupt communications. Blow up ammunition dumps."[23] Women did these things and many others. Some were drawn into the forests by the very danger posed by German occupiers, who had orders to execute certain categories of Soviet citizens, including party members and Jews; others, perhaps by the less formal structure of partisan life. Almost every detachment had some women. Most performed medical, communications, and domestic chores; but all were armed, and many fought, and performed sabotage missions. At the central partisan schools alone 1,262 women took military training, and others trained at numerous local camps. Disguised as peasant women, they moved behind German lines for reconnaisance and sabotage missions.

The most famous individual *partizanka* (partisan) was Zoya Kosmodemyanskaya, alias Tanya, who was captured in an act of sabotage, tortured, hanged, and left swinging from a tree for the local villagers to observe. A virtual media cult grew up around her name, although she was only one of many who suffered terrible deaths at the hands of the invaders. Even more spectacular, but less publicized, was the case of Elena Mazanik, a waitress and Young Communist of Minsk, who made her way into the quarters of Wilhelm Kube, the particularly savage governor of German-occupied Belorussia. Mazanik put a bomb under his bed and killed him. As in the civil war, townswomen created networks and used their jobs as shop-keepers and service personnel to gather intelligence about the occupiers and pass it on to the mobile forces in the woods. Also on record are cases of women who were reluctantly pressed into partisan service. At least one Russian women composed a pro-German leaflet that was dropped from German planes into Russian-held territory.[24]

Problems of Integration

Although the sexual problem does not seem to have loomed so large in the Russian case as the British, there is plenty of evidence that some military men, were initially skeptical or hostile about women in the service, as in all previous Russian wars, especially in combat roles. This seems to have given way to acceptance and even admiration after the women had proved themselves. Since few officers or soldiers had read much history of this phenomenon, they had to learn this acceptance all over again. Conversely, women in largely all-female units (the air regiments, the rifle-training outfit, the AA units) seem to have developed a kind of military female subculture in which things were done more casually and in a warmer context than in male units.[25] Most women served in mixed units and there is little documentation about problems of integration. One interesting feature of the Soviet situation are the husband and wife teams who fought together. Aleksandra and Ivan Boiko, she an officer and tank commander and he her driver mechanic, formed such a combat team; both survived the war.[26] Women often replaced lost husbands or brothers and were accepted, judging from the Soviet sources, exactly as such. The sources always speak of greater equality of the sexes among partisans: women did indeed share incredible hardships, take the awesome partisan oath, wear uniforms sometimes, and so on. But the equality is clearly romanticized, along with much else about partisan life and military style. The rosy Soviet memoirs are somewhat balanced by John Armstrong's study, which stresses the mistrust of women for hard missions, their unequal treatment, and the occasional "camp follower" situations, although his account seems to exaggerate in the other direction. There is evidence of in-combat marriage and cohabitation, but there is also evidence of harsh rules against sexual contact between troops.[27]

Patterns of integration are hard to find. Males served in the 596th and

587th Women's Air Combat Regiments, but not in the 588th. Women pilots and other airwomen were used in all-male units, sometimes as "wingmen" for famous male aces. There were no all-woman services or even large units in the ground forces comparable to ATS or WAAC in Britain. There were all-female training outfits and units of platoon, company, and battalion size. In the women's sniper units, about 30 percent of the officers were men but the NCOs were all women.[28] Training for infantry women could not have been as rigorous as that of the men; yet, in order to simulate battlefield conditions, women were required in basic training to march twenty to twenty-five kilometers a day, with equipment. Women were often depicted in press stories and memoirs as self-reliant and hard. A German document, based on the deposition of a captured Russian soldier, tells of tearful women pressed into service with artillery units and of men who were contemptuous of them.[29] In the partisan movement where one could expect, and perhaps even get, more equality of the sexes, there was none the less a clear division of labor whenever labor was being consciously divided (women, for example, clandestinely distributed leaflets behind enemy lines that were written by the men). In other words, as in the revolutionary movement of seventy years earlier, women proved of equal competence in those few moments when a fluid situation and the force of circumstances threw them into a central role; but since this was not taken as proof of permanent or universal ability, they were rarely forced into these roles.

Some Observations

The sources on the number of women who served in the Soviet armed forces in World War II are distressingly vague. Most accounts offer the following numbers: about a million women actually fought in the war, a figure which includes partisan and irregular war; about 800,000 of these were uniformed troops in the Red Army, a titantic figure by any measure; and about 500,000 of these actually served at the front either in combat or support roles. There is as yet no scientific way to test these figures because the Soviet regime simply issues the flat aggregates without adequate explanation of the numbers. If they are close to accurate, this means that women constituted 8 percent of the combatants in the Soviet Union during the war (there were 12 million men; and for the record, the USSR claims that it lost 20 million dead in the war, a figure exceeding by far the combined figures of killed in all the other belligerents on both sides). The Komsomol, in its five major mobilization drives, pulled in 500,000 women, 200,000 of whom were Komsomol members and 70 percent of whom saw active service.[30].

Unfortunately we have only the faintest of impressions about rank, age, and nationality from available sources. In female sniper units only 30 percent of the officers were women, although almost all the NCOs were. Of the 5,175 graduates of the First Separate Women's Reserve Rifle Regiment, 297 were officers, 986 were NCOs, and 3,892 were in the ranks—a fairly typical distribution for any group of trainees. We find captains and lieutenants in command of regiments, a unit normally headed by a colonel. But individual rank for women tells us very little. And we have no real data on numbers in each rank. Ages ranged from fifteen to fifty-one, but most who served seemed to have been very young.[31]

As to national origin of women fighters, we are again without precise figures. Some names indicate national origins—and we can be sure that Russian, Ukrainian, Belorussian, Chuvash, Moldavian, Karelian, Mordvian, Jewish, Georgian, Tatar, Armenian, and Central Asian women fought in the war. But names are sometimes misleading: for example the female pilot, Osipenko (a pure Ukrainian name) was a Tadzhik. Women of ethnic minorities were often mentioned as such in the press in order to underline the fact of a woman and a person of a national minority defending the motherland. According to Murmantseva, six thousand women of Uzbekistan (she calls them "daughters of the Uzbek people") defended their country in the armed forces. A thousand female medical workers were trained for the war in Turkmenia; half went to the front, the rest to interior hospitals. From Kirgizia 1,895 women and girls fought in the war. Except for the figure on medical workers, no indication is given of how these women of the Eastern republics served—or how their service and experience compared with those of, say, European Russia. Also, since many volunteers were party or Komsomol members everywhere, a significant number of these women were probably Russian (or Slavic) women who lived in the Central Asian republics at the time of the war, since party organs there tended to be dominated by the European, that is, Slavic nationalities. A tiny sample of 145 sniper instructors, below, simply hints that the distributions of nationalities among women fighters was probably not very different from the ratios in the population at large.[32]

Russian	120	Chuvash	3
Ukrainian	15	Mordvinian	3
Belorussian	3	Jewish	1

If performance were measured by number and kind of awards received, women would not come off very well. Some 7 million soldiers were decorated during the war, but only about 100,000 to 150,000 women. The Hero of the Soviet Union medal, the highest award for military valor, was given to over 11,000 men and to 91 women (the highest estimate). Thus while women made up possibly as much as 8 percent of the active forces, they received only 4 percent of the military awards. Figures for other awards are comparable. But this flat picture needs to be modified. Decoration for valor almost always occurs from a front-line combat action, and the majority of women did not serve in direct combat.[33]

How well did women perform? To answer this requires weighing such conflicting evidence as a mass of hyperbolic and patriotic press accounts and memoirs against the few contemptuous remarks found in German documents about the inability or unwillingness of women to fight (although even these can be matched by praise of Russian women fighters by captured German military men). Did women help win the war for Russia? Women's role in the armed forces is a variable that cannot be detached and measured in terms of its effectiveness in the total picture anymore than the performance of all junior officers, all artillerymen, all Ukrainians, or all imported American vehicles could be assessed in the overall war effort. The evidence assembled here should be sufficient to convince anyone that women played an important role in World War II, far in excess of all other belligerent nations. And that is all that can be said with assurance.

In assessing the impact of the war on women, and visa versa, it seems reasonable to isolate the historical, the ideological, and the social aspects of this relationship. The historical aspect is the national myth of female valor, the capacity for struggle, violence, and self-sacrifice, a myth that was printed on the Russian national consciousness by the role of women in the revolutionary movement over three generations. The fact that women were not given complete equality in Soviet life as a reward for this self-sacrifice is no argument against the potency of the myth itself. Women's gains after the revolution were sufficiently visible, particularly to the urban population from which it is almost certain that the major component of female combatants were drawn, to make the regime's slogans of equality believable even if far from true. The revolutionary tradition of female activism, although muffled under Stalin until the war, remained well known and was probably internalized by a large number of educated women. Underground agent Zoya Rukhadze invoked Vera Figner's name as she stood before a German firing squad.[34] Countless others seemed to yearn for the heroic activism denied to women since the civil war in their grim round of factory or office work in the purge-ridden Soviet Union. And the fact that a cadre of famous martyred heroines stood ready to be used made it easy for the regime—and the women themselves—to see widespread participation of women in the fight for Mother Russia as an inherent national tradition. Few countries could evoke this sort of legend.

The ideological message of the regime during the war also helped to recruit and to inspire feats of sacrifice among women. This message was Russian nationalism in its most old-fashioned and unadulterated form.

Marxism-Leninism, class struggle, the evils of capitalism, the dreams of a Communist society were emphatically muted soon after the war began. Stalin realized instinctively that Russians were far readier to fight for Russia than for communism. The church was given honored treatment for the first time since 1917; names of Russian national military heroes like Alexander Nevsky, Alexander Suvorov, Michel Kutuzov, and Dmitry Donskoi were exalted; the Comintern was abolished; and *Pravda's* masthead device "Proletarians of all Countries, Unite" (from Marx) was replaced by "Death to the Fascist Invaders!" Women responded—as did of course many patriotic men—to this line of propaganda with greater ease than they would have to didactic appeals to Marxist ideology. They and their menfolk were defending land, home, and family and were preserving the national keepsake for their children, not laying down the foundations for some distant arcadia of Communist egalitarianism or social justice, although many in the Komsomol clearly fought for this ideal as well as for Mother Russia.[35]

Both nationalism and historical self-consciousness had been at work in the military voluntarism of Russian women during World War I, but relatively few women actually served, compared to the experience of 1941–1945. Why? In the first place, millions of more women were engaged in productive work in factories, offices, and laboratories in the later years. Stalin's revolution from above, in addition to the vast social misery it inflicted upon the population—women included—had also pulled huge numbers of females into the industrial work force and introduced them to the rigors of machinery, industrial discipline, and "modern" notions of order, routine, punctuality, and responsibility (at great psychological cost to be sure). Second, it had educated hundreds of thousands of women in science, industrial management, economics, and technology, producing women engineers, scientists, and doctors. And, in contrast to Germany, for example, the Soviets had promulgated the rule of equal pay for equal work in industry. Although not bringing equality to women in education or industrial life, it nevertheless created a work force and a body of technicians who were utilized to great effect during the Second World War. Finally, by covering the country with a network of mobilizational organs such as the Communist party, the police, the Komsomol, and other mass organizations, it was able to reach, to preach to, and to infect huge numbers of people with its political and military imperatives, and in some cases, to coerce and order women into active service.

How much of all this—historical, ideological, and sociological—would have counted had the Soviet Union not been physically occupied by the German army and those of its Finnish, Hungarian, Rumanian, and other allies? It seems clear that the invasion, the desolation of the land, and the gratuitous atrocities of the German occupiers deepened the determination of many women to destroy or expel the invader. Russian women never heard the famous words of Heinrich Himmler who said that he did not care if ten thousand Russian women dropped dead digging tank traps for the German army as long as the ditches got dug. But Russian women in many parts of the country saw evidence enough of the German willingness to starve, burn out, or execute women and children as well as defenseless men. Rarely in modern times have enemy forces visited such wholesale destruction on a civilian population as did the Germans in Russia. The only recent parallel in Soviet memory was Stalin's own murder of millions of Russians. But the Russian case was either not understood or vaguely endorsed by a politically unsophisticated population. The German menace was, by contrast, crystal clear. Even so, many Russian men and women collaborated with the Germans until it became obvious that their policy was fundamentally genocidal. If entire families are slaughtered, entire families can also resist and repel. Although much partisan activity was carefully orchestrated, much of it was spontaneous—the first spontaneous partisan action of women since the last great occupation of Russia proper in 1812.[36]

Neither the United States nor Germany utilized female personnel on the scale of the Soviet Union either in combat or in support. America was never invaded, and Germany only after it was far too late to mount anything like a national conscription of women.[37] Women responded to the war effort in the United States, Leila Rupp tells us, because of patriotism, a longing to act, loneliness, a fairly decent incentive of economic rewards offered by American industry, and in response to skillful commercial advertising campaigns. Women also joined the armed forces but, except for the few cases of women drawn into combat accidentally, did not fight at the fronts or perform genuine combat operations. German women, much more incited ideologically by the vaunted propaganda machine of Joseph Goebbels, responded in a way that could only be called listless. Nazism offered neither a national myth of female equality nor the incentive of good wages in industry. On the contrary, it continued to stress hearth and motherhood and the sanctity of German womanliness in a wholly traditional way. Russia, painfully beleaguered for two and a half years, lacking the military-industrial might of the initial German war machine as well as the economic and productive sinew of the United States, threw into the war its greatest resources: human materials and organization.[38]

An even more apt and illustrative comparison of the Russian experience is with Yugoslavia, China, and Vietnam. Each of these societies was faced with foreign invasion and alien occupations: Yugoslavia, 1941–1945, by Germans, Italians, Hungarians, and others; China, 1937–1945, by the Japanese; and Vietnam, 1941–75, by the Japanese, then the French, then the United States. In two of them—China and Yugoslavia—there was a triangular struggle between radical national resistance (the Chinese Communists, the Yugoslav partisans), more traditional national resistance (the Kuomintang, the Chetniks), and the invaders. Like the Whites in the Russian civil war, the Kuomintang and the Chetniks tended to avoid using women as active fighters. The radical movements on the other hand used them profusely. All invoked the Russian precedent as well as their own national experience. In the Communist campaign for power Chinese women acted as workers, auxiliaries, guerrilla fighters, and straight combat personnel. In Vietnam the participation was far more complete than in China or Russia (millions are said to have participated). In Yugoslavia we have the figure of 100,000 women, one-fourth of whom were killed or executed by occupation forces and indigenous antipartisans.[39]

In all these cases, as in Russia, it was the element of national emergency, the occupation of the homeland by hated foreigners, and the use of national symbols and slogans to tap the deepest wells of love of country that seem to have most affected the mass participation of women as well as of men. On the other hand, occupation alone does not guarantee large-scale popular resistance by either sex (witness the obvious case of Denmark). Those who try to predict the future participation of women in warfare will have, therefore, to account for the unusual factors inherent in any military situation such as opportunities for popular combat (topography, for example), historical traditions, the power of ideological and national symbols, the social role, status, and educational level of women, the organizational power of the regime, and, most important, the precise geopolitical circumstance of the given war. Since the geopolitical conditions are the most difficult to foresee and yet one of the most crucial in determining the possible role of women in defense, students must exercise great modesty in making such predictions.

THE PEACETIME PERIOD

The years immediately following the war were extremely difficult for all Soviet people. Grieving women were expected to support, both emotionally and financially, the returning demobilized and often demoralized soldiers. Women were congratulated collectively for their wartime efforts, both military and otherwise, while men received recognition as individuals. Although ninety-one women received the highly esteemed Hero of the Soviet Union award, over half of these awards were delivered posthumously and only once to each woman; the majority of men receiving the award were alive and often second- or third-time recipients.

Soon after the war a decree demobilized all women in the ranks except for "those women-specialists who desired to remain in the Red Army at their war posts."[40] Strenuous jobs that had been opened to women only in the war years, such as mining, remained open to them, simply because there were no men to occupy their places. For the most part public recognition of women's sacrifices and experiences in war was not played up very much.[41] What was stressed in the postwar years were the new crucial roles for women, for instance, motherhood and the labor force. Combat experience had not been for Soviet women a path leading to greater recognition and equality in the public male sphere, but rather a stopgap measure used by a desperate regime pushed to its ultimate resource, which it did not hesitate to exploit. Women were rarely referred to in these wartime years by their functions alone; they were not specialists, fighters, or workers, but women-specialists, women-fighters, or women-workers.

Since the war, recruitment and training of women for military service in the Soviet Union has been espoused in theory but has been an afterthought in practice. In contrast to mandatory recruitment of all males, Soviet policy toward women presents military service as an opportunity and not a responsibility, unless the woman possesses certain special skills of value in wartime. Training and recruitment of women demonstate a World War II hindsight, which calls for training women as a potential reserve force to provide backup of the men if needed, and not as equally capable and well-trained comrades in combat. Thus, despite the varied and vital contribution of Soviet women to the last war effort their status is relatively unchanged from the prewar era.

An estimated ten thousand women are in the Soviet armed forces. Unmarried or childless women between the ages of nineteen and twenty-five, who are physically fit and have at least eight years of education, may volunteer for active duty. They enlist for a two-year term, which may be extended for two years, after which time they automatically become part of the reserves until the age of forty (fifty for men). Women aged nineteen to forty, with special training, such as medical or engineering, can be drafted in peacetime, called up for training or volunteer for duty, and in war may be drafted for auxiliary or special service. Thus women who have performed military service or who possess special skills must serve in the reserves after active duty.[42]

Komsomol, DOSAAF (Volunteer Society for the Support of Army, Navy, and Air Force, successor to Osoaviakhim), and other civil defense training at the preinduction level is widespread among women. However, actual recruitment preference is given to women specialists by draft boards; otherwise female applicants enlist on their own initiative. Training of women is less intense and rigorous than for men. Women are housed separately from men and receive separate classes in politics, physical training, and armed forces regulations. They can be assigned only to those positions set aside especially for them; such positions are limited in type and number. Most involve noncombat duties, since women are forbidden to serve on combat ships and planes, or even to serve as guards for any but women's barracks. Women also cannot be commissioned for officers school, which greatly reduces their chances of becoming officers, except in services where they are specially skilled in the first place, such as medical units. No active duty is permitted for women during or after pregnancy.[43]

The Soviet military forces make no effort to lure any but the most skilled women into its ranks, underlining the fact that female military personnel are still viewed today as an auxiliary, potential reserve force, to be exploited for combat use only if necessary, since more efficient use can be made of them in administrative and other backup duties. Women veterans of World War II have most often put their skills to use either in teaching or in technical fields such as engineering. The famous Zhukov Military Academy has on its faculty two female teachers who were navigators of fighter planes in the war. The Tambov Higher Military Aviation School for Pilots was named for another woman navigator of a bomber regiment. In administrative roles women are distinguishing themselves in small numbers. The first woman sea captain was appointed in May 1979. The new appointee, Alevtina Borisovna Aleksandrova, had served at sea for seventeen years prior to her most recent promotion.[44]

In terms of benefits and punishments women in the Soviet military forces are treated either equal to or better than men. Women receive the same pay, allowances, pensions, and promotions as male career personnel. Promotions are given according to qualifications and the availability of positions. Theoretically any rank in the armed forces is open to a woman. After twenty-five or more years of service women receive pensions, as do men, of 50 percent of their pay plus another 3 percent for each additional year of service over twenty-five, the total not exceeding 75 percent of pay. If they leave the service after twenty to twenty-four years, for reasons of health or reduction in force they may also receive pensions, provided they are at least forty years of age.

Women are disciplined more leniently than are men in the military. They are not subject to such things as arrest, confinement, restriction to the unit area, or assignment to extra details. They are subject instead to receiving a reprimand, admonition, deprivation of insignia, reduction in military rank, and transfer.[45] Such favored treatment evidences an ingrained feeling that women are not equal to men, but that they must be pampered or protected. This ultimately stems from the still prevailing Soviet attitude that women are less capable and less able to handle power and leadership than are men. This is also reflected in the training that boys and girls receive in school. At about age fifteen, they are both introduced to military familiarization, assembly and disassembly of small arms, field first aid, and civilian defense procedures (hardly more than air raid drills and gas mask exercises). After that boys are exposed to a much greater amount of strictly military training even before they go into the service.[46]

Does this indicate the USSR has not learned from the last war that their female population offered great military potential? Not at all. They apparently believe that in peacetime it is easier to run an all-male army, backed up by a small core of women specialists. In case of war, and always depending on what kind of war, they are fully prepared by experience, organization, national expectations, and training programs to bring into service as many women as they might possibly need, and in whatever capacity—including the most violent kinds of combat.

NOTES

1. On women partisans in 1812, see L. Bychkov, *Partizanskoe dvizhenie v otechestvennoi voine 1812 goda* [The partisan movement in the great patriotic war of 1812] (Moscow: Gospolitizdat, 1941), p. 13; and *Zhenskoe delo* [The women's cause] (August 15, 1912), p. 5. For women nurses at war, see Richard Stites, *The Women's Liberation Movement in Russia* (Princeton, N.J.: Princeton University Press, 1978), pp. 30–31, 86.

2. For women in the revolutionary movement, with documentation, see Stites, *Women's Liberation,* chapters 4, 5, and 8.

3. See, for example, the works of Atkinson, Lapidus, and Stites in these notes.

4. Murmantseva's works are cited in the notes below.

5. For women's response to World War I, see Stites, *Women's Liberation,* chapter 9, section 1.

6. "Young Girls Fighting on the Russian Front," *Current History* (May 1916): 366.

7. "Those Russian Women," *Literary Digest* (September 29, 1977): 48. See also "Warrior Women," *Literary Digest* (June 19, 1915): 1460. For Russian press accounts, see Stites, *Women's Liberation,* pp. 279–80.

8. Maria Botchkareva (Bochkareva) and Isaac Don Levine, *Yashka: My Life as Peasant, Officer, and Exile* (New York: Stokes, 1919), p. 66.

9. Full documentation on the battalions in Stites, *Women's Liberation,* pp. 295–300.

10. Ibid., pp. 305–6, 317–22. The fullest account of women in the civil war in English is Richard Johnson, "The Role of Women in the Russian Civil War (1917–1921)," *Conflict* 2, no 2 (1980): 201–17.

11. In Bessie Beatty, *Red Heart of Russia* (New York: Century, 1919), p. 112.

12. Merle Fainsod, *How Russia is Ruled* (Cambridge, Mass.: Harvard University Press, 1953), p. 104.

13. For the larger context, see Stites, *Women's Liberation,* chapters 10–12; D. Atkinson et al., eds., *Women in Russia* (Stanford, Calif.: Stanford University Press, 1977); N. Dodge, *Women in the Soviet Economy* (Baltimore, Md.: Johns Hopkins University Press, 1966); and G. Lapidus, *Women in Soviet Society* (Berkeley: University of California Press, 1978). For more details on prewar training, see: Mariya Chechneva, *Boevye podrugi moi: kniga vtoraya* [My fighting

comrades] (Moscow: DOSAAF, 1968), p. 131; *Sovetskaya voennaya entsiklopediya*, 3 [The Soviet military encyclopedia,] p. 332 (hereafter cited as SVE); "Women Flyers," *Soviet Life* (May 1975); V. S. Murmantseva, Zhenshchiny v soldatskikh shinelyakh [Women in soldiers' greatcoats] (Moscow: Voenizdat, 1971), p. 110; and G. Serebrennikov, *The Position of Women in the USSR* (London: Gollancz, 1937).

14. For policies, moods, and data on the early stages of the war, see: *The Diary of Nina Kosterina*, trans. M. Ginsburg (New York: Avon, 1968); K. Popov, "Zhenshchiny na rukovodyashchei rabote," [Women in leadership roles] *Pravda* (September 16, 1941): 3; Atkinson, *Women in Russia*, p. 125; Dodge, *Women*, pp. 51, 67; "Domashnie khozyaiki idut na predpryatia," [Housewives move into the economy] *Izvestiya* (September 19, 1941): 1; Murmantseva, *Sovetskie zhenshchiny v velikoi otechestvennoi voine* [Soviet women in the great patriotic war] (Moscow: Mysl, 1974), pp. 22, 45–46, 49, 60, 65, 218; and Alice Moats, "Russian Women at War," *Colliers* (October 18, 1941): 50.

15. Recruiting and motivation: Moats, "Russian Women," p. 51; Murmantseva, *Sovetskie zhenshchiny*, p. 149; "O mezhdunarodnom kommunisticheskom zhenskom dne—8—oi marta," [Concerning international Communist women's day—March 8th] *Rabotnitsa* [The woman worker] (March 1943): 2; M. Binkin and S. Bach, *Women in the Military* (Washington, D.C.: The Brookings Institution, 1977), p. 9; Serebrennikov, *Position*, p. 61; Chechneva, *Boevye podrugi*, pp. 134–40. See also K. Jean Cottam, "Soviet Women in Combat in World War II: The Ground-Air Defence Forces," in T. Yedlin, ed. *Women in Eastern Europe and the Soviet Union* (New York: Praeger, 1980), pp. 115–27.

16. Infantry roles: Murmantseva, *Sovetskie zhenshchiny*, pp. 127–33 and *Zhenshchiny soldatskikh shinelyakh*, pp. 98–105, 111, 116; J. D. Truby, *Women at War: A Deadly Species* (Boulder, Colo.: Paladin, n.d.); *Rabotnitsa* (October–November, 1944): 10; *Krasnoarmeets* [Red army man] (August 1943): 4; Serebrennikov, *Position*, pp. 57–58; *Ogonek* [Little fire] (February 1, 1942) and (June 28, 1942): 6; SVE 3, p. 332; *Geroini* [Heroines], 2 vols. (Moscow: Izdatelstvo Politicheskoi Literatury, 1969), vol. 2, pp. 95–101 (a useful collection of episodes and memoirs); *Soviet Military Review* (March 1971): 62–66 and (March 1974): 19.

17. Murmantseva, *Sovetskie zhenshchiny*, p. 140.

18. Ibid., p. 136.

19. For armor and other branches, see: Romana Danysh, section on the Soviet Union in "Women in Combat," Staff Support Branch, U.S. Army Center for Military History (unpublished) (Washington, D.C., 1978), pp. 33, 39, 41; Murmantseva, *Sovetskie zhenshchiny*, pp. 129, 136, 140–43 and *Zhenshchiny soldatskikh shinelyakh*, pp. 45, 120–22, 63–73; P. V. Terchkov, *Boevya destviya tankov* [Tanks in action] (n.p., n.d.), p. 2; SVE 3, pp. 332; *Rabotnitsa* (January 1945) and (April 1945); *Ogonek* (January 1944), back cover and (September–October 1945): 2; *Krasnoarmeets* (May 1943); *Geroini* 1, pp. 318–26; Binkin, *Women*, 9, *Geroi i podvigi* [Heroes and exploits] (Gosizd. Politlit., 1958), vol 2, p. 74; Serebrennikov, *Position*, p. 57; and National Archives, T 580, Roll 665, Order #447, *Auszüge aus Kgf. Vernehmungen* [Excerpts from prisoner of war interrogations], June 28, 1943, deposition of a Soviet POW in a captured German document.

20. The literature on airwomen is huge, but uneven: In English, see: A Boyd,

The Soviet Air Force Since 1918 (London: Macdonald and Jane's, 1977), pp. 4–10, 165n; *Soviet Military Review* (March 1969): 20–22, and (March 1977): 61–62, and (March 1972): 46–48, and (March 1976): 11–13; *Soviet Life* (May 1975); *Soviet Aerospace Handbook* (May 1978): 170; Danysh, "Women," pp. 24–32; Truby, *Women at War,* p. 31; *Flight International* (December 27, 1962): 1019–20; Moats, "Russian Women," *Colliers* (October 18, 1941): 18, 49–51; and V. Chuikov, *Battle for Stalingrad* (New York: Holt, Rinehart and Winston, 1964), p. 222. In Russian: Murmantseva, *Sovetskie zhenshchiny,* pp. 122, 133–37, 144–46, and *Zhenshchiny soldatskikh shinelyakh,* pp. 2–8, 47, 83–94; *Ogonek* (August 1941), and (May 17, 1942): 8, and (January 17, 1943): 7, and (April 20, 1943), and (July 10, 1943): 4; *Rabotnitsa* (June–July 1944): 12, and (October 1944): 1, and (April 1945): 11, and (January 1943), SVE 3, p. 332; *Geroini* 2, pp. 329–33; *Zvezdy nemerkhushche slavy* [Stars of unfading splendor] (Simferopol: Krym, 1967); *Krestyanka* [The peasant woman] (September 1943): 16.

21. Moats, "Russian Women," p. 51; *Soviet Military Review* (September 1968): 41–43 and (March 1974): 19; Serebrennikov, *Position,* pp. 55–56; Murmantseva, *Zhenshchiny soldatskikh shinelyakh,* pp. 33–34; *Krestyanka* (February–March 1944): 12; *Ogonek* (November 10, 1943): 2; *Geroi i podvigi,* vol 1.

22. Murmantseva, *Sovetskie zhenshchiny,* p. 217.

23. Quoted in N. J. Anderson, "Guerrilla Warfare," in *Command and General Staff School Military Review* (April 1942): 43.

24. The literature on partisan warfare is also extensive. In addition to the works cited above by Anderson, Serebrennikov, and Murmantseva, see the following titles: L. T. Kosmodemyanskaya, *The Story of Zoya and Shura* (Moscow: Foreign Language Publishing House, 1953), written by Zoya's mother; P. Lidov, *The Story of a Heroic Russian Partisan* (Moscow: Foreign Language Publishing House, 1942); *Rabotnitsa* (March 1943): 8; *Ogonek* (February 1942): 10, and (June 1942): 6, and (September 1942): 13; Binkin, *Women,* p. 9; *V groznye gody* [In the years of menace] (Petrazavodsk: Kareliya, 1964), pp. 29–31; Katherine Vinogradskaya, *A Woman Behind the German Lines* (London: Soviet War News, 1944); *Svetlyi put* [Bright Road] (Moscow: Izdatelstvo Politicheskoi Literatury, p. 218; A. Werth, *Russia at War* (New York: Avon, 1964), p. 656. The most negative view is to be found in John Armstrong, *Soviet Partisans in World War II* (Madison: University of Wisconsin Press, 1964). See also the captured German files in *Selected Soviet Sources in the World War II Partisan Movement* (Alabama: Maxwell Air Force Base, 1954), p. 155; and in National Archives, T 313/3838672305 (the pro-German pamphlet).

25. Murmantseva, *Zhenshchiny soldatskikh shinelyakh,* pp. 44–57; Ilya Kuzin, *Notes of a Guerrilla Fighter* (Moscow: Foreign Language Publishing House, 1942); E. Bochkareva et al.

26. "V sobstvennom tanke," [In her own tank] *Rabotnitsa* (April 1945).

27. Armstrong, *Soviet Partisans; Auszüge aus Kgf. Vernehmungen,* see above note 19.

28. Murmantseva, *Sovetskie zhenshchiny,* pp. 131–32; G. Krivich, *Zhenshchiny-snaipery Leningrada* [Women snipers of Leningrad] (Leningrad: n.p., 1966), pp. 36–37.

29. *Auszüge aus Kgf. Vernehmungen.*

30. Soviet figures: SVE 3, pp. 332 and Murmantseva, *Sovetskie zhenshchiny,* pp. 120–29. See also: M. Leibst, *Women in the Soviet Armed Forces* (Washington, D.C.: DDI-109-76, 1976), p. 1; Danysh, "Women," p. 22; "Participation of Soviet Women in World War II," (Washington, D.C.: n.d., DIA Information Paper), p. 1; *Information Paper: DAMI-FII* (January 20, 1978), p. 1.

31. See note 28, above.

32. Murmantseva, *Sovetskie zhenshchiny,* pp. 126, 131.

33. For figures and lists of decorated women, see: Murmantseva, *Sovetskie zhenshchiny,* pp. 264–71 and *Velikaya otechestvennaya voina Sovetskogo Soyuza, 1941–45: kratkaya istoriay* [The great patriotic war of the Soviet Union, 1941–45: a short history] (Moscow: Voenizdat, 1970), pp. 525–27.

34. Vera Figner, *V. borbe* [In the struggle] (Leningrad: Detskaya Literatura, 1966), p. 226.

35. The most detailed description of the wartime mood and the ideological tone of the regime is Werth, *Russian at War.*

36. For the general setting, the best work is Alexander Dallin, *German Rule in Russia 1941–1945* (New York: St. Martin's Press, 1957).

37. See Jeff Tuten's paper on Germany, this volume, pp. 47–60.

38. A superb treatment of German and American women at war is Leila Rupp, *Mobilizing Women for War: German and American Propaganda 1939–1945* (Princeton, N.J.: Princeton University Press, 1978).

39. See Richard Stites, "Women and Communist Revolutions: A Comparative Perspective," in *Studies in Comparative Communism* (1982).

40. *Ogonek* (October 14, 1945): 1.

41. Chuikov, *Battle for Stalingrad,* p. 222. See also Dodge, *Women in the Soviet Economy,* p. 67.

42. Leibst, *Women,* pp. 4–12; Harriet and William Scott, *The Armed Forces of the USSR* (Boulder, Colo.: Westview, 1979), p. 389.

43. Leibst, *Women.*

44. Harriet Scott, "Soviet Women in Uniform," *Air Force Magazine* (March 1976); "Weekly Economic Report," *Summary of World Broadcasts* (July 6, 1979): A18.

45. Leibst, *Women.*

46. Scott and Scott, *Armed Forces,* p. 316; personal information.

4 | YUGOSLAVIA: WAR OF RESISTANCE

Barbara Jancar

The subject of this paper* is the role of women in the Yugoslav military. At first glance the subject might be easily dismissed in one sentence. Namely, there are no women in Yugoslavia's professional army today, except for those in the medical and other support units. However, this statement completely overlooks the history of the woman armed fighter in Yugoslavia, women's present participation in the territorial forces of the Yugoslav unified defense system, and the debate now in progress in Yugoslavia about the future role of women in the Yugoslav military.

This paper proposes to examine the relationship between women and the Yugoslav military from a historical perspective with the aim of drawing some implications from past experience for the future of women in the Yugoslav armed forces. The proposition advanced is that at no time in national history, not even during the Second World War, did women achieve full and equal participation with men in the Yugoslav military. While Yugoslav women may have distinguished themselves in military performances from women in most other armed services in the world, in fact, the military roles they filled were feminized roles. Not even in death were women "equal" with men, for they gave up their lives in proportionately greater numbers than men. In war as well as in peace Yugoslav women have been assigned an identifiable "woman's place" in the defense of their country.

Sponsored by the U.S. Army Research Institute for the Behavioral and Social Sciences. The views and conclusions contained in this document are those of the author and do not necessarily represent those of the sponsor or the U.S. Government.

* I would like to express my sincere appreciation to the Yugoslav Information Center, New York City, especially to Tanya Lenyol, for assistance in obtaining for me necessary documents and materials.

To develop this proposition, the paper will first look briefly at the tradition of the woman fighter as found in the national histories of the constituent republics of Yugoslavia and at woman's participation in the Marxist labor movement in what is now Yugoslavia from 1880–1941. The paper will then explore the role of women in the National Liberation Army (NOV) during the Second World War. Finally, the paper will discuss the present status of women in the Yugoslav armed forces, focusing on developments that argue for change in that status. The emphasis will be placed on the role of women in NOV. All accounts reviewed by the author agree that women's mobilization both within and outside the partisan units was a decisive factor in the Communists' ability to broaden the social base of the war and achieve eventual victory. More important from our point of view, the record of women in the Yugoslav National Liberation Movement (NOP) constitutes one of the most complete we have on the performance of women as fighters and combat soldiers on active duty.

At the outset, a few words should be said about sources. Virtually all of those relating to the role of women in NOP are official Yugoslav publications. The Yugoslavs are justifiably proud of the achievements of the partisans and particularly of the women fighters. Most of the documents reflect this pride. The representation of problems is kept to a minimum and difficulties are depicted as obstacles that are faced and overcome, rather than as permanent or intrinsic characteristics of the wartime situation. Reports of heroic acts predominate for the Yugoslav side as accounts of atrocities multiply on the enemy side. One will thus find no overt recognition of the existence of sexual harassment or rape within the partisan forces, but there will be graphic documentation of the enemy's proclivities in these areas.

Second, the primary source data were for the most part collected during the Second World War in the middle of a violent struggle for national survival. They cannot be expected to be systematic, but reflect the uncertainties and developments of the time. Serbian documents may use different terminology for army units than do the Croatian sources. The number of women in a list of members of a particular division or brigade at a given time may not tally with the number of women whose biographical sketches follow the list. The size of army units varied in different parts of the country depending on recruitment and combat casualties, so it is difficult to compare women's participation across army units.

Finally, since these are Communist sources, the researcher is faced with an overemphasis on women involved in political work. Information on women with ties to the party and politics is almost invariably fuller than that on women with no such connections. Indeed, the selection of women given short bibliographies in the Slovenian, Croation, and Serbian series documenting women's role in the National Liberation Movement (NOP) appears to be based primarily on the degree of commitment of the entrant to the National Liberation (Communist) cause, and secondarily on the personal knowledge of the data collector.

The documents do not give a complete picture but rather a representative picture from the official Communist perspective. Within this limitation, however, the researcher is afforded the unique opportunity to study the performance of women in combat in one of the most ruthless and bloody theaters of World War II.

THE TRADITION OF THE WOMAN FIGHTER AND WOMAN ACTIVIST IN YUGOSLAVIA

Yugoslavia was formed after the First World War from the independent states of Serbia (including Serbian Macedonia) and Montenegro; and the Austro-Hungarian provinces of Slovenia, Croatia, and Bosnia-Herzegovina. Serbia and Montenegro gained their independence from the Ottoman Empire in the nineteenth century. The two states were far less developed than the former Austrian provinces that had experienced considerable industrialization under the Dual Monarchy, especially Croatia and Slovenia. The fight for independence from the Turks encouraged the tradition of the patriotic fighting woman in the southern states, while economic development spawned the Marxist and feminist movements promoting the woman activist.

Montenegro prides itself on the traditional respect accorded to women because of its *kult majke* (''cult of motherhood''), which permitted women a large degree of authority in the home, allowed them to dress in men's clothes, and let them go to war. Widows, in particular, constituted the largest segment of women among the warriors. As war depleted the male ranks, the widowed woman could achieve respect and fame by joining in the fight. A battalion of women is reported to have taken part in a battle between the Turks and Montenegrins in 1858, while a Russian journalist reported his amazement at the bravery and devotion of Montenegrin women fighters. Women are recorded engaging in anti-Austro-Hungarian activities during the Austrian occupation of 1916–1918, and thirty-seven are said to have died in Austrian camps.[1]

In Macedonia many became legendary figures, celebrated for their military prowess against the Turks. Women were also honored for their role in the nationalist movement as teachers and founders of schools to foster nationalism in Macedonian children. The best known of these is Slavka Dinkova, founder of the first Macedonian national school. Women were members of the Macedonian Revolutionary Organization (VMRO) both as terrorists and teachers, and were active in the underground during the Balkan Wars (1912–1914).[2]

Serbia also has its share of women heroes. Among these is the Countess Milice, who, in 1389, after the Serbian defeat in the Battle of Kossovo Field, was able to negotiate an agreement with the Turks that guaranteed Serbia tributary status under the Turks, while retaining titular independence within the Byzantine Empire until complete Turkish annexation in 1459. Women are reported to have become enthusiastic and loyal camp followers of their men in the struggle for Serbian independence. In the February uprising of 1804, women took part in active combat and are reported to have captured an enemy cannon barehanded.[3]

The tradition of the woman fighter from the southern territories of Yugoslavia was not matched by a comparable tradition from the north. However, in the 1870s, in particular, Serbia, Croatia, and Slovenia, saw the growth of Marxist and feminist movements, which encouraged women publicly to oppose the existing system and to speak out for women's rights. In 1909 a group of women in Macedonia gathered around the Socialist Rosa Plaveva to form the first Montenegrin women's Socialist group. Plaveva entered into correspondence with Rosa Luxembourg, bringing the outside world into the experience of the women in her group.[4] Similar groups developed in other parts of what was to become the Yugoslav Republic in 1919.

During the interwar period, the non-Communist women's movements centered around national and religious affiliations, including the national unions of Serbian, Croatian, and Slovenian women, the Union of the Slavic Women affiliated with the International Women's Congress, and the Feminist Alliance. In general, the non-Communist feminists either endorsed the existing regime or, like the Feminist Alliance, adopted a neutral stand. Thus, while women in these organizations did get out into the rural areas, they discouraged political activism, concentrating instead on the teaching of traditional skills, such as sewing and embroidery.[5]

Only the Communist party adopted a coherent policy of women's rights, which it consistently fought to implement. At the founding of the Yugoslav Communist Party (CPY) in 1919, a parallel women's group was organized dedicated to the mobilization of women to the cause of revolution. This organization persisted with only a few interruptions to agitate among women, especially in the urban areas, where women were employed in factories.

As World War II approached and the military dictatorship in Yugoslavia became more oppressive, labor unrest increased. The number of strikes rose from seventeen in 1931 to four hundred in 1936. Women participated in these strikes, and in those industries in which they predominated, such as the textile industry, they outnumbered the male strikers. Communist women actively spread political propaganda among these strikers as well as among university students. At the height of the Spanish civil war,

Communist women organized promotional drives to get money for the war and some volunteered to go to Spain to fight. In 1939 the Communists supported a large-scale campaign for women's right to vote, which attracted wide-female participation.[6]

Government persecution had severely crippled Communist membership during the early thirties. By 1939 Josip Broz Tito had succeeded in bringing it back to sixty-five hundred. But as the Fifth National Conference of that year, there were only 390 women Communists.[7] Hence, talk about women activists before the Second World War refers to a very small segment of Yugoslavian women that provided the nucleus of leadership for the mobilization of women during NOP as well as the tradition of activism in the cause of equal rights.

WOMEN'S PARTICIPATION IN THE NATIONAL LIBERATION MOVEMENT

The two Yugoslav traditions of the woman fighter and the woman activist are important if one is to understand the participation of women in the National Liberation Struggle (NOB), as the Second World War is called by the Yugoslavs. In fact, the war was not one war but three in Yugoslavia. It was a war against the invader, German, Italian, and Bulgarian; it was a war among the Yugoslav nationalities, Croat, Serb, Slovene, and the other nationalities; and it was a war between the old and the new Yugoslavia. This last turned into the political war between the Communists fighting for a Soviet-style revolution and those who sought to restore partially or wholly the old order.[8] Research indicates that among the many reasons that could be cited as to why women opted for the Communist cause the two principal ones were: (1) the Communists were the only organized force in Yugoslavia capable of issuing a transnational patriotic appeal in the nation's defense; and (2) the Communists coupled their call to national liberation with their call for this new political order where women would have equal rights and equal opportunities with men. As was the case then, with virtually all of those who fought on the partisan side, women were fighting on both a military and political front. It is important to understand that the line between these two fronts was at no time clearly delineated. Rather, like two sides of the same coin, they complemented each other.

Chinese Maoist experience notwithstanding, the Yugoslavs credit Tito with having developed a new form of warfare during the Second World War. The all-people's war, as they call it, is a war that is fought by all the people against the invader and any perceived or actual supporters of the invader within the country, such as the Chetniks. The all-people's war is at once a war of liberation and a social revolution, in which the people are mobilized not just to fight for their country but also to fight for a new form of government. Tito was both commander-in-chief of the army and first secretary of the Communist party. He directed all military and political operations. Although military strategy demanded that he flirt with the idea of a non-Communist Yugoslavia during 1944 in order to placate the Western allies, in actual fact, by the end of 1944, the Communists had conquered Yugoslavia and routed the enemy. They brought the Communist system of National Liberation Councils to every area the partisan forces liberated, the first of which was organized in the first liberated areas in 1942. The councils were unified under the Anti-Fascist Council of the People's Liberation of Yugoslavia (AVNOJ).

The participation of women in both the political and military endeavor was critical to the process of social revolution and the emergence of a Communist Yugoslavia at the end of the war. Yugoslav sources set the number of people mobilized in NOP at 3,741,000. The number of male dead was about 1.1 million, of which approximately 400,000 were in the partisan army.[9] Although NOV numbered only around 80,000 in 1941, by 1945 it had grown to over 800,000 organized into five armies.[10] By contrast, Yugoslav sources set the total number of women involved in the partisan side at 2 million, only 100,000 of whom were recruited into the National Liberation Army and partisan units.[11] Approximately 1 in 10, and later, 1 in 8, soldiers were women. The rest were organized into the Anti-Fascist Front of Women (AFŽ) (a government sponsored general organization for women who wanted to participate in the resistance). As can be seen from the statistics, the bulk of the civilian population mobilized to serve in the rear were women serving in AFŽ.

AFŽ was the successor to the Communist women's movement during the interwar period. At first, the party established AFŽ units on an *ad hoc* basis on the county or local level. As areas were liberated, these units made contact organizationally. Gradually regional units were established, until 1942, a national AFŽ Conference was held which officially set up a nationwide women's organization under one central council. Women in this movement took the place of men behind the lines. They ran the local governments, organized procurement, planted the fields, spun cloth and sewed clothes, carried out espionage activities behind the enemy lines, operated the printing presses so vital to the promotion of the revolution, and managed the propaganda and educational schools, the orphanages and the hospitals.

When the enemy overran a village, these women became the front line and suffered accordingly. Their acts of heroism in saving the wounded, evacuating the children and withstanding enemy torture are movingly recorded in the documentary materials. Many were captured by the Italians and sent to Italian POW camps. When Italy capitulated, they returned to their country to carry on the fight anew. The early days of the war in

Croatia saw the commission of some of the worst atrocities against civilians by the Ustashe (Croatian Fascists). Women were frequently the targets. Hence, women who escaped from the Ustashe camps immediately went to join the partisans. In one sense, everyone who participated and fought on the partisan side considered himself a soldier, since the war was fought not on any particular front but all over the country. Yet, the 2 million women who were mobilized into AFŽ are generally not considered military in the strict sense of the word. They did not enter the army.

While this study focuses on those who did enter the army, the vital role played by the many women who supported the partisans in the villages and cities should not be overlooked. Many of their functions are generally considered military and are performed by women in professional armies today; more will be said about these functions later. Women's contribution was especially important as the war took a higher and higher toll of the male population. Women became essential to the maintenance of the military support system as well as to the development of the new civilian order.[12] Some indication of the sacrifice made by Yugoslav women mobilized into NOP may be had when one considers that from 1941 to 1945 8.5 percent of the total female population of Yugoslavia was killed or died (many from diseases such as typhus), while 31 percent of those who joined NOP died and 25 percent of the women recruited into NOV died. Clearly, the toll on the "civilian" women was substantially higher than on the women in the military, and many times higher than that for the female population as a whole.[13]

WOMEN IN THE NATIONAL LIBERATION ARMY (NOV)

Recruitment

All the documents indicate that women joined the army willingly and enthusiastically. Indeed, they were among the first to sign up when the partisan detachments were initially organized. For example, thirty girls from the Bosnian village of Dvar signed up in the spring of 1941, and the first woman national hero was from Dvar.[14] In the July 1941 uprising in Montenegro, women actively participated on an irregular basis, providing first aid and bringing food and munitions.[15] Two women were among the first to join the partisan detachments in Macedonia in August 1941.[16] In Slovenia three women were members of the first partisan unit formed in June 1941 and all these women were among the first to lose their lives.[17] Fifty women were in the first partisan detachments formed in Serbia; the majority of these came from Belgrade and Zemun.[18]

Some indication of the growth in the number of women attracted into NOV may be seen from Croatian statistics. In 1941 only 12 women were in NOV; in 1942, 479; in 1943, 1,211; and in 1944, 6,610 women.[19] Dedijer recalls in his diary that women were so eager to join that he saw them shaking and on tenterhooks lest they be rejected.[20] Mary Reed notes in her research that women were so enthusiastic that they were bitterly disappointed when they were assigned jobs in the rear or sent to organize supplies and do menial tasks.[21]

The documents do not suggest any one reason for women's interest in NOV, but the data offer several possible explanations. Partisan life appears to have been particularly attractive to young women, even more so than to young men. When one looks at the biographical data, most of the women recruits seem to be in their late teens or early twenties. Partisan experience opened a whole new world and gave a sense of camaraderie.[22] Theatrical and musical performances were given by the professional entertainers. Brigades would compete in songfests.[23] The dangers of war brought closeness, a sense of togetherness and purpose. Partisan life also opened educational opportunities for women. One the most frequent comments found in the biographical entries is: "She learned to read and write among the Partisans." Perhaps the second most frequent is, "She took a first aid course, a radio telegrapher course, a course in codes." Most of the women medics (bolničarki) trained during the war returned to civilian life to staff the new Yugoslavia's hospitals, an opportunity which would have been far beyond the reach of most village women in prewar Yugoslavia.

A third and final reason for women's enthusiasm to join NOV was that the woman fighter came to stand as the symbol of Socialist Yugoslavia. On the battlefield Yugoslav women won equality with men, as document after document gives testimony to their bravery and fortitude under fire. Women are described jumping from cover to throw bombs under advancing enemy tanks. Women risked their lives to evacuate wounded under heavy enemy fire. Women marched shoulder to shoulder with men in the breakouts from German encirclement. Indeed, so noteworthy was woman's courage that thirty years later Djilas wrote that women partisans performed more bravely than men.[24]

It cannot be stressed too much that fighting for the partisans constituted a political act in favor of a Socialist postwar Yugoslavia. Early in the struggle the Communists confirmed their commitment to women's liberation. In July 1941 the provisional Supreme Command of the National Liberation Troops of Montenegro, Boka, and the Sandžak issued a communiqué to the effect that the right to vote and to be elected "shall be exercised by all citizens eighteen years of age and over, men and women."[25] Although relatively few in number, women were elected to the first national liberation councils. Their political and social emancipation was the product of the military campaign. One of the central tasks of the AFŽ was to propagandize the political advantages accruing to women if they joined NOP, particularly if they joined the army. By contrast, the

AFŽ was ordered by the party to do everything possible to discourage women from working for the enemy or in any way being drawn into the enemy orbit.[26]

Personal freedom and opportunity were, therefore, concomitant with patriotism for the women who joined the National Liberation Army.

Training

The documents provide little evidence of special training for women in the army. Women as well as men *borac* ("ordinary soldiers") were given a one-month introduction to war and then sent to the front. Frequent references are made to one-month "political-military courses" where both young men and young women were trained for the "tasks" imposed by NOB.[27] In 1942 a bomb factory was formed in Dvar, where twenty-five older workers supervised between fifty and sixty women in the making and using of bombs.[28] The army also offered other training courses, mentioned earlier, such as first aid, coding and decoding, and artillery courses. None of these was specifically oriented towards women and nothing in the documents suggests that women trained in any way differently than men. The courses were probably rudimentary at best and did little to teach support skills. The higher mortality rate of women to men in NOV (25 percent as compared to 11 percent) suggests greater inexperience on the part of women with the implication that women might have benefited from additional special training to develop these skills.[29] On the other hand, the higher female death rate may mean that women, for lack of a better word, were more "gutsy" in the defense of their home than men. The biographical material found in the documents is full of trenchant statements to the effect that "she joined NOV in 1943, died the same year." Or, "she joined in 1942, died in 1943."

First aid courses were by far the most frequently and perhaps the most necessary courses taken by women, according to the documents. Apparently, the courses varied in difficulty and complexity depending on the army unit to which the trainee was to be assigned. In February, March, and April 1942, for example, first aid courses were organized in Croatia for medics at the squad level. In May 1942, a fifteen-day more advanced course was organized under the direction of a medical doctor for medics at the battalion level.[30] Courses such as these continued throughout the war years. Classes apparently were kept small. As a rule, the number of participants was about thirty. While open to all, the majority of students were women.

The AFŽ played a major role in providing administrative and training personnel for the paramilitary courses. In addition to the literacy courses, the AFŽ also organized courses in first aid, radiotelegraphy, codes, telephone electronics, and mechanics. Because of its support function behind the lines, the AFŽ committees even gave instruction on such guerrilla warfare techniques as the destruction of telephone lines, rail cutting, and the destruction of roads and bridges.[31] Finally, the AFŽ committees were primarily responsible for the political training of both soldiers and civilians. A first course offered by the AFŽ organization in Lika in 1942 addressed the topic, "The aims of NOV and the tasks of AFŽ in it."[32]

Sexism in the Army

Reference to so-called sexism in the Yugoslav partisan units is absent from the Communist sources. Officially, the strictest moral code and discipline were enjoined upon party members and upon the military. In his wartime speeches, Tito makes frequent mention of the party's high moral code. Doubtless, the immediate application of social and coercive sanctions was against rape and other sexual offenses. Given the nature of armies, however, one can be sure that incidents of these offenses did occur which were not detected. It is interesting, for example, that in his recently published memoirs of the period, Djilas seems to take a certain perverse pleasure in revealing how many in the party leadership failed to live up to the Communist moral code. Djilas is particularly severe against Ranković and Tito.[33] Such comments indicate that sexual misconduct was more widespread than the party and headquarters (HQ) would have liked to admit and that it was sanctioned in some degree by the party leaders.

The party and the Supreme Military Command also officially endorsed the position that women were equal to men in military action. Order and directives notwithstanding, the evidence shows that there was male resistance to the full participation of women in military action. An editorial published in the organ of the Central Committee of the CPY *Proletar,* the March–April 1942 issue commented:

Many of our Party members hold some outdated and unworthy views that women cannot bear arms in the struggle, that they should not perform various functions in the army headquarters, etc. These are the views of the fifth column, which wants to prevent the active participation of women in the war.[34]

To buttress its position and make sure that women were not discriminated against, the Supreme Headquarters demanded that the list of persons subject to military conscription include the names of women who had volunteered to fight.

The party further attempted to ensure a nonsexist attitude among the population at large. Civilians were censored for maintaining traditional sexist attitudes or for viewing a woman partisan or AFŽ organizer as a prostitute. The frequency of party proclamations regarding the equality of women and their valiant contribution to the war effort in the basic documents suggests that the authorities had an uphill road in this regard.

By comparison, the enemy, including the non-Communist guerrilla fighters, the Chetniks and the Croatian fascist units, Ustashe, were always depicted as humiliating and degrading to women. The AFŽ was urged to publicize every known act of terrorism, rape, or other humiliation visited on women by the enemy. One story of particular horror concerned the Nazi camp at Staroj Gradiski. In their need of workers, the Nazis loaded women and children onto trucks and hauled them to the camp where they took their pleasure with them. Some one thousand women were brought to the camp and raped on Christmas Eve 1942, after which a general massacre of women and children took place.[35]

The aim of partisan propaganda was clearly to make the enemy so terrifying and the partisan side so bright, that women would volunteer to work for NOP. Dedijer enthusiastically writes that women were completely liberated in NOP and that there was no differentiation between male and female partisans: "Not a single man, even among the old peasants was against the position of women in the war."[36]

If enthusiasm for the woman fighter existed to the degree described by Dedijer, the question inevitably arises as to why the male High Command decided to exclude women from the regular military service immediately after the war. One answer must be sought in the highly conservative attitudes of the party leadership.[37] It is difficult to accept the proposition that the party and HQ wholeheartedly embraced the idea of women's liberation during the war and then callously rejected it afterwards. A more plausible explanation lies in the fact that war, particularly a war which encompasses an entire country, is a great leveler. The Communist leadership needed women in order to organize the rear, to fill the depleted front ranks, and to promote actively, not just tolerate, the Communist call to revolution. In such wartime conditions, traditional conservative attitudes were perforce held in abeyance. Once peace returned, however, the old attitudes resurfaced to find expression in official policy on the role of women in the new Yugoslav army.

Women's Military Roles

The unsystematic nature of the data has made it difficult to obtain a precise picture of the distribution of women in military roles throughout the National Liberation Army because of incompleteness of available records. The first partisan detachments were organized on an *ad hoc* basis, generally at the local or county level. Official records of these groups, which might number anywhere from ten to one hundred people, were not available to the author. The first transnational so-called proletarian brigade was organized in December 1941. Immediately afterwards, the order went out from Supreme Headquarters to all the districts involved in the fighting "to form units of the best workers and peasant elements, which can, at any given moment, join the proletarian brigades.''[38] Records of these units were not available. The proletarian brigade was the nucleus of the National Liberation Army, which officially came into being on November 4, 1942. During 1943 the partisan units were re-formed into army units resulting in the emergence of six corps by 1944. These six corps were subsequently formed into five armies. By 1945 the Yugoslav army had assumed its present form. The public documents listing the positions of women in the various military units for the most part date from 1943, no doubt because the reorganization of the army from a guerrilla force required documentation on personnel. Little information is available on the roles filled by women before 1943.

Furthermore, the materials consulted did not provide a comprehensive listing of women by brigade and division. *Serbian Women in NOP* tended to give biographies of women by place of origin. Kovačević's national study, *Borbeni put žena Jugoslavije* [Yugoslav women's militant road] identified only women who distinguished themselves by their bravery. The one source that gave the names of women recruits by brigade or division, or both, was *Croatian Women in NOB,* the second volume of which contains some three hundred pages listing women fighters by military unit with accompanying biographical material.

In an effort to gain a more realistic idea of the types of functions women were performing in NOV, I chose to study in detail the women in the Dalmation units around 1943. The results of the statistical count may be found in Table 4.1.

It must be stressed that the women listed were selective and that the table does not include all the women in the Dalmation units. Certain generalizations may, however, be drawn from the table and integrated with a more cursory inspection of the data on women in the other Croatian divisions.

First of all, as might be expected, there is a high percentage of women who served as medics *(bolnicarka)* or fighter-medics *(borac-bolnicarka);* the percentage of plain soldiers *(borac)* exceeds that of the medics by just a few points. A much lower percentage of women served as military specialists, such as radiotelegraphers, artillerywomen, or cipher officers. There is no doubt, however, that women did serve in these capacities. Third, only 6 percent of the sample—fewer women than I had anticipated—held political positions, and even fewer are identified as service workers doing traditional feminine jobs, such as cooks, seamstresses, and typists. This finding is not surprising. Since the AFŽ had the task of organizing procurement and providing food and clothing for the army, an army recruit then would be mainly entrusted with the fighting. Fourth, the table indicates that women were given responsible positions at the lower military echelons. Of the total sample 11 percent were noncommissioned officers,

Table 4.1

Distribution of Women in World War II Dalmation Army Units: 1943

BY JOB POSITION	CITED DOCUMENTS							
	Doc. 369†		Doc. 370††		Doc. 368†† 371–377		Total #	Total %
	#	%	#	%	#	%		
Bolnicarka (Medical Corpsmen)	171	72	13	18	295	33	479	40
Referent Saniteta (Chief Medic)	11	4	6	8	53	6	70	6
Borac (Fighter)	12	5	47	63	451	50	510	42
Borac* (Specialists)	16	7	3	4	34	4	53	4
Politkomisars (Commissar)**	18	6	5	7	49	5	72	6
Service Personnel***	14	6	–	–	16	2	30	2
	242	100	74	100	898	100	1214	100
Noncommissioned	35	14	7	9	69	8	111	9
Commissioned Officers	7	3	7	9	57	6	71	6
Died	18	6	27	36	295†††	33	340†††	28
Cited	18	6	–	–	–	–	–	
Medals	7	3	–	–	–	–	–	

Doc. 368, no date	First and Second Dalmation Workers Brigade
Doc. 369, Oct. 27, 1944	IX Division
Doc. 370, no date	IX Division, 4th Split Brigade
Doc. 371–	
374, Oct. 31, 1943	XIX Division
Doc. 375, no date	XX Division
Doc. 376, no date	XXVI Division, 11th Dalmation Brigade
Doc. 377, no date	Various Dalmation Units including Partisan Detachments

SOURCE: Adapted from Marija Šoljan, principal editor, *Žene hrvatske u narodnooslobod-ilačkoj borbi* [Croatian women in the national liberation war], vol. II (Zagreb: Izdanje Glavnog odbora Saveza ženskih društava Hrvatske, Publication of the Main Committee of the Union of Croatian Women, 1955), pp. 104–72.

 * Specialist include artillery, tank, radio telegrapher/cipher.
 ** Includes youth league (SKOJ) leaders.
 *** Includes typists, cooks.
 † Summary statistics tallied in the document itself.
 †† All other summary statistics in the table are tallied from the raw personnel entries on the pages cited.
 ††† These figures are underinflated since in some cases mortality information was not included.

while 8 percent of the total sample were commissioned officers at the lowest ranks. No woman in the sample held a commission higher than captain, and there were only three of these. In the total Croatian data, only three women were listed as majors. Fifth, the table suggests a very high mortality rate (about 30 percent).

The picture of the typical woman partisan that emerges from the table and the other Croatian data is of a young girl in her late teens or early twenties, fresh from a village with little education or experience, who some time in late 1942 or early 1943 enlists in NOV. If she survives the first six months, or first year and a half, she may take a first aid or other course. Eventually she may be put in charge of her *vod* ("platoon") or her *referent sanitet* ("first aid unit"). Rarely does she rise higher in the ranks. Those who enlist with more education appear to become the *politkomisars,* squad delegates, youth leaders and AFŽ council members. The data do not reveal how or why a woman becomes a captain. In one instance, the woman is a medical doctor, but in the others, there is no reference to formal education in the biographical sketch.

Table 4.2 based on a sample from one Dalmation division provides a little more information on mortality and promotion to a commission. As can be seen, 50 percent of the commissioned women officers in this division were recruited from the chief medics in charge of a *referent sanitet* ("first aid unit"). A plain woman soldier had a higher mortality rate than a medic, but in general it could be expected that in 1943, at least one out of every three women who volunteered for NOV would be killed in action. As women continued to be recruited and the severity of fighting leveled off, the morality rate fell to an average of one out of every four, still far higher than that for men.

The two tables suggest a definite pattern of sexism in the distribution of military functions. Clearly, the role of medic became "feminized" during World War II in the Yugoslav army. Men were the fighters, but if there was a single woman in the *ceta* or *vod,* she would be designated the medic. We do not know whether the role came to her by choice, or because women were the traditional nurturers in the village, and thus it was viewed as "natural" that women take care of the sick. On the other hand, it must be remembered that in interwar Yugoslavia, hospital nurses were trained nuns. While nursing may be considered a woman's occupation from its very origins, Yugoslav women did not enter nursing on a large scale until the Second World War. Hence, while one must agree that the assumption by women of medic roles is evidence of sexism, the force of the allegation is modified by the fact that training in first aid provided the women the opportunity to escape from their traditional village roles into the modern world. Moreover, nursing under guerrilla warfare conditions forced the

Table 4.2

Distribution of Casualties and Officers Among Job Descriptions from Data Document 377

TYPE OF JOB	N	%	SUM %	% LIVING	OFFICERS COMM.	NON-COMM.
Soldier	160	51			3	1
			54	79		
Soldier Specialist	10	3				4
Soldier Casualties	88	28				
			32	2		
Medic Casualties	12	4				
Medics	18	6				
			9	13		
Chief Medics	10	3			6	
Political Personnel	15	5				
			6	8	3	
Service Personnel	3	1				
	316	101	101	100	12(4%)	5(2%)

Soldier casualties/(soldiers + soldier specialists + Soldier casualties) = 88/170 = 34%

Medic casualties/(medics + chief medics + medic casualties) = 12/40 = 30%

SOURCE: Adapted from Marija Šoljan, principal editor, *Žene hrvatske u narodnooslobodilačkoj borbi* [Croatian women in the national liberation war], vol. II (Zagreb: Izdanje Glavnog odbora Saveza ženskih društava Hrvatske, Publication of the Main Committee of the Union of Croatian Women, 1955), pp. 157–72.

woman to be at once medic and soldier, whose chances of survival differed little from that of the ordinary soldier.

The distinction between sexes comes out more clearly in the comparison of the numbers of men and women serving in NOV. Official statistics set the total number mobilized at 1 million, of which women number only 100,000. There is no doubt that men bore the brunt of the fighting. As was pointed out earlier, however, there were 2 million women not in NOV engaged in administration, provisions, and maintenance in the organizations of AFŽ. These 2 million represented the overwhelming majority of the mobilized civilian population. If we include support functions carried out by AFŽ in the military effort, as we did not do earlier, then there were more women in service than men, but only one woman in twenty was actually in the front lines. The rest were providing support in the rear.

Modern armies view support functions as "woman's place" in the military, while combat is considered exclusively the male prerogative. Viewed from this standpoint, the distribution of the total number of women mobilized in NOP reflects the current attitudes of those armed forces that permit women in their ranks. Once again, however, in the case of Yugoslavia in the Second World War, the support functions cannot be considered traditionally female. Providing food and sewing were indeed part of woman's work in the village. But direct participation in administration and guerrilla warfare engagements most certainly were not.

What must be concluded from the available data is that the Second World War offered Yugoslav women the opportunity to escape from their traditional feminine roles to assume "woman's place" in the modern industrial world. Participation in both the National Liberation Movement and the army was indeed a liberating experience for the traditional village woman. But to a large degree that liberation prepared her for only complementary feminine roles in the larger society. One cannot agree with the official claim that women enjoyed full and equal participation with men in NOV. The typical woman partisan was assigned what clearly became identified as the feminine position providing the support functions.

Military Rank

Table 4.3 compares the commissioned ranks held by women with those of men in some of the Croatian military units.

Table 4.3

Ratio of Staff Officers to Total Numbers in Unit by Sex in Six Croatian Partisan Units: 1941–1945

| | RATIO OF STAFF OFFICERS (n) TO TOTAL NUMBERS IN UNIT (N) | | | |
| | Males | | Females | |
NAME OF UNIT	n/N	%	n/N	%
VIII Division, 1 Corps of the Croatian National Liberation Army (NOV)	36/1557	2.31	4/194	2.06
X Division, 1 Corps, Croatian NOV	62/2511	2.47	2/262	0.76
XIII Division, 1 Corps, Croatian NOV	22/5220	0.42	1/139	0.72
XII Proletarian Stock Brigade	23/1277	1.80	1/136	0.74
XIII Proletarian Brigade	56/3451	1.62	1/128	0.78
XVIII Croatian Brigade	19/227	8.37	2/70	2.86
Ratio of officers to total	220/14243	1.54	11/929	1.18

SOURCE: Adapted from Marija Šoljan, principal editor, *Žene hrvatske u narodnooslobod-ilačkoj borbi* [Croatian women in the national liberation war], vol. II (Zagreb: Izdanje Glavnog odbora Saveza ženskih društava Hrvatske, Publication of the Main Committee of the Union of Croatian Women, 1955), pp. 220, 241, 268, 294, 295, 317.

Two thousand women were made officers during the National Liberation War. While the table only represents a small sample of the total divisions and partisan detachments in NOV, it shows that of all male partisans there were about 30 percent more partisan male officers than there were partisan women officers out of all women partisans. The table further shows that there was a wider variation in the percent of officers to the total among the male partisans than among the women fighters.

The indication is that men had greater opportunities for promotion than women, or even that women were deliberately discriminated against. As suggested earlier, the data indicate that women officers of superior rank generally possessed nonmilitary skills, particularly in medicine. Given the fact that the majority of both male and female recruits came from peasant backgrounds with little formal education, we are forced once again to refute the official Yugoslav claim of equal participation of women with men in NOV.

WOMEN IN THE YUGOSLAV MILITARY TODAY

After World War II women were gradually eased out of the professional army. A letter to Belgrade went unanswered, so I was unable to ascertain the precise number or job status of women currently in service in the Yugoslav People's Army (YPA). Women are not subject to the draft and do not have to do the twelve or fifteen months military service required by law of all men, generally upon completion of secondary education.

Women do serve in the Territorial Defense Forces (TDF). These forces came into existence after the Soviet invasion of Czechoslovakia in 1968, when the whole system of national defense came under review. The concept of the all-people's war was then revived as the most effective means of deterring or repelling the invader, or of doing both. At its inception, the TDF had a distinctly regional character, although its command posts were staffed by YPA reserve personnel. However, the command structure went directly from the Supreme Commander to the republican commands, bypassing the YPA General Staff. In 1972 TDF was made more subordinate to the YPA; commands were passed through the General Staff, and the integration of the two defense organizations was achieved under what was called a "unified defense system."[39] Two women were made generals in the reorganized TDF.

Since 1968 all able-bodied citizens, men, women, and children, are required to undergo paramilitary training at their school or workplace. All are assigned a specific post and function for which they are responsible in the event of enemy attack. Girls as well as boys attend military science classes in school and learn to shoot. My cursory review of Yugoslav material on the People's Defense System, found, however, no pictures or discussions of women undergoing artillery or military specialist training. The pictures I did find of women in TDF portrayed them in their best-remembered NOP roles—as medics.

The role of women in the military is currently under severe scrutiny in Yugoslavia. One question of particular urgency is whether to require the draft of all women. A bill presented to the Yugoslav Federal Assembly in December 1979 urged greater participation of women in the YPA, but stopped just short of requiring the draft. The bill noted that

In contrast to the People's Liberation War, when women, on a mass scale, on an equal footing with men, took part in almost all military special duties, in fighting and in the rear, in commands and grew into leading personnel of our people's liberation army . . .today there are very few women in the armed forces or in service in them—or they are only symbolically present and represented. . . .

One reason advanced for the absence of women was that there were previously enough trained men to do the job. The bill went on to say, however, that "it is good and correct" that the opportunities be open to women, both in terms of the national interest and for women themselves. It is suggested that women not be subject immediately to compulsory military service, but that "provisions be made for such opportunities when necessary." Provisions also should be made for women reserve officers, the promotion of whom requires that women undergo a minimal program of military training in the YPA.[40]

The new law passed in early 1980, opens professional military service to Yugoslav women, but will leave enlistment on a voluntary basis. There is no indication that enlistment will lead to combat duty or training. The present inequality as regards the participation of men and women in the army is continued with the recognition that there are many jobs in the army not of a combat nature which women can perform as well or better than men, just as women did in the Second World War. Thus, despite the record of women's heroism, despite their record of combat duty during NOB, the present Yugoslav leadership does not seem much closer to giving women full and equal participation with men in the present professional army than it was during the Second World War.

SUMMARY OF FINDINGS

The Yugoslav cultural tradition of the woman fighter as well as the party tradition of the woman activist might be thought to have been strong enough to undermine the "bourgeois" feminine ideal that has captured the mind of the twentieth century in support of a strong female presence in the modern Yugoslav army.

Yugoslav women, in lesser numbers admittedly, but with equal or greater bravery and determination, did fill combat positions during the Second World War. They experienced the same war conditions at the front as did their male counterparts, and they engaged in large numbers of new occupations generally unavailable to them in prewar Yugoslavia, including administration. Most of these new occupations, however, represented "woman's place" in the civilian world of postwar Yugoslavia. The war experience thus did not truly offer women equal participation with men in military service. Woman's second-class status during NOB was given tacit recognition in their exclusion from the professional army and in their exemption from the draft after the Second World War. Thirty years after the war the question of their full participation has, finally, come once more to the fore.

The summary is sobering for anyone who supports the draft for women as well as the principle of equal opportunity in the armed forces. The conclusion is inescapable. The prevailing Yugoslav cultural and social image of women is conservative where the military is concerned, and this image tends to outweigh the combined logic of national tradition and experience. Even the presentation of the historical record cannot escape sexist overtones. The biographies of the women who fought in NOV contained in the sources take pains to show how really "feminine" these women were, when they were not engaged in desperate deeds of heroism. Women are depicted as bringing compassion and mercy to the war effort. Their role in NOP was to defend the motherland, not aggression. Women and combat were and still are perceived as total opposites.

Attitudinal change comes slowly. The new law may be the first step in Yugoslavia's acceptance of the woman fighter on a professional basis.

NOTES

1. Dušenka Kovačević et al., eds., *Borbeni put žena Jugoslavije* [Yugoslav women's militant road] (Belgrade: Kelsikografski zavod "Svezjanje," 1972), pp. 76–77.

2. Ibid., pp. 154–55.

3. Ibid., p. 223.

4. Ibid., p. 155.

5. For a discussion of the non-Communist women's organizations in Yugoslavia during the interwar period, see Pauline Albala, *Yugoslav Women Fight for Freedom* (New York: The Yugoslav Information Center, 1943).

6. Dušenka Kovačević, *Women of Yugoslavia in the National Liberation War* (Belgrade: Yugoslovenski pregled, 1977), pp. 9–26.

7. Statistics cited by Tito in Josip Broz Tito, "Nájlɛpši spomenik žaučesnice naše revolucionarne borbe jeste dosledno ostvarivanje ideala, za koje su se nesebično, herojski borile." "The most beautiful monument to the women participants

in our revolutionary struggle is the persistent realization of the ideals for which they unselfishly and heroically fought." *Žena danas: 1975—Trideset godina pobede nad fašizmom, medjunarodna godina žena, oun*. [Women today: 1975—thirtieth anniversary of the victory over fascism, U.N. international women's year] 39, no. 275 (1975), p. 65.

8. See Dennison Rusinow, *The Yugoslav Experiment, 1948–1974* (Berkeley and Los Angeles: University of California Press, 1978), pp. 3–7.

9. Figures taken from *The Second World War* (Belgrade: The Military Historical Institute, 1970), p. 512.

10. Josip Broz Tito, *The Struggle and Development of the CPY between the Two Wars* (Belgrade: STP-Socialist Thought and Practice: Kommunist, 1977), p. 94.

11. Tito, "Najlepsi spomenik," p. 16.

12. For a longer account of the involvement of Yugoslav women in AFŽ, see Barbara Jancar, "Women in the Yugoslav National Liberation Movement," in *Studies in Comparative Communism* (1982).

13. Percentages based on Yugoslav population figures for 1939 and Tito, "Najlepsi spomenik," p. 16.

14. Kovačević, *Borbeni put*, p. 52.

15. Ibid., p. 86

16. Ibid., p. 161.

17. Ibid., p. 195.

18. Ibid., p. 232.

19. Ibid., p. 127.

20. Vladimir Dedijer, *With Tito Through the War* (London: Alexander Hamilton, 1951), p. 121.

21. Mary E. Reed, "Emergence of the Political Woman in the Partisan Resistance in Croatia, 1941–1945," unpublished paper presented at the International Conference in Women's History, Women and Power: Dimensions of Women's Historical Experience, sponsored by the Conference Groups in Women's History, Center of Adult Education, University of Maryland, November 16–18, 1977, p. 10.

22. Marija Šoljan, ed., *Žene hrvatske u narodnooslobodilačkoj borbi* [Croatian women in the national liberation war] (Zagreb: Izdanje Glavnog odbora Saveza ženskih društava Hrvatske, Publication of the Main Committee of the Union of Croatian Women, 1955), vol. 1, pp. 210–11. A young woman recruit describes her first experience in the army in terms of the new-found friendships and support of her unit and unit head.

23. Dedijer, *Tito*, pp. 234–35.

24. Milovan Djilas, *Wartime* (New York: Harcourt Brace Jovanovitch, 1977), p. 210.

25. Kovačević, *Borbeni put*, pp. 63–64.

26. Šoljan, *Žene hrvatske*, vol. 1, Document 37, "On Organization and Tasks of AFŽ from CC KPH," p. 57.

27. Kovačević, *Borbeni put*, p. 128.

28. Ibid., p. 52.

29. *Second World War*, p. 512.

30. Kovačević, *Borbeni put*, pp. 128–29.

31. Bosa Tsvetich, ed., *Žhene srbije u NOB* [Serbian women in the national liberation struggle]. See also *Žene hrvatske*, vol. 1, Document 74, p. 107.

32. Ibid., vol. 1, Document 96, pp. 136–37.

33. Djilas, *Wartime*.

34. As quoted in Kovačević, *Borbeni put*, p. 52.

35. Šoljan, *Žene hrvatske*, vol. 1, Document 71, pp. 100–101.

36. Dedijer, *Tito*, p. 241.

37. The postwar conservative attitudes of the party leadership have been well documented in Allen H. Barton, Bogdan Denitch, and Charles Kadushin, *Opinion-making Elites in Yugoslavia* (New York: Praeger, 1973), particularly chapters 2 and 3.

38. Ahmet Donlagic, Zarko Atanackovic, Dusan Plenca, *Yugoslavia in the Second World War* (Belgrade: Interpress, 1967), p. 78.

39. For two discussions of the Yugoslav unified defense system, see A. Ross Johnson, *The Yugoslav Doctrine of Total National Defense* (Santa Monica, Calif.: The Rand Corporation, 1971); and Nikola Ljubičić, *Total National Defense-Strategy of Peace* (Belgrade: STP-Socialist Thought and Practice, 1977).

40. The foregoing was cited and condensed from Colonel General Branislav Joksovic, Member of the Committee for National Defense of the Federal Chamber of the Assembly of the SFRY, *Borba*, December 23, 1979, p. 14.

5 | VIETNAM: WAR OF INSURGENCY

William J. Duiker

A central feature of Communist revolutionary strategy during the recent conflict in Vietnam was the concept of a "people's war," a mass struggle waged by the entire people against the American imperialist invaders and their lackeys, the reactionary government in Saigon. In the war, all Vietnamese—rural and urban, young and old, men and women—were judged primarily in terms of their prospective ability to contribute to the common endeavor of completing the struggle for the unification of Vietnam.

One of the more familiar images of the Vietnamese people's war is that of the woman combatant. She is a member of an artillery unit protecting Hanoi from American bombing raids. She is a guerrilla fighter in South Vietnam, a rifle in her arms and her child strapped to her back. She is a member of a local militia unit in a liberated area, serving not only as wife and mother, but also as a defender of her village against an attack by enemy troops. Is this a true image? Did women play an active and even an equal role in the Vietnamese revolution? If so, what were the historical precedents? And what are the implications for the rights and responsibilities of women in postwar Vietnam?

The immediate source of Communist revolutionary strategy in Vietnam was the concept of national liberation war developed by Mao Zedong in China. When Communist party leaders first mapped out plans for a national war of resistance against the double yoke of Japanese occupation troops and French colonial authority in the spring of 1941, they were undoubtedly aware of the acquired experience of their comrades to the north, and the new strategy developed at that time was consciously patterned after the Maoist model.[1] That is not to say, however, that there was not a native precedent for the idea of a national struggle against foreign invaders. Indeed, the concept of a people's war to defeat the invading forces of powerful enemies is one of the foremost historical traditions of the Vietnamese people. The roots of this tradition are located in the periodic uprisings launched over a period of several hundred years against Chinese rule. While it is probable that a good part of that tradition lies in the realm of myth rather than verifiable history, it is nonetheless a fact that on several occasions, Vietnamese were able to mobilize a national effort to defeat invading forces and restore their independence.[2]

One of the more enduring aspects of the Vietnamese legend of the people's war is that several of the heroic figures who defended the Vietnamese nation against foreign conquest were women. The earliest, and by far the most renowned in song and saga, were the Trung sisters, whose exploits against occupying Chinese forces in the first century A.D. have thrilled Vietnamese patriots for nearly two thousand years. They were not professional warriors. The eldest, Trung Trac, was the wife of a petty nobleman who had been executed by the Chinese for his rebellious activities. The widow and her younger sister Trung Nhi then proceeded to appeal to the populace and were able to raise an army which, in A.D. 40, drove the Chinese out of Vietnam. According to legend, seven of the Vietnamese military commanders were women. One, Phung Thi Chinh, allegedly delivered a child while leading the troops at the front: "Surrounded, she delivered at the front itself, after which, putting the newborn baby on her back and brandishing a sword in each hand, she opened a bloody route in the ranks of the enemy and escaped."[3] The tradition of women warriors continued to light the pages of Vietnamese history down to modern times. During the several hundred years of Chinese rule that followed the Trung sisters revolt, women on more than one occasion took the lead in stimulating popular revolts against occupying forces, establishing a tradition that has lived to modern times. It was not only the Communists who were led to bask in its reflected glory. When the pro-American government of Ngo Dinh Diem was established in Saigon in 1954, one of the most prominent public monuments erected by the new republic was a statue of the Trung sisters at the edge of Saigon harbor. The visage of Trung Trac looked suspiciously like that of Diem's sister-in-law, Madame Ngo Dinh Nhu.[4]

By itself, too much should not be made of the tradition of heroic women in Vietnamese history. Most cultures have a Joan of Arc in their past, their greater-than-life heroines who stepped forward in moments of crisis to defend society against invading enemy forces. What is more important, of course, is whether such heroic figures represent the visible manifestation of a society in which women play a prominent part.

In traditional Vietnam, the picture was mixed. Scattered evidence suggests that women were more active in ancient Vietnam than their counterparts elsewhere in Asia. Indications are that there were no rigid distinctions between the sexes in their social roles. Whatever the case, this tradition was destined to be undermined and virtually erased by one thousand years of foreign rule. For the Chinese conquest of Vietnam had enduring consequences for Vietnamese society, its institutions, and its social values.

A more restrictive attitude toward the role of women was one of the legacies of the centuries of Chinese occupation. For under the Chinese, women's place in Vietnamese society was gradually circumscribed to conform to Chinese practice. In the Confucian view prevalent in China and transmitted to Vietnam, women were clearly inferior to men. According to the famous *san kang* ("three obediences") women were subordinate in three respects: the daughter to the father, the younger sister to the older brother, the wife to the husband. Women played no active role in politics or in the professions. Entrance into the governing class, achieved, at least in theory, through success in the regular civil service examinations, was restricted to males.

In fact as in theory, women were restricted to the home and to the role of dutiful wife and mother. As a general rule, they did not receive an education. The dominant female virtues (as defined by males) were modesty, purity, and obedience. According to Chinese law and social custom, their rights within the family were rigidly circumscribed. The husband not only possessed all property rights, he was also permitted to take a second wife or a concubine if the first wife failed to perform by producing a son.

For the most part, then, in the area of women's rights Vietnamese culture appeared to be almost a carbon copy of that of China. There were some minor exceptions, a pale reflection of the pre-Confucian past. Under the Hong Duc Code established in the fifteenth century, women, following local custom, were permitted under certain circumstances to own property and to perform ritual functions in the family.[5] In this respect, Vietnamese custom triumphed over the rigidities of Chinese law. While the point seems minor, the implications contained in the code were perhaps not entirely theoretical. According to custom, Vietnamese women occupied a more honored place in the household than their Chinese counterparts, often taking responsibility for the family budget and handling other aspects of family administration. Not infrequently they were the dominant force within the family. Under the last dynasty of the Nguyen (1802–1945), however, the position of women was again restricted. The new legal code, promulgated under founding emperor Gia Long, returned to the rigidities of Chinese law and specifically prohibited wives from owning property.[6]

The French conquest in the late nineteenth century opened a new era in Vietnamese history. Under French colonial rule, Confucian institutions and values rapidly disintegrated and were gradually replaced by those of the modern West. With such changes came a new attitude toward the role of women in society. In the early years of the twentieth century, a new Franco-Vietnamese school system opened education to women for the first time. In theory, Vietnamese girls would receive at least a primary level of instruction in their native villages, while a select few would be permitted to advance to higher levels of education; for that purpose, a girls' secondary school, the famous Dong Khanh School, was opened in the imperial capital of Huê. By the 1930s women were accepted at the only institution of higher learning in Vietnam, the University of Hanoi.[7]

The consequences began to be felt in the first decade after the First World War. Women began slowly to enter the professions. A consciousness that women, too, had rights and that they should be permitted to fulfill their own desires began to permeate the assumptions of the small but growing middle class. Popular novels written during the period began to describe women in a new light, not simply as virtuous and dutiful consorts, but as individuals with their own goals and emotional needs. The "emancipated woman" began to make her appearance, at least in the pages of Vietnamese novels. In 1913 the journalist Nguyen Van Vinh established a new journal, *Dong Duong Tap chi* (Indochinese Journal), with a special column with advice for women.[8] A decade later the first publication devoted entirely to women, *Phu Nu Tan Van,* appeared on the newstands.

While French rule had resulted in some improvements in the area of women's rights in Vietnam, it probably had little impact on the lives of the vast majority of Vietnamese women. In rural areas, feudal customs often remained untouched. Where the French presence did have some effect, it was not always beneficial. As French efforts to tie Vietnam to the world economy accelerated, women were recruited to work in factories or on French-run rubber plantations, where living conditions were abysmal, wages at near-starvation levels, and life expectancy short. The most that could be said was that their male compatriots suffered in equal proportion at their side.

WOMEN IN THE VIETNAMESE REVOLUTION

As the place of women in Vietnamese society gradually began to take on a new prominence, their potential role in the struggle to restore Vietnamese independence also came under increasing scrutiny. At first, this process was limited to the area of theory. One of the best-known Vietnamese nationalist leaders of the early twentieth century, Phan Boi Chau, aimed to transform Vietnam into a modern society based on the twin foundations of Western science and democracy. As part of that program, women would be emancipated and play an active role in the struggle to evict the French colonial regime and restore national independence. As chief publicist for his movement, he wrote pamphlets calling on all members of Vietnamese society, including women, to join together to rid

Vietnam of its foreign rulers. Yet Chau's movement fell short on performance. While his movement achieved brief popularity, there is no record of substantial female participation. Certainly there were no women among the leaders of Chau's organization.[9]

With the formation of the Vietnamese Communist movement after World War I, Chau's ideas began to be put into reality. Ho Chi Minh, the founder of the movement, demonstrated a particular sympathy for the conditions of Vietnamese women, and in several articles written before the formal appearance of the Indochinese Communist party (ICP), he cited examples of the brutal mistreatment of women in Vietnam at the hands of the French colonial oppressors. One article in particular, written in 1922 and entitled, "Annamese women and French domination," was typical, describing the sadistic cruelty of French colonial troops in raping and torturing innocent Vietnamese women. While the article made no specific reference to what women could do to alleviate their personal hardships, it was clear from his writings that he felt Vietnamese women had no choice but to unite with their countrymen in joint resistance against the colonial regime.[10]

With the formation of the ICP in early 1930, Ho and his small coterie of followers began to put such ideas into practice. Women were actively recruited into the party and into the embryonic mass organizations, representing peasants, workers, intellectuals, and women. While accurate statistics are lacking, scattered evidence suggests that women were relatively active in the movement at the lower levels, although few achieved prominence within the party. The major exception was the revolutionary Nguyen Thi Minh Khai. Born in 1910 of a scholar-gentry family from central Vietnam, she joined the party soon after its formation. An intense, single-minded revolutionary, she rose quickly to prominence and was chosen as one of the delegates to the Seventh Congress of the Comintern, held in Moscow in 1935. By 1939, then married to Le Hong Phong, number-two man in the party after Ho Chi Minh himself, she returned to Vietnam and was selected as party secretary of the ICP's municipal committee in Saigon.[11]

The enunciation of a new strategy of national liberation by the Eighth Plenum of the ICP Central Committee in the spring of 1941 represented a watershed in the Vietnamese revolution. The party then openly declared that it was waging a struggle of all the people directed at national independence. It attempted to disguise the Communist character of the leadership of the new Vietminh Front and win support from the mass of the population through moderate programs and an emphasis on nationalism.

As the end of the Pacific War approached, Ho Chi Minh directed the establishment of a new Vietnamese People's Liberation Army (PLA), later called the PAVN, or People's Army of Vietnam. The familiar Maoist three-tiered approach was adopted. At the top were the regular main force units; at the second level were lightly-armed full-time guerrillas operating on a regional basis; and at the village level, militia units were formed for self-defense purposes and to provide logistical assistance to main force troops operating in the area. It was, indeed, a plan for a people's war. Recruitment for the revolutionary armed forces would begin in the villages as active youths would be mobilized to join the self-defense forces. Those highly qualified would then be selected to serve in higher level units. While statistics are lacking, it appears that women were frequently found in the local militia units and less likely at the upper level. There were reportedly three women in the first thirty-four-man unit of the PLA, established in 1944.

With the outbreak of the Franco-Vietminh conflict in December 1946, the classic form of Vietnamese people's war began to emerge. Following the Maoist model calling for a three-stage process of retreat, equilibrium, and attack, Vietminh units retreated from the cities and other densely populated areas along the coast and into the swamps, mountains, and highland plateaus to fight a protracted guerrilla war. Thanks to extensive efforts to mobilize the population, the Vietminh were able to survive the first difficult years, and by the late 1940s, were ready to make a serious challenge to the French. The main force units, though still small in size and poorly armed, nevertheless proved to be tough and after a highly successful Vietminh campaign along the Chinese border in 1950, the French were forced gradually to the defensive. In the long run, the mobility and toughness of the Vietminh armed forces, and the extensive support provided by paramilitary units and the civilian population, were what made the difference.

Women often played a significant role in the process. They served in a variety of capacities, and were a major factor in the party's ability to mobilize support for its cause at the local level. While the number of women in main force or guerrilla units was relatively small, women performed a number of other vital tasks for the resistance. They were recruited for production tasks to replace men serving at the front; they repaired roads, served on first aid teams, and in liaison and intelligence units; finally, they comprised a substantial proportion of the transport units that carried vital military equipment and provisions to the troops at the front. In the key battle of Dien Bien Phu, for example, it was the sustained efforts of predominantly female transports units carrying artillery pieces and ammunition over mountainous trails several hundred miles from the Chinese border that permitted the Communists to sustain constant artillery pressure on the beleaguered French outpost and eventually compel its surrender.

Women were considered particularly useful in assisting Vietminh military forces to seize French outposts in rural areas, proselytizing among French troops, sabotaging villages from within, forming crowds of protesters that frequently served as a smokescreen for an upcoming guerrilla attack on government installations. The importance of such activities is suggested by the statistic provided by Bernard Fall that one-third of all French posts seized by the Vietminh during the war were taken by stratagem. Not least, evidently, in their service to the cause were Vietnamese prostitutes, who often served as spies reporting on French military activities through information provided unwittingly by their clients.[12]

The pattern established during the Franco-Vietminh conflict was repeated in the second conflict that followed a few years after the restoration of peace at Geneva in 1954.

The political centerpiece for the renewed struggle was a new united front entitled the National Front for the Liberation of South Vietnam (NLF) and established in December 1960. Like its predecessor, the Vietminh Front, the heart of the NLF was located in a series of functional associations representing the various elements in South Vietnamese society expected to be sympathetic to the insurgency cause. Representing women, a new mass organization, the Women's Liberation Association (Hoi Phu Nu Giai Phong) appeared in early 1961. The political program of the NLF set the tone for its future propaganda efforts: women were promised equality before the law, equal pay for equal work, and equality in marriage. By contrast, the alleged shortcomings of the GVN (Government of Vietnam based in Saigon) in the field of women's rights were emphasized. Women in the South were described in published statements as exploited and degraded, the victims of the "poisonous weeds" of American bourgeois culture.

It was apparent from the beginning that the party intended to make active use of Vietnamese women in the new revolutionary struggle. At least in the early years, party strategists were optimistic that the Saigon regime could be overthrown by a relatively low level of combined political and revolutionary struggle. Primary reliance would be placed on the "political force of the masses," a combination of unarmed demonstrations by the masses and low-level armed struggle conducted by lightly armed guerrillas and militia forces. Because large-scale combat might not be required, main force units might not be used, and the insurgency movement in the South could rely on local forces recruited there and supplemented by southerners trained in the North and sent South to provide experienced leadership.

Under these conditions the role of women in the new stage was likely to be significant. Women could take part in low-level armed activities and play a particularly active role in mobilizing the masses for the revolutionary struggle. To provide a framework for action, guidelines were established.

Women were expected to adhere to the so-called five goods—to take part in production, to engage in self-improvement, to raise a family, to study diligently, and to assist in the defense effort. A training school, named after Nguyen Thi Minh Khai and patterned after a similar institution in the North, was established in a liberated area to train female cadres for political and military work. The course lasted three months, and the students were selected by local chapters of the Women's Liberation Association.

It did not take long for a model figure to appear. One of the first attacks launched by the new People's Liberation Armed Forces (PLAF) took place in the province of Ben Tre in the heart of Mekong delta in January 1960. The area had been a stronghold of anti-French sentiment for years, and after the Geneva settlement had been the object of particular attention by the Saigon government of Ngo Dihn Diem, which launched a "denounce the communists" campaign, resulting (according to NLF figures) in the arrest of over two thousand Communist sympathizers. When in mid-1959 the southern leadership approved a policy of cautious military escalation, provincial party leaders responded by planning a mass uprising in the province in January 1960. One of the major leaders of the local revolutionary movement was a woman. Nguyen Thi Dinh, born in 1920, had become acquainted with the Communists through the activities of male members of her family. She became a party member in the late 1930s, and by 1945 had become a leading figure in the Ben Tre provincial committee. The following year, she personally took part in transporting one thousand rifles from the North to the area to assist the local revolutionary forces.[13]

According to her memoirs and other Communist accounts of the Ben Tre uprising, the local PLAF units lacked both troops and weapons and decided to rely on the "mass uprising" technique that had worked well during the early stages in the war against the French. The attack, launched under her direction, began in mid-January, when several villages and government outposts were seized by ruse or by mass attacks. Weapons were distributed and military units of company size were formed, many wearing uniforms disguising them as main force units from outside the province. To compensate for the PLAF's weakness in size and firepower, the leadership turned to another technique that had been successfully utilized in the uprising in 1945, namely, the mass march of thousands of women to government administrative centers to protest against corruption, government atrocities, and economic conditions. The first such demonstration took place in April 1960 with five thousand women and children marching to the capital of Mo Cay district. Government officials, surprised and embarrassed, found themselves on the defensive and unable to react against women protesters. The technique spread and was soon labeled the long-haired army (*doi quan toc dai*). The uprising eventually subsided after government troops entered the province in force, but the techniques used at Ben Tre were soon emulated in other provinces throughout the delta and in the Central Highlands. As a result of her leadership role in the movement at Ben Tre, Nguyen Thi Dinh became a celebrated heroine of the revolutionary forces and soon was promoted to the position of deputy commander of the People's Liberation Armed Forces.

By 1961 a unified command for the PLAF had been created, and the characteristic shape of a Maoist-style insurgency began to appear, with self-defense militia units formed in hamlets and villages sympathetic to the revolutionary cause and guerrilla units at higher levels. Recruits for the guerrillas were usually selected from the most active and loyal elements, whether men or women, in the village units. Figures on female participation in the various military units are scarce, but the percentage at lower levels was apparently quite high, and not infrequently women were found in positions of command. According to one estimate, 40 percent of all regimental commanders of the People's Liberation Armed Forces were women.[14] In some cases, women served in units alongside the men; in others, however, all-female units were formed to perform specific duties considered appropriate to their capacities. For a variety of reasons, there was a growing tendency to view women as a separate element in the revolutionary arsenal, presenting unique opportunities as well as distinctive problems. It was sometimes considered disadvantageous to recruit women for service in predominantly male units. Men were sometimes resentful of, or patronizing to, their female colleagues. The love interest presented special problems, as men tended to court the younger and prettier women, leading to resentment on the part of older, and frequently more experienced, women in the unit. According to some sources, also, women were often considered inferior to men in combat.[15]

On the other hand, women were particularly adept at certain tasks vital to the success of the movement. They were often superior to men in liaison work, and they made effective spies. They were useful (being more quick witted, according to one American observer, than their male counterparts) in persuading government troops to defect. Finally, women were apparently better at performing the most demeaning task of the revolution—that of transporting supplies. Men were usually stronger, and able to carry more in quantitative terms, but women were less inclined to complain of the drudgery and had greater stamina. As a result, female transport units were common, leading the American expert Douglas Pike to describe women as "the water buffalo of the revolution."[16]

They also played a central role in the political struggle. According to one history of the movement published in Hanoi:

the women played a particularly efficient role in these political struggles. They had their own political army, their own direction, their particular organization. They were at the same time combative and tenacious, heroic and intelligent, knowing how to combine toughest resistance with sweetest persuasion. They constituted a real long-haired army, particularly feared by the puppet civilian and military authorities. When they came, barehanded, to prevent the artillery from being used, when they lay on the road to prevent the advance of an armoured column, when they came by hundreds and thousands to besiege the residence of a provincial chief or a military post, carrying the corpses of children killed by the enemy in their arms, advancing resolutely in the face of machine-guns levelled at them, most of even the toughest soldiers and policemen shrank back. The participation of women in political struggles had been a decisive factor to ensure success.[17]

THE SUPPORT EFFORT IN THE NORTH

By the mid-1960s, the escalation of the conflict in South Vietnam had brought the war closer to the North. Increasing American participation in the conflict after 1964 compelled Hanoi to postpone its own domestic goals and to put its own society increasingly on a war footing in order to increase the level of its own assistance to the insurgency in the South. By the winter of 1964 the first regular units of the Vietnamese People's Army were being sent into South Vietnam to beef up Communist strength and provide replacements to compensate for the heavy casualties suffered by local Viet Cong forces.

With the mobilization of the population in North Vietnam for the war effort—the slogan of the moment was "all for the southern front"—the role of women took on increased significance. Since the establishment of the Communist power in the North in 1954, women had been targeted for an active role in the new society. In peace as in war, the Communist leadership viewed all Vietnamese as equal participants in the common endeavor, each performing the task for which he was best suited. To be sure, the regime saw itself as sincere in its commitment to achieve true equality for the female sex. The new constitution adopted in 1960 promised total equality in all fields for every Vietnamese, regardless of sex. A 1959 marriage law abolished a number of traditional practices, such as child marriage, concubining, and polygamy, and guaranteed the right of wives to own property.[18]

In education, too, opportunities for women were vastly expanded, as the government moved quickly to implement its goal of universal elementary education. As their technical capacities increased, women were increasingly recruited for professional vocations, in medicine, education, and industry. Women began to move into managerial positions and, significantly, more were being elected to people's councils at all levels of government administration. Where only 3 percent of elected officials at the local level were women in 1954, they represented almost a majority ten years later.[19]

The intensification of the war effort accelerated this process. In March 1965, as the United States began intensified bombing of the North, the government responded by calling for a total mobilization effort. Women were called upon to carry out the so-called three responsibilities: to replace men in various branches of activity in order to increase production, to manage the household, and to defend the fatherland, engaging in combat if necessary.[20] As in the South, the Communist leadership called on women to participate actively in the war effort, while at the same time drawing a distinction between the roles to be performed by the two sexes. Emphasis for women was placed on the support effort, rather than on combat itself. While some women, mostly young and single, were recruited for the PAVN, they were not as a rule placed in combat units, but in special units such as the medical corps, liaison work, or bomb defusing teams. It was general policy to discourage active combat for women.

This does not mean that women were restricted totally to civilian activities. To the contrary, women were increasingly called upon to assume the burden of local civil defense activities. With most able-bodied young men subject to conscription, women were recruited to serve on antiaircraft teams, placed in bomb defusing units, and assigned to units directed to search out and capture downed American flyers.[21] And, of course, they made up a high percentage of members of the village self-defense militia. As the village males were called away to war, often up to 30 percent of the local militia units would consist of women. It was one of the more familiar sights for visiting foreigners traveling in rural areas to see women working in the field with rifles slung over their shoulders.

The mobilization of women to serve in paramilitary tasks reached truly impressive proportions, as reports of visitors and a perusal of the North Vietnamese press attests. Female units were praised and honored in the media for shooting down American planes or capturing and bringing in American prisoners. Emulation campaigns appealed to all women to follow the heroic examples of southern guerrillas in performing sacrifices for the fatherland. By all reports, such campaigns had an impressive degree of success. *New York Times* reporter Harrison Salisbury, visiting North Vietnam in the winter of 1966–1967, recalled seeing diminutive waitresses rushing to the roof of their Hanoi hotel with rifles at the ready in response to the sound of air raid sirens.[22]

Beyond such military and paramilitary activities, of course, lay the production effort, for which women were called upon to take up the slack left by the departure of most male workers for the front.[23] As the demands of the war increased the strain on industrial production, more and more women were hired for industrial jobs, particularly in light industry. They began to move increasingly into specialized positions. According to government figures published in 1971, women were responsible for 38 percent of all industrial production as compared with 34 percent ten years earlier. They comprised 26 percent of all technical workers, 20 percent of all doctors, and 65 percent of assistant pharmacists. The change was reflected in education. By the late 1960s 28 percent of all women in the North possessed a high school degree, and 12 percent were college graduates. Thirty percent of all college students were women.[24]

Similar developments were taking place in the countryside. In collective farms women began moving into areas of administrative responsibility and to perform agricultural tasks previously reserved to men. By the regime's own figures, by the late 1960s they were responsible for over 70 percent of all agricultural production. Their role in local administration was also on the rise. By 1970 more than three-quarters of all members of village-level people's councils were women, and there were sixty-six women representatives in the unicameral National Assembly as compared with only ten in 1946.[25]

ESCALATION IN THE SOUTH

After 1963 military escalation took place on both sides, and "people's war" was gradually replaced by conventional large-scale warfare. As regular units of the PAVN played a larger role in the fighting, the techniques of guerrilla war and political struggle were temporarily ignored. By 1967, however, it had become clear that a direct confrontation with American forces was both costly and fruitless. In the fall, party leaders attempted to devise a new plan that would combine the disintegrating effects of a military offensive with the force of people's war in rural and urban areas. In the Tet offensive, launched in early 1968, the PLAF would once again plan a major role in attacks on cities, towns, and villages throughout South Vietnam. The PLAF had been weakened by high casualties, however, and recruitment in the South was at an ebb. Perhaps that helps to explain Communist directive to local Communist commanders to increase female participation in guerrilla units to 50 percent in the lowlands and to 12 percent in minority areas.[26] More stress would be placed on the recruitment of women to replace men in noncombatant positions in the PLAF so that males could be released for combat. At the local level, each village under NLF control was instructed to establish a permanent platoon of female civilian laborers to provide for food supply, care of the wounded, and liaison activities. Women were sent in propaganda teams into government areas to circulate in urban markets in order to spread rumors and sow distrust and resentment of the Saigon government.

The famous Tet offensive took place in early 1968 with uprisings and attacks on all major cities in South Vietnam. Nearly seventy thousand military and paramilitary forces took part on the Communist side, including units that had long operated covertly in government areas. There is evidence of considerable female participation in many of the attacks. The most famous was the case of an all-girl guerrilla squad that for several days held off advancing American troops as they fought to restore Saigon's control of the city. Eleven girls were in the unit, the oldest only nineteen years old. According to one Communist memoir of dubious veracity, the girls' squad killed 120 American GIs.[27]

The Tet offensive was a temporary aberration, not a sign of de-escalation of the influence of conventional war in the Vietnam conflict. Although Hanoi returned to low-level guerrilla war after the Tet offensive in 1968, party leaders were then convinced that victory would only come through the success of main force units on the battlefield. In the general offensives launched in 1976 (the Easter offensive) and 1975 (the Ho Chi Minh Campaign, which led to the collapse of the Saigon regime, the brunt of the fighting was borne by regular force PAVN units. Even at the final stage of the conflict, when the regular forces entered Saigon and other major urban centers in triumph, guerrilla and paramilitary units played only a subsidiary role in the process. While the people's war had played a vital part in the early stages of the conflict, it had been reduced, in the end, to a myth perpetuated in the minds of historians and party leaders in Hanoi. In the end, the role of women in the Vietnamese revolution was a significant but somewhat restricted one. Women were utilized as a basic force at the lower level, in both civilian and paramilitary positions, but for various reasons, differentiation of roles had not been eliminated in conventional areas. It is probable that the decision to limit female participation in combat activities was based, at least in part, on perceived differences in physique, or temperament. On the other hand, evidence from various sources suggests that difficulties caused by male attitudes in many cases may have played a significant role. If that is the case, the decision to limit female participation in combat was not necessarily based on sexist attitudes among the leadership, but more likely on the pragmatic belief that the people's war could not perform effectively if male-female tensions appeared at lower levels within the movement.

CONCLUSIONS

In few societies have women played so prominent a part in national affairs as in modern Vietnam. Active participants in the war efforts, Vietnamese women were equally active on the domestic front, and a major factor in the effort to build a modern, technologically advanced Socialist society in Vietnam. How accurate is the image? Have women achieved true equality in what was until recently a male-dominated society? They are active in many professions previously reserved to men. Their educational opportunities, in the early 1980s, approximate those of their male compatriots. In factories, offices, collective farms, and schools, they occupy positions of authority to a degree unthinkable a generation ago. Certainly, women have made great strides in recent years. They are increasingly active in government, particularly at the lower levels and are beginning to appear at the vice-ministerial level as well, and in the National Assembly.[28]

But if the sincerity of Hanoi's commitment to the expansion of women's rights seems unquestionable, there is still room for improvement, as the regime concedes. Perhaps in no area of Vietnamese society is the absence of women more obvious than at the top levels of government, and in the party leadership. Although the percentage of women in local elective bodies and even in the National Assembly, is markedly on the rise, they are conspicuous by their absence at the leadership level. With the exception of Nguyen Thi Binh, who was foreign minister of the Provisional Republican Government in the South, there have been no women in prominent positions in either the government or the party since the formation of the Democratic Republic of Vietnam in 1945. The gap is most obvious in the party—the real focus of power in Vietnam. During the course of the war, there were only three women members (one an alternate) in the seventy-four-man Central Committee.[29] There were no women in the party's ruling group, the Politboro, which for a generation has been a male preserve. Only at the recent Fourth Party Congress, held in December 1976, did the party expand its female membership on the Central Committee to five. While some might cite such figures as proof of male chauvinism, the problem is most likely less a product of sexist attitudes than of the extreme stability and longevity of the party leadership. There was little upward or downward mobility to drive the war generation, as Hanoi placed a high priority on party unity and continuity. As a result, the average age of members in the Central Committee in 1973 was in the midsixties. There was some sign of movement during the recent party congress, with both the Politboro and the Central Committee expanding their membership considerably. And, as the revolutionary "first generation" begins to pass from the scene, presumably more new faces—some of them women—will make their appearance.[30]

Based on its own stated goals, then, the Communist regime in Vietnam has reason to be proud of its achievements in the area of women's rights. While not all of the past disabilities suffered by women in Vietnam have been eliminated, considerable progress has been made in a number of areas. If reports in the Hanoi press are indicative, perhaps the major legacy of the past can be found in the lingering prejudice that still frequently exists in the minds of male Vietnamese. Old attitudes often die hard, even in revolutionary societies, and Vietnamese women still encounter discrimination and condescension, primarily in isolated villages but occasionally in administration and in the party itself.

A final point should be kept in mind. The liberation of women in the Democratic Republic of Vietnam has taken place within the framework of a highly organized society in which the rights of the individual are rigidly subordinated to the needs (as interpreted by the Communist party leadership) of society as a whole. Women in Vietnam, like all other social groups in the community, are viewed primarily in terms of their potential contribution to achieving the goals established by the state. Although Vietnamese women have been able to overcome many of the legal and cultural disabilities that hindered them in the past, neither they nor their male counterparts have the freedom to pursue their own personal goals and express their individual views and preferences as do citizens of more open societies.

NOTES

1. For a brief discussion of the roots of Vietnamese revolutionary strategy, see my "Vietnamese Revolutionary Doctrine in Comparative Perspective," in William S. Turley, ed., *Vietnamese Communism in Comparative Perspective* (Boulder, Colo.: Westview, 1980).

2. Vietnamese leaders have relied heavily on that tradition to provide a model for behavior in the modern day. For an example, see Vo Nguyen Giap, "Arm the Revolutionary Masses and Build the People's Army," *Vietnam Documents and Research Notes* (hereafter cited as VDRN) Document 106, Part I, p. 50.

3. Address by Mme. Ngo Dinh Nhu, October 29, 1956, printed in *The Times of Vietnam*, March 9, 1957, and cited in Joseph Buttinger, *The Smaller Dragon: A Political History of Vietnam* (New York: Praeger, 1958), p. 125.

4. The statue did not long survive the fall of the regime. Soon after the overthrow of Diem, mobs in Saigon ripped down the monument.

5. Richard J. Coughlin, *The Position of Women in Vietnam* (New Haven: Yale University Southeast Asia Studies, 1950), p. 2. Also see Buttinger, *The Smaller Dragon,* p. 185.

6. Coughlin, *Position of Women,* p. 2.

7. Ibid., pp. 8–9.

8. Vinh, aggressively modern in thought, did not hesitate to criticize Vietnamese women for their own shortcomings—such as superstition, proclivity for gossip, fickleness and lust, and their habit of chewing betel nuts.

9. Chuong Thau, "Nguon goc chu nghia yeu nuoc cau Phan Boi Chau" (The roots of the patriotism of Phan Boi Chau), in *Nghien Cuu Lich Su* (Historical Research), no. 88 (July 1967), pp. 29–34 (hereafter cited as NCLS). For Chau's program see Phan Boi Chau, *Tan Vietnam* (New Vietnam), in NCLS, no. 78 (September 1965).

10. Ho Chi Minh, "Vietnamese Women and French Domination," in Ho Chi Minh, *On Revolution: Selected Writings, 1920–1966* (New York: Praeger, 1967), pp. 13–15.

11. According to French intelligence sources, at least one thousand women were in the movement in the late 1930s. See Archives Nationales de France, Section Outre-mer, Service de Liaison avec les originaires des territoires de la France d'outrmer (SLOTFOM), Note Periodique, 55, August–September 1937. A Brief Biography of Nguyen Thi Minh Khai is located in Dao Duy Ky, *Nhung Nguoi Cong San Viet Nam* (Some Vietnamese Communists) 1 (Hanoi: 1957).

12. Bernard Fall, *Street Without Joy* (Harrisburg, Pa.: Stockpole Press, 1961), p. 141.

13. Nguyen Thi Dinh, *No Other Road to Take* (Khong Con Duong Khac Nao) (Ithaca, N.Y.: Cornell University SEA Data Gapaer No. 102 June 1976), pp. 2–3.

14. Arlene Eisen Bergman, *Women of Vietnam* (San Francisco: People's Press, 1974) p. 171.

15. W. P. Davison, "Some Observations of Viet Cong Operations in the Villages," Rand Report RM 5267/2-ISA/ARPA (May 1968), pp. 82–83.

16. Douglas Pike, *The Viet Cong* (Cambridge, Mass.: MIT Press, 1966), p. 178.

17. *The Failure of Special War 1961-65,* Vietnamese Studies, no. 11 (1967) p. 55.

18. William S. Turley, "Women in the Communist Revolution in Vietnam," *Asian Survey* (September 1972) pp. 788–89, citing *Nhan Dan,* December 29, 1959.

19. Bergman, *Women of Vietnam* (in English), nos. 3–4 (1970).

20. Wilfred Burchett, *Vietnam North* (New York: International Publishers, 1966), p. 91.

21. It is worth pointing out, however, that role differentiation often occurred even in such paramilitary units. Hanoi press reports note that female members of artillery teams were often assigned to carry ammunition, wipe the guns, and supply refreshments for the male members.

22. Harrison Salisbury, *Hanoi: Behind Enemy Lines* (New York: Harper and Row, 1967), p. 124.

23. By the mid-1960s at least half of all draftable males in North Vietnam were being called up for active service.

24. Bergman, *Women of Vietnam,* nos. 3–4 (1970).

25. Ibid. At the top level of government, there were five women vice-ministers.

26. "Women in the Winter-Spring Campaign," VDRN, no. 24 (April 1968), has a discussion of women's role in the Tet campaign.

27. "Eleven girls of Hue defeated one American battalion," in *Scenes of the General Offensive and Uprising* (Hanoi, FLPH, 1968), pp. 21–26. The memoirs made no mention of Communist casualties.

28. In 1973 125 of 420 members of the National Assembly were women. "Bases of Power in the DRV," VDRN, no. 107, p. 17.

29. For an analysis of the composition of the Central Committee, see "VWP/DRV Leadership 1960 to 1973, "Part I: the Party," VDRN, no. 114, pp. 1–10.

30. According to Douglas Pike the percentage of women in the party has risen in recent years from 10 percent to 20 percent. See his *History of Vietnamese Communism* (Stanford, Calif.: Hoover Institution Press, 1978), p. 97.

6 | ALGERIA: ANTICOLONIAL WAR

Djamila Amrane
Translated by Richard Stites

INTRODUCTION

Algeria was one of the last colonies on the continent of Africa to gain its independence; this occurred in 1962 at the conclusion of one of the longest wars of decolonization. The tenacity of France in maintaining its colonial hegemony over Algeria is explained by the wealth of Algeria—particularly its oil deposits and the natural gas of the Sahara—and by the fact that Algeria was a settled colony.

Two peoples of diametrically opposite economic status and way of life lived side by side: a European people of foreign origin implanted by force and a native Muslim people. The Europeans, comprising in 1954 some 984,000 people[1]—a bit more than one-ninth of the total—disposed of most of the country's riches: 66 percent of agricultural production, 75 percent of industrial production, and almost all administrative and technical jobs (93 percent of the higher officials were French). The native Algerians, about 8,450,000, formed 90 percent of the total population. They lived largely by traditional subsistence agriculture, on the foothills and highlands, despoiled of the fertile lowlands by the European settlers. This resettlement resulted in disequilibrium of the traditional economy and impoverishment that was further aggravated by a sharp demographic rise of 28.5 percent.[2] In 1954 the average income for the peasant was twenty-two thousand old francs a year per person. At the same time the number of unemployed and underemployed was estimated at about 1 million people, almost half of all males of working age. Illiteracy affected 90 percent, nearly the entire native population. Education was very weakly developed; only 14 percent of the children of school age were in primary school, and university education was enjoyed by only 589 students in 1954.

The contrast between the two communities—one affluent and educated, the other indigent and mostly illiterate—was also reflected in the political

123

life of the country. Algeria, defined as three *départements* of the French Republic and thus denied any status of nationhood, was given relative financial autonomy which was assured by an Algerian assembly. The electoral rules of this assembly are a good example of the inequality between the two peoples of Algeria. The electors were differentiated according to their ethnic origin. The assembly comprised 60 delegates chosen by the First Curia made up of French men and women and a small assimilated native elite of 58,000 (of a total of 500,000 electors) and 60 chosen by the Second Curia who represented all the Algerians designated by the colonial administration as "French Muslims," that is, 1,300,000 electors (excluding Algerian women who did not have the right to vote).

Opposition to French colonization had existed from the beginning. From the 1830s[3] the resistance movement, led by Emir Abd el-Kader,[4] took the form of sporadic armed insurrections. In 1926 the North African Star, the first nationalist party, was formed. Under the leadership of Messali Hadj[5] the party struggled for independence and for social reforms. Outlawed by the authorities, the North African Star transformed itself in 1937 into the Algerian People's party. Some attempts to improve the status of Algerians legally were made by nationalist movements, but these efforts encountered the systematic opposition of the European minority. In 1945, at the end of World War II, in which many Algerians had died fighting for France, there arose a mighty surge of hope for a peacefully negotiated liberation of Algeria from France. But the peaceful demonstrations calling for independence were harshly repressed in Algiers on May Day of that year and especially in Setif and in Guelma on May 8, the day of the armistice ending World War II.[6] The events of May 8 made the war of 1954 inevitable.

The National Liberation War of the Algerian people against French colonialism was one of the cruelest and longest of the anticolonial wars. From November 1954 to July 1962—for seven and a half years—successive governments of France tried in vain to crush by military force the national liberation movement. In the face of the armed might of France (120,000 troops in 1954 and 400,000 by 1956, equipped with modern weapons and supported by air power), the Algerian people responded with guerrilla warfare, urban terrorism, and a political campaign waged on an international scale. The mobilization of a large segment of the population, particularly women, was a determining element in the victory.

And yet, there was nothing about the status of Algerian women that could have allowed one to foresee the role they would play during this war. In 1954 women were practically nonexistent outside the home; only 2 percent of them were employed. Access to education, limited as it was for the entire Algerian population, was even more exceptional for women of whom there were hardly fifty in the university. Their right to vote was not recognized by the colonial authorities. The political parties did not have a single responsible woman in their ranks; and the militants (the local

name for the guerrilla or partisan fighters for independence) were still very
few in number.

Almost all Algerian women lived in a wholly traditional manner. In the
cities they rarely went outside their homes and almost always were veiled.
The veil was less often encountered in rural areas where women took part
in agricultural work. But everywhere they remained outside public life and
dwelled in an essentially feminine world, without ever being in the company of men other than those in their family. But during the war of national
liberation, women overturned the traditional social structures, fought at
the side of men, and rendered invaluable assistance and support to them.

SOME GENERAL DATA

It is still difficult, given the present level of research, to present a
definitive accounting of the number of female militants and their activities.
This paper will attempt a statistical approach by means of the file-card
records of combat veterans as well as an approach—less scientific but
more evocative—based on extracts from tape-recorded eyewitness testimony. The inquiry, conducted in 1978–1979 at the Ministry of Combat
Veterans, enabled a review of 10,949 index record cards of women militants. The initial results of the counting and analysis of these cards indicate
certain aspects of the militant struggle, and these form the body of the
paper.

Urban and Rural Militants

Examination of militants according to the urban-rural sector shows a
definite predominance of the rural. For 8,796 female militants in Algeria,[7]
whose base of activity is known with precision, we have the following
data:

SECTOR	SIZE OF RURAL OR URBAN UNIT	NUMBER OF WOMEN MILITANTS	PERCENTAGE
Rural	<3,000	6,856	77.9
Urban	3,001– 5,000	172	20.1
	5,001–10,000	314	(total urban)
	10,001–20,000	322	
	20,001–40,000	176	
	40,001–80,000	283	
	80,001 and over	673	
	Subtotal	8,796	100
Place of activity unknown		1,678	
Active outside Algeria		475	
	Total	10,946	

About 78 percent of the militants were active in the countryside. Some of these fought in the *maquis* (a French term from the underground resistance designating rural or mountainous regions); the others gave logistical support to the Algerian *maquis* men. About 20 percent were active in the towns. These data ought not to be interpreted to mean that rural people were more active than urban ones. They correspond exactly to the relative ratio of the population as a whole in rural and urban areas.

In 1954 the population of native Algerians living in Algeria (many worked in France and elsewhere) was 7,643,000 of whom 1,397,000 lived in villages or towns of more than 3,000 inhabitants, making the demographic weight of urbanization about 18.4 percent.[8] Estimates are that by 1959 the demographic weight of urbanization had grown to about 22.6 percent. The percentage of urban militants for both years was about 20 percent.

Age Range

It is common to associate youth, a period of total and selfless dedication, with militant activity. Women of all ages were involved militantly in the Algerian movement. The following table, based on the age of militants at the time they began active work in the movement, shows this complicated picture:

AGE	INCLUSIVE PERCENTAGE	CIVILIAN	MILITARY
14–16	7.4	5.1	19.3
17–19	12.5	8.9	31.8
20–29	28.2	27.1	33.7
30–49	41.8	47.3	13.1
50 and over	10.1	11.6	2.1
Total	100.0	100.0	100.0

All ages between fourteen and seventy are represented, with a majority between seventeen and fifty. The distinction between military and civilian shows a rather different division. If among civilian female militants the percentage of those under twenty years of age remains high (15 percent), the majority (about 74 percent) were between twenty and fifty. These were adults and mostly married women. In 1954, in spite of a slump in the number of traditional marriages, 68.3 percent of young women were married by age twenty and 89.2 by age twenty-five. In 1966 the percentages were: 8.5 by age twenty and 94.2 by twenty-five. One can conclude then that among the militants all of the women twenty-five or over and most of those twenty or over were married and had families.

By contrast the female militants in the military were younger. Almost

84 percent of them were under thirty and 51 percent under twenty. It is clear that family status is a factor that cannot be neglected. The unmarried girls could more easily break out of the family and join the *maquis* than could married ones. The fear of violation by French troops could also, in some cases, have augmented the flight of the younger ones to the *maquis* with the permission of their families.

The correlation in age between the total female population and the militant female population indicates a correspondence that demonstrates the participation of all age groups.

AGE	PERCENTAGE OF EACH AGE GROUP FOR THE TOTAL FEMALE POPULATION	PERCENTAGE OF EACH AGE GROUP FOR THE TOTAL FEMALE MILITANTS
14–20	24.3	19.9
21–30	27.6	28.2
31–50	32.3	41.7
51 and over	15.8	10.2
Total	100.0	100.0

In the extreme age brackets where it is normal to find fewer female militants, the very young (below twenty-three) and the old (fifty and over), are 41.1 percent of the overall female population but only 30.1 percent of the militant female population. The age group twenty-one to thirty corresponds closely: 27.6 percent of the female population and 28.2 percent of the female militants. But, by contrast, in the thirty-one to fifty-year-old group—the years in which all women were married and mothers—the percentage of militants (41.7 percent) is distinctly higher than the percentage for the total female population (33.3 percent) and proportionally there are the most militants. If one looks only at the civilian militants, the age group thirty-one to fifty accounts for 47.3 percent, or almost half, the female militants. This is exactly the age group where the participation of a woman, the mother of still young children, implies the maximum of devotion and sacrifice to the cause. Further it shows that women in full maturity chose political engagement only in a deliberate and reflective way. Enthusiasm and youthful exaltation cannot be invoked to explain their participation.

Women and Repression

Repression fell heavily on women. It is impossible to evaluate the violence endured by them during the scouring operations in the countryside and in the towns. Many women were beaten, raped, and even tortured inside their own homes with portable electric torture equipment. We can speak, however, of the number arrested and killed. Of the 10,949 women counted, 1,343 were imprisoned and 949 were killed. One of every five female militants suffered detention or death.

AGE	PERCENTAGE OF ALL MILITANTS	PERCENTAGE ARRESTED	PERCENTAGE KILLED
14–24	35.5	36.30	54.5
25–49	54.5	54.75	38.8
50 and over	10.0	8.95	6.7
Total	100.0	100.00	100.0

This categorization by age of victim of repression shows dramatically the sacrifices made by the younger women: 54.5 percent of those killed— more than half—were younger than twenty-five, even though this age group represents only 35.5 percent of all female militants. The young accepted more readily the need to give their lives for an ideal and thus exposed themselves to danger more than older women did. By contrast the age groups of those arrested correspond closely to those of the militants in general. Repression of this sort hit without regard for youth (some of those detained were fifteen years old) or for age (the two most prominent of the arrestees were more than seventy).

ROLE AND FUNCTION

Most of the index records of militant activity during the war against the French do not provide precise information on the type of activity engaged in, although the distinction is always made between civilian and military affiliation. Of the 10,949 cards reviewed, 3,271, almost a third (of whom 3,066 were civilian and 205 were military) give precise indications of mode of activity as the table on page 129 indicates.

The Civilian Sector

The militants of the civilian sector of the struggle were recognized members of the Civilian Organization of the National Liberation Front (the French initials OCFLN) and defined by a later decree as those who were ''structurally attached to the organization as responsible members of the Political-Administrative Committees, as Fidayine,[9] as collectors of money, liaison agents, and as those in charge of housing and sanitation. . . . Excluded from this category were sympathizers and

| FUNCTIONS | CIVILIAN | | MILITARY | | |
	NUMBER	PERCENT	NUMBER	PERCENTAGE	TOTAL
Providing refuge & food	1,958	63.9	6	2.9	1,964
Liaison & guide	677	22.1			677
Collectors of money, medicine, arms	286	9.3			286
Nurses	56	1.8	101	49.3	157
Cooks & laundresses			91	44.4	91
Terrorists	65	2.1			65
Seamstresses	19	0.6	1	0.5	20
Secretaries	5	0.2	3	1.4	8
Political commissars			2	1	2
Armed fighters			1	0.5	
Total	3,066	100.0	205	100.0	3,271

donors of money or goods and those who participated only occasionally."[10] Thus the women members of the OCFLN were responsible militants, fully engaged, as opposed to the mass of sympathizers whose aid had been nevertheless of decisive importance.

Those responsible, as their main activity, for housing, shelter, and feeding comprised the majority of the women militants, about 64 percent. A woman responsible for sheltering combatants usually worked with a group of other women, either family members or neighbors, who assisted her. Only she, however, who was designated *responsable* properly belonged to the resistance movement. There were, then, many more women than the figures indicate who carried out this humble but indispensable task of assuring safe shelter and nourishment to the combatants. It was they who housed and fed the militants pursued by the police in the towns and the *maquis* fighters in the countryside. They repeated day in and day out their daily tasks: cooking, laundering, cleaning. Theirs was a monotonous and thankless task, bereft of military glory or heroism, and yet demanding exposure to danger. During the scouring operations by the French these women were maltreated by the soldiers, sometimes even tortured and imprisoned. All witnesses—as, for example, M. Z. and B. O., both *maquis* nurses—have indicated the courage and sacrifice of these women militants. One of them, M. Z., a schoolgirl sought by the police, at age fourteen went to be a nurse in the *maquis,* recalled their work.

Women possessed political maturity and were more politicized than those of the towns. I don't know whether this is because they were surrounded by danger, but in any case, they accepted everything. Once, after a skirmish, the French mounted a particularly monstrous scouring operation. In the evening when I returned to the village I found all the houses burned. How, I asked the women of the village, are you going to go on without homes, without anything. One of them replied, "Our huts have been burned and destroyed; it's all right; tomorrow we'll put up new ones." The main thing is independence. When there had been a raid, the women always found a way through and brought us something to eat: bread sometimes with honey or whey—or maybe just bread—but they always came. . . . When a skirmish was over they helped gather up the wounded and to bury the dead.

Another woman, B. O., a nursing student who joined the *maquis* at age twenty, recalled:

At Kabylie the women were very brave; they feared nothing. When a scouring raid was announced they got us out of the area saying "Allah be with you—leave at once"; then they cleaned up, hid the gauze and washed away the spots of mercurochrome. They scattered pepper around to prevent the police dogs from sniffing out traces. . . . Sometimes we remained in the villages, dressed in civilian garb. The French soldiers took away the men, destroyed everything, mistreated the women and sometimes even the children. But no one ever uttered a word.

Liaison and guide work, usually combined, constituted the second most important function of women militants. Less suspect than men, women were effective and well suited to this role. The experience of A. K., a forty-three-year-old peasant woman without occupation, married and with two children, illustrates this very well.

I carried out liaison work for the *maquis* from one village to another. I carried their messages, sometimes twenty or thirty kilometers, traveling on foot and returning the next day. I also did some shopping for them: cigarettes, socks, food. . . . I carried it all on my head. In my courtyard there was a hiding place near the stove. One day there was a raid; they hung me from a tree and beat me. There were two *maquis* fighters and a nurse in the hiding place. I said nothing.

Many young Algerian women were European in appearance, but the habit of thinking like racists did not allow the French to believe that they could ever fail to distinguish between a native Algerian and a European. This allowed certain young women to pass totally unnoticed, and they played an important role in establishing communications within the movement. Thus Z. B., a twenty-two-year-old student, made possible the centralization of communications for the commanders of one *wilaya* ("military district"):

I was in direct contact with the military leader of the *wilaya*. I had very precise duties. Because I lived underground in the town where I was not known I served above all as liaison. Because of my appearance I was able to move among the Europeans without being disturbed. I thus became the link between the liaison agents and the commanders of the *wilaya*. I also worked as a secretary. For several months, I lived completely isolated in an apartment which served as a mail drop and lived completely alone.

Female intelligence agents were rather rare. In the countryside women, like the rest of the population, including children, apprised the *maquis* people of the movement of the enemy and acted as lookouts. The term *intelligence* appears in the records of some of the militants who were liaison agents, but without much elaboration. To my knowledge the only examples of intelligence work were the cases of militant women whom the French army asked to betray the movement and who pretended to agree in order to act as double agents. Thus Z. Z., an unemployed twenty-four-year-old mother of five served by chance as an intelligence agent. While serving the movement by providing lodgings for the urban terrorists, she was arrested and released on the condition that she would inform for the French. She served as a double agent for a few months before being arrested again.

They let me go but made me promise to provide them with all the information I could get on the combatants. With the agreement of my chief, I pretended to work for them. I began to go regularly to the barracks and got information about our own people who had been arrested and, most important, could see and identify the informers. This was important because they were not known to us. I requested and obtained a document saying that I was working for the French army and this put my house, even though it was a safe house for our people, under French protection. Unfortunately, we were arrested again a short time later.

Suppliers of medicine, money, and occasionally munitions worked above all with the *maquis*. They conveyed these items from the towns into the countryside for the *maquis*. The women collectors worked among larger groups of women, but only the deliverer was registered as a member of OCFLN and recognized as a militant. Thus for each collector, there was a larger group of assistants, mostly women. The testimony of K. K., aged twenty-four, married, mother of two children, and employed in a hospital, illustrates this:

I worked in a military hospital in Algiers and was in contact with the *maquis* of the Oued Fodda region (a small town two hundred kilometers from the capital) to whom I brought medical supplies. Most of this was antibiotics; I would open packets of sugar, put the medicine in them, and then cover it with sugar and close the packets. I also managed to steal live rounds of ammunition which I hid the same way inside bread dough. Then I would take the train to Oued Fodda with my basket filled with sugar, dough, vegetables, and so on . . . as if going for a visit.

At the station in Oued Fodda a militant woman would meet me and we would then make the journey of twenty to thirty kilometers on donkey to the *maquis* camp. I even stole military uniforms that I took to the *maquis*. Young Algerians drafted into the French army would bring me their weapons. Women also helped me. One of them worked in a cafe frequented by French military men. Soldiers came several times to search me but never found anything. I hid the bullets and the medicinal items in socks and hung them outside with the wash, so that there was nothing to be found in the house. The neighbors suspected something, but they never said a thing.

Although relatively few in the movement (only 2 percent), female terrorists played the most spectacular role. Public attention was riveted on them, especially at the time of the trials. Six of them were condemned to death but were pardoned. Terrorism is an urban phenomenon. Young girls and women had the important advantage of not arousing suspicion, and they were often indispensable. They participated directly in the armed struggle in the town either in transporting arms—sometimes right up to the spot from where the assassinations were launched—or in carrying out assassinations themselves.

The Military Sector

The militants of both sexes of the ALN (French initials for the Army of National Liberation) were clearly fewer than those in the civilian sector, only 38.9 percent of those in the records. The percentage of women was even smaller, 19 percent of women militants being enrolled in the army. How were they defined?

In order to be recognized as a member of the ALN, one must have: (1) joined it before January, 1962; (2) been registered in the ALN as a *djoundi*[11] in one of the units, as a leader in one of the political and military staffs (*wilaya*, zone, sector, subsector), as a fighter in uniform in one of the auxiliary services (guards, nursing, information, administration, ordnance, communications, engineers, or religious affairs), (3) never deserted from the ranks of the ALN.[12]

The reference here is to regular soldiers, women who abandoned home and hearth and family in order to join the *maquis*. We have seen that most of them were very young: 51 percent under age twenty and 85 percent under thirty. Their exact functions in the army were rarely indicated in the records. We have only been able to process 205 cases, about 11.7 percent of women militants in the army. But this modest sample illustrates very well the limited activity of women of the *maquis*. Two functions, both traditionally associated with women, occupied them; nursing and cooking, representing together about 94 percent of the cases reviewed.

The nurses were most often young people from the towns, high school girls or students who, after a short stint at nursing, moved into the *maquis* to work in health and sanitary operations; nurses and nursing students whom the FLN tried to recruit systematically due to the vital need of the *maquis* for medical assistance; or female militants wanted by the police in the towns who were obliged to flee into the *maquis*. (This latter group was always integrated into the nursing service.) Although not numerically impressive, nurses played a very important role both as medical assistants and, by the very fact of their engagement, as exalted and moving examples for the *maquis* and the civilian population alike. In the early years of the war, the *maquis,* whose medical service was very weak, had appealed to nurses to come and care for the wounded. In the course of the struggle the nurses expanded their mission and used their skills for the care and cure of the civilian population, especially women and children. B. O., a nurse who joined the *maquis* at age twenty, talks of life there:

By day we lived among the people, looked after the women and children and advised them in matters of child care, breastfeeding, and hygiene. At night we went to the *maquis* especially when movements of the French forces had been made known to us. We sometimes walked ten hours to find this mountain or this hiding place. We never stayed more than twenty-four hours in one village. . . . I also took care of wounded *maquis* men. I recall one burn victim whom I had nursed for some time: the enemy had passed through a settlement in the Kabylie region, destroyed everything, doused it with petrol and set fire to it. This militant had enormous blister burns; his entire body was covered with third degree burns and he died. I believe he died of dehydration. . . . Once in the region of M'Sila-Barika we found ourselves in a stretch of flat land without any trees or villages, with no place to hide. We marched at night and in the daytime hid ourselves in *kasmates,* big holes in the ground about a meter in circumference, sometimes less. We had to slide down and at the bottom was a sort of dugout shelter. We could not stand; we had to sit, huddled together. It was very hot, but we could not move until nightfall. When night fell, someone from outside came and lifted the earthen and brushwood cover from our hole and let us out. We did some exercise in order to loosen up and then marched all night to the next hole.

The extremely harsh conditions of life in the *maquis,* especially after 1957–1958 with the extension of forbidden zones,[13] forced the military leaders of the movement to evacuate the nurses to Morocco or Tunisia.

The cooks and laundresses of the army were women of rural origin, who had been integrated into the life of the *maquis* but who, like the nurses, had kept to functions considered feminine. Political commissars and armed combatants among women were exceptional. The *maquis* had been forced to appeal to nurses for help. But they never lacked fighting men, only weapons for these fighting men. This explains why women, physically and psychologically of low aptitude for the life of combat, were not used as soldiers. The image of the armed female combatant was not the reality but a myth based no doubt upon a few exceptional individual cases that struck the popular imagination. Female militants who bore arms (as transporters of weapons, assassins, or fighters) represented no more than 2 percent of the 3,271 cases studied.

The work summarized in these pages and based upon 10,949 cases cannot be considered exhaustive. But if the card index of the Ministry of Combat Veterans does not offer a complete listing of the female militants, the number available is high enough to allow us to affirm that it is a representative sample. A more refined computation, which remains to be done, and the further use of questionnaires will allow more precise data in the future.

CONCLUSION

The war of liberation revealed not only that women were capable of assuming responsibilities and of struggling just like men, but also that the men recognized the place of women at their side. One would have thought that with independence the status of women would have undergone a sudden transformation. In fact, the new laws did not lay down barriers to reform. The constitution provided that "all citizens are equal in law and in obligations. Any discrimination based on sex, race, or occupation is forbidden. . . . Women must participate fully in the building of socialism and in national development." Women were granted access to all occupations. The National People's Army, which could have been the sector least open to women, accepted them into its advanced school of engineering, pilot training, and in hospitals. And yet, twenty years after independence, the participation of women in the economic and political life of the country is still weak and low. Only 3.7 percent of women of working age are employed. If the proportion of working women had remained steady, by contrast their representation in political life has regressed. The first National Constituent Assembly had 10 women of a total of 194 members, or 5.15 percent. In the 1980 National Assembly, this percentage is only 3.95 (10 women of a total of 253 members). In the local legislative bodies, they occupy 3 percent of the seats and 1.4 percent of those in communal assemblies (the lowest local unit).

The most dramatic change has occurred in the realm of education of children, particularly of girls. In 1980, 60 percent of Algerian girls are in school. This figure, lower than that for boys (88 percent) represents enormous progress. The university accepts about fourteen thousand young women out of a total of fifty-five thousand students. And it is really the access of women to education that makes for genuine change in the status of Algerian women. The female militants, fighting alongside the men, were not merely a passing phenomenon, linked to the exceptional fact of a war; their participation in the war of liberation represents a jump in the evolution of the position of women. But the best guarantee of a deeper transformation is the changes in economic and educational opportunities for women.

NOTES

1. The census of 1954.

2. Ibid.

3. French occupation of Algeria began in 1830.

4. Emir Abd el-Kader led the armed resistance struggle against the French from 1830 to 1847.

5. Messali Hadj was a dominant figure in the Algerian nationalist movement from 1926 until the 1950s.

6. The French colonial administration gave the figures of 103 Europeans killed, 1,500 Algerians killed, and 1,476 Algerians condemned in this incident. The figure for Algerians killed is certainly too low. French historian Charles Robert Ageron estimates four to five times as many Algerians killed over the official figures. Algerians estimate 54,000 Algerians killed.

7. Of the 10,949 militants reviewed, 475 were active only outside Algeria (in France, Morocco, and Tunisia).

8. The census of 1954.

9. *Fidayine,* that is, terrorists.

10. Decree No. 66-37 of February 2, 1966, relative to social benefits for combat veterans of the War of National Liberation.

11. *Djoundi,* that is, soldier.

12. See the decree cited in note 10 above.

13. The forbidden zones were areas prohibited by the French authorities to the civilian population. Entire villages were evacuated and their inhabitants relocated into hastily built sites known as regrouped villages. The French army subjected the forbidden zones to frequent bombing raids and mortar shelling.

7 | ISRAEL: THE LONGEST WAR

Anne R. Bloom

INTRODUCTION

Israel's army was established on May 26, 1948, by decree, shortly after the declaration of the independence of the new state. Its roots, however, date back to the first decade of the twentieth century when pioneering and security were closely connected in both concept and practice.

It is the thesis of this paper that women have played a significant role throughout the development of the security forces. The debate about the extent and nature of their participation is not a development of latter-day history: it has always existed in vigorous polemics among the different groups within the *Yishuv* (the Jewish population in pre-Israel Palestine) and has continued uninterrupted since the establishment of the state. More impressive than the changes has been the remarkable consistency, for nearly a century, in the arguments for and against women's integration into the various aspects of defense. Without the guidance of a clear policy their role has evolved, more of process than of planned conception.

At the source of this process is the traditional cultural separation of the two worlds of men and women.[1] Not the same as the ''domains'' that are described in the definition of the universal status-concerns of women,[2] the woman's world is not labeled as secondary to men's by traditional Judaism. Separate, yes, but also intrinsic and equally important in the Jewish family, an entity that supersedes in value the individual whether man or woman:

Research for this paper was supported by a mini-grant from the Inter-University Seminar of Armed Services and Society, and by the Harry Frank Guggenheim Foundation, whose grant supporting the larger project, ''Israeli Women and the Military,'' enabled work on the history to be undertaken.

Thanks are due to Moshe Lissak and Rivka Bar Yosef for their assistance, and to the many present and former members of the Israel Defense Forces, who generously gave their time and shared their experiences.

The complete Jew is an adult with a mate and offspring. No man is complete without a wife; no woman is complete without a husband. For each individual the ideal center of gravity is not in himself, but in the whole of which he is an essential part.[3]

In a very real sense, therefore, at the beginning of the process we describe for women's participation in Israel's military forces, women were, in Jewish life, equal to men. Their equality was one of value, however, not of function.

The matter is complicated further by misconceptions about the boundaries of the separate Jewish male and female worlds. Jewish women, for example, played important economic roles in the *Shtetl* (the small-town Jewish community of Eastern Europe), often serving as the major providers for their families. It remains true, nevertheless, that Jewish men represented the family in the community and in the outside world, and prestige was vested primarily in the male role.

"Women's emancipation" was a defined issue among intellectual and revolutionary circles in nineteenth-century Europe. It was not in early Zionism. For the latter, the problem of Jewish existence was the fundamental and overriding social issue on which all energies were concentrated. Equality of the sexes was more or less taken for granted, while the press of pioneering in a harsh environment supplied a further impetus toward equality among the participants.[4]

Against these cultural values and pioneering realities, the role of women in Israel evolved. As the numbers and types of immigrants grew, so did the complexities of women's participation. The military, a domain that historically, regardless of culture, tends to be a male monopoly, proved to be a critical test of Israel's social attitudes concerning the relative position and appropriate function of the sexes.

The cultural attitudes and individual choice represent only one part of the historical evolution of the military role of women in Israel. At least equally important to the influence of political and religious ideology have been economic, social, and demographic realities.

The important central fact is that women have been part of the Israeli defense system from its origin, and as of 1981 they remain so. As one traces the patterns of development of the Israeli army, it is clear that women as a class have never been treated the same as men in matters of defense (or in any part of the social structure of Israel). Women have, however, penetrated the military sectors in so significant a proportion that security problems and actions have never been in the hands of the male establishment alone. The patterns of development in the role of the woman soldier, the trends and meaning of these patterns, are, in our judgment, the central problem for analysis here.

The method of this paper is primarily descriptive. Starting a century ago, the five migrations that are customarily identified with the modern return of the Jewish people to Israel are briefly defined with particular attention to those ideological factors that were to influence the new state's social and political institutions. Against this general historical background, the analysis shifts to the organization of security, tracing the specific defense institutions from the earliest formally constituted force, Hashomer, to the interim, sometimes secret, organizations of the mandatory period, and finally, the official military organization of the state of Israel, the IDF (Israel Defense Forces). Throughout, the focus is on the patterns of participation of women, up to and including the CHEN (Chail Nashim or Women's Army Corps), the current women's defense organization of Israel. This portrait is the basis for interpretation of the current structure of the Israeli women's defense roles.

MIGRATION TO ERETZ ISRAEL

Developments in Israel's military strategy and strength are inseparable from nonmilitary, political, and social factors in Eretz Israel.[5] Therefore, to understand the role of women in settlement and defense, it is essential to review briefly the patterns of immigration ("Aliyah"), dating from 1880.

Members of the first Aliyah (1882–1903) were part of the Jewish masses on the move. They came to Palestine often as families with strong ties to their heritage, hoping to reproduce their spiritual life as Jews within the physical environment of that heritage. They were capitalist in orientation, settling in villages, often needing assistance from outside funds.

The second Aliyah (1904–1914), also from Russia, was a counterforce to the earlier settlers. Mostly unattached young people, fresh from an atmosphere of revolution, their imagination was fired with possibilities of Socialist change. They came from families who could spare them economically and who could support them at least emotionally. Eretz Israel was an opportunity that combined their youthful ideological enthusiasm with their past, providing them with a reality for their own development. They would not only settle the land, they would also build a new society.

As small a group as they were, they defined the image of the pioneer, the *halutz,* an image that persists, as an individual who could endure and sustain personal self-sacrifice, not needing immediate rewards, for the sake of the community. This ideal remains a value, even though the society has undergone enormous changes.

The third Aliyah, following World War I (1919–1923) reinforced the ideology and concretized it into a way of life solidifying the kibbutz (that is, collective settlement) and *moshav* (collective farm) as forms of agricultural settlement. Many had been trained in pioneering in their country of origin preparing them to join established settlements, to build and guard new ones. They represented a creative force, ready and willing to do any work needed by the country.

During the fourth Aliyah (1924–1931) the influx of Halutzim dropped and the numbers in the middle class rose. This group, people of small means, entered commerce and industry, as well as becoming artisans. Although they shared the pioneering spirit, most of them settled in Tel Aviv or other towns rather than in agricultural settlements.

Members of the fifth Aliyah (1932–1944) were predominantly urban immigrants, many who felt the press of Hitler. They brought with them skills as well as capital, helped to develop industry and trade, and opened factories. They became private farmers as well as enlarging existing agriculture. Many were established professionals, physicians, lawyers, and musicians who infused Western culture into the country.

The Yishuv, which developed its defense and security organizations, fought the War of Independence, and laid the foundations of the state, is composed of these diverse groups. Many who shared the pioneering spirit did not necessarily share methods and goals. Labor was dominant in ideology and politics, but always had two other forces to contend with— a bourgeois, middle-class, urban group as well as religious Zionists who had their own agenda.

THE ORGANIZATION OF DEFENSE: HASHOMER, 1907–1920

The initial defense organization, Hashomer, began in 1909. Consisting at first of only a few dozen people, it was actually the expansion of Bar Giora, a secret organization started in 1907.[6] Records and pictures usually portray ten men of Bar Giora, dressed in Bedouin clothing, as the core group of Hashomer. Indeed, they took as their model the behavior of the warrior Bedouin, translating it into the ideal prototype of a courageous Jewish defender ready to move when needed. At least two women were members of Bar Giora, Manya Shochat and Esther Becker.[7]

In 1909, at a conference in Mescha, Bar Giora became Hashomer, with the purpose of forming a guild of Jewish watchmen. Its constitution contains no mention of methods, tactics, or policy. Rather, it states, "any Jew of sound body and mind who had had six months' experience was eligible for membership; but he must agree to place his duty to Hashomer above all personal concerns and swear to obey orders promptly and without question."[8] Shmira, ("guarding") was viewed as more than a vocation; it was an essential national service.

As Hashomer membership grew and watchmen's jobs increased, the woman's role in guarding was heatedly debated. Many men supported women in their demands for equal participation, while others questioned and even ridiculed the idea.

As in all the activities of the second Aliyah, the women in Hashomer were role innovators. "They had no one after whom to model themselves . . . no way of knowing which way was better and which way worse, what work they should do and what work they should not do."[9] They sought active defense participation and equal responsibility, constantly arguing for their rights, but they were not always successful.

In effect, there were two distinct types of roles for the women associated with the Hashomer. The first is represented by Manya Shochat and Rachel Yanait who, along with some of the others, became full-fledged members. These women were participants at meetings and were trusted with the discussion of the purchase and hiding of arms and with organizational and operational matters. The second group were the "wives" of Hashomer members, clearly delegated to second-class status, not allowed into those meetings.[10] At the annual conferences, debates about training and the use of weapons by female members persisted but, although all the women desired to take an active part, no clearly favorable resolution was reached.

The women of Hashomer infused the concept of role equality into the national psyche, but they also showed the men that they would settle for less than they asked for. They set the precedents for the dichotomy between ideology and behavior, thus creating a confused mythology.

HAGANAH: 1920–1940

The conclusion of World War I ended the Ottoman Empire and the Turks' control of Palestine. The British Mandate offered the Yishuv a short-lived hope for peace. The Balfour declaration articulated the concept of a national homeland for the Jews, but the British did nothing to implement it. Instead the Arab attack became more coordinated and more sophisticated, while the British could not or would not act in time to stop the bloodshed.

The attacks of 1920 on Tel Hai and Kfar Giladi and in 1921 on Jerusalem and Jaffa made clear that Hashomer was inadequate to the new security demands. Political and strategy debates ensued. The prevailing attitude that won out was to include all able-bodied Jews, male and female, to participate in defense, in a new secret organization called Haganah (literally "defense").

The Haganah, responsible for all matters concerning defense, had three objectives: to acquire arms, to provide military training to members of agricultural settlements, and to set up self-defense organizations in towns and cities. Its first major test came in 1929 when a new wave of Arab violence swept the country. As a result, a National Command with membership apportioned along party lines was formed. The National Command was given authority to pay permanent cadres, to purchase arms, and to supervise a professional staff.[11] In addition, the first underground workshops for local manufacturing of arms were begun where hand grenades, bombs, cartridges, and tear gas were manufactured.[12]

WOMEN IN HAGANAH: 1930–1940

Even after Haganah developed a National Command, its authority remained limited and ineffective.[13] Members were not professionals but rather volunteers. Training, which usually took place in the evenings and on weekends, depended on local leadership, and groups acted as local defense forces when needed. Given so loose a structure, women's roles depended largely on the local situation.

Primarily because Haganah was a secret organization and because decisions, plans, and strategy were arrived at in process, there are few precise records of these early years. We are dependent on diaries, depositions of individual members, and interviews particularly to describe the role of women. The reported pattern was as follows: A young woman joined the Haganah at approximately seventeen years of age. She was usually recruited either through membership in a youth movement or by recommendation of two people vouching for her as an individual who was reliable, responsible, and strong enough to handle assignments and keep secrets, and dedicated to the cause.[14] How different her training and assignments were compared to her counterpart in those early years, it is difficult to tell.

She learned discipline and organization and then was taught to handle weapons and to clean and care for them. Most often she was trained in communications and first aid. Women learned and then taught all the techniques of transmitting information, from the personal (and often dangerous) carrying of messages, to training carrier pigeons, signaling, and the use of transmitters, to stringing wires for telephone connections. In first aid as well, they were not only responsible for medical assistance when the need occurred, but for the organization of the medical facilities. During those years they were always few in number. Illustrations of what they did can be gleaned from the autobiographical statements of members from various parts of the country. From Tel Aviv:

I joined the Haganah in High School. My friend entered the first aid group and I was active in communication service. At that time I was taught to use weapons and especially to clean them. Later I was responsible for storing weapons in my place. In 1933 I organized all the production of weapons in Tel Aviv and was responsible for it. In 1936 when there were new disturbances I joined the group at the "front" and organized the first aid.[15] [Shoshana Ron]

In Haifa:

Haganah women were a direct link from the Hashomer woman. I was not given to hero worship, but they were my role models. They nurtured us, my generation, and gave us the assurance that if they could do it, so could we. In 1933, when I finished my studies, I joined the Haganah. We fought against separation and wanted mixed platoons of men and women. There were those who disagreed, and they were sent to prepare sandwiches and do first aid. We wanted to take part in combat and fought for the same training. This training took place in cellars, in the Technion (the Israel Institute of Technology). I was then sent to Juara for officer training, where there were about four women to forty men. Women in the Haganah were devoted, disciplined, and conscientious. It was natural for them to do what they did, not because they were feminists, but because they felt strongly for what was being fought for.[16] [Mina Ben Zvi]

The most difficult test for the Haganah, up to that point in its history, came on April 19, 1936, when, beginning with an Arab general strike, anti-Jewish attacks started in Jaffa and spread throughout the country. For the next three years, these attacks continued, affecting the British as well as the Jews.

In response to this challenge, Yitzhak Sadeh, in the summer of 1936, set up a smaller and unofficial mobile unit with young volunteers from Haganah, called the Nodedet ("Patrol"), designed to attack Arab guerrilla bands based in their own villages rather than fight only in defense. This was a shift from the practice of restraint (havlagah) that Haganah had been committed to.

Shoshana Spector, who later became a member of the General Staff of the Palmach, tells of her experience in the Nodedet. She was the "one girl among Yitzhak Sadeh's boys." They were her friends with whom she had grown up.

We went to the course together (first rank of commander). We were about 34. In this course, practical experience was in the field. We had a village to defend and naturally I went out with them—it was natural that I was in the course—and natural that I went out with them because that was the experience of the course.[17]

During these years, the attacks were virulent, and the danger was everywhere. Meeting the enemy at your own door or going to his was the issue. In either case, fighting took place.

Sarah Kahn was a member of Kibbutz Ein Hashofet. She was sent by her kibbutz to the first countrywide course for women commanders, to enable her to train other women. She wrote:

I was assigned to the first group of five women and twenty-five men to guard the site during the riots. Everyone had a position and went to guard as soon as the alarm was called. There was a barbed wire fence around a small hill surrounded by pill boxes. In the center was a two-story fortified house, an old Arab house we reinforced. The roof we used as a fort. We carried our guns all the time. The attacks were usually at night and we fired back from our position. . . . Women took equal part with the men at that time. Protecting was done on the home ground. Later we found it important to get the enemy outside the home ground. Then the women stayed home to guard, while the men went out. There was a change of tactics throughout the country in 1937 and 1938.[18]

By 1939 the Arab attacks subsided, and the British withdrew their tacit cooperation with the Jews. In May 1939 a White Paper was issued in England limiting the immigration of Jews into Palestine to a fixed number of seventy-five thousand persons over the subsequent five years. Thus, just as the Nazi oppression of the Jews in Europe had become unavoidably clear, the British shut the door to Palestine.[19]

WORLD WAR II: 1940–1945

In 1940 the 463,535 Jews[20] in Palestine faced formidable enemies. Although there was a moratorium on the immediate conflict with the Arabs, the leadership was fully aware that the lull was only temporary. In addition, the frustration and anguish caused by World War II required decision and action.

In the 1939 White Paper the British had dealt the Yishuv a deadly blow with a policy that seemed not only partisan but also inhumane in the light of developments that threatened to destroy all of European Jewry. Yet, the Yishuv could not retaliate against the British by supporting Hitler.

David Ben-Gurion provided the statement that guided the community and motivated individuals. From his declaration, "We will fight the war as if there is no White Paper and we will fight the White Paper as if there is no war,"[21] the Yishuv mobilized and prepared itself for future sovereignty.

The decisions taken by the Haganah during this period had significant consequences for the future state. In all areas, women volunteered and accepted assignments as did men. Although women never equaled men in actual numbers or in proportional representation, those who were involved were indeed significant. In the decade 1941–1951 women played their most active role in defense.

AUXILIARY TERRITORIAL SERVICES (ATS)

In December 1941 the National Service Act was passed in England conscripting unmarried women aged twenty to thirty into the ATS.

Because the British were more reluctant to send their own women to the Middle East than they were to have Palestinian women serve in their armed forces, recruitment for the ATS in Palestine started the first week in 1942. Women from ages eighteen to fifty were eligible for service. Many women volunteered, enlisting either directly through British offices or through Jewish authorities. The total recruited numbered four thousand, about nine hundred of whom were WAAFs (Women's Auxiliary Air Force).

Following the original British pattern, a cadre of women was to be selected and trained first. They in turn would be the officers and the NCOs to train those who followed. Of the first group to volunteer, sixty-six were finally selected, including three who were Christian Arabs and three Armenians. Among the Jewish sixty, one-half were Haganah members, while the others had been recommended by the various women's organizations. A deliberate attempt to include kibbutz women in this leadership group was met with resistance.

The kibbutz arguments against recruitment came primarily from men who felt that women should serve locally in the Haganah or, if they did go, should serve only as nurses and doctors, but not as drivers for officers.[22] Despite the fact that most of the women did not agree with the arguments presented, they accepted the decision of the kibbutz authorities.

Some kibbutz women did revolt against these attitudes. "I became ashamed, remembering all our discussions around the question of women's recruitment. Our friends regard this as a matter of the 'women's question': should women be defended; should a protective arm be created around them? They have not regarded this as the expression of the independent Jewish woman who knows her destiny."[23]

The recruitment, which went ahead without the kibbutz cooperation, attracted mostly city dwellers and Haganah and Histadruth (General Federation of Jewish Labor in Palestine) members. Some joined for the opportunity to fight Hitler and to be part of a more global response, others for a chance to search for lost relatives. More recent arrivals to Palestine without other means of support saw service as an opportunity to gain skills.

On a personal level, the women faced many obstacles. Each of the individuals interviewed for this paper reports having heard accusations of ATS recruits being loose women. If not outright prostitutes, they were labeled adventure-seekers, or seen as motivated to catch a husband, or as escapees from unhappy marriages. Many families whose women joined were ostracized. Without strong family support, particularly from fathers, it would have been impossible for most of them to go.

In contrast to all the apprehension regarding their women's "exposure to the temptations of rude and licentious soldiery,"[24] the Yishuv relaxed as reports came in of the ATS women fulfilling their dual mission with distinction. Indeed, the task was twofold: first, on the official level, to carry out their assignments within the British military framework; and second, to fulfill their own national needs, by retaining and strengthening their identity as a Jewish group and continuing any assignments the Haganah requested.

From reports brought from Egypt, the ATS women were highly praised by the local British command. One English colonel was reported to have said to an official visitor:

Look here, I really don't know what I could have done without your girls. I tried every conceivable element. . . . I tried my own soldiers, but they did not do half of what your girls do. A lot of hard work has got to be done . . . and I thought your girls would be too gentle to be ordered about, but they do it and stand for no nonsense.[25]

Throughout their service they continued to be Haganah members. Messages were passed when necessary, skills, such as decoding and teleprinting, were learned that would prove useful later on, and the transfer of arms was arranged.

It is probably safe to say that the four years of service for these women enabled many of them to have careers of distinction in the new state. Their most obvious contribution was the organization of CHEN, the women's army. Because of the controversy surrounding the British influence in the IDF, the ATS image does not have the same aura of heroism as does the Palmach.

THE PALMACH

On May 19, 1941, by Emergency Order No. 2, the Palmach (assault companies) were created for the execution of any special or dangerous duty assigned them by the High Command of the Haganah. By November 9, 1941, six companies were established, with four based in agricultural areas, one in Tel Aviv, and the sixth in Jerusalem. While these companies were mainly from agricultural settlements, the Jerusalem company had, in addition to kibbutz members, people from HISH (field forces), especially students. These six companies remained the core groups to which members were added.

The early days of the Palmach were shaky, due mostly to lack of funds. In the spring of 1942, the British, threatened by Rommel in Africa, offered assistance for training the Palmach. With this aid, Palmach members were doubled. They were now based in kibbutzim, where they worked part-time (to help pay for their support) and trained. In effect, this arrangement allowed the Palmach to become a standing force stationed in training bases, living under a military regime.[26]

When the question first arose regarding the recruitment of girls to the Palmach, the Haganah chief of staff issued explicit instructions against it. During the winter of 1941–1942, Israel Livartovsky, the commander of the Jerusalem company, disobeyed the order and assembled a small group of Jerusalem girls, the first women's formation in the Palmach. According to Bauer:

In the spring of 1942, the girls were court-martialed by the Jerusalem regional commander for "illegal entry into the Palmach." They achieved "legalization" on May 3, 1942 by decision of the National Command.[27]

While the National Command agreed to include women (limiting the number to 10 percent of the total group), it did not say what the function of the female recruits would be. Sarah Braverman writes:

Each one of us saw ourselves as a guinea pig. We were more or less one unit in each company. In training we were spread as individuals, one in a kita (squad), two in a machlaka (platoon). The main opinion was that the Havera (female member) could participate in all the activities that the Haver (male member) did, so we were trained in all the professions, using the rifle, pistol, grenades, stens and in physical training. We shared all the experiences and our effort was unbelievable.[28]

In September 1943 the first first convention of Palmach women was held in Mishmar Haemek to evaluate the past and plan for the future. They were fully aware that the failure of one woman would cast doubt on the entire group and the failure of the 10 percent could end women in the military.

The recommendations were geared toward improving the method of absorbing women into the military framework. They were not intended to separate women into specific functions, nor to prevent those who were fit from joining combat. Braverman states:

The defense of the land cannot be without the full participation of the human potential which anyway is very small. Anybody who puts down women as fighters should remember that he is putting down fifty percent of the fighting potential of the Yishuv.[29]

In early 1944, to solve its internal problems of recruitment and financing, the Palmach changed its system of membership. At the end of 1943, the Palmach had 1,113 members, far short of its goal of 5,000.[30] Financial support from the British was no longer forthcoming. The decision was therefore made to call up the Hachsharot, the youth movement groups preparing for settlement in the kibbutzim. While the kibbutzim would assist in financing their training, the members of the Hachsharot would work part-time to pay their way.

The composition of these groups consisted primarily of young boys and girls, from urban middle-class or well-established working-class families. They all shared Socialist ideas of collective living and dedication to public service. On a personal level there were close social attachments with high moral and cultural standards, stamping the Palmach even more with ideological fervor.

One-half of each *garin* ("core group") was female. An agreement signed in 1944 by the Palmach and the youth movements guaranteed that the enlistment of all the girls would occur and that the autonomy of each group would be preserved. As Bauer wrote: "Throughout 1944–48, the Palmach became the home address for all young Jewish men and women who were ready to fulfill what they themselves called "the duty of our generation."[31] It is important to note that the youth movements organized only a small percentage of the young generation, but these volunteers were the trend setters for their age group. They reinforced the ideology of their parents, many of the third Aliyah, living out their parents' dreams of a homeland, as well as their own reality.

Irgun Zvi Leumi (Irgun or Etzel)

By 1943 relations with the British began to cool considerably. The war had turned in favor of the Allies, and the immigration termination date (March 1944) of the White Paper was approaching. Within Palestine the tension was mounting as the knowledge and the extent of the Holocaust spread. Meanwhile the British began to search once again for secret arms caches in the kibbutzim. The lines were drawn. Britain intended to fulfill its immigration policy and the Yishuv intended to fight them on it.

In the actual means of the struggle there were differences between the Haganah and the Irgun, a separate Jewish military group, dissident within the Yishuv. The Irgun saw the British as the main enemy, with Arabs only inflamed by them. It was against the British, then, that Irgun "operations" were carried out.

While at the end of its existence, Irgun had a membership of five thousand, no more than two thousand, 20 percent of them women, were involved in actions during the height of the struggle.[32] These four hundred women were distributed among several branches dealing with propaganda, information, education, and medical and combat units. Their jobs consisted of putting up posters with anti-British information on walls, transferring ammunition from place to place, and maintaining contact between members who were in the deep underground. These assignments were often dangerous; the first woman caught with a bomb was an Irgun member, Rachel Ohevet Ami, who served seven of her fifteen-year sentence.

Some women were part of the combat units, although there was great reluctance among the men to involve them in direct combat action. For example, a few women joined the unit that attacked the radio station at Ramallah (May 17, 1944). The action, deep in Arab territories, involved no Jewish settlements. Because the risk to the injured without access to medical attention was great, the women who could administer such aid were taken. These women were armed and trained for such actions.

E. Lankin, a member of the Irgun High Command, stated:

It was because of the reluctance of the men that the girls were not included more often in the "actions." They were a wonderful group of girls, who without hesitation performed their duties under the most difficult conditions. They often showed greater zeal, greater responsibility than the men . . . this I saw . . . and there were some girls who were better in the action than some of the men.[33]

THE WAR OF INDEPENDENCE

The United Nations resolution to partition Palestine into a Jewish and an Arab state with Jerusalem in an international zone, triggered a war between the Jews and all of their surrounding Arab neighbors that was to continue for sixteen months, from December 1, 1947 until March 10, 1949.

In every sense, this was the culminating event for all of the defense preparations and experience of the previous half century. For women, there was an interweaving of patterns that, on the one hand, were continuous with the prior history, and, on the other, shifted toward those that were to dominate their role in the official defense forces of the new state. The past and the future came together.

It was in the Palmach, itself the most active branch of the Yishuv's forces, that women participated closely with men, in the largest numbers, and continued throughout the conflict to fulfill the roles for which they had been trained. Elsewhere, the story was different, changing from relatively full participation early in the conflict toward a more specialized and limited division of labor.

From the beginning, the war was very costly for the Yishuv, taking more than 6,000 lives. Of these, 2,000 were civilians. Among the four thousand soldiers who lost their lives, 114 were women.[34]

At the outbreak of hostilities, the Yishuv's available manpower was 6,990 HISH, 26,700 HIM (Home Guard), 9,447 Gadna Youth,[35] and 2,220 Palmach in active units, with 1,000 in reserve.[36] By February 1948 the Palmach group expanded to 4,035, "including twenty percent girls who were classified at the highest level of physical capability, and ten percent boys and girls with a low profile."[37] Beginning in June 1948, there were 6,000 mobilized Palmach members, including 1,200 women.

For the first six months of the war, Palmach served as the defensive screen behind which the rest of the Army could mobilize and stabilize. Its units were trained in infiltration, surprise attack, and assault. Women participated at all levels.

In leadership roles, both in combat and training, women were included. As officers, five women commanded combat units, two in Harel Brigade and three in Yiftah Brigade. All remained in Palmach units until the end of the war. At a central training camp where most of the raw recruits were male, the commander, Major Dvora Spector, was described as a "real professional."[38] One of the most important assignments was in communication. Meir Pa'il, a Knesset member and colonel in the reserves, reports: "Women were excellent—there was not a single incident of a female soldier not behaving correctly under fire."[39]

In the Battle of the Roads, women made up one-third of the *Fulmanim,* the name by which the convoy escorts were known. They hid ammunition, operated the wireless, administered first aid, and fought when attacked. The job was arduous and hazardous. One veteran reports that she was on a convoy every day for four and a half months. As a wireless operator, she rode in the first armored car. During an ambush, when the commanding officer froze in psychological shock, she became the link between Jerusalem and others in her convoy. In effect, she took command.[40]

In actual function, Palmach women divided in the following ways: those who (1) participated in the battles as fighters and/or commanders; (2) took part in the operations as saboteurs, wireless operators, medics; (3) were in the *mishlatim* ("outposts") caring for the fighters' needs, serving as drivers, in welfare and culture assignments, teachers of Gahal ("soldiers from abroad intending to settle in Israel"), or preparing food; and (4) served at the base, teaching, cooking, training, and performing secretarial and administrative work.

For the non-Palmach Haganah women, on the other hand, the precise record of their functions has still to be documented. Some facts are clear. They were distributed among the brigades, as secretaries and adjutants, close to the commander. Hanna Eshel, who was in a fighting battalion, gives the following description:

There were about 800 men, 20 women—signallers, nurses, secretary for the battalion. I was trained in a signals course; we carried 17 kilos on our back and went with them to attack in Jaffa. We were in the battle but never used our guns to attack—we were at the front with radios. This was true at Tel Hashomer, and at Lod Airport, I was up in the tower with my Walkie-talkie—a few women, mostly with the men.[41]

HISH fighting units did include women. In the company sent to defend Ramat Naftali in the north, Ada Ben Nachum played a cardinal role in saving the settlement. When attacked by the Lebanese infantry and armored cars, she used a Piat (Projector Infantry Anti-Tank) to hit the first armored car, causing the others to retreat. The Piat was a spring-loaded contraption, according to Gunther Rothenberg, "with a disconcerting characteristic that if it was pointed below horizontal, the bomb would slip out of the projector tube."[42] This made the weapon dangerous for the person firing it, and the subject of real fear among the members of Ben Nachum's group. Given these conditions her action appears all the more courageous.

The available facts, taken together, comprise a record of impressive achievement by Israeli women in the war. To a large extent the Palmach women remained in action until the end of the war, although this was not so for the Haganah women. Esther Herlitz tells of her experiences in the spring of 1948, when she and another former ATS officer were asked to form a women's battalion in Jerusalem. She reports:

One of the things we had to do was to take the Haganah girls out of the front line. It was a decision about which there is controversy till this day. In Jerusalem one woman was killed in Sheik Jarrah and another taken prisoner in the old city—both were soldiers. Of course it is difficult to say where is the "front" and what is "non-front." But the decision was to take them out of the fighting units. Ben Gurion's explanation was that for everyone in the front line, you need so many in the rear. Since boys would be better fighters, that was the arrangement. The Haganah girls didn't like it, especially the radar girls. It kept them from getting good jobs in the army, in lower ranks, and out of decision making posts. They resented it."[43]

The time for the volunteers was over. Now women were part of the state's "manpower pool" from which the regular army could be created. The shift from a volunteer to an official state defense institution was to be a critical one, in ways hard to predict, for the eventual role of women in the Israel Defense Forces.

CHAIL NASHIM (CHEN) IN THE ISRAEL DEFENSE FORCES

Soon after he proclaimed the birth of the state of Israel, Ben-Gurion moved to unify the Jewish fighting forces. His goal was to create a professional and depoliticized army based on the British model, while retaining and strengthening the pioneering spirit within the new state. Controversy regarding women in this new army arose immediately. The first issue to be debated was whether they should be included at all, and second, if indeed they were, how would they function.

The question of inclusion arose primarily from the religious bloc. During the debate in the first Knesset, Rabbi Levin called female military service "an absolute contradiction to the spirit of Israel."[44] The fact is that there are no religious laws that forbid women to bear arms. The underlying reasons for opposition are social and moral, and the definition of "women's place." Ben Gurion, a secularist, believed that the Bible occupied a central place in the life of the Jewish people and was, therefore, willing for the Jewish state to come to terms with its religious minority. Regarding women, the Second Aliyah Zionist in him could offer them equality, while the nonreligious biblical Jew could define them in their rightful place. He states:

We are told that women are not drafted into any other army in the world. We, too, have no intention of putting women into combat units, though no one can be sure that, should we be attacked and have to fight for our lives, we should not call on services of every man and woman. But the law in question deals with a peacetime situation, and we want to give women only the most basic training.[45]

The Defense Service Law of 1949 was enacted by the Knesset on September 8 of that year. It was amended several times. From 1959 the law stipulated that:

1. Women who reach the age of eighteen are eligible for conscription to serve for a period of twenty-four months.
2. Married women and mothers of children are exempt as well as women for whom religious convictions preclude their serving.
3. Deferment of service is available to women studying in institutions which the army accepts. Their full period of military service upon graduation is required, regardless of their future marital state.
4. Reserve service is obligatory. After the term of national service, a woman is obliged to serve in the reserve until the age of thirty-four (in actuality women perform such service only until twenty-four years of age) or until the birth of her first child.
5. Unmarried physicians, dentists, surgical nurses, physiotherapists and occupational therapists serve until the age of thirty-four.[46]

Within these broad outlines, policy for recruitment and utilization of women evolved as the army developed. The organization of CHEN preceded the law by approximately sixteen months. Early in May 1948, a group of women who had been active in the earlier defense forces were asked to organize a women's corps.

Just as there was controversy regarding means of balancing the British and Palmach influence in the IDF as a whole, so were these differences apparent in CHEN. Two lines of thought were in conflict from the outset. The first approach was to duplicate the ATS pattern, with the women's corps entirely separate. Under this plan, the female soldiers would be sent to serve in men's units, but all other aspects of their military life would remain under CHEN jurisdiction. Included in this were separate store-houses, technical schools, as well as training and judicial responsibilities. The second proposal, offered by the Palmach, was for total integration of the female soldiers into those units in which they served, minimizing the separateness.[47] Organizationally these two plans were merged during the first two years, making CHEN the responsible authority for training and judicial matters, while all work assignments became general army man-power decisions.

More significant within CHEN, however, were conflicts between the two approaches regarding style, attitudes towards military life, and rela-tions of officer and recruit. Probably most crucial of all was the extent of military training. The ATS women were inclined to emphasize the auxiliary aspect of women's participation in the war, while at the same time setting high standards for achievement in all the undertakings. Although not serving in combat was an accepted fact by them, the range of jobs women could do was broad in scope. Military discipline and looking like a proper soldier would produce high level performance, they argued.

One woman commander tells how she attended the first officers course, was given a ribbon, made a camp commander and started to help form an army in Mt. Carmel, Haifa. "We reproduced everything from the British Army exactly in the same way. From the "Order of the Day" to the payroll, to saluting, to insisting on the way the uniform was worn. This is what we knew."[48]

For the Palmach women standing at attention and all other military ways were anathema. A commander who organized the camp in Tel Aviv tells of her debate with a Palmach officer:

She wanted to teach the girls, the first day they came in, shooting and throwing bombs. I said to her, let me first organize things so they know where to go, teach them what the army is and what the army expects from them. At the very beginning we only had the girls for a few days, but I had to give in, and find a day for training with rifles.[49]

The argument revolved around just how far the "self-defense" in train-ing concept would be translated into military "action" and how seriously "military behavior" was to be taken in the newly formed army. The change from underground to a regular army was difficult and painful. Gradually during that first year, many Palmach women returned to their kibbutzim or went on to university and other studies. The leadership in CHEN was left primarily in the hands of the former ATS women; from the start until 1970, the commanding officer of the women's corps was always a former ATS officer.

HOW CHEN OPERATES

The Women's Corps is not a corps in the true sense of the term, but rather an administrative cadre governing training assignments and military careers of women in the IDF.[50] The highest officer, a colonel,[51] is on the General Staff, under the manpower branch. She advises the chief of staff on problems of training and supply, leave and vacation, housing and hygiene, and all general conditions of service pertaining to women in all services (land, sea, air, military settlements, and youth battalions).[52] Each of these units has a CHEN chief officer who advises the male commanding officer in charge regarding the women in that unit. Manpower decisions are made in each separate branch of the service. Therefore, whether or not women are utilized in various professions are decisions made outside of CHEN, by men. The women's corps only advises in this area.

Regarding this, the report on the status of women has recently pointed out that:

When Zahal (IDF) was first established, the State recognized the right of the girls to serve in all jobs on a voluntary basis. As time elapsed the equality has disappeared. The only considerations are needs of army efficiency and economic ones. On this basis jobs are opened and closed to girls. As a result the IDF is lagging behind other armies which are more resourceful in absorbing women.[53]

Out of the 850 different jobs that are presently estimated to be available in Zahal, women can fulfill about 270. The occupations fall into three categories: (1) secretarial, administrative, clerical, which are occupied by approximately 65 percent of the women; (2) technical and mechanical; (3) operational. The latter two categories absorb the remaining 35 percent.[54]

The primary consideration remains "to supply the fixed quota of girls to whichever army branches need manpower that year," Dalia Raz, a former chief CHEN commander, stated.[55] Two other factors enter into a recruit's placement; her own preferred choice and her total profile, a combination of a medical and quality index.[56]

Two areas of responsibility belong to CHEN alone. The first basic training for all recruits is dealt with by its personnel. More important, CHEN is the sole judicial authority for all women soldiers, regardless of where they serve. The recruit is directly responsible to the commander under whom she works, a person who is most often a male. That commander cannot, however, punish or judge her without consultation and consent of a CHEN officer. This brake on his ultimate authority regarding female soldiers causes him difficulties he does not encounter in dealing with male recruits. "It makes him mad—and at the very least it's a great inconvenience," one senior CHEN officer stated about this situation.[57]

The ambivalence by commanders towards female soldiers is clear. On the one hand, women are seen as excellent workers, conscientious, dedicated and able, often far superior to their male counterpart. On the other hand, the special privileges they must be granted (according to official rules of the army) create additional difficulties not encountered with a male recruit. On the personal level, just as women create a "humanitarian" atmosphere within the units, so do they curb the clubby atmosphere of the man's world doing a "man's" job. Just how far these organizational and interpersonal aspects restrict the utilization of women on a larger scale needs to be analyzed.

COMBAT ROLE

While actual combat and front-line combat support had been debatable tasks for women in the prestate period, the formation of the IDF put an end to the debate. All jobs involving combat, jobs that have to be filled under bad conditions, and jobs where physical demands are regarded as too great for females are closed to them.[58]

The implications of this decision are far-reaching beyond the issue of actual fighting in a conflict. It is important to note the meaning of combat in the IDF.

The officer, whatever his actual job, is thus defined (as an image, if not a description of reality) as a combat leader. It goes without saying that combat activities also had the highest prestige, induced by the fact that they also are given the highest priority. If a civilian, employed by the IDF, in his professional capacity (say, as a psychologist) also is an officer in the reserves, he will typically during his annual call-up be sent to his combat unit. Economically, it would probably be more profitable for the IDF to keep him in his professional job at the reservist's low pay, rather than conceding his professional services for the 45 days during which he is a platoon leader. But the norm of priority to combat is the dominant one.[59]

In reality, it has been pointed out that it is at the very most only 15 percent of the army that goes into battle, but the image is a powerful one.

Women only participate in that image by "freeing a man for combat," which is repeated to her as liturgy. The effect of this is real. For example, since 1977, women have become tank instructors. They can teach how the motor works, how to drive the tank, how to repair it, how to use all the equipment in the tank. The teaching takes place in a classroom and then in the tank. There is general agreement that the female instructors, like their male counterparts, know everything about the tank. While the male instructor is allowed to go out into the field, however, the female instructor is prohibited from doing so. He feels what he teaches and she feels the lack of this experience. There is agreement that she would be a better teacher in the classroom if she taught the course the additional step, but because the field is considered combat training she is prohibited from doing so.[60] Keeping women out of combat was a decision made when the IDF was organized. The reasons given are explanations for the decisions, but, in fact, they are insufficient to explain the rule.

The prevailing explanation offered within CHEN is the fear of women being taken prisoners, based upon previous experiences. Yet documentation regarding such incidents are difficult to find. Dr. Meir Pa'il, a former commander, writes in the *Jerusalem Post*:

I feel obliged to respond to Mr. Schull's [a journalist] comments about the "horrible fate of the few girls who did fall into Arab hands alive." To the best of my knowledge those few Jewish girls, soldiers and civilians, who happened to fall alive into Arab armies' hands were treated in a respectable manner. The most important case concerning the question occurred some time before the Six Day War, when a bus carrying about 30 women soldiers happened to cross the Lebanese borders by mistake, was captured by Lebanese armed forces and brought back after a few days to Rosh Hanikre. According to the girls' report, the Lebanese treated them honorably. So, I neither "forgot nor ignored" anything in considering the question of importance of women's service in army combat formations in general and in the IDF in particular.[61]

Binkin and Bach wrote, "the character and composition of a nation's military system mirror the society that it is established to protect and defend."[62] CHEN has truly reproduced what is present in Israeli society, and indeed is its mirror image. Women are equal in value, but not in function. In modern society it is of course in "function" where the status and the power are. But so familiar is the reproduction, that Israeli society does not even question CHEN's underlying structure.

SUMMARY AND CONCLUSIONS

The Israel Defense Forces Spokesman, the official publication of the armed forces, opened its February 27, 1980 issue describing CHEN as follows:

Sorry to disappoint you if you have been influenced by the Hollywood image of Israeli girl soldiers being Amazon-type warriors accoutred in ill-fitting male combat fatigues and toting sub-machine guns. Today's female soldiers are trim girls, clothed in uniforms which bring out their youthful femininity. They play a wide variety of noncombatant, though thoroughly essential roles within the IDF framework and within certain sectors of the civilian community.

This picture of the "charming" female soldiers has been carefully fashioned in all interviews and communiqués regarding CHEN women. It is a far cry from Esther Becker, Manya Shochat, Rachel Yanait, and the other

Hashomer women who spoke so strongly eighty years earlier for the right of women to bear arms equally with men. It has also served to place the contributions of those women who fought—whether in or near front lines— into a historical and long past era. Although many of these earlier women are still alive, they are viewed by the recent generation like yellowed pictures of a bygone era.

The shift in the imagery has served to answer the critics, reassure the skeptics, and put a brake on the achieving female.

Reinforced by protective legislation, the woman soldier's life remains sufficiently circumscribed to allow her both to do national service and return to society understanding her role as a woman. She receives the double message. In Zuckoff's words,

. . . it's good for Jewish women to be strong and aggressive when the Jews are in danger and she's acting in the people's interest. . . . If we go through the Bible and legends carefully we see that whenever Jewish survival is at stake, Jewish women are called upon to be strong and aggressive. When the crisis is over, it's back to patriarchy.[63]

What were some of the forces at work to create the picture that we now see?

The cultural tradition, based in the religion, must be considered one of the significant influences. Within this context, male and female roles have always been separate and distinct. Because the bulk of the population (from the Second Aliyah through the present) has always been secular, it is easy to understate this influence; and because it has found expression in subtle and unexpected ways, it is often oversimplified when recognized.

Israel's Jews are Israeli by citizenship, but Jewish by nationality. The "peoplehood" concept has been translated into legal terms, so that although most people are not religious, they are still Jewish. Moreover, Jewishness at the base is connected with religious precepts. As Berl Katznelson maintained: "A generation that creates and innovates does not throw the heritage of previous generations on the rubbish heap . . . but may keep the tradition by adding to it."[64]

In fact, however, before the state, the religious groups were a dormant force. They did not surface as a real political force until the state was created. Only then, because of their strategic position in coalition politics, was their true power brought into being. For women in the defense forces, the impact of this shift was great. Because it was based on voluntary participation, the woman's issue as it related to defense never had to be fought before on a national scale. Only on personal bases was it a struggle, within the voluntary armies. Now, however, the religious bloc used religious notions about women as a bargaining tool.

When, in 1949, women were officially accepted in the IDF, the first reaction was that the battle had been won. What the leaders of this struggle did not recognize immediately was the danger of being precipitated into a truly national debate. The battle for women's belonging in the armed forces, far from won, was only then joined, to be fought over the next thirty years until, in July 1978, Amendment No. 13 of the Defense Service Law of 1959 liberalized the exemption.[65] The religious group, by focusing the lawmakers on the question of conscription versus nonconscription, has deflected attention away from the issues of what women do in the armed forces. The forward thrust of the evolution has been effectively blunted, and women put on the defensive.

The structural changes from Yishuv to state were reflected in the IDF as well. However, the hope was that many of the functions of the Yishuv security organizations would be carried over into the new professional army.

Zahal was given the primary function of guarding the state, but, as Ben-Gurion wrote, that was not its only function. "The Army," he said, "must also serve as an educational and pioneering center for Israeli youth—for both those born here and newcomers. It is the duty of the army to educate a pioneer generation, healthy in body and spirit, courageous and loyal."[66] This was a vision of an army as a citizen's academy.

The IDF, therefore, emerged as an institution with dual functions. Its primary function of guarding the state was never forgotten, as it forged its citizenry into a formidable army. In addition, Zahal served an educational role that was intrinsically to socialize recruits in the basic values of the society. Thus, on the one hand, the emphasis of the IDF development was on professionalization, creating a meritocracy designed for a competitive society where individual competence is highly regarded. On the other hand, the IDF assumed responsibility for educating its recruits, for social and welfare problems of its members and for the integration of highly diverse immigrant populations into the society. As Zahal has played out this dual character, males dominate in the sphere of the professional meritocracy, and the women recruits are funneled into the sphere of social maintenance and the ideological side of military functions. As experience shows, with the professionalization of an occupation, women are expected to be the idealists.

Ben-David has illustrated this point with the case of the unionization of teachers and nurses in Israel.[67] Attempts at the improvement of working conditions and salaries in these occupations were regarded as immoral efforts "to raise the price of an essential service and turn what ought to be a mission into a business." In Ben-David's interpretation, "The only way the quality of manpower, or indeed, the supply of manpower can be maintained, given such a set of circumstances, is by using cheap female labor and appealing to certain kinds of idealism to which women, badly handicapped in occupational careers, are sensitive."[68]

To date this has been the accepted position by the professional women who serve in the IDF as well as by the society at large. Whether this will shift depends upon several factors already present in embryonic form. First, the growth of influence from the women's movement in other countries is increasing. Within Israel, issues that were ridiculed not too many years ago are taken seriously now. Second, the need for women in professions outside the feminine area is anticipated because of manpower shortages. Serious training within the army for women will have to be addressed on a larger scale than the "experimental" approach now being taken. Third, the professional military women who serve in Kevah[69] will begin to deal with some of their questions regarding rank (to go above colonel), power (to go beyond *advisers*) and access to decision-making roles.

The most telling point of the story of women's participation in the defense of Israel is perhaps that their utilization has been both *ad hoc* and pragmatic. The attempt to study the issue systematically through careful documentation concerning both their contribution within the army and value to the society appears not to have been dealt with. Given the significance of the army as a social institution in Israel, such an effort to understand the armed forces' past and to control its future is warranted.

NOTES

1. Mark Zborowski and Elizabeth Herzog, *Life Is With People* (New York: Schocken Books, 1952), p. 128.

2. Peggy R. Sanday, "Female Status in the Public Domain," in Rosaldo, Michelle Zimbalist and Louise Lamphere, eds., *Woman, Culture and Society*, (Palo Alto, Calif.: Stanford University Press, 1974), p. 190.

3. Zborowski and Herzog, *Life Is With People*, p. 124.

4. Daphne Nundi Israeli, "The Women's Movement in Palestine, 1911–1927." (Paper presented at the Ninth World Conference of the International Sociological Association, Upsalla, Sweden, 1978), p. 3.

5. Meaning literally "the land of Israel." Cf. S. N. Eisenstadt, *Israeli Society* (London: Weidenfeld and Nicolson, 1970). This book is the main source of the subsection on Aliyah.

6. Lotta Levensohn, *Hashomer: The First Jewish Watch in Palestine* (New York: Vaad Bitachon, 1939), pp. 9–13.

7. Esther Becker, "The History of the Watchman's Family," in Matti Meged, ed., *Sepher Hashomer* (Hebrew) (Tel Aviv: Dvir Co. Ltd., 1936).

8. Levensohn, *Hashomer*, p. 20.

9. Israeli, "Women's Movement," p. 9.

10. Precise figures of women members and wives are discrepant. *Sepher Hash-*

omer includes twenty-eight women out of one hundred members. Cf. Meged *Sepher Hashomer.*

11. Gunther E. Rothenberg, *The Anatomy of the Israeli Army* (London: B. T. Matsford Ltd., 1979), p. 24.

12. Zeev Schiff, *A History of the Israeli Army, 1870–1974* (San Francisco, Straight Arrow Books, 1974), p. 12.

13. Ibid., p. 13.

14. Interview, January 1979, with Esther Herlitz.

15. *Sepher Toldat Ha-Haganah* (The History of the Haganah), vol. 3 (Tel Aviv, Ma'arachot, 1956).

16. Interview, September 1978, with Mina Ben Zvi, Haganah officer.

17. Interview, August 1978, with Shoshana Spector.

18. Geraldine Stern, *Daughters from Afar* (New York: Bloch, 1958), pp. 151–2.

19. Yehuda Bauer, *From Diplomacy to Resistance* (New York: Atheneum, 1973), pp. 16–67.

20. Dan Horowitz and M. Lissak, *Origins of the Israeli Policy* (Chicago, University of Chicago Press, 1978), Appendix 1.

21. David Ben-Gurion, *Israel, a Personal History* (Tel Aviv, American Israel Publishing Co., 1972), p. 54.

22. Yoav Gelber, *Volunteerism in the Yishuv* (Ph.D. diss., Hebrew University, Jerusalem, 1977).

23. Rivka Rabinowitch, "On the Women's Recruitment," Givat Haim Diary, March 27, 1942, in Gelber, *Volunteerism.*

24. Major Lewis Rabinowitz, *Soldiers From Judea: Jewish Units in the African Campaign, 1941–43* (London: Gollancz, 1945), p. 48.

25. Moshe Shertok, "The Path of Glory," *The Pioneer Woman* (May 1943), pp. 4–6.

26. Bauer, *From Diplomacy,* p. 188.

27. Ibid., note p. 401.

28. Sarah Braverman, in Zvi Raanan, ed., *The Army and War in Israel and the Nations* (Hebrew) (Tel Aviv: Sifriat Poalim, 1955), pp. 767–69.

29. Ibid., p. 768.

30. Bauer, *From Diplomacy,* pp. 292–304.

31. Ibid., p. 304.

32. Interview, August 1978, with E. Lankin.

33. Ibid.

34. Ministry of Defense, Tel Aviv. Eighteen of these women killed were members of Palmach.

35. Gadna (Gedudei Noar) Youth Corps of high school boys and girls aged fourteen to seventeen, who are given premilitary training.

36. Pa'il Meir, Min HaHaganah L'Zva HaHaganah (The Emergency of Zahal), Zmora, Betan, Modan, Tel Aviv, 1979, p. 241 (Hebrew).

37. Ibid., p. 233.

38. Interview, August 1978, with Meir Pa'il.

39. Ibid.

40. Interview with a Palmach woman, June 1980.

41. Interview, April 20, 1980, with Hanna Eshel.

42. Rothenberg, *Anatomy of the Israeli Army,* p. 37.

43. Interview, January 1979, with Esther Herlitz.

44. David Ben-Gurion, *Israel.* See also, for statement from Arab Knesset members regarding conscription of women, pp. 373–74.

45. Ibid., p. 376.

46. CHEN: Israel Defense Forces spokesman, February 27, 1980.

47. From interviews with former CHEN officers and soldiers. (Anonymity requested.)

48. Interview with Col. Stella Levy (Ret.), July 1980.

49. Interview with a former CHEN officer, July 1978.

50. CHEN: IDF spokesman, p. 1.

51. This position is always filled by a woman, responsible directly to the chief of staff. She serves in the professional manpower branch, as does the chief of education, the head of religion and the judge advocate. In an interview with a retired general who was present when the original ranks were distributed, I asked why the highest ranking officer of CHEN is only a colonel. His answer was, "When ranks were designated the women didn't fight for anything higher, as did the others."

52. Samuel Rolbant, *The Israeli Soldier* (New York: T. Yosaloff, 1970).

53. Report on the Status of Women, Prime Minister's Office (Jerusalem: August 1978), p. 101.

54. A high-ranking CHEN officer gave these figures, June 1980.

55. Delia Raz, *Jerusalem Post,* International Edition (November 16, 1976).

56. Included in this "Kaba," as it is known, are medical profiles, IQ scores, knowledge of Hebrew rating, educational level. The quality groupings range from 41 to 56; 41–47 are the lowest, 48–50 are medium, while 51–56 are the highest score, reached mainly by high school graduates. Individuals who rank 55–56 are in the top category, making them officer quality. Twenty percent of the female recruits score at this level, while only 10 percent of the male recruits do so. Report on the Status of Women, August 1978.

57. Interview, June 1980, Tel Aviv, with CHEN officer.

58. Report on the Status of Women, August 1978,

59. E. O. Schild, "On the Meaning of Military Service in Israel," in Michael Curtis and Mordecai Cherkoff, eds., *Israel: Social Structure and Change* (New Brunswick, N.J.: Transaction Books, 1973), p. 428.

60. Interview with the two instructors in armored corp., July 1, 1980.

61. *Jerusalem Post,* June 22, 1978.

62. Martin Binkin and Shirley J. Bach, *Women and the Military* (Washington, D.C.: The Brookings Institution, 1977), p. 1.

63. Aviva Cantor Zuckoff, *Response* (Summer 1973), no. 18.

64. Horowitz and Lissak, *Origins of the Israeli Policy,* p. 149.

65. Amendment No. 13 frees a woman who declares she is religious from army service. While previously she had to appear before a committee and answer questions to obtain an exemption, her own declaration is now sufficient.

66. Amos Perlmutter, *Military and Politics in Israel, Nation Building and Role Expansion* (London: Frank Cass & Co. Ltd., 1969). Quotation from Ben-Gurion is cited here.

67. Joseph Ben-David, "Professionals and Unions in Israel," in Eliot Freidson and Judith M. Lorber, eds., *Medical Men and Their Work* (New York: Aldine Alberton, 1972).

68. Ibid., p. 36.

69. Kevah is the professional branch of the three-tier form of the IDF. The other two consist of the conscripts and reservists.

PART II | THE THREAT OF WAR

8 | GREECE: RELUCTANT PRESENCE

James Brown and
Constantina Safilios-Rothschild

INTRODUCTION

In the old Greek tradition, women were never the social equals of men, having the same rights and responsibilities. Beginning with the nineteenth century, however, whenever the Greek nation faced a long period of intense crises that entailed serious manpower shortages, Greek women behaved as women of other nations have under the same conditions.[1] Namely, they stepped out of the traditional roles of wife and mother to make important decisions, to play crucial social roles, and more significantly, to fight alongside or instead of the men as *antartes* ("underground guerrilla fighters") resisting the occupying Turkish or German armies.[2] Greek history has not always recorded with great detail or consistency the important role played by Greek women fighters when the risks were very high, except to underline the courage and sacrifice that had been shown by Greeks, *even* by women. The only type of historical accounts available are short sketches of the unusual, striking, fighting exploits of a few exceptional women, rather than the more ordinary participation of great numbers of women in fighting; these depictions reflect a pattern familiar in eras and societies in which the "nonfeminine" behaviors of women must be explained away as unique and extraordinary events.[3]

The history of the Greek War of Independence in the nineteenth century reports the heroic fighting of the women of Mani and Kiafa in critical battles and singles out women such as Manto Mavrogenous and Laskarina Bouboulina, whose statues stand in the War Memorial in Athens together with those of male heroes of that war. Mavrogenous, a beautiful and wealthy woman from Mykonos who manned two ships and chased the pirates away from the island and then organized a small army, and, dressed as a man, took part in several attacks against the Turks.[4] After the death of her husband and son, Bouboulina (1783–1825), an upper-class woman from Spetses, sailed the family ship herself and took part in sea battles until she was killed.[5]

Because women's bravery and active participation in the War of Independence is explained away as exceptional behavior or as an additional duty of a good wife in time of crisis or emergency, their heroism had no consequences for the status of women. This disregard persisted even into the twentieth century. The 1928 census of Greece found one-third of all women illiterate (and three-fourths of those were over forty years of age, without political rights, and struggling to escape the Muslim-style sex segregation, subordination, and general subservience of women.[6]

After the War of Independence, the next important transition point for Greek women was the long period of crises, wars, and civil wars starting with the 1940 Greek-Italian War, followed by the resistance movement during the German occupation from 1941 to 1944 and the civil war from 1944 to 1949. Women usually transported ammunition up the steep mountains of Epirus, and, when the occasion demanded, they fought along with men and served in a variety of combat and noncombat roles in the organized underground resistance movement, especially during the civil war. While women had no official military status in the Greek army,[7] in the organized resistance groups and in the Communist revolutionary army known as the National Republican Liberation Army (ELAS) during the civil war they were trained as officers and distinguished themselves as lieutenants and battalion leaders. Historical accounts of their performance and interviews with surviving men and women who were resistance or revolutionary fighters document women's endurance in long and arduous mountain marches and under very harsh living conditions: their ability to carry heavy loads of arms and ammunition; their bravery and risk taking as well as their persistance in fighting even after they were wounded;[8]* and their ability to withstand pain and torture without breaking down or disclosing information, even though this resulted in hideous death.[9]

Fifteen percent of the revolutionary army during the civil war of 1945–1949 was composed of women[10] and 250 women have been honored as resistance heroines during World War II.[11]

The end of the civil war in 1949 marked a turning point for the status of Greek women. The active participation of rural as well as urban women in the resistance movement and the civil war in many ways helped "liberate" Greek women from a number of traditional constraints and estab-

---

*A male lieutenant of the revolutionary army in the civil war said in an interview, "In the beginning, I hesitated and did not want to have women in my unit, but now I don't want to go to battle if I have not secured some women revolutionaries in my groups. When the women are in the front, they have such an enthusiasm that everybody becomes more motivated to fight."

lished their competence in a variety of "masculine" tasks and endeavors. Starting with 1949, birthrates began to decline even in the absence of any kind of family-planning services. In 1952 Greek women were given full civil rights and the vote, and in 1956 two women parliamentarians were elected for the first time.[12] Women's access to education became increasingly similar to that of men, so much so that by 1971 illiteracy among the ten-to-fourteen-year-olds almost disappeared and an equal percentage of twenty-to-twenty-four-year-old boys and girls had finished high school.[13] In addition, the number of women university students increased throughout the 1950s and '60s and many more of them entered traditionally masculine fields, such as agriculture, architecture, physics, chemistry, and some engineering specialties. By 1971 more women than men had entered law, pharmacy, and dentistry, and in the late 1970s about 50 percent of students in training to become sea captains were women.[14] Another major change in the lives and options of Greek women, especially the more traditional rural and low-income urban women, came about through migration to Western Europe, particularly West Germany and Switzerland, where in 1968 42 percent of the Greek workers were women.[15]

In spite of all these advances in the status of Greek women and the fact that the 1975 Greek constitution guarantees full equality of the sexes, women in Greece in the late 1970s still had an unequal and inferior status to men occupationally, economically, legally, and informally. In the mid-1970s only slightly more than one-fourth of the women worked, and those who worked were consistently paid less than men either because the national collective contracts specified different rates of pay for men and women for the same type of work, or because women's promotions were delayed or entirely bypassed. In 1971, for example, women industrial workers received only 62.3 percent of men's wages.[16] Furthermore, the prevailing sex role stereotypes and longstanding, institutionalized inequalities led to powerful and persistent sex discrimination in all settings and in men and women interactions. The Greek civil law in the mid-1970s defined women in many aspects of familial and social life as second-class citizens dependent on men, regardless of the many attempts to change the laws and diminish built-in inequalities.

It is within this context that the passing of Public Law 705 in 1977 and the serious and acrimonious debates in Parliament that it promulgated must be examined.

THE PRESENT CONSCRIPTION OF GREEK WOMEN

The mandate of Public Law 705 provides for the conscription of women in both war and peace. In the absence of war, women can join the armed forces on a voluntary basis, but in the event of war or general mobilization conscription may be compulsory for women between the ages of twenty and thirty-two.[17] In November 1978 women were for the first time officially admitted into the Greek armed forces on a voluntary basis. The first women recruits completed their training in March 1979. By that year's end a total of 875 women had volunteered and their number was expected to double by 1980.[18]

The law was proposed and eventually passed because of a "national need," namely, the decreasing size of the Greek army and the zero population growth that had made the meeting of future manpower requirements problematic. Based on 1980 projections the birthrate will continue to fall[19] resulting in shrinking numbers with which to meet military recruitment needs. The acceptance of women in auxiliary, noncombat support, logistical, and administrative roles in the armed forces could release men for combat.

When the proposed bill was being debated in Parliament, the women's organizations opposed it because it was believed that in the absence of legal and economic equality between the sexes in other domains conscription would represent an additional imposed obligation without the benefit of corresponding social and economic rights. They argued that the recruitment of women into the armed forces with sex discrimination not eliminated would not enhance their status but would instead make them pawns. Leftist women's organizations have also been worried about the significance of this bill in terms of possibly increasing militarism within the Greek society. Opposition to the possible compulsory conscription of women in case of war continues in the 1980s, particularly if the age allowance is lowered to eighteen.[20]

Another concern indicated by some professional women's organizations was that enlistment in the armed forces would represent an attractive career alternative to lower middle-class working and low-income urban and rural women, provided they were adequately paid, trained in valuable skills and given a chance for promotion.[21]*

The concern, therefore, clearly voiced in the media, was that the armed forces would create an additional proletariat—one composed of women with vested interests in militarism for self-advancement.

WHO ARE THE WOMEN VOLUNTEERS?

This study will primarily use data and interviews obtained directly from the first two classes of women recruits, and observations from the first four recruit classes.[22] As previously stated, at the end of 1979 the total number of women recruited was 945 (army 413, navy 188, air force 344);

---

*These categories of women have less access than men of the same social origin to educational and employment opportunities because of limited financial resources, which are used to educate sons rather than daughters, often regardless of ability.

in 1980 this figure was doubled.[23] Volunteers are required to serve for fourteen months, after which they may, if they wish, reenlist for three more years. Provisions in the law specify that women may be eligible for officer status. Thus far, only the air force has taken this issue under advisement; the army and navy have given it no serious consideration at all. While in service, the women are subject to the same regulations as the men, except in those areas that the law specifies do not "conform to their sex and mission." After completing their basic training, the women are eligible for specialty noncombat positions. Specifically, Presidential Decree 468/1978 provides seventy-five specialties in the army (for example, clerks, interpreters, "communications men," medical technicians, sewing machine handlers, crypto-machine handlers, thirty-four in the navy (for example, administrators, technicians, chauffeurs, masons, telephonists), and thirty-four in the air force (for example, clerks, interpreters, radio and teletype technicians, medical technicians, dieticians). Article 4 of this decree specifically states: "Women are placed according to the judgment of the Armed Forces Branches in all services, except combat units."[24]

Table 8.1

Profile of Female Recruits into the Armed Forces of Greece

PROFILE OF RECRUITS	ARMY	NAVY	AIR FORCE
Age (average)	21.8	21.0	22.3
Residence			
Village	53.2%	40.8%	18.6%
City (Athens, Thessaloniki)	16.2%	44.7%	44.3%
Islands	7.1%	8.6%	5.5%
Provincial Towns	23.5%	6.0%	31.6%
Employment			
Student	33.3%	43.2%	44.0%
Private Employment	37.8%	36.4%	42.0%
Unemployed	21.2%	6.8%	6.0%
Other	5.1%	2.3%	4.0%
No Response	3.0%	11.4%	4.0%
Education			
Less than Trade School	0.0%	0.0%	2.0%
Trade School	25.3%	16.9%	18.8%
High School	65.7%	72.8%	64.0%
University	7.0%	2.3%	16.0%
No Response	2.0%	8.8%	1.0%

SOURCE: Survey conducted by the Hellenic National Defense General Staff, 1979.

The women recruits have primarily attended either a trade school or high school. It should be noted that the question was poorly phrased in that it does not elicit from the respondent actual graduation from these institutions. Also, the recruits mainly come from the villages and small towns of Greece (except those in the air force). These data are similar to those from their male counterparts, both enlisted and officers.[25] We may hypothesize that those who came from the rural areas tend to come from humble circumstances. Preliminary indications of fathers' occupations point to farmers, tradesmen, laborers, and craftsmen. Very few of the women recruits' fathers were professionally trained or were former officers.

One reason these women joined may be because of the perceived social mobility offered by the armed forces. Simply to leave the village or provincial town behind and go to Athens may be a further and perhaps more general reason why they volunteered. When the recruits were asked, "Give the primary reason why you joined the military," their responses were as follows:

	ARMY	NAVY	AIR FORCE
For a military career	55.6%	62.0%	56.8%
Patriotism	11.1%	16.0%	11.4%
Experience	9.0%	6.0%	15.9%
Training	3.0%	0.0%	2.3%
Civil Service Benefits	1.0%	4.0%	4.5%
Other	1.0%	0.0%	4.5%
No response	19.0%	12.0%	4.5%

It is not at all clear precisely what the implications of joining the armed forces "for a military career" may be. We only speculate that this is a complex term that includes personal, social, and economic reasons.

When the women were asked to indicate secondary reasons for enlisting, their responses clearly indicated that they did so in the order of patriotism, experience, career opportunity training, and civil service benefits. It would appear that these initial groups did not view civil service benefits as all-important, although each recruit would receive a 5 percent bonus on civil service examinations that they would take in the future.

It is quite clear that patriotism was an issue to them. This may be partially explained by their rural backgrounds, which implies that these women's ideology is "fundamentalist" in nature and that theirs is a basic trust and loyalty to the nation. A further explanation may rest in the still-festering confrontation between Greece and Turkey as a result of the 1974 Cyprus crisis. The roots of this hostility are historical and permeate all Greeks' value structures.

One fact of interest in our data is the percentage of women in the army who were unemployed at the time of their enlistment. With Greece's employment rate in the nineteen years age group at 6 percent and in the twenty to twenty-four age group at 4.4 percent, the higher level indicated by this category of women reflects the fact that the less skilled and less educated women enlist in the army than in the other armed forces, a pattern similar to that for men. Because the rates of women's recruitment were not meeting expectation, at the end of 1979 women were offered economic incentives (a low level salary) in order to increase motivation. We do not know how these incentives have affected the composition of those recruited in terms of such issues as education, prior employment, and status.

THE TRAINING CYCLE

What happens to the woman enlistee when she enters the Greek armed forces? Although upon entering she may ask to join a particular service, it is the military itself that makes the final determination. The training is broken down into two phases. During the first five weeks the recruits are socialized to military life. The women's basic training course is similar for all services. It is a spin-off of its male counterpart, although it is much easier and in many areas quite superficial.[26] The five weeks' course consists of marching and drilling, daily physical conditioning, room preparation and inspection, personal hygiene, education in military rules and regulations, individual tactics, assembling and firing the rifle, range practice with the rifle, moral education, first aid, and chemical-biological-radiological warfare.

Although a portion of the women's basic training course consists of combat training, it is simplified and cursory and not analogous to the training that males receive. These topics are an integral part of the training program, but the actual implementation is not always followed. The daily training periods are often changed without much forethought and planning. One female military observer on the U.S. Army Women's Training Assistant team to Greece reported that the "women did a lot of sitting around." Overall, the basic training program was not too well organized, and many decisions regarding training were made on a day-to-day basis.[27] For example, the first group of recruits received no training manuals but were given handouts. This has now been rectified. Other problems have also been noted. Very little in the area of tactics and field training was taught. The first two groups of recruits did not participate in any kind of overnight bivouacs. Furthermore, these women received very little sex education and no lessons at all in how to be a woman soldier. An attempt is now being made by the General Staff to correct some of these conditions.

A typical day of basic training is as follows:

0630	Reveille
0645	Breakfast
0700–0720	Preparation time
0730–0800	Physical exercise
0845–1330	Training
1300–1600	Lunch and time to relax
1600–1700	Training
1700	Supper
2130	Roll call
2200	Lights out

When the women were asked what changes they would recommend for future training classes, overwhelmingly they indicated that the basic training course should be toughened and include more discipline. The top five recommendations made were:

	ARMY	NAVY	AIR FORCE
Same as men	9.2%	4.2%	7.1%
Tougher/more discipline	35.8%	50.0%	31.4%
Better organized	15.8%	13.2%	20.0%
More weapons	5.0%	5.6%	7.1%
More night training	5.8%	6.5%	8.6%

Many of the respondents indicated that weapons training was a necessity and that this training gave them more confidence in their own ability. Most wanted to pull guard duty (83.7 percent), although they are now prohibited from doing so. In fact, several women commented that guard duty would make them feel that they were real soldiers. The women felt overall that their general training was too easy (56.1 percent) and that physical training should be much harder (61.7 percent).[28] Clearly, women expect to be trained to be soldiers and to have a "military career," as they reported; their experience must be quite frustrating and disappointing.

Other serious problems exist in the basic training programs. The commanding officers of these women's units are males, who also conduct most of the training sessions. Rarely is a woman officer allowed to teach, and in those rare cases they serve as executive officers or platoon leaders in the basic training units. Recently, a nurse (captain) asked for a lateral transfer from the Nurses Corps to the air force. As yet, no disposition of this case has resulted. In fact, a visiting advisory team (headed by a female colonel) "noted a reluctance on the part of some male officers to accept the existence of women in the military."[29] This could become a crucial issue once these women are sent to their permanent assignments. A woman who successfully completes basic training and specialty training and sees neither career advancement nor acceptance as a soldier or officer is not likely to elect to make the military a career.

Once the basic training course has been completed the recruits are sent to branch specialty schools. The number of specialty courses are limited but more are being planned. In fact, the Greek government originally specified that the first few groups of volunteers would be used for only clerical, administrative, communications, and medical duties. This, then, is reflective of the specialty courses that have been developed. The length of these specialty tracks will differ (for example, doctor's aide, twelve weeks; switchboard operator, four weeks; teletype operator, eight weeks; typist, six weeks), and the training at the specialty level is somewhat more vigorous than in the basic course, especially that training received in the medical specialties. Other courses are now being planned by all services (for instance, air force, meteorologist; army, pharmacist).

THE INTEGRATION PERIOD

Upon completion of the specialty course, assignment is to a unit located in the large cities (Athens, Thessaloniki, Patras, and so on), or if possible near the trainee's homes.[30] If they are close to home, permission is given for them to reside there. The army has now created an all-women's unit in Thessaloniki, which is commanded by a woman officer (Nurses Corps). She is not actually designated the commanding officer but carries the title of womens' adviser. As of 1981 no plans have been made to train women as officers, or to admit them into their military academies, or place them in a direct line of command. In essence, then, what exists is a male commanding officer who is responsible for both male and female personnel. However, this is where the similarity ends. The women are provided with better quarters and less harassment, and no guard duty. They do share the recreation areas and the dining hall with their male counterparts. If these conditions persist, then serious enlisted male morale problems will undoubtedly surface. The male personnel have been drafted and must serve from twenty-four to thirty-two months depending on the branch of service.

Furthermore, very little in the way of programs exists in the development of NCO training beyond that which is now in effect to provide women NCOs as a cadre for the training center. In fact, the selection process for NCOs is not based on ability—the decision is made by the training cadre of male officers. None of the women NCOs attends any specialty tracks or receives any form of leadership training. The lack of a published program for NCO training is apt to have a seriously negative impact on enlistment and retention of women in the armed forces.

THE NURSES CORPS

The women officers from the Nurses Corps who are serving as part of the training cadre are the only role models that the women enlistees have, with the exception of the very few women NCOs. These nurses are part of the elite special nurses corps that is commanded by a female lieutenant colonel. This corps was established in 1946 and then worked exclusively with the army. In 1956 a policy change authorized their assignment to the navy and air force. In 1971 the corps was unified under one directorate, consisting of about three hundred women.

As the *After Action Report* indicates, "these experienced military women have not, for the most part been effectively utilized. They were, and are, primarily utilized as 'baby sitters' for the recruits with no assigned duties or responsibilities."[31] This has created a very serious morale problem among this group. They feel that they have been degraded professionally by being transferred from responsible positions in the Nurses Corps to positions of virtually no responsibility within the Women's Training Center.

Some changes have taken place. The air force has made the nurse adviser the executive officer of the training center and given her full responsibility and authority to function. The army is utilizing two young lieutenants in the training of the women, although the two senior nurse officers are in limbo with no real responsibilities. Thus far the army and navy General Staffs have not seen fit to assign a senior nurse to serve either as commanding officer or executive officer of the women's Training Centers. If the nurses assigned to these programs become disenchanted, their attitudes could seriously and dangerously affect the future of military women in Greece.

DISCUSSION AND CONCLUSION

At the end of nearly two years of recruiting women into the Greek armed forces, a number of negative features have emerged. Women are not fully integrated into all units, and they are certainly not on an equal level with their male counterparts. And the basic ingredients necessary to institute this equality are lacking. The women who volunteer, however, expect to be treated as equals, to shoulder the same responsibilities but also enjoy the same rights. They also view their enlisting as opening upward mobility channels, which do materialize within the present setup. Promotion to a noncommissioned status is informal with little specific criteria needed to qualify. Women's promotions to officer status are nonexistent, and no plans to do so in the future are in the offing. Based on the current situation in Greece, where over 90 percent of the officers are graduates of the military academies, strong consideration should be given to opening competitive examinations to women for future admittance to the service academies. In the short run, the Greek General Staff should consider promoting women who are qualified to reserve officers status, in order to provide role models for the enlisted women.

It would appear that if this separateness trend persists, as it has since the initial induction of women, then the logical conclusion might lead to a separate women's service. This, in the author's opinion, would be regrettable. If women are to be fully accepted into the armed forces of Greece, they must be an integral part and not a separate service. They should receive the same training, and, as much as possible, be required to perform the same duties as their male peers and be held equally responsible for their conduct.

The present situation of women recruits in the Greek armed forces representing a marginal and partial acceptance is the least conducive to the breaking down of sex role stereotypes and prejudice. On the contrary, it underlines women's inferior position and their fitness for only auxiliary, "feminine" services and jobs rather than the core, military roles and tasks. Under the present conditions, men's attitudes can be expected to be quite negative and to remain negative since the women lack the institutional basis to reach equality and to be respected as equals. Clearly, the Greek women want to be full-fledged soldiers and officers and the history of Greek women indicates that they can be effective and brave soldiers and officers. If the present situation is continued, women cannot be expected to enlist in great numbers and those enlisted will not stay. Only equality of men and women in the military can help meet the defense needs of Greece.

NOTES

1. Jean Lipman-Blumen, "Role De-Differentiation as a System Response to Crisis: Occupational and Political Roles of Women," *Sociological Inquiry* 43, no. 1 (April 1973); and Constantina Safilios-Rothschild, "The Social Setting of the Modern Greek Family," *The Dynamics of the Modern Greek Family* (Athens: National Centre of Social Research, 1982).

2. Dina Takari, *The Social and Occupational Position of Today's Woman,* privately printed (Athens; 1978) (published in Greek), pp. 33–35.

3. Iris Avthi-Kalkani, *The Professionally Working Greek Woman* (published in Greek) (Athens: Papazissi, 1948) pp. 16–18.

4. *Greater Greek Encyclopedia,* vol. 16, 2nd ed. (Athens: Phoenix, 1963) pp. 785, 786.

5. *The Greek Merchant Marine (1453–1850)* (Athens: National Bank of Greece, 1972), pp. 102, 409.

6. *Statistical Yearbook of Greece* (Athens: National Statistical Service of Greece, 1928); and *Statistical Yearbook of Greece* (Athens: National Statistical Service of Greece, 1968).

7. Greece in 1946 established an Army Nurse Corps, and in 1956 the nurse corps was expanded to include the navy and air force. It was in 1971 that the nurse corps was unified under one directorate headed by a female lieutenant colonel.

8. *La femme grécque au combat* (Athens: a Greek Monograph privately printed, 1975); Ed Psimenou and Pip Ziteithou, *Greek Women: World War II, 1940–1944*, mentioned in Takari, *The Social and Occupational Position of Today's Woman* pp. 34–35.

9. Psimenou and Ziteithou.

10. Ibid.

11. *La femme grécque.*

12. Avthi-Kalkani, *Professionally Working Greek Woman,* pp. 37–40; and Safilios-Rothschild, "The Social Setting of the Modern Family."

13. *Statistical Yearbook of Greece* (Athens: National Statistical Service of Greece, 1972), Table V: 1, p. 101.

14. Ibid., Table V: 9, pp. 112–14; and Constantina Safilios-Rothschild, "A Cross-Cultural Study of Women's Marital, Educational, and Occupational Option," *Acta Sociologica* 14, no. 1 (May 1969): 23–37.

15. M. Livi-Bacci and H. M. Hagmann, *Report on the Demographic and Social Pattern of Migrants in Europe, Especially with Regard to International Migrations* (Strasbourg, France: Council of Europe, 2nd European Demographic Conference, August 31–September 2, 1971).

16. Loukia Moussoueou, *The Modern Greek Woman* (published in Greek); (Athens: Office of Inter-Church Aid to the World Council of Churches, 1976) and Takari, *The Social and Occupational Position of Today's Woman,* pp. 62, 75.

17. The age limit may be raised to fifty years of age in cases where women possess special skills that are needed.

18.   Data provided by the defense and military attaché, Embassy of Greece in a letter to J. Brown, dated January 21, 1980.

19. Enlisted men are conscripted into the Greek armed forces to serve for twenty-seven months. Also officer recruitment has declined in the last five years. See James Brown "Greek Civil-Military Relations: A Different Pattern," *Armed Forces and Society* 6, no. 3 (Spring 1980): pp. 389–414.

20. "Problems of Drafting," *Contemporary Woman* 10 (September–October 1979): 44–46.

21. Constantina Safilios-Rothschild, "The Options of Greek Men and Women," *Sociological Focus* 5, no. 2 (1972): 71–83.

22. The first class of volunteers consisted of 220 women (110 army, 55 navy, and 55 air force). The second class was somewhat larger numbering 322 women (144 army, 28 navy, and 150 air force).

23. Defense and military attaché's letter dated January 21, 1980.

24. The combat arms in the Greek armed forces are defined as follows: army— infantry, armor, artillery, engineers; navy—ship assignments: air force—fighter squadrons.

25. Brown, "Greek Civil-Military Relations: A Different Pattern."

26. The women have special housing facilities that are cleaner and more spacious than their male counterparts'. Each uniform is individually tailored. The fatigue uniform was identical to that of the male uniform and did cause some problems for

the women wearing them. The army training center is at Goudi, the navy's is at Skaramangas, and the air force's at Agios Andreas.

27. Women who excelled in basic training did not receive any kind of incentive recognition.

28. *MTT Greece: After Action Report,* U.S. Department of Defense 21 (May 1979): 8, 9.

29. Ibid., p. 6.

30. Most were assigned by the army in the Athens area. A women's unit was created by the army in Thessaloniki. The navy will assign most of them at Skaramangas (near Pireaus) and the air force will assign their women at Ellinikon Airport, Athens.

31. These women are not saluted by their male peers, but do receive the rank and pay of their male counterparts. *MTT Greece: After Action Report,* p. 4.

9 | JAPAN: CAUTIOUS UTILIZATION

Karl L. Wiegand

INTRODUCTION

That Japan can be included in a book that surveys the use of women in the military establishments of a variety of countries indicates the strides women have made in that stereotypically male-dominated society. Women have occupied positions other than nurses in the Japanese Self-Defense Forces (JSDF) only since 1967. At no time before 1967 have Japanese women been trained to replace men in any military functions. They have been conscripted for war work and fire-fighting brigades, and they have nursed soldiers at home and, to some extent, overseas. Unlike the case of many of our Western women, however, they have never been trained in administrative and service specialties to replace or supplement soliders either at home or abroad. Such use of women would have been almost unthinkable. Reischauer ascribes the genesis of this attitude as follows:

Confucian philosophy and the long feudal experience combined to restrict the freedom of women and force them into complete subordination to men. Women, who in the age of swordsmanship were obviously less capable of fighting than men, were gradually pushed out of the feudal structure and into a peripheral and sup-plementary role to men. Confucianism, which was the product of a patriarchal and strongly male-dominated society in China, saw women as important for bearing children and perpetuating the family more than as helpmates or objects of love. Confucianism tended to be puritanical, considering romatic love to be weakness and sex as merely a mechanism for maintaining family continuity.[1]

While the Second World War was not an occasion for the utilization of women in the Japanese military establishment, it did create conditions

The research for this report was partially funded by a grant from the Inter-University Seminar on Armed Forces and Society. Their support is gratefully acknowledged.

179

that were to undermine the old order and pave the way for the emancipation of women. It was in the civilian economy that this occurred.

The shortage of manpower during the period made it imperative for women to take over the jobs hitherto performed by men and they carried out the task quite adequately, providing that there should be no discrimination in whatever form on the grounds of sex.[2]

After the war the new constitution of Japan was promulgated. Article 14 of that constitution states that: "All of the people are equal under the law and there shall be no discrimination in political, economic or social relations because of race, creed, sex, social status or family origin."

In the spirit of the new freedoms supported by that constitution women have progressively broadened their opportunities in Japanese society. It is in the context of this general societal advancement that women's roles in the military should be viewed. Thus, in the following sections, a brief survey of women's activities in Japanese society will be given before their work in the military establishment is addressed. A sketch of the evolution of Japan's postwar military organization will also be given.

There is practically no English language literature dealing with women in Japan or women in the Self-Defense Forces. I obtained data about this topic during interviews with members of Japan's prime minister's office, the Ministry of Labor and the Defense Agency in October 1979. Other general comments are based upon personal observations and discussions during the three and one-half years I served in Tokyo and visited Japanese military bases as the United States air attaché at the U.S. Embassy, 1974 to 1977.

WOMEN IN POSTWAR JAPAN

As a result of the quality granted to women by the constitution the Election Law of Japan was revised to permit women twenty years old and older to vote. On April 10, 1946, they exercised that right for the first time and thus launched themselves into the political life of Japan.

The extent to which Japanese women have taken advantage of their postwar opportunity to enter the political life of Japan has shown a consistent increase in terms of voting rate. Between 1946 and 1977 they progressed from a voting rate lower than that of males by 11 percentage points to a rate that exceeded the male rate by about 1.5 percentage points. During the same period, however, the number of women elected to the House of Representatives decreased while the number of members of the House increased from 466 in 1946 to 511 in 1976. In the House of Councillors the number of women elected has fluctuated between 11 and 19 while the number of members of that body has remained constant at 252.

The percentage of women in local public bodies (Prefectural Assemblies, Municipal Assemblies and Town/Village Assemblies) is somewhat similar to their representation in the national legislature (the Diet), all ranging between one-half and one and one-half percent. Generally, there is an increase in the percent of women to be found in public bodies as the size of the areas represented by the body increases. At the same time there has been no dramatic increase in the participation rate of women in these bodies between 1946 and 1977.

While equality of the sexes has not resulted in dramatic numbers of women entering political bodies, there has been a great increase in the percent of women participating in senior high school and college education. The percent of girls entering senior high school has more than doubled between 1950 and 1977, at first lagging behind boys but finally surpassing them. A similar relationship can be found in the percent of senior high school graduates who enter higher education.

Occupations that have shown major gains of women between 1960 and 1975 are those that would naturally absorb the greater numbers of educated young women, namely, teachers, pharmacists, social workers, and accounting clerks. There has been, however, no sign of significant inroads into traditionally male endeavors, such as, technicians, physicians, lawyers, and managers.

It is particularly revealing to note the number of female applicants accepted for career government positions. These are truly government professionals who, if they stay in their respective ministries, will be the top managing bureaucrats of the future. The number of women taken into the thirty-three ministries and major offices of the government of Japan (excluding the Defense Agency) is only 287 in the eleven-year period from 1968 through 1978. While this is a relatively small number, these women represent a commitment on the part of the government to provide greater career opportunities for women.

There may be a rather large number of women in the labor force and the constitution may declare equality of the sexes in Japan, but, on the average, women earn only about half as much as men. This discrepancy is normally explained by stressing that women are predominantly in unskilled, noncareer jobs, and pay is largely based on longevity. Since men work longer than women, men will naturally earn more than women on the average. This may be a valid explanation but it only illustrates the vast gulf that exists between the *de facto* working worlds of men and women in Japan.

There are many prominent, successful women in Japan. They can be found in government, in business (principally merchandising and food marketing) and in higher education; however, they stand out for their uniqueness in this male-oriented society. The government is aware of the slow progress made by women and supports the movement to provide more opportunity for Japanese women. By proclamation the prime minister launched the International Women's Year in Japan in 1975. A "Resolution on the Enhancement of the Social Status of Women in the International Women's Year" was adopted by both houses of Japan's Diet in 1975 on the initiative of women representatives. A "Government Headquarters for the Planning and Promoting of Policies Relating to Women" was established in the prime minister's office. It is headed by the prime minister and is composed of representatives of the deputy ministers and four civilian advisers, all of whom are women. The people within the headquarters wrote a National Plan of Action in January 1977 based on the needs and problems unique to Japanese women. This plan, in consonance with the United Nations Decade for Women, provides a ten-year program to improve the legal status of women, to achieve increased participation of women in political, economic, social and cultural activities, to improve the consideration of women's health, to ensure economic stability for the aged, and to promote international cooperation in women's affairs.

This summary of the activities of women in the postwar era is meant to provide a background for viewing their incorporation into military service. Before the data on that topic are presented, however, another setting-of-the-stage is needed. The establishment of a military organization in postwar Japan will be reviewed.[3]

JAPAN'S DEFENSE FORCES SINCE WORLD WAR II

During the period between the promulgation of Japan's postwar constitution and the Korean War all official pronouncements about the possession of military forces were dominated by Article 9 of that consitution. War and the threat or use of force as a means of settling international disputes and the maintenance of land, sea, and air forces for such purposes were renounced. With the outbreak of the Korean War, however, a renewed concern for Japan's internal security was awakened in the Japanese government, partly at the insistence of the U.S. occupation government, and a National Police Reserve was formed in 1952. After the U.S.–Japan Peace Treaty was signed the Defense Agency Establishment Law and the Self Defense Forces Law were promulgated, formally creating a Defense Agency (headed by a civilian minister of state called director general) that controlled and administered three Self-Defense Forces— ground, maritime, and air. The mission of these forces, according to the 1954 laws, was to defend Japan against direct and indirect aggression, and, when necessary, to maintain public order. This was the government's first official acknowledgment of its responsibility for Japan's external defense.

In the years following the establishment of the Defense Agency and the Self-Defense Forces the size of these forces has grown in response to the provisions of a new U.S.–Japan Mutual Security Treaty (1960) and a succession of defense build-up plans and white papers. Table 9.1 shows the growth in the authorized and actual strength of the Self-Defense Forces over the years. Throughout these documents two basic principles prevail: reliance upon the U.S.–Japan Mutual Security Treaty for Japan's regional defense; and Japan's own responsibility for defense of its land.[4]

Table 9.1

Strength of Japanese Self-Defense Forces (Ground, Maritime, and Air): 1954–1979 (Thousands)

YEAR	AUTHORIZED	ACTUAL	REMARKS
1954	152	146	Self-Defense Forces established
1955	180	178	
1956	197	188	
1957	214	211	All U.S. ground combat troops withdrawn
1958	222	214	1st Build-up Plan
1959	231	215	
1960	231	206	Security Treaty Revised
1961	242	209	
1962	244	216	2nd Build-up Plan
1963	244	213	
1964	246	216	
1965	246	226	
1966	246	227	
1967	250	231	3rd Build-up Plan
1968	250	235	
1969	258	236	
1970	259	236	
1971	259	234	
1972	259	234	4th Build-up Plan
1973	266	233	
1974	266	237	
1975	266	238	
1976	266	236	
1977	268	240	
1978	268	239	
1979	268	238	

SOURCE: Defense White Papers and Personnel Bureau, Japan Defense Agency.

WOMEN IN JAPAN'S SELF-DEFENSE FORCES

As early as 1952, after establishment of the National Police Reserve, nurses were recruited into the ground component. Later, as hospital units were formed, the number of nurses was increased, and in 1958 the training of nurses within the Ground Self-Defense Force began. To meet the need, however, accredited nurses were still recruited from outside the force.

Accompanying Japan's economic success in the 1960s was a decrease in the number of volunteers for military service and in 1967 Defense Agency leaders decided to begin recruiting women for the Ground Self-Defense Force. In 1974 the Maritime Self-Defense Force and the Air Self-Defense Force also began recruiting women. Table 9.2 shows the officer, enlisted, and medical women strength for males and females in the Self-Defense Forces for the period 1967 through 1979. By 1979 the total number of women had reached nearly three thousand or 1.24 percent of the total force.

Table 9.2

Distribution of Men and Women in the Japanese Self-Defense Forces: 1967–1979

| YEAR | OFFICER & WARRANT OFFICER | | NCO & ENLISTED | | MEDICAL WOMEN | | TOTAL | |
	Male	Female	Male	Female	Nurse	Other	Male	Female
1967	33,006	14	197,874	0	250	294	230,880	558
1968	33,395	14	200,883	77	260	306	234,278	657
1969	33,606	13	201,039	344	253	309	234,645	919
1970	34,608	19	200,131	576	247	300	234,739	1142
1971	35,736	16	197,249	753	244	303	232,985	1316
1972	36,918	29	194,366	986	245	359	231,284	1619
1973	38,116	40	193,113	1157	252	402	231,229	1851
1974	39,317	59	195,717	1334	246	457	235,034	2096
1975	40,671	72	194,629	1802	250	496	235,300	2620
1976	41,446	89	191,820	1923	261	522	233,266	2729
1977	41,676	111	195,678	1702	262	553	237,354	2628
1978	41,359	131	194,878	1974	282	569	236,237	2956
1979	40,624	123	194,909	1906	315	588	235,533	2932

SOURCE: Personnel Bureau, Japan Defense Agency.

Of particular interest is the selectivity that the Self-Defense Force can practice in recruiting women. Table 9.3 shows the ratio of applicants to acceptees for the force between 1968 and 1978. The low ratio for men remains rather constant throughout the period while the ratio for women is consistently higher than that for men and much more variable.

Table 9.3

Ratio of Applicants to Acceptees in the Japanese Self-Defense Forces: 1968–1978

YEAR	OFFICER		ENLISTED		NURSES
	Men	Women	Men	Women	
1968	N/A	N/A	1.9	12.3	25.9
1969	N/A	N/A	1.8	8.4	19.8
1970	N/A	N/A	1.9	6.9	16.1
1971	N/A	N/A	2.1	5.5	8.8
1972	7.3	4.0	2.1	5.5	9.6
1973	5.8	2.7	2.2	3.2	7.2
1974	6.4	3.8	2.3	3.0	7.9
1975	8.3	2.8	2.4	5.2	14.1
1976	10.5	7.7	2.3	7.0	18.1
1977	12.5	13.0	2.0	8.6	21.5
1978	15.0	21.3	2.2	9.5	26.3

SOURCE: Personnel Bureau, Japan Defense Agency.

Although there is an authorized strength for the total Self-Defense Force, as the data of Table 9.1 indicate, this authorized strength has never been attained because of budgetary limitations. Within the total authorized strength there is no "authorized" strength for women. The number to be recruited is adjusted from year to year to adapt to projected shortfalls in the number of men to be recruited.

The mental, physical, and educational standards for women serving in the force are high. Recruits must be between the ages of eighteen and twenty-five and when the number of volunteers is high only high school graduates are selected. NCO candidates must be at least junior college graduates, and officers must be university graduates. They serve two or three years as a minimum.

Basic training for ground force women lasts four months and includes weapons training with the rifle. Ground force officers have stressed to me that the weapons training that women receive is for familiarization only. There is no intent to use women in combat; however, they are trained to defend themselves.

After basic training ground, maritime, and air women are trained for and used in the following areas:

Administration	Aircraft Engine
Personnel Management	Maintenance
Languages	Communication
Archives	Electronic Techniques
Counseling	Intelligence
Supply and Accounting	Photography
Aircraft Fuselage	Map Reading
Maintenance	Computers
Aircraft Electronic Technique	Physical Exercise
Aircraft Weapons	Meteorology
Maintenance	

Self-Defense Force women are permitted to marry and have children while remaining on active duty (maternity leave is limited to six weeks before the birth and six weeks after). Marriage and child rearing has been acknowledged as something of a problem for the force; however, personnel policies try to accommodate the needs of married women. Husbands and wives are generally stationed together (this accommodation is not too difficult in a country that is small and has no forces stationed overseas). Women are stationed only at the largest installations. The Japanese assert that the housing required for women cost about three times that for men and that it is, therefore, only cost effective to station the women in relatively large numbers at the larger bases. The women are subject to the same code of discipline as men and the rates of pay for both are equal for equivalent ranks.

DISCUSSION

The social change that takes place to give women freedom and opportunity can receive its impetus from factors both external and internal to the society and the institutions within the society. The case of Japan can be characterized as an example of external impetus being nearly the sole factor giving rise to this change. The postwar constitution with its recognition of the rights of women was externally formulated by the occupation authority and "accepted" by the government of Japan. Under the aegis of that constitution a relatively modest but consistent movement to achieve equality of opportunity for women within Japan's social institutions has been active.

The most recent external factor to provide impetus to the women's movement in Japan was the Women's Year and the United Nations' effort to raise the consciousness of women to their rights and opportunities throughout the world. In private conversations members of the prime minister's office and the Labor Ministry have admitted to me that the women's movement in Japan is principally a top-down effort. The top echelons of government are pushing for greater opportunity for women because they want Japan to be viewed as a progressive modern nation among the industrialized countries of the world. Thus, women's emancipation in Japan has been achieved principally by constitutional proviso and by international pressure, not by an aggressive internal pressure from organized women's groups fighting for that emancipation.

Just as the emancipation of women was an externally imposed accomplishment in Japan, the reinstitution of a military establishment was the result of external pressure. There was much public opposition to this establishment at its beginning and there is little enthusiastic support for it today. At best it can be said that the Japanese appreciate the need for a defense force and tolerate its existence in today's troubled international environment.

Factors external to the military establishment (but within the Japanese economy) forced its leaders to consider and finally to decide to put women in uniform. The failure to get enough male volunteers coupled to some extent with the general movement to give women greater opportunity forced the military to open its rolls to women. The success of that decision is acknowledged by younger Japanese officers and plans exist for increasing the number of women in the forces over the next few years.

There are other more remote factors that may be operating to influence women's opportunities in Japan's defense forces. Just as Japan is a highly technological society so is its military. This increased technology allows little excuse to exclude women from military service on the basis of their frailty. Another factor has been the difficulty of the Japanese to identify a real military threat to their nation. In the absence of an imminent threat the Japanese military may feel that they can accept women into that most sacrosanct of Japanese male-dominated institutions.

Regardless of the source of the impetus to open the defense force to women, there is evidence that the military is increasingly being viewed by women as an acceptable alternative when they seek job opportunities. The data in Tables 9.1 and 9.2 show that from 1975 the size of the defense force remained rather stable and the number of women in the force varied by only a few hundred. On the other hand the ratio of applicants to acceptees rose from 2.8 to 21.3 for officers, 5.2 to 9.5 for enlisted ranks, and 14.1 to 26.3 for nurses. It appears that the word is getting out to the increasing number of women completing high school and college that military service is acceptable employment.

Given the long history of male dominance of the governmental and military institutions of Japan (family life is another story) it is natural to wonder how males tolerate management by women. My interviews with the highest ranking women in both the governmental and military services reveal that the Japanese have accommodated to women managers in a typically Japanese way. It makes no difference what the sex of the incumbent of a position is, the incumbent receives the respect due the position. This is not to say that all men have accepted women as equals, but it does establish the general tone of the feeling toward women as they gradually work their way up the grade structures of the civil and military institutions.

Although the infusion of women into the military in the short span of barely a decade represents a significant accomplishment in this country whose history spans centuries of male dominance, there has been no recognition of this accomplishment by the principal protagonists for women's opportunity in the government. Not a single official nonmilitary publication reports on or recognizes these women. This was not a purposeful exclusion. It was simply an oversight. As one female government official remarked to me, "We never thought of them." Nevertheless, women in the Self-Defense Force have achieved equality of opportunity for training, for pay, and for advancement (to the grade of lieutenant colonel or commander). They are being employed in an increasingly wide range of jobs, and those jobs are becoming increasingly attractive to high school and college graduates. They have come to be accepted and valued within the military establishment.[5]

NOTES

1. E. O. Reischauer, *The Japanese* (Tokyo: Charles E. Tuttle Co., 1978), p. 205.

2. *The Status of Women in Japan* (Tokyo: Women and Young Worker's Bureau, Ministry of Labor, 1979), p. 1.

3. The material in this section is derived from *Status of Women in Japan*.

4. This summary is drawn mainly from the official Japanese Defense White papers issued in 1970, 1976, 1977, and 1978; Martin E. Weinstein, *Japan's Postwar Defense Policy, 1947–1968* (New York: Columbia University Press, 1971); and Makoto Momoi, "Basic Trends in Japanese Security Policies," in Robert A. Scalapino, ed., *The Foreign Policy of Modern Japan* (Berkeley: University of California Press, 1977).

5. I wish to thank the many members of the Japan Defense Agency and the Embassy of Japan in Washington for their assistance in accumulating the data supporting the opinions reflected in this and the preceding section of this report. Similar gratitude is due selected members of the prime minister of Japan's office and the Ministry of Labor.

10 | DENMARK: THE SMALL NATO NATION

Henning Sorensen

The utilization of women in the Danish armed forces reflects the trends in most North Atlantic Treaty Organization (NATO) countries toward both greater use of women and toward a volunteer rather than a conscript force. The historical background in Denmark is different, however, from that of the English-speaking NATO nations and the Netherlands and France, in that Denmark did not use women during World War II.

Historically, the Danish armed forces have been composed of male conscripts; women have not been subject to conscription. A role for women in the Danish forces began in World War II when women were active in the resistance movement; since then, the role of women has grown.[1] In 1946 Home Guard Associations, composed of men and women, were founded as private, volunteer organizations. In 1948 these private organizations were disbanded and reorganized as the established, official Home Guard Corps under the Department of Defense. Since that time the duties of the women members of the Home Guard have become progressively more military.

Women were first enlisted in the regular Danish armed forces in 1972; Denmark was the first NATO country, of those that did not have women in their military during World War II, to do so. In the following year, a decision was made to have the standing army composed entirely of volunteers. The standing force was to be largely devoted to combat assignments, which has restricted the utilization of women, since women cannot, by law, be assigned to units that have combat as their primary task. Compulsory national service was retained, for men only, but the term of service was reduced to only nine months. After completion of their com-

Sponsored by the U.S. Army Research Institute for the Behavioral and Social Sciences. The views and conclusions contained in this document are those of the author and do not necessarily represent those of the sponsor or the U.S. Government.

pulsory service, the conscripts enter the mobilization force, which has few women, in part because of its origin.

THE RESISTANCE MOVEMENT

Women played an active part in the Danish resistance movements. They were involved in illegal information activity, such as publishing and distributing illegal pamphlets and books; in sabotage activities; in receiving weapons dropped by the British Royal Air Force; in performing courier services; and in providing transportation, which helped more than six thousand Jews to escape. The only resistance activity in which women were not involved was membership in military groups.[2] Women seldom headed a resistance group; they served as secretaries or couriers for resistance leaders.[3]

Exact figures for the number of persons, men or women, in the Danish Underground Force is unknown, as the resistance movement was illegal.[4] Nevertheless, it is possible to estimate the number of women in the military units of the resistance movement. The total number of active freedom fighters during the five years of occupation has been estimated to be ten thousand people.[5] From this total number, two methods can be used to estimate the number of women. First, I have counted the number of Danish men and women registered in the indexes of books on the resistance movement.[6] According to this procedure, the resistance movement consisted of between 1 percent and 7 percent women. Second, I have compared female to male prisoners.[7] Of six thousand Danes deported to German concentration camps and prisons, sixty were women interned at Ravensbrück and Stutthof. In the Danish Concentration camp at Froslev, five thousand persons were prisoners, of whom about 150 were women.[8] Accordingly, 10 percent of the deported Danes and 3 percent of those interned were women. If these figures reflect the numbers of women in the resistance movement, between one hundred and seven hundred women were active. It must be admitted that more than half of the number of women were interned for reasons other than being an active resistance partisan, but this is also true of the male prisoners.[9]

THE WOMEN'S HOME GUARD

The Danish Home Guard is composed of both men and women who are organized separately. It is a voluntary, civilian organization, and the training and activities of the members are conducted on weekends and in the evenings.

The foundations of the Women's Home Guard were laid in 1946 with the establishment of the private, volunteer Women's Home Guard Associations, the backbone of which were members of the resistance movement and women who had fled to Sweden and organized themselves in the Danish Brigade. In 1948 the private male and female Home Guard Associations were dissolved by the Home Guard Act, which stated that all private defense contributions should be organized in the established official Home Guard Corps under the Department of Defense. The Women's Home Guard is organized into three sections: the Women's Army Home Guard, Danmarks Lottekorps, DLK (named "Lotte" following a Scandinavian tradition); the Women's Naval Home Guard, Kvindeligt Marinekorps, KMK; and the Women's Air Force Home Guard, Kvindeligt Flyvekorps, KFK.[10]

The number of women enlisted in the home guard has fluctuated over time. A period of growth from its foundation in 1946 was followed by relative stagnation between 1963 and 1975. The percentage of women has, however, steadily increased in relation to the number of men enlisted in the home guard (see Table 10.1).

Table 10.1

Number of Women and Men in the Danish Home Guard: 1957–1981

	1957	1967	1979	1981: (APRIL)
Men	55,100	60,700	62,200*	63,050*
Women	8,400	8,840	10,700	10,745
Total	63,500	69,540	72,900	73,795
Women as % of men	15	14	17	17

SOURCE: Elaborated from Søren Wissum and Steen Borup-Nielsen, "Level of Manpower, The Danish Home Guard." Paper, 1975; and P. A. Heegaard-Poulsen, "Hjemmevaernet" [The Home Guard], (Copenhagen, 1978) and an interview with Lieutenant Colonel Gurli Vidø of The Women's Navy Home Guard Corps and Colonel Bodil Westerholm of The Women's Army Home Guard Corps (January 1980).

*This figure includes the 1,500 women of the Ground Observer Corps at the end of 1979 and the 1,725 women in April 1981.

The percentage of female officers to female enlisted personnel and NCOs differs for each of the three services. The officer rate of the Women's Army Home Guard is decreasing, from 7 percent in 1957 to 3 percent in 1981, a reduction of more than 50 percent. The Women's Naval Home Guard has also experienced drastic reduction in percentage of officers, from 10 percent in 1957 to 6 percent in 1981. This reduction in the number of officers resulted from a reorganization of these two services to conform to the organizational pattern of the male Home Guard Corps. The percentage of officers in the Women's Air Force Home Guard has remained fairly constant, 10 percent in 1957, 11 percent in 1967, and 12 percent in 1981 (see Table 10.2). The rate for the male home guard units has been constant at 6 percent.

Members of the Women's Home Guard may be designated to the armed forces. This designation of women helps to meet the needs of the armed

Table 10.2

Number of Women in the Women's Home Guard by Rank: 1957–1981

	DLK (ARMY)	KMK (NAVY)	KFK (AIR F)	GROUND OBSERVER CORPS	TOTAL
1957:					
Enlisted	5,420	750	695		6,865
NCO	833	73	52		960
Officer	437	84	69		580
Officer rate	7%	10%	10%		(8,405)
1967:					
Enlisted	5,456	839	1,069		7,364
NCO	783	85	161		929
Officer	347	61	141		549
Officer rate	5%	6%	11%		(8,840)
1979:					
Enlisted	6,400	1,250	1,250	(1,500)	8,900
NCO*	850	200	250		1,300
Officer*	250	50	200		500
Officer rate	3%	3%	12%		(10,700)
1981 (April)					
Enlisted	6,456	1,168	1,323	(1725)	10,672
NCO	889	168	227		1,284
Officer	239	83	192		514
Officer rate	3%	6%	12%		(12,470)
Designation rate	15%	50%	95%		(2,770)

SOURCE: Elaborated from Søren Wissum and Steen Borup-Nielsen, "Level of Manpower, The Danish Home Guard," Paper, 1975.

* The majority of officers and NCOs in the home guard are men and women holding a military rank beside their civilian job. For instance, of the five hundred officers in 1979 only about thirty had full-time employment in the home guard as officers.

forces for personnel. The Women's Home Guard constitutes an important base of resources for the armed forces. Without this system of designation from the Home Guard Corps, the regular Danish forces would need to enlist many more women. Members of the Women's Home Guard decide for themselves whether to serve in the home guard or to be designated to the armed forces. This recruitment procedure cuts down on the armed forces budget, an important consideration given the Danes' reluctance to increase the budget for the armed forces. The home guard enjoys substantial support from political leaders who are willing to finance the increased volunteer accessions to the guard.

The principles of performance of women in the Women's Home Guard are stated in the "Home Guard Regulations nr. 270–10, March 1978" and correspond to the female functions in the armed forces. Within this framework, the functions of women designated from the Home Guard to the armed forces are determined by the armed forces unit commander (see Table 10.3).

Table 10.3

Types of Functions for Women in the Women's Home Guard and the Armed Forces: 1946 and 1972

	1946—WOMEN'S HOME GUARD			1972—THE ARMED FORCES		
	Army	Navy	Air Force	Army	Navy	Air Force
Military Production (radio-equipment)	X	X				
Administrative Staff Communication	X	X	X	X	X	X
Medicine, Medical Care, Nursery	X	X	X		X	
NBC-Service*	X	X	X			
Catering	X	X	X			
Education, Weapon Instructors				X	X	X
Transport	X	X	X	X		
Radio Telephony, Teleprinter			X	X	X	
Control of Shipping, Airplanes (Weather Service)		X	X	X	X	X
Logistic		X				X

SOURCE: Based on Jørgen Braemer, "An Introduction to Enlisted Women in the Danish Armed Forces." Paper presented at the Thirteenth International Symposium of Applied Psychology, Lahr, Germany, April 1977.

* Nuclear, biological, and chemical warfare service.

The designation of members of the Women's Home Guard to the armed forces has resulted in the higher officer rate of the Air Force Women's Home Guard. Air force officers have evaluated the importance of the functions of the Air Force Women's Home Guard Corps so highly that their positions have been classified as equivalent to officer rank.

The overall trend has been for the three Women's Home Guard Corps to become oriented more toward military tasks. This evaluation can be supported by the high designation rate, especially for the Air Force Women's Home Guard. Moreover, it can be found in the increased integration of the Women's Army and Navy Home Guard with the male home guard and consequently with more direct military tasks. Furthermore, the proclaimed aims of the Army Women's Home Guard have changed. In 1946 three functions were stated: first, social and humanitarian work; second, assistance in emergency and catastrophe situations; and third, military support to the armed forces. The Civil Defense Act of 1949 excluded the civil emergency assistance function, and the social and humanitarian efforts have decreased over time, leaving military support to the armed forces as the central task. In 1951 the minister of defense became the commander of the home guard.

On the other hand, the integration of the Women's Army and Navy Home Guard with the male home guard pattern reduced the actual number of female officers with military assignments since the number of officer slots was reduced. Moreover, the number of Army Women's Home Guard personnel designated to the armed forces has been reduced drastically because the army is not organized operationally toward combat roles, which are closed to women. This means fewer educational and designational possibilities.

WOMEN IN THE ARMED FORCES

The legislative basis for employing women in the armed forces is an act governing military personnel of the armed forces, which was passed in 1962 and renewed by the act of 1969. This legislative provision was not exploited until 1971 when the Deparment of Defense laid down further regulations governing enlistment and employment of women in the armed forces. Table 10.4 shows the growth in the number of women in the Danish armed forces. Related to the total stength of the regular forces, women were 1.4 percent in 1972 and 1.9 percent in 1981.

As a main principle, enlisted women have the same obligations and conditions as corresponding male personnel. This principle applies to enlistment education, employment, training, payment, and the like. There are, however, certain limitations to this principle explained in part by the fact that women, unlike men, are not subject to compulsory national service or, as conscientious objectors, to service in the unarmed civil defense. As a consequence, the Department of Defense has applied to the Equal Position Council for a dispensation from the Equal Treatment Act passed in 1978, in order to maintain the status quo.[11] The Equal Position Council, waiting for further information, has not made a decision.

In Denmark the armed forces do not classify jobs in the same way as the U.S. armed forces. In principle, all jobs are open to men and women on an equal basis according to the "Law nr. 174 of May 16, 1962," which was renewed in 1971. The only restriction is that women will normally not serve in military units with specific combat tasks or, formulated more officially, "Female military personnel will not be used in positions which imply the possibility of direct utilization in combat activities."[12]

In practice, two modifications can be noticed. Women can be assigned to military units with mainly combat tasks, but not to combat positions. However, women in these situations serve rather close to the military and combat functions. Another exception to the overall restriction of women from combat functions is an attack upon a unit or barracks with female personnel. In this situation, it is generally accepted that the women would participate directly in the fighting.

A final decision as to when, how, and in what numbers women should be functioning in the armed forces has not been made. The years since the introduction of women in 1972 are regarded as a period of gaining experience. Therefore, the exact and specific listing of which jobs women may perform does not exist as in the United States.[13] The overall principle is, however, that women enlist and are educated and placed (except for the above-mentioned limitations) under the same rules as men (see Table 10.3)

Female soldiers of the three services, army, navy, and air force, are employed in more varied functions than their female colleagues in the Women's Home Guard. Two main functions seem, however, common for all female personnel of the three services: staff and headquarters service and work as instructors for both men and women. This staff service for the women may, to some extent, cause inconvenience for the job rotation of the men.

Since women have been accepted into the armed forces, they have successively been promoted. In 1972 there were no women officers, in 1981 the number of female officers, including officer-cadets, was sixteen (see Table 10.4). There are more female officers relative to other female enlisted personnel (3 percent) than male officers to male personnel, draftees, enlisted, NCOs (1.7 percent). The higher rate of female officers does not reflect equality in elite positions, however. On the contrary, the highest rank for a female officer is lieutenant.

The enlistment of women in 1972 was, of course, a shift toward a new employment policy of the armed forces. But as far as I see, the roles and

Table 10.4

Development in the Number and Rank of Women in Military Units in the Armed Forces: 1972–1981*

	ARMY	AIR FORCE	NAVY	TOTAL
(1972–1974 Oct.)				
Enlisted	94	94	25	213
NCO	12	1	0	13
Officer	0	0	0	0
1977 April				
Enlisted	276	118	30	424
NCO	28	7	5	40
Officer	0	0	0	0
*1979 May***				
Enlisted	176	102	26	304
NCO	42	8	3	53
Officer: B***	6	2	1	9
A	4	1	1	6
1981 (March)				
Enlisted	403	171	28	602
NCO	45	12	5	62
Officer: B***	4	2	1	7
A	8	1	0	9

* Including officer cadets.

** Excluding professional volunteers, named "konstabler."

*** A-branch officers (commissioned officers) have an academic training, including the ranks from first lieutenant to general/admiral. B-branch officers (NCO) have a shorter training and have tasks especially in relation to the company. They have ranks from second lieutenant to major.

functions of women have not changed greatly. The increasing numbers of women in Denmark are employed mostly in traditional female positions as clerks and communicators, as they are in the United States.[14] A real change in the function of women in the armed forces would be their designation to combat units.[15]

ATTITUDES TOWARD WOMEN IN THE ARMED FORCES

Repeated surveys show that three-quarters of the Danish population believes that it is "desirable that we have the armed forces."[16] These data have been collected in 1976 and 1977, some years after the introduction of female soldiers, but the rate of about 75 percent has, however, been constant for many years with or without women in the armed forces.[17]

One research study on the attitudes toward female soldiers has been conducted.[18] A representative portion of the personnel in seven military units in the army and the air force where women were serving were interviewed to illuminate some consequences for leadership and cooperation stemming from women's employment. In November and December 1974, 188 men (111 enlisted, 45 NCOs, 32 officers) and 71 women (67 enlisted and 4 NCOs) were interviewed. The results of the research showed that no change in rules of leadership or cooperation were needed.[19] Moreover, a key point in explaining different attitudes among military male and female personnel seems to be the type of leadership. Leadership units that indicated good or excellent agreement with the progressive principles of leadership established by the services had a positive attitude toward women's service—women improved efficiency, created a friendlier climate, strengthened cooperation. In leadership units that could only be characterized as "fair" in their agreement with progressive principles, women were to some extent regarded as a hindrance to the practical performance of the work, making problems of cooperation between enlisted men and women.[20]

This study also examined whether or not women were treated equally with men and reported two findings. On the one hand, according to the observations of the male enlisted group, the officers and the NCOs consciously or unconsciously, treated women better than they treated men. On the other hand, the normal procedure of assigning persons to jobs according to their abilities, for instance, you do not give a heavy machine gun to a little guy, was not applied to women. The officers seemed to feel that all enlisted women should be able to do the same work.[21] No effect of these attitudes on the part of the officers was reported.

CONCLUSION

The rather modest number of women in the armed forces—680 or 1.9 percent—is not a sufficient picture of the numbers of women in the armed forces. To this number should be added the Ground Observer Corps of about 1,725 women and the 2,770 women designated to the armed forces from the Women's Home Guard. This designation of women from the home guard helps to meet the needs of the armed forces for personnel. The figures show not only that the armed forces undoubtedly could utilize more women, but also that the Women's Home Guard constitutes an important base of resources for the armed forces. This recruitment procedure can be explained by the manpower reduction in the armed forces combined with the greater willingness of political leaders to support the home guard. These two facts seem to be of greater importance to the number of women in the armed forces in Denmark than the type of armed force, all-volunteer or enlistment, or the type of party system, one-party or multiparty, as Goldman has suggested in "Women in the Armed Forces of Industrialized Nations."

Generally, women are employed in the armed forces of a country for two reasons: either they are the only labor force available, a reason of quantity, or they are the best personnel available, a reason of quality. I do not think that these reasons are sufficient to explain the employment of women in the Danish armed forces. Regarding quantity, in 1972 Denmark did not have a recruitment problem.[22] On the contrary, there was a sizable surplus of young men available for the armed forces (see Table 10.5). In addition, Denmark has experienced unemployment, especially among teenagers. The armed forces could also fill their personnel needs at little cost by the designation of women from the home guard. Finally, the most fundamental support for this position is the fact that although the armed forces were allowed legally to enlist women as early as 1962, they did not do so until 1971.

Table 10.5

Number of Draftees, Physically Fit, and Conscientious Objectors in Denmark: 1970–1976

YEAR	TOTAL NUMBER OF ACTUALLY DRAFTED FOR NATIONAL SERVICE	TOTAL NUMBER OF PHYSICALLY FIT FOR NATIONAL SERVICE	TOTAL NUMBER OF CONSCIENTIOUS OBJECTORS
1970	24,700	29,100	2,450
1971	27,000	30,000	4,200
1972	19,700	35,000	3,350
1973	18,500	22,600	4,000
1974	18,200	22,400	4,160
1975	11,300	29,700	3,130
1976	10,800	20,100*	1,480

SOURCE: Steen Borup-Nielsen and Søren Wissum: "Conscription and Conscientious Objection in Denmark." Paper (July 1977).

* This figure includes only the period from January to June 1976.

Nor do I find quality to be a reason for the enlistment of women in the Danish armed forces. Although the inclusion of women results in positive benefits—increased efficiency, and the like—the fact that women cannot be attached to combat units limits their usefulness to the armed forces. My conclusion is that the introduction of women soldiers in Denmark in

1972 was the result of forces outside of the military establishment. And since the military is reluctant to increase the numbers of women and their assignments (a suggestion of the Danish Secretary of Defense to increase their numbers from five hundred to three thousand and to open service in combat units to them was rejected by the Defense Command), new steps in offering women equal opportunity in the military will have to be based on civilian ideology and initiatives. It cannot be expected from the male-oriented and dominated military system.

NOTES

1. The increased utilization of women in Denmark is found in other countries; see Nancy Goldman, "Women in NATO Armed Forces," *Military Review* (1974): 72–82; Nancy Goldman, "The Utilization of Women in the Armed Forces of Industrialized Nations," *Sociological Symposium* (Spring 1977): 1–23; and Jean A. Klick, "Utilization of Women in the NATO Alliance," *Armed Forces and Society* 4, no. 4 (1978): 673–78.

2. Jørgen Barfoed, manager of The Freedom Museum, Copenhagen, stressed the courier service of the women as an important contribution (telephone conversation, July 17, 1979).

3. For an example of a local female resistance movement leader, see Kate Fleron, *Kvinder i modstandskampen* [Women in the resistance movement], 2nd ed. (Odense: Sirius, Risskov, 1964), pp. 56–71, 80–86. See also Frode Jakobsen, *I Danmarks Frihedsråd, bd I og II* [The Danish freedom council] (Copenhagen: Gyldendal, 1975), pp. 115, 219; John Oran Thomas, *The Giant-Killers: The Danish Resistance Movement 1940–45* (London: Michael Joseph, 1975), pp. 70–80.

4. For further literature on the recruitment of persons into the resistance movement, see Olfert Dickmeiss, *En redegørelse for modstandsorganisationen "Holger Danske" s opståen, malsaetning og udvikling indtil maj 1945* [A description of the resistance movement organization "Holger Danske's" emergence, aim and development to 1945] (Copenhagen: Historisk Institute, Kobenhavns Universitet), request no. 123. Lars Møller, *En kritisk undersogelse af rekrutteringen til den aktive modstand mod den tyske besaettelse og det dansk-tyske samarbejde 1940–45, med saerligt henblik på at belyse sammenhaengen mellem den almene okonomiske/sociale udvikling og rekrutteringen, 1976* [A critical research on the recruitment of the active resistance against the German occupation and the Danish-German cooperation with particular respect to illuminating the relation between the general economic and social development and recruitment] (Copenhagen: Institut for Historie og Samfundsvidenskab, Odense Universitet), request no. 5. Ib Damgaard Petersen, "Modeliten, Traek af den danske modstandsbevaegelses opstaen og udvikling 1940–45" [The resistance elite. Perspectives of the emergence and development of the Danish resistance movement 1940–45] (Institute of the Social Sciences, University of Copenhagen, 1978). The book is based on "Perspectives of the Emergence and Development of the Danish Resistance Movement 1940–45" with an English summary on pp. 155–80 (Institute of the Social Sciences, University of Copenhagen, 1974); *Laerebog* 2 (1978).

5. According to a telephone conversation with Jørgen Barfoed, manager of The Freedom Museum at Copenhagen, July 18, 1979.

6. *Basaettelsens Hvem Hvad Hvor* [The who, what and where of the occupation], bibliographical chapter (Copenhagen: Politikens-Forlag, 1965), pp. 385–476, lists 152 Danes, of whom 2 were women; the index, pp. 480–88, names 406 Danes, including 6 women. See also John Oran Thomas, *The Giant-Killers;* its index lists 367 men and 28 women or 6 percent.

7. *Besaettelsens,* p. 275; six thousand Danes were deported, six hundred died; p. 271, thirty-five women were in Ravensbrück, seven at Stutthof.

8. Up to 150 women were in prison at Frøslev at one time, Kate Fleron, *Kvinder i modstandskampen,* p. 151.

9. Kate Fleron, "Kvinder i Frøslev," [Women in Frøslev] in Jørgen Mågård, *Fanger i Frøslev 1944–45* [Prisoners in Frøslev 1944–45] (Copenhagen: Nationalmuseet, 1974), p. 171. "Accoding to information in October 1945, twenty-six Danish women died in German concentration camps and prisons. Of twenty women the Office for Special Affairs does miss information." Eighteen women of the resistance movement on "active duty" were interviewed in 1945 shortly after the German surrender. Together these figures give a female death rate of about 7 percent.

10. DLK (Danmarks Lottekorps, The Women's Army Home Guard), "Tjen dit land," [Serve your country] (Jubilaeumsudgave 1946–1956) [Jubilee publication], pp. 8, 13. See also pp. 204–5, this volume for a discussion of Lotta.

11. The "Act of Equal Treatment of Men and Women Regarding Their Occupation" was passed in 1978. A short introduction to the act and its implications was delivered by Kristen Thorbal, *Juristen* 13 (July 1, 1979): 303–97, together with a critique of the act for encouraging legalized hypocrisy, given by H. G. Carlsen, *Juristen,* pp. 308–11.

12. PIT 358.286/PIT 19562 from the defense command to my inquiry of July 11, 1979.

13. See Kate A. Arbogast, "Women in the Armed Forces: A Rediscovered Resource." in U.S. Air Force Academy, Department of Political Science, John E. Endicott and Roy W. Stafford, eds. *American Defense Policy.* (Baltimore, Md.: Johns Hopkins University Press, 1977), pp. 489–95. Arbogast discusses women in the armed forces, their relative strength, function, and so on. Many former all male bastions were opened in 1972 for women and the first female general officer was promoted. See also office of the Assistant Secretary of Defense (Manpower, Reserve Affairs and Logistics) *Use of Women in the Military,* (Washington, D.C.: Department of Defense, 1977); "More Jobs Now for Women in the Military," *U.S. News and World Report* 51 (1973); "Women: The Recruiter's Last Resort," in *Recon* 2, no. 9 (September 1974); "Skirts for 20%," interview with Congressman Otis Pike, *Armed Forces Journal,* p. 110.

14. See Nancy Goldman, "The Utilization of Women in the Military," *Annals* (March 1973): 107–16; Nancy Goldman, "The Changing Role of Women in the Armed Forces," *American Journal of Sociology* 78 (January 1973): 892–911; and Melody Kay Lemmon, "The Unchanged Role of Women," *ERIC* paper.

15. See M. D. Feld, "Arms and the Woman: Some General Considerations," *Armed Forces and Society* 4, no. 4 (1978): 557–68: "What is actually being debated

[women in combat units] is the symbolism of civic culture and the values through which a state mobilizes its social resources."

16. Military Psychological Service (MPT) 1977, "Refolkningens holdning til forsvarstanken maj 75 og Okt 76." Paper (1977).

17. For the record, this aspect of attitudes towards women in the armed forces is confined only to the armed force and not to the Women's Home Guard. In the United States the literature on attitudes toward women in the U.S. armed forces is comprehensive. More than half the annotated works in Edna J. Hunter et al., "Women in the Military—An Annotated Bibliography," *Armed Forces and Society* 4, no. 4 (1978): 695–716, are attitude surveys, mostly dealing with attitudes toward women in combat, women's efficiency, satisfaction, and career opportunities.

18. Jørgen Braemer, "Kvinder i forsvaret. Arbejdspsykologisk studie af militaere enheder meod kvindeligt stampersonel." (Unpublished paper, Copenhagen 1975), pp. 7, 10, 79.

19. Jørgen Braemer, "Enlisted Women in the Danish Armed Forces." (Paper, Copenhagen, 1976), p. 3. (This paper is the English Summary of note 18.)

20. Jørgen Braemer, "Kvinder i forsvaret," p. 78.

21. Jørgen Braemer, "Enlisted Women in the Danish Armed Forces," p. 12.

22. See Goldman, "Women in NATO Armed Forces." Recruitment problems as a major reason for employing women in the armed forces are generally pointed out. See Arbogast, "Women in the Armed Forces," p. 489; Goldman, "The Changing Role of Women in the Armed Forces"; Goldman, "The Utilization of Women in the Armed Forces of Industrialized Nations."

11 | SWEDEN: THE NEUTRAL NATION

Kurt Törnqvist

INTRODUCTION

The history of women at war is long but disconnected. Between the Amazons of the ancient world and the modern woman in the defense forces only a few female figures are known to have taken part in military activities. In Britain Boadicea, a queen who after her husband's death in A.D. 60 led a revolt against the Romans, appears to have been the only woman to have led armies into battle.[1] In Sweden, according to a medieval legend, Blända of Värend led a female crowd in cutting hostile Danish troops to pieces after a feast, which she had arranged.[2] And in 1520 after her husband's death Kristina Gyllenstierna took over the defense of Stockholm against the Danes.[3] Joan of Arc seems, however, to have been more religious than martial, and Florence Nightingale was more domestic than destructive. Actually, until the emancipation of women in the twentieth century, women in Sweden, as in the rest of the world, rarely made any contribution to war and military defense.

During the last century this has changed. In Sweden today women have a clear-cut role to play in the defense forces. The relations of women to these forces have changed tremendously during the last sixty years. This is quite remarkable as Sweden has not been in war since 1813, more than 160 years ago.

Thus, the change in Swedish women's relations to the defense forces cannot be the result of a need to utilize women as military personnel during war. Why then has this change occurred?

There is not just one answer. Even though Sweden itself has not been in war, it was affected by the world wars. There are, however, reasons other

Sponsored by the U.S. Army Research Institute for the Behavioral and Social Sciences. The views and conclusions in this document are those of the author and do not necessarily represent those of the sponsor or the U.S. Government.

than war for utilizing women as military personnel. For example, in Sweden the change, in part, reflects the influence of other nations such as Denmark, Norway, and Belgium, which in the late 1970s initiated the use of women in this capacity. It also reflects the influence of the United States and Britain which have, during this period, increased their utilization of military women. Also, Swedish society has changed tremendously since World War I, as have women's roles in the family and workplace. It seems reasonable that women's role in military activities would also be affected.

In the development of the utilization of Swedish women as military personnel, we can discern three steps. The first started just after World War I and consisted of providing domestic service during exercises to soldiers who were in voluntary officers' training. The next step was taken during World War II when Swedish women became voluntary substitutes for soldiers in the regular defense forces. The third step is a recent development that has taken place during the 1970s. Women have been integrated in the regular defense forces and employed to do the same jobs as men.

VOLUNTARY DOMESTIC SERVICE TO SOLDIERS IN VOLUNTARY OFFICERS' TRAINING

In 1901 the army reserve, which was the older group in the conscript army, was transformed into a home guard. But it was an organization on paper only because trained officers were not provided. Instead persons within the home guard without officers' training were selected as commanders. Because these people were worried about their ability to act as commanders, the idea of voluntary officers' training was born and started in local areas. In 1912, when international tension began to increase, a national organization of regional associations was founded for this purpose.[4]

In 1914 the government gave this organization financial support, but the grant was not sufficient. Individual contributions had to be added. After World War I when it was commonly recognized that the League of Nations as a guarantor of eternal peace was a myth, the Swedish government decided in 1921 to drop the grant. This step resulted in financial difficulties for the home guard, which could not be completely remedied by individual contributions and national fund raising.

It was against this background that the Swedish women's organization for the support of the voluntary training of officers was founded in 1924. In 1925 this new organization was recognized by the government and given a small grant. This recognition contributed to a rapid growth of local associations, and a new popular movement was born.[5]

The idea for this movement came from Finland. During the Finnish civil war in 1918 some women started to aid their men in the Defense Corps by carrying weapons, food, and other supplies. In 1918 several female committees were founded in Nyland in southwest Finland. They organized themselves into associations called Lotta Svärd. By 1920 every district in Nyland had its own Lotta Svärd association.[6]

Lotta Svärd was a soldier's widow and a sutler in the Finnish war in 1808–1809 when Sweden lost Finland to Russia. She is commemorated in a famous poem by the Finnish-Swedish poet Ludvig Runeberg. She gave the soldiers not only material aid but also moral support. Lotta Svärd became a symbol for the Finnish women in their support of their fighting men. She also became a symbol for the Swedish women in their support of the voluntary officers' training. Inspired by their Finnish sisters, some Swedish women founded a similar association in Stockholm in 1924. And soon the Lotta movement spread to a number of other places.

From 1924–1942 the Lotta women supported the soldiers in three main areas. They started out by raising money and providing financial support for voluntary officers' training. The Lotta women, by spirit and service, gave moral support to the men. Their organization became an important instrument for the formation of public opinion and the dissemination of information about defense matters, particularly among women. The women served coffee and hot food to the soldiers in the training fields and camps and later they trained to use military field kitchens to cook for the men on military exercises and in training courses. Soon cooking for the soldiers and officers in training became the most important task for the Lotta women. The soldiers and officers were most grateful not to have to peel potatoes, cook food, and wash dishes when, tired, they returned from their field training. Later the Lotta associations started courses in nursing, mending, and other domestic services in order to serve the soldiers in these areas.

Swedish women began their integration in the military service by leaving their kitchens, homes and families and moving into the training fields and military camps in order to give the soldiers and officers, who often were their husbands, fathers, or brothers, traditional domestic services.

The Lotta women did not receive military training in the use of weapons, but on exercises they performed the same cooking duties as the military male cooks. They were given a uniform and trained to march in parade formation. They were not a military reserve, however, and did not belong to the home guard. The Lotta women were a kind of voluntary military personnel. There was and is no conscription of women in Sweden.

By 1929, 13,041 women were members of the Lotta movement and were organized in 99 local associations. In 1939, 26,223 members belonged to 169 local associations. During this period the members were recruited mainly among middle-class or upper-class women.

VOLUNTARY SUBSTITUTES FOR SOLDIERS IN THE REGULAR DEFENSE FORCES

During World War II Sweden maintained extensive military preparedness in order to preserve its neutrality. During this period many more Swedish women became involved in activities related to military service and in more fields than before. New organizations of women serving the defense forces in various ways were founded, and the women became more closely related to the forces.

While the old field kitchen activites continued to be of great importance, women began to replace soldiers in several functions within the forces. In civilian life women also replaced men who were called up for military service. Thus, many Swedish women voluntarily became substitutes for men, both in military and civilian occupations. They proved they could perform well in many jobs that earlier had been reserved for men. This period therefore was important for Swedish women in the development of equality between the sexes both in civil life and in the armed forces.

Sweden's Lotta Corps increased its membership more than four times during the war to about 110,000 in 500 associations in 1943. The organization mainly served the army. During the war, a number of sister organizations developed. The Naval Lotta Corps was established in 1939,[7] while the Air Force Lotta Corps was founded in 1943[8] and the Home Guard Lotta Corps in 1940.[9] Many of the women serving the home guard were working- or farming-class people, and during the war the other Lotta Corps began to recruit members not only from the middle or upper classes but also from the workers and farmers. In 1942–1943 Sweden's Lotta Corps separated from the Voluntary Officers' Training Organization and became an independent national organization. It changed its name to The National Organization of Sweden's Lotta Corps (Riksförbundet Sveriges Lottakårer).[10]

The women in this Lotta Corps were trained in many areas. Besides the traditional kitchen service, mending, and nursing, new fields were opened for women. Some of these fields, such as office work and telephone service, were similar to women's civilian jobs. But some areas were quite new. These included air defense service, which involved looking for hostile airplanes and coordinating the reports in central places; communication and signal service in the field; service in the tactical and air defense control system to direct airplanes; the naval defense control system to direct war ships in fights; and maintenance. In all these services women replaced male soldiers who were then free for other military duties. In many of these services women had no previous experience in their civilian lives but had to be trained within the defense forces.[11]

Many of the women in the Lotta Corps were more closely connected with the defense forces through contracts. A system was organized in which the Lotta woman could sign either an A- or a B-contract. The Lotta woman with an A-contract bound herself for permanent service in the defense forces during wartime. She signed a contract with a military authority and was drafted. The Lotta woman with a B-contract bound herself for temporary defense work and signed a contract with her own Lotta Corps. The contracts were for four years; for Lotta women with an A-contract they extended to fifty-five years of age and for those with a B-contract up to sixty-five years of age. About 20 percent of the Lotta women had an A-contract and about 25 percent a B-contract. Still they did not belong to the military authority or to any home guard; they were members of a voluntary female defense organization.

There were other female defense organizations of importance. One is Sweden's National Federation of Female Motorcar Corps founded during the war. Members were trained in transport and motorcar service.[12] The women in this voluntary organization served as drivers in the defense forces, thereby releasing a number of soldiers for other military duties.

Another female defense organization is the Swedish Blue Star, whose main purpose is animal care and animal medical care during times of war and peace. It was originally founded in 1917 as an offshoot of the international Etoile Rouge founded in Geneva in 1914. The Swedish organization changed its name from the Swedish Red Star to the Swedish Blue Star in 1941. During the war-preparedness period, many star sisters served in the defense forces in medical care for horses and dogs.[13]

During the war-preparedness period, Swedish women were able to demonstrate their abilities in many new occupations in industry, transport, farming, and the defense forces; earlier these positions had been filled or dominated by men. The women were ambitious and proved to be very good in these new occupations, much better than expected. The Lotta women improved telephone service. Many women went straight from their daytime office work to serve for several hours in the underground telephone centrals at night. Also due to the shortage of trained nurses, the Lotta women were asked to fill in. In spite of short training, they performed very well.

As women were utilized as substitutes for men in military occupations, they became much more integrated in the defense forces. Still the women belonged to voluntary organizations and were not a part of the home guard. They did not learn to shoot, although there were female associations for shooting training. The government did not consider militarizing women serving the defense forces, not even those who had signed an A-contract.

These female defense organizations cannot be compared with other volunteer occupations for women of the leisure class. In the women's military associations, the work was much harder and more training was needed. During the war about 150,000 women were utilized in the defense forces: the total number of soldiers in the defense forces was about 700,000.

The utilization of women in the Swedish defense forces during World War II was also greatly influenced by the way in which some nations in war utilized women for defense purpose, such as Great Britain and the United States.[14]

EMPLOYMENT OF WOMEN IN THE DEFENSE FORCES TO DO THE SAME JOBS AS MEN

The third step in the development toward the integration of women in the Swedish defense forces started in the 1970s. It meant two things: first, women would no longer serve the forces only in domestic service or as substitutes for male soldiers but would in some instances do the same jobs as men.

The discussion about the role of women in the defense forces had intensified in the 1960s in connection with the problem of female compulsory military service. Three factors precipitated this discussion of women's role in the defense forces. First, the movement toward equality called for women to fulfill the same defense duty as men. This movement also called for reforms to counteract the division of men and women in different professional categories. Second, in order to forward the equality between the sexes, the special laws protecting women were removed. These laws had led to recruitment based on sex instead of individual qualifications and thus had become a barrier to women's opportunities for advancement. Third, women are employed as military personnel in the armed forces of other countries. The problem of affording enhanced tasks in the defense forces therefore became an issue of increased importance.

The starting point was the proposal by the chief of the air force in March 1969 asking permission to employ women in military and civil-military positions within the air force. There were two reasons for this proposal. One was the shortage, within the air force of employed personnel, although not conscripts. This shortage occurred because of the unpopularity of military jobs in the late 1960s as a result of the antisocial and antimilitary attitudes that developed during the Vietnam War, the student protests, and the strong left-wing trend. The second reason was that equality between the sexes had become a more prominent issue. In order to get a broader and better foundation for recruiting, the air force chief wanted to give men and women a chance to compete on equal terms for those officers' positions that were considered fit for women. The chief, therefore, suggested that all officers' positions that did not involve fighting be opened to women. Women could not be pilots with fighting tasks in wartime or heads of fighting ground forces.[15]

The proposal was referred for consideration to various military and civil authorities, most of whom supported the principal issue of employment of women in military positions. It was also discussed in the Parliament, which referred the issue to the Committee for Compulsory Military Service of 1972. In its report of 1973, the committee stressed the importance of equal training or education for men and women for military professions. It recommended a review of the current conditions and instructions for recruiting and training women in military and civil-military positions.

This report was also referred to military and civil authorities for consideration. In 1975 the Parliament once more dealt with the problem. The result was that the government in March 1975 appointed a special committee on Women in the Defense Forces to work toward enabling women to be employed in the defense forces. This committee was called "Beredningen för det fortsatta arbetet om kvinnan i försvaret" (Drafting Committee for Further Work Concerning Women in the Defense Forces).

The report of the committee was delivered in 1977. It contained recommendations about basic principles for employment of women as officers, detailed suggestions for employment of women as officers within the air force and certain personnel corps common to the defense forces (that is, medical, administrative, and messing functions), suggestions for employment of women in fiscal and catering work, for practice service, for employment in the Emergency Troops of United Nations and for recruiting women to the industrial defense service of the home guard. The issue of female compulsory military service was not dealt with by the committee. There is no need for so many new soldiers in Sweden's army organization, and these costs could not be covered by the allowance assigned to the Defense Department by the Parliament.

Nor did the committee deal with the issue of employing women in combat positions, a difficult problem because very often there is no clear-cut difference between fighting and nonfighting positions. As of 1980 no other Western country has opened combat positions to women and many people did not think Sweden should do it. To accept women as officers but not in fighting positions, is, of course, illogical and unsatisfactory. But the development should be considered as a step-by-step process toward a long-range goal.

The principal recommendation by the committee is that women be placed under the general orders and the basic demands that are in force for men. Women who are going to be employed as regular officers should pass admissions tests, basic training equivalent to the training for compulsory military training, and regular officers' schools. Women who have passed the regular officers' training must be able to be used as instructors and leaders of large units. Demands that are not necessary and that are unfair to women should be eliminated.

When working to improve women's opportunities to develop within the defense forces, one must start from the principle of equality laid down by the government and the Parliament about everybody's right to work and personal development. One does not aim at employing a certain number of women. Instead women and men will compete on equal terms for those positions that are suitable for both men and women. The aim must not be to employ women in order to release men for other tasks. Women should not be considered a reserve force. The aim is not to increase the number of positions but rather to keep the employment of women within the financial frame of the defense forces.

Military service could not be said to be particularly popular among women and the right to serve in the military has not been sought by many women. But serving as officers in the defense forces is a logical result of the work to increase equality between the sexes.

In order to get the public's view of women in the defense forces, the Swedish Board of Psychological Defense Planning (Beredskapsnämnden för psykologiskt försvar) took an opinion poll in the fall of 1976. Asked how important employment of women in the defense forces was to increasing equality between sexes, 58 percent (men 60 percent, women 56 percent) considered it important. The positive attitude was most common (71 percent) in the youngest age group, eighteen to twenty-four years of age. Asked if they thought that certain positions for officers could be opened for women, 62 percent (men 60 percent, women 64 percent) said yes. Eighty percent (men 80 percent, women 81 percent) were of the opinion that male and female officers should have the same promotion system, and 79 percent (men 75 percent, women 82 percent) believed that women as officers should be in command of both men and women. But only 40 percent (men 36 percent, women 44 percent) were of the opinion that female officers also should hold fighting positions, while 49 percent (men 54 percent, women 43 percent) said no. On these last two issues women were positive to a larger extent than men, but otherwise there was no significant difference between men and women. This opinion poll indicates that the committee's suggestions are in line with existing opinion about female roles in the military today. Thus, opportunities seem to exist to institute changes in women's roles.[16]

The committee has studied different positions within the air force and found that some of these could be considered fit for women. All positions as air force technicians and master mechanics are recommended to be opened for women. Positions as officers of tactical and air defense control system and of communications service are also considered fit for women if they do not require pilot training and experience. Positions as air traffic control leader, aeronautical engineer, and meteorologist are also suggested suitable for women. Aeronautical engineers are trained along two different lines, the air line and the ground line. The aeromedical factors that should be considered on the air line are not yet clear enough for a judgment about positions as aeronautical engineers on the air line. The positions also include pilot training, which is another hindrance.

Positions as troop instructors and as pilots with fighting tasks are at the present not considered suitable for women. In reaching the decision about the pilot position, not only aeromedical reasons but also ergonomical problems were considered. Among other things, the seat in the cabin is constructed only to suit men.

On the basis of this report, the Parliament in the fall of 1978 decided that in 1980 opportunities should be opened for women to become regular officers within the air force. In order to give information to young women interested in these professions, the army and the air force arranged summer training camps in 1979. February 4, 1980, was a unique day in the history of the Swedish defense forces because the first women officers' candidates enrolled for admission tests at the enlistment center in Solna outside Stockholm. Eighty women undertook the three-day enrollment test. Out of these eighty women twenty-five to thirty will be admitted. It is the same test as the men have to undergo. The women will compete with the men on the same terms for the two-year officers' course at the officers' school. They will first have to take a basic training course for one year at the air force regiment in Uppsala. The first such course started in June 1980.

This development will continue. In spring 1978 the government gave new instructions to the Committee for Further Work. The starting point for the second stage is that all officers' positions within the army and the navy in the long run should be opened to women. Individual fitness should be the only criterion for selection and recruiting of regular officers.[17]

In December 1980 the Committee for Further Work Concerning Women in the Defense Forces delivered its final report.[18] The committee suggested that all positions for officers should, in the main, be open to women as well as men and eligibility should be based on ability. "Medical obstacles," such as pregnancy and those found in certain extreme environments such as in tactical air service and in certain parts of submarine service, are the only acceptable reasons for excluding women.

The committee suggested that the reform should be realized in three steps. It should begin in 1983 with basic military training within the following professional areas:

The Army: Signal Troops and the Army Service Corps
The Coast Artillery: Sea Front Artillery Service, Radar and Communications, and Medical Service (shared with the Navy)
The Navy: Battle Management Service, Communications, Maintenance, Surface Attack Service

The committee further suggested that the following occupation areas should be open to women only after gaining knowledge of their ability to serve in the areas previously open to them, or when the "medical obstacles" for the particular occupation have been surmounted:

The Army: The Infantry, The Cavalry, and the Armored Troops
The Coast Artillery: The Coast Light Infantry Corps and the Ground Fighting Service
The Navy: Submarine Service and Submarine Technical Service
The Air Force: Pilot Service and Service as Flying Air Force Engineers.

The opening of remaining positions for officers should, according to the committee, depend on the decision of the Commander-in-Chief.

The Government agreed with the suggestions of the committee and in July 1981 sent its bill concerning the employment of women as officers within the Defense Forces to the Parliament.[19] On November 5, 1981 the Defense Committee of the Parliament concurred with the Government's bill without any objections.[20] This means that the Parliament in 1982 will pass a resolution which will open, *in the main,* all officers' positions in the Swedish Defense Forces to women.

WHY DID THIS DEVELOPMENT HAPPEN?

What are the causes for these changes? There are, of course, many. In the first phase, World War I, the War of Independence in Finland, and the change in government policy withdrawing the grant to voluntary military training, were all influential, as was World War II during the second phase. In the third, the Vietnam War, although not relating directly to Sweden, played a certain role.

Then there is the general social change from 1920 to 1980. The changing role of women in the defense forces is in a certain sense a mirror of that social change. As society changed, the role of women changed, with their emancipation continuing at a slow but steady pace. More women got better educations, and many of them entered the labor market. Soon they invaded traditionally male trades and professions, and sought the same rights, in society and in the labor market, as men. The efforts towards equality between sexes became stronger.

At the same time, the character of war changed, and military technique and the military profession changed accordingly. In many military jobs strong physical capability was no longer as important as educational, technical, and other professional skills. Defense could often be carried out at a distance with the aid of technical innovations and communication aids. In addition, there were examples from other coutries where women were utilized in the military profession. Being in the forefront of development, Sweden could not neglect the experiences of other countries that utilized women in their defense forces. All of these developments converged when the air force suffered a shortage of employed personnel.

NOTES

1. *Encyclopaedia Britannica,* vol. 3 (Chicago: 1973), p. 820.
2. *Bonniers Lexikon,* vol. 2 (Stockholm: 1966), p. 560.
3. *Bonniers Lexikon,* vol. 6 (Stockholm: 1966), p. 564.
4. Gustaf Lindström, *Bakgrunden, Svensk Lottarörelse 1924–49* [Background, the Swedish Lotta movement in 1924–49] (Stockholm: Riks förb undet Sveriges Lottakårer, 1949), p. 8.
5. Ibid., p. 9.
6. Armas Appelgren et al., eds., *Skyddskårister och lottor i svenska Nyland* [The voluntary defense corps and the Lotta women in the Swedish-speaking Nyland, Finland] (Helsingfors: Nylands södra skyddskärsdistrikt, 1944), p. 287.
7. *Svensk Lottarörelse,* p. 45.
8. Stig M. H:son Björkman, ed., *Sveriges Kvinnliga beredskap* [Sweden's female war-preparedness] (Stockholm: Spectator, 1942), p. 40; *Svensk Lottarörelse,* p. 54.
9. *Svensk Lottarörelse,* 38.
10. Ibid., pp. 43–44.
11. Ibid., pp. 55–59, Militär lottautbildning [Military training of Lotta women].
12. *Sveriges kvinnliga beredskap,* p. 99.
13. Ibid., pp. 68–69.
14. Great Britain, Air Ministry, *The W.A.A.F. in Action* (London: A & C Black, 1944); Mattie E. Treadwell, *The Women's Army Corps* (Washington, D.C.: Office of the Chief of Military History, 1954). Nancy L. Goldman and Richard Stites, pp. 30–36, this volume; George H. Quester, pp. 219–29, this volume.
15. Statens offentliga utredningar [Government's official report] (SOU) 1977, 26. *Kvinan och försvarets yrken* [The woman and the professions of the defense forces], (Stockholm: Liber Förlag, 1977), pp. 12–13.
16. Kurt Törnqvist, *Kvinnor och försvaret* [Women in the defense forces], (Stockholm: Beredskapsnämnden för psykologiskt försvar, 1977).
17. Kerstin Ekman, *Beredningen Kvinnan i Försvaret* (BKF) [The committee concerning women in the defense forces] (Bilkåristen: June 1979), Nr. 2, p. 15.
18. Försvarsdepartementet [The Ministry of Defense], *Kvinnan och försvarets yrken—slutbetänkande, avgivet av beredningen för det fortsatta arbetet om Kvinnan i försvaret.* Ds Fö 1980:5, Bilagedel Ds Fö 1980:6 [The women and the professions of the defense forces—final report, the committee for the further work concerning the women in the defense forces, Ds Fö 1980:5, Appendix Ds Fö 1980:6] (Stockholm: Liber Förlag, 1980).
19. Regeringens proposition 1981/82:3 om anställning som befäl inom det militära försvaret, m.m.; beslutad den 9 juli 1981 [The government's bill 1981/82:3 concerning the employment of women as officers within the Defense Forces etc.; given on July 9th, 1981] (Stockholm: Norstedts Tryckeri, 1981).
20. Hans O. Alfredsson, *Öppna hela försvaret för kvinnliga befäl* [Open the

defense forces as a whole for female officers], *Svenska Dagbladet* [The Swedish daily], November 6, 1981; Försvarsutskottet betänkande 1981/82:6 om anställning av kvinnor som beväl inom det militära försvaret, m.m. (prop. 1981/82:3), [Report 1981/82:6 by the Defense Committee of the Parliament concerning employment of women as officers within the military defense etc. (Bill 1981/82:3] Riksdager 1981/82, 10 saml, Nr 6 [The Parliament 1981/82, vol. 10, no. 6].

PART III | AMERICAN DILEMMAS AND OPTIONS

12 | THE PROBLEM

George H. Quester

My intention in this chapter is to draw on the very limited experience the United States has had with women in the military, to see how the issue of a female combat role has been handled in the past, and to find some evidence as to how women would do in combat. The preliminary finding is short and to the point. Women have been allowed almost no combat role, but when they have somehow moved into such a role, they cannot be said to have done any worse than men. In recounting how the substantive issue of female military service has arisen in the past, we will also be drawn into the process by which this issue has been handled, amid broader inferences on how Congress and the American public have progressed in their views about male and female roles in our society. Beginning as an analysis of the American experience with female military service, this chapter thus necessarily also becomes a discussion of American attitudes on gender stereotypes.

Hovering in the background of the discussion, with great importance for the female military service issue, is also the changing American attitude since the Vietnam War on military service and foreign policy in general. The shift from a draft to a volunteer army has been of great significance in its own right, but it has also been a symptom of still broader convulsions in American attitudes.

UNIFORMED WOMEN, AWAY FROM COMBAT

Discussions of female military service in the United States, and the possibility of combat participation, have a tendency to begin in a manner very similar to discussions of black participation. A series of legendary tokens are introduced by which each major war of our history is covered (for example, Molly Pitcher as the woman of the American Revolution, Christopher Attucks as the black), thus to establish that such participation is a part of our tradition, and not some sort of total departure from the American character.

Yet the hard data is typically more difficult to come by. While such references to history have a function, they cannot be allowed to obscure the facts. Regarding the question of female participation, American military history has been an overwhelmingly male experience.

To summarize an easily established situation, there has been no substantial participation of females in the American armed forces in the past, and there has been next to no participation in combat. Auxiliaries of female nurses were added to the army in 1901 and navy in 1908, but these were not given status as full components of the military until 1944. While the U.S. Navy actually went ahead to enlist some women in the navy and marine corps during World War I, the army did not follow suit, despite the urgings of General Pershing, who sought to free men for combat service. Congressional opposition emerged when the proposal drew publicity, while the Navy Department had gone about its own modest enlistment of women earlier and more quietly.[1]

At no point did anyone in the United States propose the use of females in combat. Nurses, by definition, might be drawn closer to the front, for there would be found the wounded needing their treatment. Yet the morality of the world had already legislated substantial exemptions for medical personnel, male or female, from the rigors of combat. While sometimes observed only in the breach, the avoidance of firing at Red Cross flags and medical facilities was still often observed in practice, in what in many respects was a more gentlemanly age. There was thus a correlation, at least a weak one, between the idea that medical service military personnel should not be shot at and the idea that women could be allowed to become medical service personnel.

At a later point, we shall turn to the special case of the participation of American women in espionage and sabotage in World War II. Female Americans played no role to speak of in World War I. As a sign of American feelings in the matter, however, one should note the extensive British propaganda successes scored in the United States with the case of Edith Cavell, a British nurse accused by the Germans of espionage in Belgium, and then shot. The British, of course, vehemently denied that the nurse was a spy, but (whatever the credibility of this denial) made a great deal of the fact that it was barbarous for a *woman* to be subjected to such punishment. (Showing how the Allies could have their cake and eat it too, the French government a little later executed Mata Hari on charges of espionage for the Germans, on flimsy evidence indeed; at this point, the Germans became barbarous for having *employed* a woman in espionage.) The American view on this underscores a general naiveté which was to persist for some decades to come, a naiveté about the role of women and the need for their protection, a naiveté also about the nature and costs of war.

At the end of World War I, the women in the navy and marine corps were discharged, and the U.S. military then became an all-male sanctuary again until the 1940s. Various plans and proposals were developed in the interwar years for a mobilization of women in the future, based on projections that any new war might indeed sorely tax the American manpower base.[2] But such proposals, like many other interwar contingency plans, simply went nowhere, as the grave situation that would cause them to be needed did not yet loom on the horizon.

Much of this indifference to the issue then changed in 1940, of course, with the rapidity of Hitler's conquest of Europe, causing Americans to conclude that great preparations for future war would now be in order. Moves were thus made to establish women's auxiliary services for each of the military services, entitled the WAAC (Women's Auxiliary Army Corps) in the Army, WAVES (Women Accepted for Voluntary Emergency Service) in the navy, with additional auxiliaries for the marines and coast guard. Again, the initial move entailed less than full membership in the military for females, with different rank structures, lesser subjection to military law and discipline, and markedly lower level of military pay and benefits.

As the war moved ahead, it became increasingly obvious that many complications could be eased, and greater efficiency achieved, if these auxiliary units were to be made full-fledged components of the military. Hence in 1943, the WAAC became the WAC (Women's Army Corps), with similar metamorphoses for the other military services.[3]

Yet the ban on combat service remained in effect, even as these other steps were taken. As each change in the status of female military service ran the gauntlet of congressional scrutiny, again and again it encountered protestations of deep aversion to the idea of females in combat, exacting executive statements and legislative constrictions to reassure that such combat participation would be avoided.

It is thus not wrong to offer this generalization that the primary resistance to the participation of American women in combat during World War II, and before, and since, has been found in the U.S. Congress. The executive branch and the professional military would have generally preferred legislation that left planning unencumbered by such special anti-combat rules for females, but Congress, even in the worst months of World War II, seemed to take great pride in demanding and legislating assurances that women would be spared.[4] While the most vehement of the congressional debate in this vein often came from congressmen from the South, the pattern was not predominantly regional; southern congressmen tended by seniority to be powerful, but also to be more visible as spokesmen for their colleagues.

A possible explanation of such attitudes would, of course, be that these senators and representatives were simply responding to constituent pressure. Yet this does not ring true, since one finds little evidence that an incumbent would have been likely to lose his seat if he had voted the other way on the issue; the results of public opinion polling indeed suggest a substantial open-mindedness about the question in the populace at large, with a strong feeling that women should serve in the military:

March 10, 1944

The army can either draft 300,000 single women aged 21–35 for the WACs for nonfighting jobs, or it can draft the same number of married men with families for the same work. Which would you favor?[5]

Draft single women	75%
Draft married men	16%
No opinion	9%

By Sex:
Men

Draft single women	72%
Draft married men	19%
No opinion	9%

Women

Draft single women	78%
Draft married men	13%
No opinion	9%

Apart from opinion polls, another indicator might be found in the plot lines of Hollywood-produced war movies after the bombing of Pearl Harbor. There was, of course, a persistent need to incorporate female characters, simply for the needs of film entertainment value, just as later films on trips to the moon or Mars always incorporated the indispensable female scientist. Nonetheless, such films are filled with American nurses demanding to be up close to the front line, alongside their brothers and sweethearts, or with female guerrilla soldiers in the Soviet Union and China and France, or generally with female military personnel wanting to share as many burdens as possible with their military brothers.

EXCEPTIONS TO THE RULE: WOMEN IN COMBAT

An account of female participation in combat thus becomes a survey of exceptions to the rule. The inclination of the professional military to test congressional and public resistance to such roles is shown in an interesting experiment with the Anti-aircraft Artillery (AAA). This unit, deployed to shield Washington, D.C., against German or Japanese air attack was integrated with female personnel on a trial basis in 1942, the entire experiment being shielded from publicity lest an aroused Congress step in to veto it.[6]

Given that such personnel would be involved in "combat" only if senators and representatives were being bombed, this hardly would seem like such a radical departure from the American way of life. Other countries had tended to see antiaircraft duties as a natural entry point for women into the military, for an enemy air attack by its very nature would have already been bringing war to the women and children of the country being defended. As a test of whether female personnel could adjust to the special rigors of preparing for a shooting war role, the experiment seemed a clear enough success, with no serious problems. As an opening wedge for a combat role, however, the experiment was destined to go no place, since the Luftwaffe would not cooperate by attacking North America. The antiaircraft defense of the continental United States was thus thinned out as American forces penetrated North Africa and Europe, and whatever precedents had been set in 1942 and 1943 had no follow-up.

A more lively and visible precedent might have been set with the projected use of female pilots to ferry aircraft from the United States to combat zones. A formal structure was established in the WASP (Women Airforce Service Pilots), which at its peak included some 1,830 female pilots under the direction of Jacqueline Cochran. What happened to the WASP illustrated how much of the history of female participation in the military has been the result of quirk and happenstance, rather than predetermined major pattern.[7]

The WASP, like the WAAC, was not yet a military body but an auxiliary. As the WAAC was upgraded into the fully military WAC, the question naturally arose as to whether the WASP should become part of the WAC. Cochran at this juncture instead demanded that the WASP be established as a separate female military service, analogous to the separate Army Nurse Corps, with its own colonel as commanding officer. Whether this was based on good reasons, or simply on old-fashioned bureaucratic imperialism, the result was that it called congressional attention to the special nature of the WASP, with a predictable result that resistance arose to the idea of *any* female piloting of military aircraft, even to their ferrying on the way to combat. As the U.S. Army Air Force was at this point discovering that it had overestimated its needs, and was actually now accumulating a surplus of male pilots, the incentives for any challenge to congressional ire on this issue were entirely lacking, and Cochran's female pilots were destined to see no further service.

Again, using women as ferry pilots might have been the beginnings of a more active combat role. Sooner or later, what had been expected to be a ferry mission would have encountered an enemy interceptor aircraft, and would have had to take evasive action, or otherwise protect itself.

Even if combat had not been encountered, it would have struck some Americans that flying is dangerous even at the stages preparatory to combat, for example, bringing aircraft across the North Atlantic or across "the hump" of the Himalaya, for test flying new aircraft to make sure the defects have been found.

Apart from the demise of the WASP, however, it is an interesting fact that the Army Air Corps, later named the Army Air Forces, generally surged in front of other portions of the army, and ahead of the navy, in the employment of female personnel. On a host of ground-breaking decisions, the Army Air Force's thus took the lead, ranging from the integration of military grades to the breakdown of sex-defined job classifications.

The explanations for the leading role of the air force are mixed. One could begin by noting how this service tends to be less "military" than the others, breaking free of tradition generally, just as it had to break free of tradition on the mode of transportation used in combat. A service so heavily mortgaged to technological innovation might thus always place less stock on any conventional wisdom about inherent psychological attributes, or on any traditional notions of what amounted to military prowess.

A second explanation, still also very relevant today, notes the larger tail-to-teeth ratio for aerial combat, as compared to combat on land or on the sea; a great deal of the technological and human effort of aerial warfare consists in getting ready for combat, paying off then in a battle waged by relatively few people. If the opposition of the U.S. Congress or public was to seeing women in actual combat, then a much larger fraction of job possibilities was still left as theoretically open to women. This holds just as true in 1980 as in 1945, as a current estimate of "noncombat" positions open to females would run as high as 76 percent for the air force, as compared to perhaps 50 percent for the army and 38 percent for the navy.[8]

A third explanation for the comparative World War II experiences, again far less deterministic and much more idiosyncratic, is simply that the U.S. Army Air Corps, later the USAAF (U.S. Army Air Forces), was commanded by an officer, General H. H. Arnold, who happened to be open-minded about the possibilities of employing women in military service. Some commanders in other service components were as open-minded on this question, but many were not.

The manner in which women in the WASP might thus have drifted into combat is illustrated by some of the more venturesome deployments of WAC personnel attached to the ground forces. There were several instances where female personnel on their way to Europe and North Africa were on board ships torpedoed by German submarines, with the females having to be rescued and fished out of the ocean just as their male counterparts. Such personnel deployed forward were of course also in danger from air raids in North Africa, or V-1 and V-2 bombs in London (along with the Arab women of Oran and the British women of London, of course). In Italy, women were often deployed within thirty miles of the front lines, which were rather static. One can speculate about what American reactions would have been if there had been a similar close-to-the-front deployment in Belgium at the time of the Battle of the Bulge.

Nurses also had to be deployed within reach of the front lines, even at a time when the Red Cross flag did not protect very much against enemy bombing or shellfire. The front-line provision of medical service was, of course, still to be provided by male medics, a kind of medical paraprofessional, which for long had no equivalent in American civilian life. The chances of a nurse being captured or wounded were thus not extraordinarily high, and not high enough to rouse the indignation and concerns of the American Congress and public.

The pattern of policy here is thus broadly consistent, amid a series of minor inconsistencies based on the flukes of the bureaucratic process, or the incomplete oversight by the legislative branch. To the extent that there was a plan, it seemed the intention of Americans that women should be kept out of combat; including them would somehow sacrifice American standards of civilization. (It is interesting to note that this attitude also prevailed in Germany and Japan, countries on the losing side, which might have thus seemed in more desperate straits toward the end. Britain, by contrast, felt much more impelled to mobilize its women for military duties, albeit not yet combat; the USSR went the furthest, by advertising its employment of females in combat.)

The minor inconsistencies emerge because the military leadership itself did not want, all in all, to be tied down by too many iron-clad rules. In the process of staying free of such rules, the military occasionally and inadvertently exposed females to combat rigors. The cases where rules are imposed or not imposed by the Congress thus often turn out to depend on timing, and on the happenstance of greater or lesser publicity being drawn to the question at the crucial moment. This is the only good way of explaining the difference between the army and the navy in World War I, or the fate of the WASP women pilots in World War II.

A final driving force, quite interesting in light of what has happened since World War II, is that females themselves seemed consistently eager to win greater military roles for themselves, that is, to avoid the binding rules intended by Congress. Women's aim was not just to leave their generals free to make their own decisions, but also to get into the front-line positions that produce full acceptance and gratification in a military career. A most important generalization about World War II is that the morale of female personnel was usually higher as they were closer to the front.[9] Such a finding might be puzzling for any dedicated antimilitarist who wishes to give everyone an exemption from enemy bombing or artillery fire or submarine attack. It will be far less puzzling for someone familiar with the internal social attitudes and status determinants of the military.

Morale correspondingly was lower for females who were indelibly stamped as rear-area troops or typecast as capable only of doing "women's work." Morale correlated also with the extent to which a unit was kept busy, since feeling purposeful for the war effort was an important part of what had led women to volunteer for the military in the first place. One could, of course, be kept busy at locations far removed from an active combat front, for modern war has a great deal of necessary preparatory activity prior to any actual output in combat. Yet the odds were that one was more likely to feel overmanned and redundant at a rear area, and quite unlikely to feel redundant closer to the front.

Morale among female military personnel also went down wherever evidence emerged that Americans in general, or male military personnel in particular, were not taking the female participation seriously. In some cases the setbacks took the form of prejudices among commanding officers, who either resisted being assigned female personnel or who failed to assign meaningful work roles to them after they had been assigned. In other instances, the setbacks came with rumors assailing the moral styles of female personnel, with rumors of high pregnancy rates and rampant promiscuity, or assertions that the sole intent of adding females to the armed services had been to provide sexual companionship for the males doing the fighting.

Some of such negative feedback was inherent in the circumstances. With large numbers of men sharing military deployments with small numbers of women, social arrangements were bound to make the females a scarce commodity, raising issues of whether officers had unfair advantages as compared to enlisted men, or whether marriages should be encouraged or discouraged. Since a large number of females in the service would be involved in secretarial tasks, moreover, working for male officers just as secretaries work for business executives in the private sector, speculation was bound to emerge about whether such work relationships were likely to evolve into sexual harassment as well. An illustration of the sensitivity of the possibilities came with the intention of Colonel Oveta Culp Hobby as WAC commander that commissions be awarded only to persons passing through the WAC's officer training programs, rather than also being handed out on any direct-commission basis. While the policy was generally adhered to, some blatant exceptions arose; several American general officers decided to have their secretaries commissioned in the WAC, secretaries who were not even American citizens. The decisions, upheld by General Marshall, include General Eisenhower's British secretary, Miss Summersby, and several Australian secretaries assigned to Generals

George C. Kenney, Richard K. Sutherland, and Richard J. Marshall.[10]

The low point of WAC morale apparently came in mid-1943, in what was for a time feared to be an Axis-inspired whispering campaign alleging widespread pregnancy among WAC personnel deployed overseas. The facts did not at all support such rumors. Given the morality of the times, and the needs of military discipline, female detachments were generally given quarters and living rules more like cloisters than barracks, often physically removed from male barracks, always guarded, and otherwise protected. The rumor campaign, after investigation, did not turn out to have been the product of Axis-dispatched outside agitators, of course, but merely of the natural biases of American servicemen and civilians.[11] The damage to female morale was thus less that women were being used as sex objects, but rather were *seen* as sex objects, that is, not seen very interestingly or convincingly as soldiers.

THE SERIOUSNESS OF AMERICAN ATTITUDES

What then did the American people really want to have happen on the issue of women in combat, during World War II, or before, or after? One answer is probably that most Americans had not given any serious thought to the subject.

The frivolous treatment accorded the subject of women in the armed forces, even when shielded from combat, is astounding when compared to what we are experiencing today. However naive we might interpret Americans as being in the 1980s, the change from the 1940s is enormous. Even in the darkest days of World War II, press conferences on the plans for a Women's Army Corps would often degenerate into questions about women's outerwear and underwear. A steady fare of cartoons in service and civilian publications about the arrival of women on military posts underscored the lack of seriousness with which the issues were viewed.[12]

Such prurient and trivial responses show how much America has changed in the years since, in at least two different ways. First, discussions of sex were obviously far more constrained than they are today, with the result that surrogates regularly had to be utilized; the possibilities of female military personnel being mixed with males thus became a ready-made outlet for those feeling short of risqué rumor.

Second, perhaps even more significant, in the 1940s Americans still had not adjusted to what the full costs of war might be. Even after the disasters of Pearl Harbor and the loss of the Philippines, the United States wound up mobilizing its economy to a far lesser extent than did Britain or the Soviet Union.[13] Sparing females from all exposure to combat was thus a luxury that Americans were still not yet ready to surrender, because the demands of winning World War II did not yet dictate it.

WOMEN IN ESPIONAGE

Apart from this quite meager set of uniformed-service exceptions to the rules against female combat, however, there is another very interesting set of female roles in espionage and sabotage, in the Office of Strategic Services (OSS) and its sister services. The role of females was not trivial, and it certainly was in no way token. Indeed, this female war role subjected women to risks of death or torture exactly parallel to those for males, and amounted to a blatant violation of the general attitudes of Congress described above.

Why was espionage/sabotage activity for women such an exception to the general American pattern we have described? To begin, such operations virtually by definition had to be secret; the same secrecy that confounded the Germans and the Japanese also kept the American public and Congress from knowing the details, at least until after war's end, when the stories of individual heroism could be published in an atmosphere which brooked little criticism. The exemption of the intelligence services from congressional scrutiny was, of course, not total; yet the OSS, for example, encountered the most criticism on its employment of known Communists as agents, and next to none on its employment of women.[14]

A second factor easing the way for the participation of women comes in the inherent nature of intelligence operations, which are located either at a safe distance from the front lines of combat, or in the definite lack of safety of being deep behind enemy lines. There was thus less likely to be any continuing debate about "how close" women should be allowed to the front lines.

Spies and guerrillas fight out of uniform, whether or not they are full members of an army in terms of table-of-organization and retirement privileges. In espionage, therefore, there was bound to be less debate than in service *per se* about whether females were military or paramilitary or auxiliary, subject or not subject to military discipline and barracks inspection.[15] (The concomitant of not having to wear a uniform was, of course, that the intelligence operative, male and female, had no protection under the so-called Laws of War when captured by the enemy, but could be executed or worse.)

An important additional explanation for the most imaginative employment of females here was simply that the OSS, like its allied intelligence services, was constantly short of qualified operatives, and thus in a somewhat different situation from the uniformed combat services. Someone fluent in a European language, able to operate a radio, and brave, would not be redundant to the intelligence networks needing to be established. Whether the task was organizing guerrilla forces, or gathering data, or simply serving as a courier to relay messages, qualified people were at all times welcome.

Yet another factor came with the ties to indigenous underground movements, which tended to include women guerrilla fighters. If a part of the United States had been occupied, American women would obviously have gotten into combat too, as indigenous guerrillas. As things stood, it was not at all unthinkable to parachute a British or American woman into France to help coordinate with the French guerrillas.

The number of such combat-involved females was of course small, just as the total of all intelligence operatives was small. Yet they outnumber the uniformed females who were involved in combat. The performance of females in OSS nonetheless gives us some sense of what is possible, what work women are capable of doing, what prejudices men are capable of shedding.

As one reads through accounts of intelligence and sabotage operations behind the lines during World War II, one finds almost no instance where male operatives found themselves trusting their female comrades less and refusing to serve with them. "An agent is an agent" seemed to be the general rule.

The enemy in such operations was always close at hand. The fear was largely of how one would be treated when captured, and how one could stand up under torture. Few people anywhere can predict how long they will be able to endure pain; the men who entered the espionage field were serious enough to realize that they could be no more sure of themselves than of a female collaborator.

Part of being a successful operative also, of course, entailed keeping a cool head in face of the threat of capture, of not becoming careless, of not panicking. Again, one finds no tangible evidence that women were generally given any lower grades on this scale than men. While the bias of the whole world would have been that "women are naturally more emotional than men," the business of working behind the enemy lines was serious enough to make such biases lose relevance.

Some intelligence operatives, usually not those who were American nationals, would be working with their spouses close at hand, basically in the same family and business situation as before the war had begun. Since a majority of intelligence operatives were male, it would follow that a majority of such spouses (many of them being left in the dark about the espionage or sabotage operations under way) would be female. Spouses (female and male) generally behaved less well after apprehension than the actual operatives, for the screening and training were missing in their case. Any image we have of women breaking down more frequently under interrogation after capture thus stems basically from this anomaly.

There is another good reason why an intelligence service would want to include females, a reason which relates to the biases the world has had about the role of females, but only quite indirectly. A war zone soldiered entirely by males has always wanted to have females around for the sexual companionship they offer, and the "camp follower" role is an old one. Where it would have been difficult to explain the presence of an additional male agent in place, it would often be more easy to justify the presence of an additional female, acting in roles ranging from hostess to girlfriend to prostitute.

The suspicion of some Americans that their sisters and daughters were wanted in the combat zone as sex partners is thus not verified here in the straightforward sense. American male intelligence agents did not want a female partner along merely to while away the hours. Yet the presumption for a number of women recruited for this service was that they might indeed have to be ready to put patriotism ahead of the standard morality of the 1940s; they would at least be entering a zone in which the enemy who did not know they were intelligence agents might presume that they were not constrained by sexual morality.

Too many novels and too many bad movies have been based on the Mata Hari theme of sexual favors being exchanged for espionage data, and a serious observer of the question should be on his guard here, against yet another of the leering kinds of speculation about women in combat zones that has plagued analysis of the topic in the past. But the realities for once are not totally removed from the legend. The company of an attractive woman was a scarce resource in the Europe occupied by the Germans and their allies, and this could be exploited to get female agents travel permissions and access to data which would otherwise have been unattainable.[16]

In all discussions of intelligence operations, it can be a mistake to overestimate the activity behind the enemy lines, as compared with the amount of work needing to be done back in Washington or London or Bombay or Chungking, analyzing the data as it comes in. Sabotage, by definition, has to be accomplished entirely behind the enemy's back, but a large fraction of espionage is accomplished in a nation's own rear areas.

This portion of intelligence, of course, involves no female exposure to combat. The record of female participation was nonetheless not unimpressive, but again more significant and more weighty than that permitted within the regular army and navy. The best comparison of sex roles on this end of intelligence work might have been with the gender distribution at any American university at the time. Where females had established themselves as experts and specialists, despite all the discouragements of our culture, they were put into work roles quite like those of men. No one apparently felt that women were to be discounted or handicapped at such applied social science, simply because the application was in a context of war and military matters.

Some of the speculation about the possibility of women in combat relates to the sheer physical stamina that may be required for moving weapons about, hacking their way through the bush. An evaluation of such speculation would obviously have to note that some men are stronger than others, but also that some women are physically stronger than some men. One would not want to assign any job to an individual who was not physically up to it; the result might then not be a military force equally divided between males and females, but it would probably not be an all-male force either.

A very different objection often advanced alleges certain psychological traits of women; they are judged to be more emotional, more afraid of pain and violence, less coldblooded and steel-nerved in moments of crisis, and so on. The meager evidence we have from the performance of women in espionage and sabotage suggests that women can be as brave and as coldly homicidal as men, whenever their patriotism calls for it.

Being part of an underground is admittedly not as physically arduous as being part of an infantry patrol. Yet in most other respects it resembles the patrol, in the crucial need for mutual confidence among its members, in the alternation of long periods of waiting and boredom with short periods of extreme tension, and in the crucial need for discipline. Women have not passed this test in the military in the past because they were not asked to take the test; in the OSS and parallel services, however, they did.

Our analogy with an infantry patrol, of course, raises one crucial factor, the need for mutual trust and acceptance if women are to be an effective addition to a combat team. By definition, intelligence operatives will on average be a little more intelligent or knowledgeable than infantrymen, a little less prone to suspicion and bias and stereotype. Perhaps the most serious problem for women in combat will, in the end, be less what they can do and more what their fellow soldiers think they can do; unfair as it is, this could remain a serious problem indeed, since combat situations depend on mutual confidence.

To summarize, intelligence operations are not the same as combat, but they are as good an approximation as we have. Such work behind the enemy lines is in some ways less demanding than combat at the lines, and in other ways more, such that the history is an imperfect test. It is nonetheless a test that women did not fail.

THE PATTERN SINCE WORLD WAR II

The aftermath of World War II saw a rapid and almost total demobilization of American armed forces, and it is thus no surprise that the female component was also substantially reduced. From a high point of 265,000 women in the uniformed services in 1945, out of a total of 12 million total U.S. military personnel, the female contingent was reduced to 14,000 by 1948.[17]

Numbers aside, a good part of the progress in World War II was not undone. Congressional action in 1948 established the female branches of the military services on a regular and continuing basis, despite a few last traditionalist suggestions that these instead be made reserve or auxiliary components.

Yet much of the earlier capriciousness of the process was also still in evidence. In a seemingly random manner, the legislation establishing the female branches of the U.S. Navy and the newly separate U.S. Air Force specifically forbade the employment of women in combat, while no mention was made of this in the new legislation on the female branches of the U.S. Army or the Marine Corps. (The latter services nonetheless stated that they interpreted the wording of the air force and navy legislation as the intent of Congress for themselves as well.)

Women served with the U.S. forces deployed to Korea after 1950, and to Vietnam after 1963, but never explicitly "in combat." Given that combat in Vietnam was of the guerrilla rather than front-line variety, with terrorist attacks ranging even into downtown Saigon, the females of the U.S. military did again share some of the perils.

The legislative barriers enacted at the end of World War II still basically remain in effect today in the 1980s, even as the world has in the meantime gone through some enormous changes. As an attempt at a historical account, this section thus can close with only a very brief summary of how these changes brought us through the 1970s.

Perhaps the most important factor is one of delayed action. Namely, that the American *birthrate,* after rising during the immediate postwar baby boom, dropped significantly in the 1950s and 1960s, with the result that the cohort of "military-age males" some eighteen to twenty-five years later may inexorably be smaller than what is thought needed for the proper-sized U.S. military establishment.

A second factor has been a general turning against compulsory military service, primarily because of the casualties suffered in the Vietnam War, but also in larger part because more modern and more urbanized societies have greater inclinations to resent and oppose compulsory service in general. Getting individuals to volunteer has thus become an important part of maintaining a military service; the task is not so easy, especially in face of the smaller male cohorts. Inevitably, therefore, this has made civilian planners and professional military officers develop more open-minded ideas about the employment of female volunteers.

A third factor has been the growth of a sexual permissiveness in the United States. Based in part on the development of new contraceptive techniques and in larger part on the breakdown of some traditional notions of morality, the new wave would strike any observer from the 1940s as almost unbelievable. At its less engaging side, it has been symptomized by a flood of pornography. At its better side, it has immunized Americans against a great deal of the tittering sexual humor that got in the way of serious discussion of male-female issues in earlier decades.

A fourth factor, enormous in its general importance, although somewhat slower and more indirect on the military question, has been the women's liberation movement. The movement has been generally significant for championing equal access to employment for women throughout the civilian economy. In more general terms, it has played an important role in further reducing the tendencies of Americans toward innuendo or rumor based on ribald perceptions of sex differences.

On the legal front, by pushing the Equal Rights Amendment (ERA) to the Constitution, the movement has forced Americans to consider the possibility that women in the future would be as liable as men to compulsory military service (if the draft should ever be reestablished) and (as volunteers or as draftees) as liable to service in combat. Opponents of the ERA indeed sought to alter it to specify an exemption of females from combat (perhaps out of sincere concern for the issue, or perhaps in an effort to make it look less "equal" and, therefore, less worthy of ratification by the states). The alterations were, however, defeated by supporters of the amendment, either because they genuinely felt that women should share all the military burdens in the future, including that of combat, or because they feared that such alterations would indeed be used against the ERA in the ratification debates.

The ERA may be ratified, or it may fail. In either event, it will have played a role in testing American attitudes again on the questions of female military service, and in forcing Americans to think seriously about such questions. If the amendment passes, it will be very clearly arguable that congressional bans on female combat service will have become unconstitutional.

A fifth significant factor has been the willingness of important military officers to take the lead in pushing aside old ideas and traditions on the roles of women. Easily the most important of these for publicizing the issues was Admiral Elmo Zumwalt, who, as chief of Naval Operations (CNO), caught the public eye and antagonized many of his fellow admirals, by substantially changing U.S. Navy policies affecting blacks and women.[18]

Observers often had difficulty in categorizing Zumwalt's performance as CNO. Seemingly a radical or at least a liberal on personnel policies, Zumwalt nonetheless looked very traditional or hardline on the more central questions for the U.S. Navy, namely budget and the threat of the Soviet navy. Those concerned with presenting a less hawkish or more arms-control oriented viewpoint on the budget questions thus tended to see Zumwalt's opening of naval pilot training to females, and similar moves, as a smoke screen designed to lull the American left into not watching him as closely as it should. It indeed seems to have been the case, at the end of the Vietnam experience, that Zumwalt alone of the principal military officers could give addresses on American campuses without serious heckling or hostility.

A contrary view of Zumwalt, and of other officers expressing similar views, would be that the issues of better treatment of minorities and females in the military are not merely some sort of sham, but rather deeply held views. A reading of Admiral Zumwalt's memoirs indeed suggests a seriousness about his stands on the issues, amid a complicated personality that cannot so simply be labeled "liberal" or "conservative." An admiral who truly and hawkishly wants to maintain a navy to match that of the Soviet Union might very sincerely want to make the fullest use possible of female personnel.

The impact of these five factors was certainly significant. In the wake of the congressional passage of the ERA, one had already seen another landmark event in the admission of female cadets and midshipmen to the service academies, preceded even earlier by their admission to Reserve Officers' Training Corps (ROTC) programs. In terms of straightforward female participation in the military, even with the continuing bans on combat service, the rise in percentages through the 1970s was quite remarkable, as shown in Table 12.1.[19]

Table 12.1

Total Number of Women as Percent of Total U.S. Military Personnel: 1971–1980

1971	1972	1973	1974	1975	1976	1980
1.6%	1.9%	2.5%	3.5%	4.6%	5.2%	8%

Depending on how one interprets some distinctions between reserve and active service, the United States now indeed has moved into the position of leading the world in terms of female percentage participation in the military.[20] Israel might have been everyone's guess as to the global leader, but the United States probably now leads Israel if the calculations are done in terms of "person-weeks" of service, divided between "man-weeks" and "women-weeks." While Israeli women are indeed drafted for service (the only country in the world doing this) they find it much easier to get exemptions than do men and cease to participate in active units and reserve units at an earlier time.[21]

As for "combat," the military services in the 1970s were again probing congressional resolve on the issue, once more, in effect, "nickel-and-diming" the crucial distinctions in ways that make it difficult for the legislative branch to object. The navy moved ahead in 1974 to train female pilots, with the air force following some years later. Women have been allowed to participate in armored warfare schools and in general combat infantry training. Maneuvers and experiments in general were under way, officially to test the ability of women to adjust to combat situations, unofficially to ease the way past congressional or public opposition to the idea.

UNCERTAIN PROJECTIONS INTO THE 1980s

The continued increase in female military service in the early 1970s was somewhat paradoxical, for, with the withdrawal from Vietnam, it came at a point of reduced rather than increased mobilization of U.S. military resources in general. The aftermath of World War I by contrast had seen a total phasing-out of the female military, and the aftermath of World War II saw a substantial reduction.

The aftermath of Vietnam was quite different, however, politically, psychologically, and strategically. Unlike 1919 and 1946, the United States did not have any total victory happily obviating a need for military preparedness; rather it had a slow defeat, preceded by great doubts about whether the United states should have wanted to win in the first place.

U.S. foreign policy since 1970 has thus been burdened by serious internal contradictions. The distrust of earlier American foreign policy motives left the draft in limbo. Memories of the American defeat, accentuated by new rounds of apparent Soviet adventurism around the globe, conversely soon enough suggested a need to bolster U.S. armed forces. Such a combination, rendered even worse by the demography of a declining birthrate in the 1950s, made a turn towards additional female military participation quite plausible, with projections in the Carter administration suggesting a figure of 13 percent by 1983.[22]

Ronald Reagan's defeat of Jimmy Carter's bid for reelection only partially resolved such contradictions, but brought a different set of perspectives to bear. Even more than Carter, Reagan campaigned on a need for greater U.S. military preparedness, either by a volunteer army or a draft. Yet Reagan and his backers, more conservative than the Democrats on a host of domestic issues, also came into office much more skeptical again about the plausibility of women in combat, or even in military service generally, and soon announced a decision to stop well short of the Carter projections for female recruitment.

The old taboos and attitudes are thus surely not yet dead.[23] That even the Democrats in Congress had not yet become fully serious about a military role for women was shown as early as in the 1980 response to President Carter's request that men (and women) again be registered for the draft, in the wake of the Soviet armed invasion of Afghanistan. The Congress was very quick to brush aside the suggestion that women be included in such a registration for compulsory military service. The Reagan administration then shows signs of endorsing such a confirmation of more traditional attitudes within the executive branch as well.

CONCLUSIONS

The following implications seem to emerge from the history we have surveyed here: (1) Women had not been allowed any major role in the military of the United States in the past, but the growth of their role in the 1970s was quite impressive and important; (2) Women have been allowed no explicit role at all in combat to date. But they have in various small ways moved into *de facto* combat roles. The evidence from such *de facto* combat roles must be tentative, but it suggests that women, indeed, would not fall apart emotionally in combat and would not show themselves to be any less fit for military action than their male counterparts.

The United States has itself gone through a major transition over the past fifty years in its views about sexual morality and about the role of women. Americans have not yet resolved their naiveté and inconsistency here, but one result of the change is that issues of female military combat participation can now draw more serious attention than before, so that the possibility may never again be dismissed out of hand.

Americans are also still entangled in coming to terms with the nature of international politics, and the appropriate American foreign policy required in response. The so-called lessons of Vietnam, which suggested for a time that no one, male or female, need bear arms anymore, are being reexamined now in the light of continuous armaments investments by the Soviet Union and continuous threats of military action around the world. As decisions are made on the nature of the truly appropriate American military response, the integration of females into the military will continue to be one of the important questions needing to be addressed.

NOTES

1. A good overview of much of this experience can be found in Martin Binkin and Shirley J. Bach, *Women and the Military* (Washington, D.C.: The Brookings Institution, 1977).

2. For an extended discussion of the plans formulated in this period, see Mattie E. Treadwell, *The Women's Army Corps (U.S. Army in World War II: Special Studies)* Washington, D.C.: Office of the Chief of Military History, Department of the Army, 1954), pp. 6–15.

3. Ibid., pp. 256–68.

4. Ibid., p. 220.

5. George H. Gallup, *The Gallup Poll* (New York: Random House, 1972), vol. 1, p. 435.

6. See Treadwell, *The Women's Army Corps,* pp. 301–2.

7. Ibid., pp. 285, 784–85.

8. Binkin and Bach, *Women and the Military,* pp. 24–28.

9. Treadwell, *The Women's Army Corps,* pp. 366–67.

10. Ibid., pp. 393–94, 413.

11. Ibid., pp. 191–218.

12. Ibid., p. 48.

13. For an overview, see Patricia C. Thomas, "Women in the Military: America and the British Commonwealth; Historical Similarities," *Armed Forces and Society* 4, no. 4 (Summer 1978): 623–47.

14. A good general survey of the OSS activities can be found in R. Harris Smith, *OSS: The Secret History of America's First Central Intelligence Agency* (Berkeley: University of California Press, 1972). For more anecdotal material, see Robert Hayden Alcorn, *No Banners, No Bands* (New York: David McKay Co., 1965).

15. For some interesting, albeit anecdotal, accounts of the female role in espionage, see J. Bernard Hutton, *Women in Espionage* (New York: Macmillan, 1971) and A. A. Hoehling, *Women Who Spied* (New York: Dodd, Mead, and Co., 1967).

16. For a somewhat sweeping and opinionated assertion that sexual attractiveness must be most or all of a female's role in espionage, see Oreste Pinto *Spy-Catcher* (London: Werner Laurie, 1952), pp. 19–22.

17. Binkin and Bach, *Women in the Military,* p. 10.

18. See Elmo R. Zumwalt, Jr., *On Watch* (New York: Quadrangle, 1976), especially pp. 216–65.

19. Binkin and Bach, *Women in the Military,* p. 15.

20. A good overview of the state of female participation by 1980 can be found in "Women in the Military: Should They be Drafted?" *Newsweek* (February 18, 1980), pp. 34–42. For a more extended discussion of these recent developments, see the chapter by Jeff M. Tuten, this volume, pp. 237–65.

21. See Anne R. Bloom, this volume, pp. 137–62.

22. *NOW National Times* 14, no. 3 (March 1980): 1, 4–9.

23. For an eloquent statement of what still may be dominant American attitudes, see George Gilder, "The Case Against Women in Combat," *New York Times Magazine* (January 28, 1979): 29–31, 44, 46. See also Judith Galloway and Edward D. Wheeler, "Point Counterpoint: Women in Combat; The Need for Cultural Reconditioning," *Air University Review* 30, no. 1 (November–December 1978): 58–68.

13 | THE ARGUMENT AGAINST FEMALE COMBATANTS

Jeff M. Tuten

PURPOSE

In response to changes in U.S. social values and political, economic, and military pressures, combat exclusion restrictions on servicewomen have been steadily eroding in recent years. Moreover, the erosion has been particularly swift since 1970. This paper examines the causes and extent of this trend in an effort to judge whether the combat exclusion policies should be further relaxed, strengthened, or abolished.

BACKGROUND

Each of the U.S. armed services now excludes female members from active face-to-face combat. The nature and extent of the exclusion varies with each service. For the navy, marine corps, and air force, the exclusion is mandated by law. The law does not prohibit the army from employing women in combat. The army, however, has repeatedly assured Congress that it would not send its female soldiers into the trenches.

Why women were being excluded from combat has rarely been stated. Until recently, warfare was so clearly recognized as "men's work" that few people really thought to ask. When women began to enter the military, it became necessary to deal with the what, why, and how of excluding women.

The services have difficulty in defining what combat actually is in order to exclude women from it. In earlier centuries when weaponry was simple and its reach measured in tens or hundreds of yards, combat definitions were much easier. Before this century, the large majority of soldiers in the field and sailors at sea were combatants in the pure sense of the word. In battle they fought closely with their adversaries and attempted to kill or

237

capture them. Consequently, all soldiers and sailors were generally considered combatants. Thus, we can derive the first of three components of combat that have traditionally governed the exclusion of women—that of *function*. A combatant is one whose duty involves direct action designed to kill or capture members of an opposing enemy force. Because almost all members of field forces had primary or secondary combatant functions, a female combat exclusion policy could and did equate with a military exclusion policy.

But what of those few soldiers and sailors whose function is and was explicitly other than killing or capturing the enemy? What about the physicians and their field assistants? By function, they are noncombatants, yet, they share all the hardships and dangers of the combatants because they are intermingled with them. The U.S. armed services have traditionally forbidden the employment of women as front-line medics because of the place in which the noncombatant function is performed. Similarly, women have been prohibited from serving as noncombatants on warships or as members of military air crews. Thus, we derive the second and third components of the combat definition—*colocation* with those engaged in active combat and the associated *level of danger*.

The *function, colocation,* and *level of danger* rules form the framework of past and present U.S. policy regarding the exclusion of women from combat. Simply stated, the rule has been that women would not be permitted to participate directly in military activities designed to kill or capture the enemy or to share the hardship and danger of the soldiers and sailors who were doing so. The *function, colocation,* and *danger* rules for many years prevented any female membership in the military services. Then, after women were admitted (first as auxiliaries and, subsequently, as servicewomen) the rules served to limit both the duties they were allowed to perform and the units and localities in which they could perform them. The logical basis and application of these rules are now, however, being challenged.

HISTORICAL PERSPECTIVE

It is difficult to imagine the current women-in-combat debate taking place even a generation ago. At the turn of this century, American women could not vote, much less serve in the nation's armed services. Only forty years ago, there were no servicewomen except for nurses. In 1980 we find President Carter seeking authority to register women for a possible future draft. We find the military services under great political pressure to further increase their female content. We find litigation rising to the Supreme Court challenging the constitutionality of drafting only males for future wars. Obviously, American attitudes on the nature and role of women in our society have changed, and have done so with startling speed. The question is: Should we take the final step and remove all barriers to employing women in combat?

The historical record is quite clear. War and soldiering, with few if any substantial pre-twentieth-century exceptions, have been an exclusive male preserve. One can point to the Amazons of Greek mythology but few real exceptions are recorded.[1] Moreover, the pattern has been ubiquitous. The soldiers of Moses, Pericles, Darius, Alexander, Caesar, Gengis Khan, Charlemagne, Wellington, and Washington were male only. The same has held true in primitive tribes throughout the world, across time. Sitting Bull's warriors were men. So were the warriors of aboriginal Australia, New Guinea, and so on. The pattern is too widespread and complete to have been a function of chance.

Pre-twentieth century man seems never to have seriously questioned the reservation of war for the male sex. He, wisely perhaps, left this to us. It was accepted that men were the hunters while women were the keepers of the home and bearers of children. Men had the hunting instinct while women's driving instinct was maternal. Men were aggressive while women were passive. In short, the innate emotional differences between the sexes suited men for war while ruling women out.

So, too, in the minds of our ancestors, did physical differences. Patently, women were smaller, weaker, slower, and had less physical endurance than males. All these attributes were essentially disqualifying in the era when all combat was characterized by strenuous physical activity.

Thus, for the five thousand years or so that we know about, women were not only excluded from combat but this exclusion was also accepted as right and natural. If someone had questioned this historic, unwritten exclusion policy, one can easily imagine the reply: "Women's unsuitability for combat is made apparent by the fact that they have never engaged in it. Thus, *a posteriori,* women are unsuited for combat."

WAR IN THE AGE OF TECHNOLOGY

The industrial revolution, with its still increasing explosion of technology, has produced profound changes in civilization. It is probably safe to say that George Washington would have felt more at home with the technology and sociopolitical attitudes of Athens in the age of Pericles or Republican Rome than with that of America today. For one thing, warfare in 1775 was much more like that described by Thucydides than that waged today. The bows, spears, swords, and catapults of Athens were not very distant in concept or in destructiveness from the muskets, bayonets, swords, and cannons of the American Revolution. In both periods, standing armies tended to be small or nonexistent.[2] Armies raised for active campaigns were small relative to the populations that produced them.

The direct effects of war were generally confined to the soldier and sailor participants. Moreover, the costs of equipping and sustaining expeditionary forces were relatively modest. Apart from wars involving migrating populations, wars were rarely "total." The active participants and those who supported them by industrial and agricultural activities were small minorities of the national populations.

The mushrooming technological and industrial advances of the twentieth century have caused sweeping changes in the nature of warfare. War has become more diverse in the skills it demands. There were no computer specialists, radar repairmen, or X-ray technicians in Washington's army, or in Pershing's American Expeditionary Force for that matter. Today, such occupational specialties are legion. The result has been a continuing decline in what soldiers call the "tooth-to-tail" ratio. As the years pass, decreasing percentages of the members of modern military forces are assigned missions that bring them face to face with their adversaries.

For a large number of military tasks, the requirement for muscular strength, agility, and physical endurance has been reduced or eliminated by technology. In many areas, mechanical power is replacing muscle power. The army's new XM-1 tank, for example, weighs over fifty tons. It requires about as much physical strength to drive as the average family sedan. (Changing or replacing the track is, however, a backbreaking job requiring strength, endurance, and a complete vocabulary of obscenities.)

Technology has expanded the range and destructiveness of weaponry. Thus, those endangered by warfare are no longer just the soldiers on the battlefield and "within the sound of the guns." The advent of long-range artillery, aircraft, and, finally, the intercontinental missile have enlarged the battlefield until it encompasses all the territory of nations at war. Now all residents of a state at war are potential targets.

War in the twentieth century requires the direct and indirect participation of larger percentages of the warring states' manpower and materiel resources. World War I probably consumed more iron and steel than the entire world population had up to that point. The USSR suffered over 19 million dead—over 10 percent of its population—in World War II. The systematic mobilization of industry and labor in support of warfare is essentially a twentieth century phenomenon. Armies are larger and so is their per capita consumption of goods and services. Because of this effect, the size of a state's total male and female manpower pool and its productivity have become a major determinant in the outcome of war. Hence, the rise of "Rosie the Riveter" and her World War I predecessors. Both world wars were, therefore, powerful agents in bringing about changes in women's roles in society.

WOMEN'S CHANGING ROLE IN THE TWENTIETH CENTURY

The industrial and technological revolution's effects were, of course, not confined to the military. Our national economic, political, and social systems have been substantially altered in this century. Among the most visible changes have been those involving the national perception of the role that women can and should play in society. The contrast between the status of women in Western industrialized nations in 1901 as opposed to 1982 is startling. Nowhere is the change more marked than in America. This development has required a sweeping change in our views on the psychological and physiological differences between the sexes. These changes, for better or worse, are overturning the conventional military beliefs and traditions accumulated over the centuries.

American women's growing emancipation has been both expedited and mirrored by their inclusion in the military services. Their progress was slow and intermittent until the decade of the 1960s. The army inducted its first women when it organized the Army Nurse Corps in 1901. The navy followed suit in 1908. Both have remained in active service to the present. Army and navy nurses did not, however, receive full military status until early in World War II.

Pressed for personnel with clerical and administrative skills during World War I, the navy was the first U.S. military service to admit women to full membership in terms of uniform, rank, and status. About thirteen thousand "Yeomanettes' and "Marinettes" were recruited. They were restricted to shore duty. Moreover, they were discharged immediately following the war. The army considered enrolling women during the war but rejected the idea. Thus, with the disbanding of the Yeomanettes and Marinettes, women in the service were again confined to the Army and Navy Nurse Corps.

During the 1920s and '30s, there was very little interest in enlisting women in the military. In 1918 the U.S. military services had roughly 4,315,000 uniformed personnel on active duty. By 1933 that number had dwindled to about 244,000.[3] Given the size of the services and prevailing economic conditions, male recruits were available in more than ample numbers. At the same time, women who had entered the labor force in response to World War I production demands were squeezed out by the Great Depression.

The onset of World War II gave powerful impetus to the employment of women both in military service and in industry. Within ten months after Pearl Harbor, all services, including the coast guard, had formed women's auxiliary organizations. By the end of the war, 266,256 women were on active duty in the WAACs, WAVES, USMCR, and SPARs.[4] Throughout the war, their performance was impressive. They served mostly in the United States, but about 5 percent were deployed abroad and were employed in all military theaters of operation. They were prohibited from participating in any form of combat, however, and were never assigned to locations close to the front. Moreover, they were always segregated in female-only units and detachments, never integrated into male units except for the nurses in field hospitals. In the main, they served in the so-called women's traditional skills as nurses, clerks, and communicators; they also served in small numbers in some nontraditional skills as aviation mechanics, drivers, and parachute riggers. Nevertheless, the large majority of military occupational specialties were closed to women. In May 1945 slightly fewer than 2 percent of the 12,124,000 U.S. active duty military personnel were women.[5]

Equally impressive, if not more so, was the performance of American women in the civilian work force in World War II. Exhorted by an intensive and sustained propaganda campaign and lured by relatively high-paying industrial jobs, women entered the labor force in unprecedented numbers. In 1900, 20 percent of American women over fourteen years of age were employed. They composed 18.1 percent of the total U.S. labor force. In 1940, on the eve of World War II, their participation rate had risen to 27.9 percent and they constituted 25.6 percent of the civilian labor force. Thereafter, the absolute number of women in the work force, their participation rate, and their share of the total civilian labor force increased steeply through 1944. In that year, 36.5 percent of American women over fourteen years old were at work. They then constituted more than a third of the nation's civilian workers.[6,7]

In effect, women replaced men in the labor force, freeing the latter for military service. Primarily because of the influx of women, the United States was able to maintain a civilian labor force of prewar size (about 55 million workers) and, at the same time, field military forces of over 12 million. Viewed in terms of total contribution, the role of American servicewomen takes on a different perspective. At their peak strength, they composed less than 2 percent of the military forces and less than 1.5 percent of the total female work force. Had the government elected to do so, it could have employed our 266,000 servicewomen in the civilian labor force and freed an offsetting number of men for military service. Thus, without denigrating the excellent performance of U.S. servicewomen in World War II, it is clear that the United States could have just as easily fielded an all-male force. Obviously, the question in America's largest military mobilization was not whether to employ women in combat but whether to employ them in uniform at all.

WOMEN IN OTHER WORLD WAR II ARMIES

The British conscripted women for war service. Peak strength reached 437,200 in 1945.[8] The British never gave serious consideration to the employment of women in combat. They were never armed or given weapons training. As with the Americans, the large majority served within the United Kingdom in the traditional jobs—medical, communications, clerical, and administrative. Considerable numbers of volunteers were, however, assigned to active antiaircraft batteries. There, they manned searchlights, fire direction, and communications equipment but did not handle the guns.

The Germans made extensive use of servicewomen in World War II. As with the U.S. and British forces, most served within Germany while a relatively small number were deployed to subjected territories and active combat theaters. The Germans were even more protective of their servicewomen than were the Americans and British. They were not allowed near the front or in areas of partisan activity and served only in closed groups. They were strictly forbidden the use of weapons even in self-defense. Indeed, the Germans never accorded their servicewomen full military status, maintaining throughout the war that they were auxiliaries serving with the forces but not in them. The great majority served in the traditional female skill areas but, later in the war, substantial numbers were assigned to antiaircraft duties. Like their British counterparts, they were in crews on barrage ballons, searchlights, and fire direction apparatus but were not allowed in gun crews. Unlike the British and Americans, the Germans never militarized their nursing services. They relied instead on nurses drawn from the Red Cross and the religious orders.[9]

Among the major participants in World War II, only the Soviets formally employed women as combatants.[10] Faced with appalling losses and serious manpower shortfalls, they conscripted women starting in 1941. Soviet statistics are sparse and vague, but about 800,000 women appear to have served in uniform. At their peak, they constituted about 8 percent of Soviet forces. Most were assigned to combat support duties rather than direct combat. The Soviets did, however, form a number of all-female combat units, including a fighter aircraft regiment, two bomber regiments, and an infantry regiment. Little reliable information on the performance of the female combat formations is available. It is known that the percentage of Soviet servicewomen assigned to combat units was relatively small. The Germans were shocked to find them on the battlefield and were contemptuous of their fighting performance.[11]

POSTWAR EXPERIENCE

Following World War II, the nations of the world quickly demobilized their forces. Many nations that had employed women in uniform disestablished their programs and returned to all-male military services. The United States very nearly did so. Indeed, the various women's components had been viewed as temporary establishments when organized in 1942. The statutory authorization for the Women's Army Auxiliary Corps was scheduled to expire in 1948.

In June 1945 U.S. military forces had totaled slightly more than 12 million personnel including some 266,000 women. By June 1948 military strength had fallen to about 1.4 million of whom only about 14,500 were women. In early 1947 the draft law had expired and the services were unable to recruit enough males to maintain authorized strengths. The military leadership, therefore, sought authority to convert the women's components of the various military services into small but permanent establishments. (This was the first instance of male recruiting shortfalls resulting in a resort to women; it would be repeated later.) Congress responded by passing the Women's Armed Services Act of 1948. The act, at military suggestion, imposed a 2 percent ceiling on enlisted women as a proportion of the force. The ceiling on female officers was set at 10 percent of female enlisted strength (exclusive of nurses). The law also imposed grade (that is, rank) limitations and prohibited women from serving as commanders. Ironically, the nation resumed conscription of males less than a month after the passage of the Women's Armed Services Act and, for the next twenty-six years, there were to be no recruiting problems. The combat exclusion policies developed during World War II were continued unchanged. Women served in small numbers, in traditional skills, and with broadly drawn prohibitions against their employment in combat or their undue exposure to the dangers of combat through proximity.

In the latter half of the 1960s, the limits on the numbers of women in the U.S. armed forces and the roles that they were allocated began to be reexamined. The initiative did not spring from the uniformed services. Rather, it came from the more politically sensitive ranks of the Office of the Secretary of Defense and the service secretariats. Thus, the question of the servicewomen's role joined a host of others in the adversary relationship that is so frequently characteristic of the relationship of the uniformed military to their civilian superiors. The former tend to be conservative in outlook and reverent of tradition. The latter, led by political appointees, are less cautious and perhaps more attuned to national social and political trends than their uniformed subordinates. In any event, civilian defense officials have, over the years, generally pushed for expanded female military participation with fewer restrictions.

In 1967, at the Department of Defense's request, provisions of law that limited the ranks that servicewomen could hold were removed. Additionally, Congress lifted the 2 percent women's content ceiling. These were the initial steps in a progression of events that has led the United States to quintuple the number of servicewomen since 1967, while reducing male strength by one-third.

Over the same period, the military services have, with considerable reluctance and foot dragging, changed their definitions of combat in order to open previously closed job specialties to women. Concurrently, assignment policies have been revised to allow servicewomen to serve in previously all-male combat units from which they have traditionally been excluded.

THE 1970s—A DECADE OF CHANGE

The United States entered the 1970s with military forces totaling more than 3 million, which included about 41,500 women. Combat exclusion policies were broadly drawn and rigidly enforced. The army and marines employed their limited numbers of servicewomen in female-only units. No women could be assigned to division level or smaller units. Only 185 of the army's 482 military occupational specialties were open to women. In the marines, the entire Fleet Marine Force (three-fourths of total corps strength) was closed to women.

The navy strictly interpreted Section 6015, Title 10, U.S. Code, which then stated:

The Secretary of the Navy may prescribe the manner in which women shall be trained and qualified for military duty in the Regular Navy, the military authority which they may exercise, and the kind of military duty to which they may be assigned: *Provided,* That they shall not be assigned to duty in aircraft while such aircraft are engaged in combat missions nor shall they be assigned to duty on vessels of the Navy except hospital ships and naval transports.

This restriction almost totally closed all seagoing billets to Navy servicewomen. Together with force rotation requirements, it restricted female strength to less than 5 percent of the navy.

Title 10 also established restrictions on the employment of air force servicewomen.

The Secretary of the Air Force shall prescribe the military authority which female persons of the Air Force may exercise, and the kind of military duty to which they may be assigned: *Provided,* That they shall not be assigned to duty in aircraft while such aircraft are engaged in combat missions.

The air force, in 1970, interpreted this section in a way that precluded assignment of women to any air crew duties regardless of the type or mission of the aircraft. Air force regulations specifically forbade assignment of women to positions that included "combat operations by actually engaging the enemy and/or delivering weapons upon the enemy."[12]

In terms of percentage of total air force specialties from which women were barred, the exclusion was minor. Only about 6 percent of total air force jobs were restricted.[13] (This is because the numerical tooth-to-tail ratio in the air force is relatively minute.) Nevertheless, the 1970 actual female content in the air force was only 1.7 percent.[14]

During the 1970s a number of events and conditions combined to change the roles and levels of participation of women in America's armed services. Probably the most powerful agents of change were the demise of the draft and the growth of the women's rights movement.

The decision to end conscription was announced in 1970 and implemented in 1972. Military manpower managers recognized from the start that they faced an uphill battle in recruiting sufficient male volunteers to maintain required force levels. It was clear that, in order to maintain the All-Volunteer Force, the female component would have to be substantially increased. At the same time, the women's rights movement was emerging as a powerful lobby seeking equal rights for women in all aspects of American life, to include the armed forces. The result was a convergence of goals that has produced results beyond those anticipated by either the military or the feminists. (We will see later that the increases in women in uniform have been so great that they are now beginning to worry both the uniformed military and some feminists.)

Women would have to be admitted to previously closed jobs if their numbers were to be substantially increased. The services were painfully conscious that they knew very little about how well women could perform nontraditional military tasks. To their credit, they made strenuous and sustained efforts to learn. The army alone has performed three massive field studies involving thousands of personnel.[15] Study and research efforts in the other services have been comparable.

Military leaders and decision makers used known values—male performance standards—as the norm. Historical data and experience factors are such that male performance under varying circumstances and levels of stress can be predicted within narrow bounds. The various studies, tests, surveys, and exercises have been designed to determine how women perform compared to men and how well units including women perform compared to all-male units. Table 13.1 is illustrative of the type of information being sought. It is reprinted from the "Evaluation of Women in the Army—Final Report," March 1978.

As can be seen from the issues, in 1978 the army was still striving, as

Table 13.1

Arrangement of Issues for Evaluation of Women's Capabilities

MAJOR ISSUE	SUBAREAS OF CONCERN
Physical	Size-Strength-Grip-Arm and Leg Length-Endurance-Coordination
Medical	Pregnancy/Lost Time-Menses-Hygiene Birth Control-Profiles-Stress
Psychological	Emotionality-Aggressiveness-Toughness-Mechanical Ability-Confidence-Self-Image
Social/Organizational	Fraternization-Female Leadership Capability-*Male Leadership Capability-Motivation-*Intra-Service Marriage
Management	Facilities-Clothing and Equipment-Utilization-Training and Education-Sole Parents-Recruiting-Promotions-*Female Warrant Officers-*Limits on Female Content in Units
Reserve Components	Reserve Unique Areas

* Significant concerns that surfaced during the evaluation.

were the other services, to determine how much women could do and would do under stress. Additionally, the effect of women on male performance was—and remains—a matter of concern.

PHYSICAL AND MEDICAL CONSIDERATIONS

Since 1970 much has been learned regarding the physical and medical capabilities of women in the military setting. Basically, women have turned out to be somewhat tougher and more capable than the male military leadership thought they would be and much less tough and less capable than the leaders of the women's movement claimed they would be.[16]

Exhaustive work has been done in defining male-female anthropometric differences. The results are clear. Men are substantially larger, heavier, stronger, and faster. Men have greater physical endurance. A larger percentage of their body weight is devoted to muscle and bone mass. They can carry heavier loads longer distances at greater speeds. They can throw heavier objects (such as hand grenades) farther and more accurately. Finally, they can do all these things under greater extremes of temperature.

It should be noted that these male physical advantages are genetic—no amount of physical conditioning will change them. Start with two 140-pound eighteen-year-olds, a male and a female, in average physical condition. The male will be stronger and faster and have more stamina. Put them into intensive physical training. At their respective physical peaks, the male will have *increased* his relative physical superiority over the female.[17] Thus, immutable physiological differences favor the employment of men in tasks that require physical strength, speed, power, and endurance. Few would deny that these physical attributes are essential to the soldier or marine in ground combat. Closing with the enemy and destroying him is a very physical endeavor, and modern technology has not changed that at all—nor is it likely to. Therefore, without even coming to psychological, sociological, or management considerations, we can support a major conclusion: *The exclusion of women from front-line ground combat is mandated by their lesser physical capabilities.*

This exclusion is not based upon any gallant desire to shield women from the horrors of war. Rather, it is dictated by the requirement to *win*. If two ground combat forces meet in battle and one is composed, in part, of physically inferior personnel, the other force has a distinct tactical advantage. The physically weaker unit will be defeated. Equal opportunity on the battlefield spells defeat.

The point has previously been made that smaller percentages of armies now actually participate in front-line ground combat. Large numbers of personnel serve in what the ground forces call combat support (CS) and combat service support (CSS) roles. The U.S. Army classifies infantry and armor units as combat; artillery, military police, and engineers as combat support; and other battlefield functions, such as medics and maintenance, as combat service support. In the U.S. Army and U.S. Marine Corps, the smallest self-contained unit combining all arms and services is the division. An army-mechanized division normally deploys five infantry battalions of about 850 men each, four tank battalions of about 550 men, and an armored cavalry squadron of about 850 men. There is a combat aviation battalion of 800 personnel. These units are the front-line combat elements of the division. Combat support units include four artillery battalions of about 550 men each, a low-altitude air defense artillery battalion, a combat engineer battalion, and a military police company. Finally, combat service support elements include a supply and transportation battalion, a signal battalion, a medical battalion, a maintenance battalion, a finance company, and an administration company. The division commander has three brigade headquarters that exercise command over the ten combat battalions. The entire division consists of about 15,000 soldiers of whom roughly 7,500 serve in the combat battalions, about 2,500 in the combat support units, and the remainder of about 5,000 or so serve in various command and control headquarters and combat service support units assigned to the division.

A few years ago, all division duty assignments were closed to women in the U.S. Army. Now, about a third are open, including duty positions in the brigade headquarters that command and control the fighting battalions.

On first inspection, this seems to do no violence to the ground combat exclusion rule postulated earlier. However, a closer look reveals otherwise. This is because the battlefield is simply not a neat and tidy place that permits CS and CSS soldiers to perform only their assigned noncombat duties.

Even the most cursory examination of twentieth-century combat experience reveals that all divisional troops may be called on at any time to fight as infantry. This was true at the Kasserine Pass in North Africa, at the Battle of the Bulge, and on countless other occasions during World War II. It was true throughout the Korean War and the war in Vietnam. Nor is the "every soldier an emergency rifleman" rule unique to U.S. ground forces. All armies implicitly view all of their soldiers except medical personnel as emergency infantrymen.

In fact, the army's civilian leadership has admitted that many of its servicewomen will be thrust into ground combat roles. Testifying before the House Armed Services Committee on February 26, 1980, William Clark, Principal Deputy Assistant Secretary of the Army (Manpower and Reserve Affairs) said:

The Army accepts the fact that women may be exposed to combat as a result of their assignments and that some women may become battlefield casualties, given the expected fluid nature of today's and tomorrow's battlefield. Nevertheless, the Army does not propose to change its policy that would require the assignment of women to combat MOSs or to combat units who would be routinely engaged in close combat.

Commitment of divisional and higher echelon combat support and combat service support personnel as riflemen (or should we say riflewomen?) will become necessary under a number of circumstances, for instance, when:

1. The enemy penetrates the division's forward defenses and CSS troops must be committed as ground combatants to stop or expel him,
2. CSS troops must be fed into the combat battalions to replace losses, and/or
3. The enemy air assaults into the division or corps rear area and CSS units must be committed to contain/destroy the enemy's airhead.

Military history is replete with examples of these kinds of employment of CS/CSS troops in ground combat. But the problem with respect to current U.S. ground forces is broader and even more compelling. General Bernard Rogers, then army chief of staff, testified in 1979 before the Senate Armed Services Committee that the U.S. Army was 500,000 trained men short of those needed to repel a Warsaw Pact attack in Europe.[18] Moreover, the trained military manpower shortfall is most severe in the ground combat specialties—infantrymen and armor crewmen. Consequently, the army has developed plans for the wholesale diversion of men with CS/CSS specialties to replace anticipated losses in engaged combat battalions.[19] Some will be given brief combat retraining, others will go straight to the front.[20]

Now consider the consequences of the steadily increasing percentage of women in the army and the increasingly narrow definition of combat. The pool of males in CS and CSS jobs who can be shifted to combat duties is shrinking daily, both within divisions and throughout the army. It is quite obvious that the army is rapidly backing itself into a position that will make the commitment of women in ground combat unavoidable. To the extent that women serve in division level units, the combat exclusion argument is already moot. Table 13.2 shows the numbers of enlisted women currently assigned to U.S. Army divisions.

All this flies in the face of the demonstrated fact that women are substantially inferior to men in the physical requirements of ground combat. It is inevitable that divisions and corps with admixtures of women in CS/

Table 13.2

Enlisted Females Currently Assigned to Regular U.S. Army Divisions: June 1980

DIVISION	ENLISTED WOMEN ASSIGNED
1st Infantry Division	678
2d Infantry Division	398*
3d Infantry Division	894
4th Infantry Division	739
5th Infantry Division	456*
7th Infantry Division	478*
8th Infantry Division	779
9th Infantry Division	604
24th Infantry Division	339*
25th Infantry Division	401*
82d Airborne Division	107
101st Airborne Division (A/A)	686
1st Cavalry Division	434
1st Armored Division	838
2d Armored Division	678
3d Armored Division	872
TOTAL	9,381

* Divisions which consist of two, rather than three, active brigades.

CSS units will be measurably less combat effective than all-male units.

Beyond the strength, stamina, and speed differential, other physiological differences will militate against the employment of women in combat. Among these is women's capability of becoming pregnant. During calendar year 1977, 14.5 percent of the army's female officers and enlisted women became pregnant. Now it is obvious that American public opinion has, in recent years, become more liberal in its views on women in the military. It is unlikely, however, that the body politic will *ever* permit the employment of pregnant women in combat. Indeed, the issue arose during the Joint Chiefs of Staff war game conducted in 1978. During the now famous Exercise NIFTY NUGGET in 1978, army personnel managers were forced to "evacuate" over a thousand pregnant soldiers from Europe at the very time there was a desperate manpower shortfall there. Concurrently, thousands of other servicewomen could not be deployed with units that were being "deployed" to Europe—because they were pregnant. Such a situation would inevitably be repeated in an actual mobilization and deployment.[21] This state of affairs would merely be ludicrous if the army had a surplus of trained nonpregnant replacements. It becomes tragic in light of the huge existing trained manpower shortfall. All military services face the same problem of deployment.

There also is the spectre of intentional pregnancies by servicewomen to avoid deployment to the front or remaining there. It would be an easier and more pleasant alternative than desertion to Sweden.

PSYCHOLOGICAL AND SOCIAL/ORGANIZATIONAL CONSIDERATIONS

Efforts to determine the psychosocial consequences of the employment of women in formerly all-male military units have been intense. Service concerns are well expressed by Richard Gabriel in the March 1980 issue of *Army Magazine*.

The fact is that combat effectiveness is only partially, and probably only a small part, the result of well-applied technical skills. Most skills in the military, especially combat skills, are learnable by virtually anyone within six to eight weeks. But military unit effectiveness and cohesion are far more the result of sociopsychological bonding—anthropologically, male bonding—among soldiers within combat groups.

Without this crucial bonding, units disintegrate under stress no matter how technically proficient or well-equipped they are. The key variable in the effectiveness of a military unit is not the technical abilities of its troops, although a certain level of technical competence is required, but the ability of troops to maintain cohesive bonding groups under fire. With regard to the role of women, if examined in terms of technical competence, the question is misplaced.

and:

What is devastatingly certain, however, is that we have tinkered with the very foundations of our military forces without any sound sociological or psychological research from which to predict the results of our organizational restructuring. Driven by ideology and the equation of military tasks with civilian business, we have proceeded to integrate females in our military forces with scant regard for the possible consequences.

What evidence is available suggests strongly that the complete integration of women in the military, especially in ground combat roles, may have devastating consequences for the levels of cohesion and effectiveness that can be expected of integrated units. There are, for example, no historical models for the use of females in warrior bands.[22]

Gabriel has been quoted at length because the issue he raises lies at the heart of the combat exclusion issue. It would do so even if women were physically equal or superior to men. The question of the effect of female integration on the cohesion and fighting qualities of the combat group is particularly relevant to the air force and navy. In these services, large numbers of combat jobs do not require physical capabilities beyond those of women. Women's advocates who admit female physical limitations naturally point to such combat assignments and ask why women should not be employed in them.

A number of problems face the researcher trying to assess the effect of women on fighting-group combat effectiveness. Foremost is the problem of extrapolation. The sustained stress of actual combat cannot be duplicated. Therefore, researchers are forced to employ field exercises and attitude surveys. None of the results can be fully trusted because the grinding fear and stress of combat cannot be simulated. In the absence of such hard knowledge, it is obvious that the inclusion of women involves the risk that the combat effectiveness of mixed units, be they combatant ships or combat air squadrons, will be reduced. Moreover, it is highly unlikely that the extent of such a combat capability degradation can be known before it is too late to reverse it or overcome its consequences. Thus, on the basis of the foregoing, we can formulate a second major conclusion: *Women should not be integrated into combat formations unless it is demonstrated that their presence will not degrade combat performance.* Again, the intent is not to shield women from war—it is to shield warriors from defeat.

Beyond the effect that women might have on male fighting performance, there is the question of women's aggressiveness and fighting spirit. Here, it is interesting to note, the feminists themselves are divided. Writing in *The Nation* earlier this year, Jean Bethke Elshtain described the dichotomy.

The dilemma confronted by the feminist "second wave" from the 1960s to the present on the question of women's "nature" and its relation to issues of war and peace can be stated somewhat as follows: The assertion of identical male and female natures (men are not born "men" and women are not born "women" but become such through interaction with a social environment that reproduces men and women along recognizable, distinguishable and stereotypical lines) has the advantage of reducing naive assumptions concerning women's innate goodness but the disadvantage of having to look to men as examples of what women can or shall become once they are "liberated." There are feminists to whom this is unsatisfactory, either because they accept the "natural-difference" hypothesis or because they hold that "feminine principles" or a specifically female way of thinking, which one contemporary feminist theorist dubs "maternal thought," have indeed emerged over the years and have been run roughshod over by the male-dominated society. This group of feminists insists that the whole thrust of the women's movement should be to articulate those principles or to legitimate a specifically female way of seeing, one tied inescapably to women's traditional functions as mothers and keepers of the hearth.[23]

Feminists such as Mary Jo Salter favor the innate female difference hypothesis. In the June 1980 *Atlantic,* she wrote:

It seems a far-fetched reaction to a call for draft registration, perhaps, for me to reiterate Woolf's question. But I think it is an explosive question for the new generation of women who are both draft-eligible and professionally inclined. To be man's equal, must we share his wardrobe of three-piece suits and military uniforms? It may be understandable, but is certainly regrettable, that "equality" in so many cases means conformity to the male habit. To earn the right to speak our minds, must we agree that we've always been "highly combative," or that we ought to let them teach us how to be? Too often we've been told that to be dedicated professionals, we must eagerly sacrifice all for our jobs and neglect our children (if our offices allow us time to give birth at all). Now, to be dedicated citizens—and feminists—we must accept the male notion of citizenship as including compulsory military service.[24]

The American Civil Liberties Union (ACLU) Women's Rights Project position is more environmentalist in its view of women's nature. Suzan Blank wrote the following in the April 1980 issue of *Civil Liberties.*

Beyond these past and present cases is the most sexist issue of all—the exclusion of women from combat. Many Americans, President Carter seemingly among them, take as a given that women ought to be barred from combat duty. The ACLU Women's Rights Project does not agree.

Diana Steele points out that, especially with the recent technological changes in weaponry, which make combat as much a matter of technical expertise as physical strength, women are capable of most feats of physical combat—and, like men, they can be trained for modern-day fighting. In fact, at West Point, women are already receiving the same combat training as men—with only a few differences, such as karate lessons instead of boxing.

Only a small proportion of combat positions involve actual hand-to-hand fighting. Many positions provide support for frontline troops, or places for personnel who are being rotated off combat duty. If women are barred from all such positions, they miss out on many chances both for enlistment and advancement in the military.[25]

Where lies the truth? Are women innately less aggressive and combative than men? Or are women the victims of cultural conditioning that represses their natural warlike instincts to levels below those typical of males? Robert Ardrey has proposed a theory that suggests that both the above factors are operating together.

Cultural traditions are also a part of our environment. If there is a tradition, as in almost all African tribes, to kill twins as soon as they are born, then you will not find many twins around, and if you pursue the tradition through a sufficient number of generations the genetic potentiality to twin should be considerably reduced. In this sense the cultural anthropologist is correct: Variations between the cultural traditions of human populations must, if pursued for a sufficient number of generations, have a selective effect on the quality of a population's gene pool. The capacity for a human population to form cultural traditions which become a significant selective force in a particular environment has probably contributed to the rapid rate of human evolution. To underrate the long-term genetic consequences of a cultural tradition is as dangerous as to overrate the short-term conclusiveness of cultural determination.[26]

This formulation would suggest that the widely held belief that women as a group are less naturally combative is due to a combination of cultural conditioning and natural selection operating for thousands of years. There is a growing body of scientific knowledge which supports this conclusion. The evidence suggests a linkage to male hormones. Kenneth Lamott addressed the cultural versus chemical issue in an article in *Horizons* in 1977.

. . . Anyway, social conditioning is suspect as the entire explanation, since there are reasons for thinking that biology is at work here, too. Aggressiveness is a biologically determined trait that is found more often in men than in women. Evidence of male aggressiveness comes from anthropologists, ethnologists, and endocrinologists. It appears in virtually all human societies. The evidence of male aggressiveness in other mammals and in birds argues that it is not a characteristic of human society alone but a natural attribute of maleness. Finally, from studies with laboratory animals—rats, monkeys, and others—comes direct evidence that aggressiveness is influenced by the level of male hormones; that is, increased androgens result in increased aggressiveness.[27]

Actually, the root causation of the male's higher aggressiveness is of little importance. That the male of the species is more combative is a fact of life in contemporary society—and one that must be reckoned with in addressing the women in combat issue. Even if female submissiveness is nongenetic and nonchemical but, instead, purely environmental in origin, the fact remains that women are less aggressive. They are the product of that "repressive" male-dominated environment *now*. That being the case, it would be necessary to reprogram the current generation of military-age women to suit them for combat. That is, of course, an impossible task. Further, it is not one the American people would allow even if it were possible to accomplish. Finally, it is not likely that the nation will undertake to restructure its entire cultural pattern in order to prepare its future generations of women to be warriors. Yet, combativeness and aggressiveness are necessary traits in the combat soldier, sailor, and airman. The conclusion is obvious: *Servicewomen should not be assigned combat missions, even in all-female units.* Unless, of course, we can get an agreement from our adversaries that our female units will only have to fight their female units.

CURRENT EXCLUSION POLICIES

However, the political pressures on the uniformed services to increase female content continue to grow. They are struggling to maintain required strength levels in a volunteer environment. A return to conscription is an obvious solution, but it is not one most legislators are willing to consider publicly. Rather, considerable political goodwill can be had by championing the cause of women's equality and expanded military opportunities for women. These increased opportunities have been created by reducing the scope of the combat exclusion.

The current army combat exclusion policy is as follows.

Women are authorized to serve in any officer or enlisted specialty, except those specified at any organizational level, and in any unit of the Army, except in Infantry, Armor, Cannon Field Artillery, Combat Engineer, and Low Altitude Air Defense Artillery units of battalion/squadron or smaller size.

The key features of this policy are as follows:

Brigade level headquarters positions, except those documented for closed specialties, are opened to women.

Medium and high altitude air defense artillery battalion positions are opened to women.

Missile and rocket field artillery battalion positions are opened to women.

All aviation positions, except aerial scout and attack helicopter pilots, are opened to women.

Some Eighty-second Airborne Division positions are opened to women.

In October 1978, at the request of the secretary of the navy, Congress amended Title 10, U.S. Code, Section 6015 to read as follows:

Women may not be assigned to duty in vessels or aircraft that are engaged in combat missions nor may they be assigned to other than temporary duty on vessels of the Navy except for hospital ships, transports, and vessels of a similar classification not expected to be assigned combat missions.

In April 1979 the secretary of the navy issued SECNAVINST 1300.12, which is printed in part below:

1. *Purpose*. This instruction prescribes the guidelines under which Navy and Marine Corps women may be assigned to duty in ships and aircraft of the Navy.

2. *Background*. Previously, the assignment of Navy and Marine Corps women aboard ships and aircraft was severely restricted by reference (a) prior to its recent Amendment. This restriction deprived the sea service of the proper utilization of highly motivated, dedicated, and capable women. Navy women are a valuable personnel resource contributing significantly to the attainment of the Service's mission.

3. *Policy*. It is the policy of the Department of the Navy that women members, officers and enlisted, will be assigned to billets commensurate with their capabilities unless such assignment is precluded by law. Accordingly, with respect to duty on ships and aircraft, women:

a. May be permanently assigned to duty in hospital ships, and vessels of a similar classification not expected to be assigned combat missions. The phrase "vessels of a similar classification" includes auxiliaries and service craft as set forth in SECNAVINST 5030.1H. A listing of such vessels, currently available for the assignment of women, is included at enclosure (1). Enclosure (1) will be subject to frequent review and will be modified or added to as appropriate to ensure that women are authorized for permanent duty assignment to all vessels not precluded by operation of law.

b. May be assigned to temporary duty to any ship or squadron in the Navy provided that unit is not expected to have a combat mission during the period of temporary duty. For the purpose of this instruction, "temporary duty" includes both "temporary duty" and "temporary additional duty" as defined by reference (b) and involving written orders. Assignment of women to ships for temporary duty is authorized in performance of and for the period required by their normal military duties. Such periods of temporary duty are not to exceed 180 days.

c. Will be authorized to participate—including landing on shipboard flight decks under conditions permitting temporary duty on naval vessels—as crew members or passengers in aircraft engaged in training or support not expected to be assigned combat missions during the period of the assignment. Women may be assigned to permanent duty in squadrons containing such aircraft and also be assigned to support billets in shore-based combatant aircraft squadrons where such assignment would not require them to participate as crew members in combatant aircraft missions.

d. May be assigned for duty in rear echelon billets for combat service support functions which would not require them to deploy with the assault echelon of the command should a contingency arise. . . .

e. Will not be assigned to combat duty or, if assigned temporary duty on a vessel which is assigned a combat mission, every reasonable effort will be made to disembark them prior to execution of such mission. For this purpose, a "combat mission" is defined as one which has as one of its primary objectives to seek out, reconnoiter, or engage the enemy. The normal defensive posture of all operating units is not included within this definition.

4. *Action*. The policy outlined above . . . delineates units to which women legally may be assigned, but this instruction does not mandate assignment of women to any unit or unit-type. Specific plans and long-term policy guidance directives for assignment of women shall be developed by the Chief of Naval Operations and the Commandant of the Marine Corps within the policy contained herein. These plans and directives shall be submitted for Secretarial approval, and shall be structured to ensure that women of the Navy and Marine Corps are assigned and utilized to the fullest extent possible in order to maximize Service benefit and provide rewarding careers.

There followed a list of sixty-nine navy ships to which women could be assigned. Included are fleet ocean tugs, destroyer tenders, submarine tenders, and a host of others, including the training aircraft carrier U.S.S. Lexington.

The marine corps for the first time began to assign women to previously restricted Fleet Marine Force (FMF) units. The most recent marine corps policy guidance was promulgated in January 1980. The operative sections are printed below.

3. *Non-FMF Assignments*

a. Women Marines may be assigned to any non-FMF unit/duty station for which qualified by grade, MOS, or other special criteria.

b. Women Marines may be designated as enlisted crew members and assigned duties aboard base and command support aircraft (C-9,T-39 and UC-12B).

4. *FMF Assignments*

a. Women Marines will be trained to provide essential support of combat operations. However, women Marines will not be assigned to any unit within which they would likely become engaged in direct combat with the enemy. Accordingly, women Marines will not be assigned to the following units or any sub-element thereof:

Infantry Regiment
Artillery Battalion
Reconnaissance Battalion
Force Reconnaissance Company
Tank Battalion
Assault Amphibian Battalion
LAAM Battalion
FAAD Battery/Platoon
Air/Naval Gunfire Liaison Company
Combat Engineer Battalion
Marine Air Support Squadron

b. Women may be assigned to other combat support/service support units in a designated hostile fire area as long as such assignments will not routinely expose them to direct combat action. The normal defensive posture of any unit in a hostile fire area is not prohibitive in this regard. Women Marines could therefore be employed in the general proximity of division headquarters but not be assigned to support units/elements that would be expected to maneuver with the infantry regiment or its subordinate units or be colocated with the infantry regiment in fortified positions (e.g., Helicopter Support Teams, LSU Detachments, Counter-Intelligence Teams, Interrogator-Translator Teams, etc.).

c. Women Marines may be assigned to any aviation squadron for the purpose of providing the service/support function for which they are trained.

(1) However, women Marines will neither be assigned nor be allowed to perform duties as a member of the flightcrew of any aircraft.

(2) Women Marines assigned to units involved in the WestPac unit deployment program, may participate in such deployments provided air transportation to/from WestPac is directed for the unit. Women Marines may not participate in Marine Amphibious Unit (MAU) deployments to either WestPac or the Mediterranean.

d. In the event a combat contingency arises, women Marines will not be permitted to deploy to the contingency site with leading elements assigned to provide assault support. Women Marines will be permitted to deploy to the contingency site once rear-echelon support areas are established.

The marine corps policies parallel those of the army except that female marines are restricted from assignment at regimental headquarters level while they are allowed at the army's comparable brigade headquarters. Also, female marines are restricted from all flight crew duties. Further, the marines limit female membership to 10 percent in FMF units. Nevertheless, it is clear that by assigning women to divisional CS/CSS units the marines, like the army, have crossed the great combat exclusion divide. Women will fight; they just will not do so routinely.

Only the air force appears to be comfortable with its rapidly expanding female population. The secretary of the air force has requested that the Congress amend Section 8549, Title 10, U.S. Code along the same lines as Section 6015 was adjusted for the navy. Meanwhile, the air force has changed its interpretation of the current provisions of Section 8549 to permit much wider employment of air force women and has, like the army, already begun to train female pilots and assign them to squadrons that do not have attack missions.

Still, the civilian leadership in the Office of the Secretary of Defense continues to press for even less restrictive combat exclusion policies. Consider the statement of M. Kathleen Carpenter, deputy assistant secretary of defense for equal opportunity, made in February 1980.

The Secretary of Defense supports repeal of the combat exclusion laws, in order to give the Secretary of the Air Force and the Secretary of the Navy the same flexibility in the assignment of women that the Secretary of the Army currently has. The issue is not one of immediately placing women in combat roles, but removing an artificial barrier so that the military services can determine how best to utilize a valuable personnel resource.[28]

At the same time, the civilian leadership of the Department of Defense is steadily raising both the absolute and relative numbers of women in the services. Ms. Carpenter forecasts 238,000 servicewomen by 1985—13 percent of the total force.[29] This year, for example, the Office of the Secretary of Defense mandated still another increase in army female end-strength by fiscal year 1986. The army protested, saying, in part:

A further increase in the number of enlisted women in the FY 86 timeframe will have negligible near term impact on the force, however the Army is not sure how many women can be in the force and still accomplish its primary mission of ground combat. The Army and the enlisted women in it must be given time to gain experience in the service in general and with duty in formerly male only combat support and service support units in particular.[30]

WARTIME REQUIREMENTS

It can be seen that the services, in order to increase peacetime female content, have had to reduce combat exclusion restrictions to open previously closed duty assignments. Women's rights' advocates sometimes claim that manpower shortages would force us to use women in these assignments in a major war in any event. Therefore, they say, we should start in peacetime in order to be ready.

A glance at the nation's population projections coupled with wartime military force expansion plans shatters this argument. Contingency war plans do not call for force levels as high as those the United States achieved in World War II (12 million). The U.S. population was 140 million in 1945 but reached approximately 220 million in 1979. If the same ratio of males were called in 1980 as were called in World War II, it would produce an all-male force of over 18 million—much larger than anticipated requirements.

That sufficient males are available was recently made clear by the testimony of Richard Danzig, principal deputy assistant secretary of defense (Manpower, Reserve Affairs and Logistics) before the Senate Armed Services Committee. Mr. Danzig was testifying in favor of the president's plan to include women in the peacetime draft registration. He was questioned by Senator Jepson regarding the need for women in manning the wartime force.

Senator Jepson. Are you associating your advocacy of registering women with the military need?

Mr. Danzig. I think that the case for registering women does not stem from a need to have numbers of people to man the military forces of the United States.

Senator Jepson. So, your advocacy for registering women has more to do with equity in response to pushy groups at this time?

Mr. Danzig. That's right. It is quite right that if it were not for equity, if there were no such idea, I would not be in favor of registration of women. That is what animates my feeling.[31]

CONCLUSIONS AND CONSEQUENCES

It is clear that the influx of women into the military services is not a product of military need. It is equally obvious that the combat effectiveness of the nation's military forces is ultimately at risk. To the extent that the United States increasingly relies on women to man its peacetime forces, we jeopardize our ability to defend the country.

We have already, through the semantics of combat definitions, begun to count women as *de facto* combatants. It matters not at all whether this has been done for reasons of well-intentioned desire for social "equity" or for pure political expediency. The result is the same.

The U.S. armed forces have more female members now than any other nation in the world—both in actual numbers and in percentages. We now have more servicewomen than all the Warsaw Pact states combined. We have fifteen times more women in our forces than the Soviets have in theirs. And our disproportionate reliance on women is increasing.

At the same time, we have the least stringent combat exclusion policies of any nation in the world. Even the Israelis, who face serious manpower shortages, have stricter prohibitions against women in combat.

Those combat exclusions that we have managed to retain remain under attack. Moreover, the standing military forces are becoming increasingly feminized. As our peacetime female content grows, we increase the likelihood that, faced with major shortages of trained men, we will have to abandon remaining combat exclusions. Yet, everything we know about physical and psychological differences between the sexes indicates that women are less well suited for combat.

RECOMMENDATIONS

The question is whether to halt or reverse the erosion of policies that exclude women from combat. Ultimately, the answer hinges on the primary purpose of the defense establishment. If the primary purpose were to provide jobs on an equal opportunity basis, then the answer would be to press on and grant women full warrior status. But, the primary function of the U.S. armed services is to provide for the common defense—not to redress perceived social and sexual inequalities in our society. More bluntly—*the primary function of the military services is to defend the American society, not to change it*. To the extent that we use the military as a testbed for social experimentation we risk the security of the nation.

Therefore, the answer to the question posed above must be yes. We must reverse the current trend toward eliminating women's combat exclusions.

Such a reversal may only need to be temporary. As we learn more about the effect of women in military units we may elect, with due caution, to expand the combat role allotted to women. Full combat status should not be granted, however, until we have had the opportunity to experiment using various mixes of women in selected combat units under actual combat conditions.

This will require that we wait until we fight our next war. Female volunteers can be assigned to various units in combat. Their performance, and that of the units to which they are assigned, can be evaluated. If the performance is equal to or exceeds that of all-male units, then all combat exclusions should be revoked.

Until such time as this definitive combat test is completed, we should remove women from all army and marine divisions and other units that might operate within divisional areas of operation. Moreover, a ceiling should be placed on the total female content in each of the military services. These ceilings should be designed to ensure that sufficient males are available in combat support and combat service support functions to meet emergency demands for combat casualty replacements. To this end, women should be restricted from sea duty and air crew assignment in all services.

These measures will not be popular with politicians or feminists. They are not egalitarian. They are, however, necessary in light of the dictates of national security.

UPDATE

The preceding paper was completed in October 1980. President Carter was in the fourth year of his term. The number of women in the services continued to increase in percentages and absolute numbers. His appointees within the Department of Defense continued to press the military services and the Congress for further diminution of female combat exclusion policies. The Supreme Court had agreed to rule on the constitutionality of the male-only registration and there appeared to be considerable likelihood that male-only sign-up might be struck down. In short, in late 1980, the influx of women into the military services continued in spite of the fears of experienced military leaders that we were proceeding too fast or too far, or both.

A year later the situation had changed dramatically. The Reagan administration acted quickly to slow the headlong rush to increase the female content of the military and dilute combat exclusion policies. The army was first to act to slow the pace. In March 1981, William Clark, acting assistant secretary of the army for manpower and reserve affairs announced that the army was abandoning the Carter goal of raising female strength to 87,500 by 1986.[32] Clark, testifying before the Senate Armed Services Committee, stated that the army was fearful that further increases in the women content would hurt combat readiness.

By the end of March it was apparent that all the services shared the army's concerns and that the Defense Department was prepared to "reassess" the ambitious Carter goals.[33] By May it had become official. Lawrence Korb, assistant secretary of defense for manpower, reserve affairs, and logistics was quoted in the *Washington Post*.[34] "Past female recruiting goals were based largely on theoretical models. What's happened is now we have some experience. I think it's an appropriate time, at the beginning of an administration when you are having a force expansion, changing doctrine, to take a look and say, okay, let's stop and see if these models should be changed." He went on to say, "Just what I've picked up from talking to people in the field [is] that maybe we were a little bit too eager, and [doing] a little too much, maybe, wishful thinking." Also, "I just don't think our society will ever want to have women in front-line combat, and as long as you don't have that, you're really sort of limited as to the jobs that you can give them."

In a parallel policy decision, the Reagan administration elected not to pursue the hold-over Carter initiative to repeal remaining statutory combat exclusions.[35]

Finally, in midsummer, the Supreme Court ruled that no constitutional bar to the selective registration of men for possible military conscription exists.

From the above it is apparent that the current administration has sided with those who believed that combat readiness should take priority over feminist desire for full equality, even on the battlefield.

NOTES

1. Only one substantial exception can be found. This was the female army of King Gezo of Dahomey (1818–1858). His army was chiefly composed of highly trained and disciplined female infantry. They comprised about one-fourth of the total female population.

2. During most of George Washington's two terms as president, there was no standing army or navy. During the two years in which active forces were on duty (1794 and 1795), they never exceeded 6,000 men out of a population of approximately 4 million. Military strength during the War of 1812 peaked in 1814 at only 46,858 out of a U.S. population of roughly 8 million. This amounted to one serviceman per 170 citizens contrasted to one serviceman per 11 citizens in World War II.

3. *Selected Manpower Statistics* (Washington, D.C.: Department of Defense, 1979), p. 60.

4. Martin Binkin and Shirley J. Bach, *Women and the Military,* (Washington, D.C.: The Brookings Institution, 1977), p. 7.

5. *Selected Manpower Statistics,* pp. 62, 112.

6. *Historical Statistics of the United States, Colonial Times to 1970* (Washington, D.C.: U.S. Bureau of the Census, 1970).

7. Leila Rupp, *Mobilizing Women for War: German and American Propaganda, 1939–1945* (Princeton, N.J.: Princeton University Press, 1978), pp. 79, 189.

8. Nancy Goldman, "The Utilization of Women in the Armed Forces of Industrialized Countries," *Sociological Symposium* (Spring 1977): 16.

9. Franz W. Seidler, *Frauen zu den Waffen—Marketenderinnen, Helferinnen, Soldatinnen* [Women to arms: sutlers, volunteers, female soldiers.] (Koblenz/Bonn: Wehr & Wissen, 1978), pp. 156–62.

10. Binkin and Bach, *Women,* p. 124. Female participation in partisan combat activities was extensive in the Soviet Union and Yugoslavia.

11. Seidler, *Frauen,* p. 209. See also Griesse and Stites, p. 75, this volume.

12. Air Force Regulation 35–30.

13. Binkin and Bach, *Women,* p. 23.

14. *Selected Manpower Statistics,* p. 113.

15. Specifically, the studies were the "Women in the Army Study" (WITA), The "Women Content in the Army—REFORGER 77" Study (REF-WAC 77), and the "Evaluation of Women in the Army" (EWITA) Study.

16. The author conducted informal interviews with male and female military staff officers charged with testing and evaluating female physical capabilities. He also solicited the views of members of the women's movement and representatives of the Defense Advisory Committee on Women in the Services (DACOWITS).

17. For a more complete examination of relative physiological differences, see James A. Peters and others "Summary Report on Project 60: A Comparison of Two Types of Physical Training Programs in the Performance of 16- to 18-year-old Women" (U.S. Military Academy, May 3, 1976). See also Binkin and Bach, *Women*.

18. Some manpower analysts believe the shortfall may be even larger. See Kenneth J. Coffey, *Manpower for Military Mobilization* (Washington, D.C.: American Enterprise Institute for Public Policy Research, 1978), p. 23.

19. John J. Fialka, "The Grim Lessons of NIFTY NUGGET," *Army Magazine* (April 1980): 17.

20. The army experienced a similar problem in 1944 when a severe shortage of combat infantrymen developed. Between October 1944 and May 1945 over 100,000 men had to be hurriedly transferred from the army air forces and service forces for retraining and commitment as infantry. See Robert R. Palmer et al., *The United States Army in World War II, The Procurement and Training Ground Combat Troops* (Washington, D.C.: Historical Division, Department of the Army, 1948), p. 82.

21. The army servicewomen's pregnancy rate was 13.8 percent in 1978 and 10.5 percent in 1979. Army planners anticipate the rate will rise substantially in coming years. This is because the army, in May 1979, lowered female enlistment criteria (educational and intelligence standards) to the same level as those governing male enlistments.

22. Richard A. Gabriel, "Women in Combat? Two Views," *Army Magazine* (March 1980): 44.

23. Jean Bethke Elshtain, "'Amazon' vs. 'Earth Mother'?: Women, War, and Feminism," *The Nation* (June 1980).

24. Mary Jo Salter, "Annie, Don't Get Your Gun," *Atlantic* (June 1980): 83.

25. Suzan Blank, "Combat is Not for Men Only," *Civil Liberties* (April 1980): p. 6. The Diana Steele mentioned in the quote is an ACLU Women's Rights Project attorney.

26. Robert Ardrey, *The Territorial Imperative* (New York: Atheneum, 1966), p. 33.

27. Kenneth Lamott, "Why Men and Women Think Differently," *Horizons* (May 1977): 41–45.

28. M. Kathleen Carpenter, "New Directions for Equal Opportunity," *Defense 1980* (February 1980): 15.

29. Ibid., p. 15.

30. 1979 internal army memorandum to Office of the Secretay of Defense commenting on the Manpower and Logistics paper (copy in author's possession).

31. U.S. Congress, Subcommittee on Manpower and Personnel, Senate Committee on Armed Services, Hearings on the President's Plan for Registration Under the Military Selective Service Act, April 2, 1980, unedited stenographic typescript, Alderson Reporting Co., pp. 99, 100.

32. *The Army Times,* March 9, 1981, p. 2, col. 1.
33. Ibid., March 30, 1981, p. 4, col. 1.
34. *Washington Post,* May 13, 1981, p. 4, p. 1.
35. *The Army Times,* August 3, 1981, p. 4, col. 4.

14 | THE ARGUMENT FOR FEMALE COMBATANTS

Mady Wechsler Segal

The purpose of this paper is to discuss the issue of whether combat roles in the U.S. military should be open to women. The major arguments on both sides of the issue will be presented and weighed. While this topic has been the subject of much debate, both in the public policy arena and in social scientific writing, the issue is still alive and undecided. Contrary to the beliefs of many Americans, this is not an issue that can be debated for years before we arrive at a decision. Despite the current combat exclusion policy, there are women in jobs in the U.S. military that will place them in combat should war break out where they are stationed or where their units are planned to be deployed. As pointed out by Grace King, as well as Jeff Tuten, many women in the army who are in combat support and combat service support military occupational specialties are currently at risk of combat.[1]

What distinguishes the combat support and combat service support jobs that women now occupy from many of those from which they are excluded is not the degree of risk of their being killed, but rather the degree to which the jobs involve offensive or defensive combat potential. Women are permitted to occupy jobs that are likely to require them to be in combat in defensive positions. They are excluded from jobs and from units that in wartime routinely participate in offensive warfare. Thus, the combat

* An earlier version of this paper was presented at the meetings of the Inter-University Seminar on Armed Forces and Society, Chicago, Illinois, October 23–25, 1980.

The opinions or assertions contained herein are the private views of the author and are not to be construed as official or as reflecting the views of the Department of the Army or the Department of Defense.

Helpful comments were made on earlier drafts of this paper by M. Camp, William J. Gregor, Jesse J. Harris, Linda Jellen, Frederick J. Manning, David H. Marlowe, Martha Marsden, Jacob Romo, Joseph Rothberg, David R. Segal, Robert Shoenberg, Judith Stiehm, and Terry Willett.

exclusion policy does not realistically exclude women from combat, but only from certain types of combat.

THE NATURE OF COMBAT

It is most important in any discussion of the issue of women in combat to realize what our underlying assumptions are about the nature of combat. Many such discussions assume that when we speak of combat, we are referring to certain types of infantry combat or, sometimes, armor. This is the sort of assumption that leads to mental images of women in trenches. These images, in turn, create negative emotional reactions, since this type of combat is the most odious to many and is seen as least appropriate for women. It is crucial that we recognize the variety of combat jobs that exist and the many types of warfare to which we, in the twentieth and twenty-first centuries, are potentially subject.

Combat varies by the type and size of the zone in which death can be caused and, related to this, by the degree to which there is a distinction between combatant and noncombatant. Hand-to-hand combat is at one extreme on both of these dimensions. At the other extreme is widespread thermonuclear warfare, where "civilian" populations are subject to the same risk as military personnel. The most likely type of modern warfare is somewhere between these two extremes.

Women are currently excluded from operating offensive line-of-sight weapons and from other jobs in units that use such weapons. At the same time, women are in jobs and locations that have the same potential for placing them in the lethal zone, although in defensive capacities. We certainly cannot assume that being a few miles from the current forward area of battle protects anyone from combat. Women in specialties such as tank turret repairman, radar technician, long-range missile crewman, and military police (to name but a few) can be expected to be in battle. Even women in the "traditional" female specialties, such as the medical and administrative ones, may still be in the line of fire. Thus, we allow women to be in positions where they can be killed by enemy fire, but we bar them from those positions in which they can initiate attack.

Part of the reason for the present situation of women at risk of defensive combat but not offensive combat is the problematic nature of deciding whether a particular job in a particular unit or place is a combat job. In all the armed services some job specialty categories are always considered combat jobs; these are currently closed to women. There are many other specialties that are, however, open to women in some units but not in others. The units, including ships and aircraft, from which women are excluded, are those most likely to have a combat mission, that is, "to seek out, reconnoiter, or engage the enemy."[2] The definition of "combat job" has been established under pressure to increase the job specialties and unit assignments available to women, without considering them "combatants."

Many discussions of women in combat assume that women are currently noncombatants and that a policy shift to assigning them to offensive combat roles (namely, to offensive combat jobs or to support jobs in offensive combat units) will change their status to that of combatants. Some people even assume that assigning any women to combat roles will remove the protective noncombatant status from all women, even civilians. These assumptions may be true in a precise, definitional sense of the term *noncombatant,* but they are no longer true in the consequences of the status of noncombatant as defined by international laws of war. Noncombatants, both civilian and military, used to be protected from the risk of injury or death in war. In many types of modern warfare noncombatants do not have this protection. It is highly unlikely that an enemy attacking the United States or its allies is going to spare women solely because they are women, regardless of which roles women play in our military.

CITIZEN EQUALITY AND MILITARY EFFECTIVENESS

In deciding whether women should be in combat, the potential effects of the decision on two major goals are generally considered. One of these goals is to ensure equal rights and responsibilities of all citizens; the other is to ensure the combat effectiveness of our military. Although observers differ in the relative weight they give to these goals, both are important criteria we should use to judge arguments about potential outcomes. The proponents of women's participation in combat tend to stress equal citizenship for men and women. The opponents of women in combat tend to emphasize the reduction in military strength and national defense that they see as a likely outcome of women in combat units.

One of the basic principles on which our nation was founded is the full participation of all its citizens in all aspects of the life of the nation. The rights of citizenship in our society are viewed as connected to civic responsibilities, including military service.[3] One of the ways minority groups have achieved more equal citizenship rights is by individual members of those groups serving in the military, especially in combat roles. The "opportunity to serve in the combat branches" is "associated with the notion of civic and personal fulfillment."[4] We often hear the statement, "If you want equal rights, you have to accept equal responsibilities." This admonition is currently being directed at women and serves as the basis of many young men's opinion that if they are subject to military registration then young women should also be expected to register. The exclusion of women from combat roles serves not only as a major barrier to the careers of military women, but also to all U.S. women achieving full status as citizens.

Emphasizing the importance of combat inclusion for citizens, Maury Feld argues that "the case for accepting women for combat assignment cannot be argued on a pragmatic basis; nor at least on strictly military terms."[5] Opposition to this view comes from those who believe that the presence of women in combat units poses serious threats to our national security.[6] These writers do not necessarily deny the citizenship argument; rather, they stress the overriding importance of maintaining an effective fighting force. They argue that combat effectiveness would be substantially reduced by women in combat jobs. Indeed, they believe that the U.S. military has already been weakened by the recently increased numbers of military women and by the assignment of women to combat support and combat service support jobs.

Opponents of women in combat do not necessarily agree on the basis for that opposition. Even those who argue that reduced military effectiveness would result from the inclusion of women differ in the emphasis they give to the reasons for such weakness. Some stress the physiological characteristics of women that make them less suited to combat than men; some emphasize psychological differences between men and women; others are concerned about potential disruptions to the interpersonal relationships and cohesion of combat units. If, on the basis of credence given to these concerns, we exclude all women from combat while seeing men's participation as a citizen's duty, we thereby deny men and women equal status as citizens. It is, therefore, important to evaluate the validity of these concerns. We turn now to some of these specific arguments, with discussions of their current validity and the likelihood for change in the future.

PHYSIOLOGICAL CHARACTERISTICS OF WOMEN

A number of physiological characteristics of women are seen as limiting their capacity for combat. It is important to recognize that not all women possess all of these limitations. Some women possess none of them, and most women possess them only some of the time.

Physical Strength

The first characteristic that is often cited as limiting the combat performance potential of women is their lack of physical strength, especially upper body strength. The average young woman today is weaker in upper body strength than the average young man. There are several aspects of this difference which would, however, argue for its rejection as the basis for excluding women from assignment to combat roles.

If a certain level of physical strength is required for a particular job, then this should serve as one of the selection criteria for the job. Rather than assuming that all women are incapable of performance by virtue of the average woman's lack of capability, specific requirements should serve as the selection criteria, not gender. By the same token, we cannot assume that all men are capable of performing jobs that require a high level of upper body strength. Not all young men are strong enough to perform as combat infantrymen. We must be careful not to confuse a difference in average physical strength between men and women with a situation in which all men are strong enough and no women are.

On the other hand, given the current large difference in average physical strength between young men and women, certain situations may require the use of gender as a screening criterion. In the event of a mass mobilization, where large numbers of potential recruits or conscripts, or both, have to be processed in a relatively short period of time, it is inefficient to test large numbers of women to identify the few who have the requisite physical capabilities. Since a situation of mass mobilization does not currently prevail, this is the time to study the ways to narrow the gap between the physical performance of men and women by raising women's capabilities. Innate sex differences may preclude the possibility of equalizing men's and women's physical strength and stamina. Some of the sex differences that currently exist, however, are due to the effects of body conditioning, rather than biological necessity.

Dennis Kowal's study on injuries during army basic training show that women experience a higher rate of injuries than men and that a major cause of women's injuries is lack of prior fitness and conditioning. Kowal suggests preenlistment screening to identify those men and women most at risk, coupled with remedial training before the more strenuous physical regimen of basic training.[7] An experimental program along these lines could aid in ascertaining what degree of improvement is possible with adult women.

If the trend toward increased participation of young girls in sports continues, we may expect American women in the future to be more physically fit as adults. Girls and women in the United States have historically been unlikely to participate in any sports and have been excluded from many particular sports. Until quite recently, only certain sports have been considered appropriate for girls and women. In the 1970s there have been many changes in this situation. Most notable is the extent to which children are engaged in organized sports that include both girls and boys, both in school programs and extracurricular programs in sports, such as soccer and baseball. Some women have also moved into sports previously defined as for men only, such as boxing, wrestling, and weight lifting.

Perhaps more important for the anticipation of future trends in women's physical performance is evidence that sex differences have been considerably reduced among trained athletes.[8] While the performance of both male and female Olympic athletes continues to improve, women have been improving at a faster rate than men in the same sports.[9] Such evidence demonstrates that performance differentials previously attributed to innate differences are affected by sex role socialization and physical training. As there are changes in which activities are socially defined as appropriate for girls and women and as girls increase participation in athletic activities and training, the physical performance gap between males and females, at the upper level and the average, will be narrowed.

It is also the case that jobs can be redesigned and new technologies developed to allow for performance by weaker people. This was commonly done for factory work during World War II, when women were performing jobs previously held only by men. The necessity of using women in jobs, because men were not available to fill them, produced changes in the jobs, such as the introduction of lifting machinery to substitute for physical strength. While this type of redesign and technology development may not be possible for all types of combat jobs now requiring great upper body strength, it is not inconceivable that some progress can be made.

Not all military jobs currently closed to women depend on physical strength. Women are barred from service in any job aboard navy ships with offensive combat missions and from flying combat planes in the navy and air force. Such exclusions cannot be justified by citing differences in physical strength between men and women. Indeed, navy women are permitted to perform some jobs in shore billets, within the severe constraints on numbers imposed by current sea-shore rotations for men, but are excluded from those same jobs on ships. Such jobs require technical skills, not physical strength.

Pregnancy

It is a fact that most women are physiologically capable of becoming pregnant, while no men are. Being pregnant is seen as a handicap to the performance of combat jobs. We must keep in mind the enormous range of individual differences regarding what women can and cannot do while pregnant, as well as the range of types of combat jobs.

It is probably safe to conclude that some (but only some) women can continue strenuous activity in the early months of pregnancy and that few can or should (for their own and the unborn child's health) be in certain combat jobs in the later months. As with other conditions that require the reassignment of personnel, contingency plans must be made for the reassignment and replacement of pregnant women when their pregnancy interferes with their job performance. We must be careful, however, not to assume that no pregnant woman can do her job and automatically reassign every woman as soon as she becomes pregnant.

The average American woman is pregnant for a very small proportion of her life and some women never do become pregnant at all. Also important is the fact that people in combat jobs do not spend most of their time in combat, further reducing the incidence of pregnancy interfering with job performance. The fact that most women can get pregnant is no reason to exclude all women from a particular job, just as the fact that men can get the flu or venereal disease is not used to exclude them from a job.

Menstruation

The menstruation of women in combat will be considered as an issue for three reasons. First, it is frequently mentioned in informal discussions as a combat problem. Second, I believe that this issue is one that underlies some of the opposition of military men to women in field situations, whether combat or not. Third, it is an issue that must be dealt with realistically for preparation for field situations.   The crucial question is how menstruation will interfere with a woman's performance of her duties. The answer is that for most women, most of the time, menstruation does not change their behavior very much.[10] Perhaps even more important for combat situations, women under stress or undergoing strenuous physical training may not menstruate at all. Such is the experience of women cadets at West Point, for example.[11]

It may be possible that in appeals to their male supervisors some women use their menstruation (or claim to be menstruating) to get out of unpleasant duties. Since most men are quite ignorant of the facts of menstruation and are embarrassed by discussing it, this is a very useful ploy for some women. I do not mean to argue that no women function at less than their usual level during some parts of their menstrual cycle. There is great variation in women's reactions to menstruation, however, partly as a function of their attitudes toward menstruation and to social definitions.[12]

It should also be recognized that men experience physiological and psychological changes in cyclical patterns. Less is known about male cycles, partly because men do not have a physiological symptom as unambiguous as menstruation. That we know less about male cycles than female cycles does not, however, mean that they are any less debilitating in the mood changes that accompany them, even though they are not explicitly used as an excuse.

The real problems of menstruation in field situations are probably those of inconvenience, lack of privacy, and lack of cleanliness. There are potentially many ways to deal with these problems. Research needs to be done to ascertain what problems women in the military are currently experiencing with regard to menstruation, what solutions they have attempted, how successful they have been in overcoming the problems, and how the military can begin to address unsolved problems. For example, materiel research effort can be directed towards developing new devices for absorbing menstrual flow that can be left in place for sufficient amounts of time to make them more convenient. We must also recognize that female military nurses have had a long history of functioning in wartime under primitive, unsanitary conditions[13] without questions being raised about menstruation interfering with the performance of their duties.

Child Care

The issue of care of minor children is often raised by opponents of women in combat since women traditionally have been the primary care-takers of children. Obviously, arrangements have to be made to ensure children's welfare in their parents' absence. This need not be seen as a problem involving all women and no men. Not all women have children. Specifically, in front-line combat units, troops are drawn primarily from among those who are young enough to be most physically fit, usually eighteen to twenty-one years old. Certainly, at these ages, most women are still not mothers. Furthermore, the failure to raise this issue with regard to males is based on the untenable assumption that children need their mothers more than they need their fathers. This assumption is espe-cially challenged by the growing number of single fathers, including those in the military.

If our goal is to ensure adequate care for young children, several types of policies can be adopted. For example, we can choose not to assign any parents of minor children to combat jobs or to any jobs that require frequent or prolonged absence from their families. Alternatively, as is currently done, we can require soldier-parents to make arrangements for the care of their children. Another possibility is for the military to provide child care for use by its personnel when their jobs necessitate deployment. It is not necessary for present purposes to debate the merits of the various possible policies. Rather, we need to recognize that the problem is not applicable to all women, that it is not peculiar to women, and that it should not be used as the basis for excluding women from voluntarily holding any particular jobs, including combat jobs. It is no more appropriate to bar all women from combat jobs because of the necessity of absence from families than to bar women from civilian jobs that require frequent travel, middle-of-the-night emergency call-ups, or the like.

PSYCHOLOGICAL CHARACTERISTICS OF WOMEN

Ability to Perform under Stress

It is sometimes assumed that women would be less capable of performing under the stress of combat than men. There is currently no evidence to substantiate such a claim. But there is a great deal of evidence that military women have performed on a par with their male peers in difficult circumstances and in situations of severe psychological pressure. Instructive here are the well-known REFWAC and MAXWAC studies[14] as well as documented descriptions of the reactions of women in World War II, including those who were prisoners of war.[15] Kalisch and Scobey summarize the experiences of female American military nurses in wartime, including the "squalid and verminous living conditions" and having to "witness the pathetic results of the physical violence of modern warfare."[16] The fact that "American nurses proved their physical and emotional stamina while performing their jobs under combat conditions"[17] is often forgotten in discussions of women's potential for withstanding the stress of combat.

In addition to such evidence of the ability of American military women to withstand psychological stress, some historical documentation shows that women in other countries have performed on a par with men in combat, albeit not in equal numbers.[18] Recent studies also document the ability of American policewomen to cope with situations of potential and actual physical violence.[19]

We have no evidence on how young American women today would behave in the extreme situation of infantry combat fighting side by side with young men. If we have no evidence that women are inferior or superior to men in terms of their psychological stability to withstand the effects of combat, then there is no reason to assume that they are inferior. The conventional approach in research and in law is to assume that no difference exists between groups until a difference is demonstrated.

Even if we find a difference between the average man and the average woman in the ability to function under stress, we should use that ability and not the person's gender as the basis for the selection or rejection of the person for a job. Obviously, this requires us to develop a measure of this ability.

Stereotypically Feminine Personality Characteristics

Certain personality characteristics are components of the stereotypical ideal of the American woman. These include, but are not limited to, warmth, nurturance, submissiveness, passivity, and lack of aggressiveness. It is unclear whether these traits are actually still believed to be desirable in women by the majority of the American people. It is even less clear that these traits actually describe the way women are. There is a continuum on each of these traits along which each man and woman falls. It is certainly true that not all American women are at the supposedly "feminine" end. Indeed, being at the extreme "feminine" end on these traits would interfere with the successful performance of many other jobs, such as teacher, doctor, executive, lawyer, police officer, and bill collector.

It is also the case that many men are more nurturant, submissive, and passive than are many women. There is no reason to exclude women who are psychologically suited to a job automatically, while at the same time automatically including all men, whether or not they are suited to the job.

Desire to Participate in Combat

There is also the question of whether American women desire to participate in combat. The probable answer is that most women who would be eligible for combat jobs do not want them. Some women would, however, be willing to take combat roles. Even more important, few men actually desire to participate in combat (and those who crave combat are not likely to be the best soldiers). If willingness to serve in combat is to function as the basis for participation for one category of people, then it should be the same for other categories. If duty determines that individual desires not be the major factor for men, then there must be some strong justification for exempting women from such obligation other than a lack of desire.

The Potential for Change

The military has traditionally been a virtual exclusive province of men, characterized by prototypic masculine subcultural norms. It is, therefore, not surprising to find that the average young woman today is less inclined, and perhaps less suited, to military service, especially combat, than the average young man. It is also not surprising to encounter resistance, both within the military and outside, to equal treatment of men and women with regard to military service. In making policy decisions, rather than being content with adapting to the status quo, we must consider the potential for change in the future.

A great deal of social change in the past two decades has been in the actual and normatively expected roles for American women. The rate of participation by women in virtually every societal institution has increased, as has the acceptance of women in previously all-male statuses within those institutions. The change is most dramatic in the proportion of women who are in the labor force. It can also be seen in women's roles in such institutions as government, religion, and the family. While women still tend to be concentrated in traditional female occupations (for example, clerical work, retail sales, service, teaching, nursing, and social work), there is increasing recognition of women's abilities in male-dominated arenas, such as mathematics, science, police work, corporate management, and sports, as well as in the military.

The greater the acceptance of women in these predominately male areas, the greater the number of girls and women in the future who will aspire to participate in these areas and who will develop the requisite capabilities. It is not possible to make exact predictions about how long it will take for the socialization of girls to undergo these profound changes, or to specify the precise limits to such socialization. It is instructive, however, to examine some aspects of the socialization process that are relevant to anticipating trends for the future.

The effects of socialization have been clearly demonstrated in the differences between males and females in achievement in mathematics, science, and technical fields such as engineering and computer science. These areas, like the military and sports, have been traditionally socially defined as male domains. Girls have been taught that achievement in these areas is inappropriate for them. As a result, beginning in secondary school, girls and women have performed less well in courses in mathematics and science. The further into secondary school they go, the greater has been the gap between the performance of boys and girls in these areas. It has also been the case that girls and women have taken fewer courses in these areas, on the average, than boys and men.[20]

There is a great deal of evidence that girls are influenced in their course taking and achievement in mathematics and science by the attitudes and expectations of others, including parents, peers, teachers, and guidance counselors.[21] The positive influence of female role models has also been demonstrated.[22] As old stereotypes break down and the expectations communicated to girls change, we can expect more girls to pursue study and careers in previously male fields.

While such social change is slow, there is some indication that it has begun with respect to mathematics. In a national survey conducted in 1978, thirteen-year-old girls and boys did not differ significantly in the number of years of high school mathematics courses they intended to take.[23] It remains to be seen whether this cohort will actually achieve its objectives or whether it will be subjected to the social pressures of the past. Nevertheless, these results point to a narrowing of the gap between male and female achievement in mathematics. Such evidence, taken together with indications of greater female participation in other predominately male areas, suggests a gradual increase in the future in the number of women with the psychological attributes, technical skills, and motivation for successful performance in the military, including combat. Indeed, the faster and more thorough the integration of women into the armed forces, the more rapid such social change will be.

INTERPERSONAL DYNAMICS

Interpersonal dynamics in a group affect combat effectiveness; we do not know the degree to which the presence of women is likely to affect these dynamics. It is well known that the performance of a group engaged in coordinated activities is usually more than the sum of the task performance of the individuals who comprise the group. There is evidence that high group cohesion and morale improve performance in combat and reduce the incidence of psychiatric breakdown in combat.[24] We know much less about the effects of various gender compositions on group cohesion.

The results of the MAXWAC and REFWAC studies showed that the proportion of women in combat support and combat service support units had no effect on measurable unit performance in field training exercises.[25] These results surprised many people who assumed that raising the proportion of women beyond some minimal level would be detrimental to performance. Some remain unconvinced even by this evidence and insist that these trials were not adequate tests because they did not involve actual combat. In order to evaluate this argument, we need to consider what would be different in actual combat in the interpersonal relationships in fighting units.

The willingness to engage in actual combat, to kill and to risk being killed, depends upon a very strong devotion to the group. This commitment to the group is seen as depending, among other motivations, on male bonding.[26] The presence of women would interfere with the process of devotion of the men to each other, as women are outsiders who are not privy to the male subculture. There may also be competition among the men for the sexual favors of the women. No real evidence exists to support or refute these arguments. One point is clear: if men believe that women are not part of their group and that they cannot function with women around, this belief will disrupt such functioning and may hinder actual ability to cope with the stress of combat, thereby serving as a self-fulfilling prophecy.

Let me offer an additional explanation for men's resistance to allowing women in combat units. I conjecture that there is a psychological differentiation between the "real world" and combat that enables some men to survive the enormous psychological stress of combat. One survives by preserving a mental picture of the normal world back home to which one will return from the horror world of combat. One is engaged in an elaborate game (albeit one with very high stakes) and when the game is over, one can go home to an intact world. One of the major components of the world back home is women, "our women," who are warm, nurturant, ultra-feminine, and objects of sexual fantasy. Women (at least "our women") are not part of war. Indeed, one of the reasons for fighting is to protect our women and the rest of what is in that image of the world back home. If we allow these women into combat with us, then this psychological differentiation cannot be maintained, and we lose this psychological defense.

I would also conjecture that, in less extreme form, this differentiation exists for many men between work and family. It may be one of the reasons for resistance to women in various male-dominated civilian occupations. This would be especially true of blue-collar jobs where male subcultural norms govern interpersonal interaction (for example, construction, fire fighting, and auto mechanics). I also believe that this differentiation is one of the mechanisms used by male cadets and midshipmen at the military academies to survive the rigor of cadet training, especially during the first year.[27] This would account for some of the resistance to women cadets and for some of the reactions to them (especially negative stereotyping of them as too masculine).

If these speculations are accurate, I do not know precisely what effect women in combat would have on combat unit cohesion. I suspect that the effects have already been felt in military units that used to be all male but now have women, including the academies. Various processes of social change resulting from gender integration have probably already begun and will continue to proceed in creating new styles of interaction in face-to-face working units. It is certainly hoped that women's presence in groups will not automatically result in low cohesion. New images of the "real world back home" may supplant the old ones. These new images may then serve the same psychological functions.

The concern that women in combat units will reduce unit cohesion is reminiscent of arguments that have been used in the past to justify excluding women from other occupations. It was not so long ago that women were excluded from law, medicine, police work, and fire fighting (to name a few). This exclusion was based partly on women's supposed inability as individuals to perform the jobs adequately and partly on the potential disruption of men's interpersonal relations if women were included. While such arguments were accepted in the past, they have now been shown to be fallacious. While women have certainly not been fully integrated into these occupations, and while many men are not happy with women's presence in these jobs, few would today be willing to advocate publicly their exclusion. This unwillingness is based on the normative changes in our society and on the evidence that women's performance in these occupations has been unexpectedly successful.

Even outside of combat situations, there are certain interpersonal problems already existing in the military that deserve attention. The lack of acceptance of women by many military men creates problems for the women. As in other predominantly male settings, military women often face prejudice from male superiors, peers, and subordinates and face certain male behavior that creates stress for the women. Such behavior includes differential treatment of women that interferes with their job performance and sexual harassment of varying degrees. These problems also exist in institutional settings other than the military, but they must be addressed in the military before women can function most effectively.

The interpersonal problems associated with the gender integration of previously all-male settings, which are being experienced by military men and women, are similar to problems that were experienced in the process of the racial integration of the U.S. armed forces. That is, the current stage in the process of gender integration appears to resemble an earlier stage of racial integration. In the first half of this century, black men were underrepresented in the military and were largely excluded from combat jobs. Moskos, in a summary of the history of the roles of black men in the U.S. military, notes that during World War II blacks were in segregated units and most were in combat support and combat service support jobs.[28] Moreover, "even black combat units were frequently used for heavy-duty labor." As late as 1945 and 1950, reports by two army boards "concluded that practical considerations required a maintenance of segregation and the quota system" and "recommended that black personnel be assigned exclusively to support units rather than combat units."[29] The end of racial segregation came as the result of President Harry Truman's 1948 desegregation order and the combat manpower needs of the Korean War.

Much attention and effort in the military have been focused on achieving racial equality and interracial harmony. The racial polarization of the early 1970s was attacked by formal institutional policies, such as the establishment of the Defense Race Relations Institute and the development of equal opportunity officer and NCO positions.

While the process of gender integration of the military is not expected to be identical to racial integration, there are noteworthy similarities. Many of the arguments being advanced to justify exclusion of women from combat are reminiscent of those used in the past to bar black men from combat. Research evidence on prejudice and discrimination has yielded some general principles that are applicable regardless of the particular group that is the object of the negative interpersonal reactions.[30]

The cohesion of military units in general, and combat units in particular, need not be based on the exclusion of women. The bonds that tie soldiers to their groups often derive from respect for their fellow group members, based on performance that contributes to the goals of the group (including survival). Such mutual interdependence and affective regard can develop in mixed gender groups. DeFleur's study of the Air Force Academy shows that over the course of the first four years of gender integration, there has been some increase in male acceptance of and interaction with the women. Women are far from being fully accepted and integrated, however, a situation at least partially attributable to the lack of interdependence among cadets.[31]

Intragroup cohesion also depends on having a definition of those who are considered outsiders by the group. Such exclusions need not include all women, just as they need not include all members of other categories, for example, college men or blacks. Rather, women who are seen as poor soldiers (or as not being soldiers) are excluded, while women who are seen as good combat soldiers can be fully integrated into the group. That is, male group members can view female group members as their fellow soldiers, while seeing other women as outsiders. Research and policy should be directed towards understanding the conditions under which cohesion, integration, and mutual regard are most likely to develop.

SOCIAL VALUES

The discussions above address the issue of how military effectiveness may be affected by a combat role for women by focusing on women's individual capabilities and on potential effects on interpersonal dynamics in combat units. Quester has aptly observed that often "moral issues are hiding behind alleged statements of practicality. The world has long felt that women should be protected from combat, regardless of whether or not they might be good at combat."[32] Such underlying social values may well be more important than practical issues of military efficiency in determining the attitudes of the American public and the decisions of policymakers with regard to women in combat. The impact of women in combat on some of these values is considered in this section.

Survival of the Species and of Society

One basic social value that is sometimes seen as at variance with women in combat is the preservation of the species, or at least our society. In this view, women are seen primarily as the breeders for the next generation and as being responsible for cultural transmission to the young. Since only women can bear children and they are the traditional caretakers of the young, protecting women from combat is a way of ensuring the survival of the species.[33]

Given the potential of biological, chemical, and nuclear warfare, excluding women from direct combat roles does not necessarily ensure their survival.

While the biological production of a new generation requires more women than men because a few men can impregnate many women, the survival of our society with its culture relatively intact requires that just as many men as women survive. That is, the societal values of monogamous marriage and legitimate births prohibit mere biological reproductive solutions. Men's roles as parents in our society go way beyond mere biological fathering to include caretaking and socialization functions.

American women spend a very small proportion of their lives bearing and caring for young children, due to the processes of increased longevity, lower infant and child mortality, and smaller family size. One could still argue that the childbearing and child-rearing years for women coincide with the years when they would be most likely to be combat soldiers, but, women are starting their families later than used to be the case.[34] Furthermore, the health risks of women bearing children when they are relatively older (that is, twenty-five to forty years of age) have been substantially reduced through a variety of medical developments.

Some of the vocal opponents to women in combat point to historical and anthropological evidence that only men are the warriors in almost all societies that have existed or that exist now.[35] This is taken as proof that this is the way things ought to be; however, we must not confuse the way things have been with the way they must or should be. We must also not assume that what has been true for nonliterate, preindustrial societies is applicable to modern industrial societies. It is also the case that in almost all societies, men have had power over women, in some cases absolute power. Men have been the rulers and the property holders. Indeed, women have been viewed as property, and as war booty, not as citizens. Such 'tradition' must not be used as the basis for exclusion from combat.

Preservation of the Stereotypical Female Ideal

Excluding women from combat may help to ensure the preservation of certain aspects of our stereotype of the ideal woman. This stereotype has both psychological and structural components. On the psychological side, there are the personality traits that are the antithesis of the attributes of the ideal warrior. Excluding all women from combat roles can be seen as one way to ensure that some members of society will retain these characteristics. These traits may include: warmth, nurturance, helpfulness, passivity, sensitivity, compassion, submissiveness, dependence, understanding, and gentleness. If all members of society are eligible to be warriors, then these traits may have a lower probability of surviving. It is unclear whether these characteristics will survive anyway. If these traits are valued in our society, then we should ensure their existence to some degree in all members of society, especially our leaders. Since our leaders are overwhelmingly male, we should be seeking ways to prevent our boys and men, as well as our girls and women, from developing only the personality traits that are the polar opposites of the ones listed above. Currently, our socialization of children, especially boys, stresses dominance, aggressiveness, competitiveness, strength, independence, achievement, success, individuality, and so on. Of course, these traits are also valued. Perhaps our ultimate goal should be to encourage the development of both of these sets of traits in all members of our society, without regard to their being male or female.

The structural component of the stereotypical feminine ideal revolves around the role of housewife. Despite the fact that this role is currently played by only a minority of American women (and then only for a small proportion of their lives), it persists as a cultural ideal. Most women do become wives and mothers, but they are also employed members of the labor force, just as most men become husbands and fathers as well as workers. It has become increasingly normative for women to expect to work outside the home for most or all of their adult lives. The modal U.S. family pattern today consists of a husband and wife and children, with both parents in the labor force. We also have a growing number of families with other patterns, such as the single-parent family and the childless couple. The point is that the fulfillment of the stereotypical ideal of the working husband/father and the nonemployed housewife/mother is becoming rare.

Thus, to exclude women from combat roles on the grounds that such roles are incompatible with the role of housewife requires justification. We must be able to demonstrate that combat jobs are more incompatible with being a wife/mother than are other jobs. We must also be able to demonstrate that all women desire to be wives and mothers. We must also be able to demonstrate that combat jobs are more incompatible with being a wife/mother than they are with being a husband/father. We now have a situation in which we can require fathers to participate in combat, while not allowing any women to, regardless of their family responsibilities.

Preservation of the Stereotypical Male Ideal

Some resistance to allowing women in combat roles derives from the desire to preserve our cultural stereotype of the ideal man. One traditional way for men to prove they are masculine is through the role of warrior. The military in general, and combat in particular, is a masculine proving ground. If women are fully integrated into the military, then this arena loses this function. A young man cannot prove he is a man by doing something that young women can do.[36] The negative attitudes of men toward women in the military, especially in a traditionally all-male setting like ROTC and the academies,[37] can be attributed in large part to this desire to maintain the military as a mechanism for establishing adult male gender identity.

One important component of the stereotype of the ideal man, and of a male-dominated society, is the protection of women.[38] Men feel they have failed to live up to this ideal if they allow their women into combat. In addition, if women are members of combat units, then the men in the units may act to protect the women in ways that interfere with the functioning of the units.[39]

In assessing the degree to which male protectiveness of women is indeed a value in American society, the prevalence and tolerance of violence against women suggest that this ideal is often not attained. Women are often raped on the streets of our cities (not to mention on our college campuses) and we have a serious and widespread problem of wife abuse. The responses of government agencies and institutions of higher education to these problems indicate that protection of women is low on the list of priorities for financial commitment. The high incidence of such violence against women may indicate that women in combat also face the danger of physical attack by their fellow soldiers.

When wartime conditions prevail, the protection of women is given less emphasis. American military women have served in combat zones and, in 1945, the United States, with substantial public support, came very close to drafting civilian nurses because of a shortage of military nurses.[40] It is likely that wartime exigencies in the future would arouse public opinion in favor of women in offensive combat roles.

Public Opinion

Some of the underlying dynamics of public opinion on the issue of women in combat can be seen in the discussion above. That is, some or all of the considerations already discussed serve as the basis for many people's attitudes on both sides of the issue. As is the case for most issues of public policy, not all Americans are in a position to have access to all the information relevant to the issue of women in combat, and policy will not be determined by a popular referendum. Again like other public policy issues, however, public opinion is a force in shaping policy so we must look at the attitudes of the American public.

Two issues regarding women's service in the U.S. military have been included in public opinion polls. One is the question regarding assignment of women to combat roles, the other concerns compulsory military service for women. While these two issues are analytically distinct, they have often been intertwined by the wording of questions in public opinion surveys, both recently and in the past.[41]

A recent national survey of 560 Americans aged eighteen to twenty-four conducted by the Gallup organization included several questions on military registration and the draft. One of these questions covered women in combat: "If women are drafted, should they be required to take combat roles as men are, should they be given combat roles only if they volunteer for them, or should they not be eligible for them?" The distribution of responses, by the gender of respondents, was as follows:

	Male	Female
Given Combat Roles As Men	12%	9%
Only if Volunteer	61%	74%
Not Eligible	26%	16%

Clearly, a majority of the young men and women polled favor the inclusion of women in combat roles on a voluntary basis. However, this question starts with a situation of women being drafted. This same survey included two questions concerning military registration, one on registration of young men and one on registration of young women. The two questions were as follows: "Would you favor or oppose the registration of the names of all young men so that in the event of an emergency the time needed to call up men for a draft would be reduced?" and "Would you favor or oppose the registration of the names of all young women under these circumstances?" The percent of "favor" responses to these two questions were:

	Male	Female
Registration of young men	77%	73%
Registration of young women	54%	48%

Here we see less support for registering women for the draft than for registering men and less support for registering women than for allowing them to "take combat roles" if they are drafted.

We must keep in mind the international circumstances at the time this survey was conducted (Americans held hostage in Iran and Russian troops in Afghanistan) and the fact that this sample included only eighteen to twenty-four-year-olds and is, therefore, not representative of older Americans. However, the sample does represent the population most at risk of being drafted.

We can only speculate about what the responses would be to a question of whether women currently serving in the military should be allowed to volunteer for combat jobs. I would conjecture that a majority would favor such a voluntary assignment. I would also predict, on the basis of past surveys, that the following question would produce a majority of favorable responses among young people and among older Americans: "Would you favor allowing women to volunteer for combat jobs rather than requiring men to take such roles?" Another question which might be asked is: "Would you favor drafting young single women for combat roles rather than drafting young married men with children for such roles?" Such a question might well produce a majority of most groups in favor (except, perhaps, young single women).

The circumstances that prevail at the time a survey is conducted have a strong impact on the pattern of public response. During times of perceived national emergency, the public is more likely to favor sacrifices on the part of both men and women than during times where there is no perceived threat to national security.[42] The more imminent the threat, the greater the likelihood of public opinion favoring compulsory military service for men and women and voluntary assignment of women to combat roles. This would be especially true if distinctions are made among various types of combat jobs, as some types of combat jobs are likely to be seen as more appropriate for women than others.

Attitudes of Allies and Potential Adversaries

The decision regarding the assignment of American women to combat roles also requires consideration of how such an assignment would be viewed by our allies and by our potential enemies. Even if our military could be as effective with women in combat as with only men, the perception of our military effectiveness by allies and adversaries is crucial to our national security. If our military is viewed as weak because of the inclusion of women in combat roles, our international posture can be just as critically affected as if we truly were weak.[43]

On the other hand, our military can be seen as ineffective for reasons other than the roles of military women. The military's "crisis in command"[44] refers to men, not women. Much concern about weakness derives from perceived inferiority to the Soviet Union in weaponry. The current debate in the United States regarding the state of effectiveness of our all-volunteer force is being monitored by other nations. The increased reliance on female personnel is only part of this discussion. The attention given to the so-called low quality of male recruits, high attrition rates, low levels of individual commitment to the armed forces, nondeployability of troops, and shortages of personnel in our active duty forces and reserves probably contributes more to perceptions of weakness.

The argument has also been made that our potential enemies would be less likely to surrender to combat units that include women than to all-male units, and that this would prolong combat and increase casualties. The basis for this argument is unclear. Presumably it is based on the supposed views of women as inferior in the cultures of our enemies, thereby resulting in the loss of honor to men who surrender to armed forces containing women. Very little evidence is available either to support or refute this argument. A similar argument used to be offered as a basis for excluding women from regular patrol duty on domestic police forces. The experience of the last decade demonstrates that the presence of female police officers has not increased the danger to officers during arrests.[45] Indeed, in certain critical situations, it has had the opposite effect.[46] While the two types of situations are not totally comparable, this evidence is more convincing than the speculation on the other side.

CONCLUSIONS

The issue of whether to assign women to combat roles is a complex one that is too often oversimplified. Both individual and collective concerns are relevant. Military effectiveness is a goal; so is justice and civic responsibility. There are credible arguments on both sides that cut across any arbitrary analytical distinction between types of objectives. Values, attitudes, and emotions may not be based on rational analyses, but they too must be considered. The goal here has been to summarize the relevant arguments in such a way that they can be evaluated in light of our values and the evidence we can bring to bear on achieving our goals.

Discussions of the issue of women in combat, from all viewpoints, should be applied to policy decisions. Even if the short-range decision is to continue to exclude women from certain combat roles, the trend of social change in women's attributes and roles indicates that it is likely that such a policy will be untenable in the long run. Any assignments of women to combat jobs or combat units, or both, should not be made haphazardly, but rather with great forethought given to the conditions that will maximize the likelihood that these women will function effectively and their units will function as effective wholes. Our attention needs to be continually addressed to mustering all the wisdom and evidence available to guide us in specifying those optimum conditions.

NOTES

1. Grace M. King, "Women in Combat: The New Reality" (Paper presented at the meetings of the Inter-University Seminar on Armed Forces and Society, Chicago, Illinois, October 1980). See also Jeff M. Tuten, this volume, especially pp. 248–49.

2. Department of the Navy, Office of the Secretary, "SECNAV Instruction 1300.12" (April 18, 1979).

3. See, for example, M. D. Feld, "Arms and the Woman: Some General Considerations," *Armed Forces and Society* 4, no. 4 (August 1978): 557–68; David R. Segal, Nora Scott Kinzer, and John C. Woelfel, "The Concept of Citizenship and Attitudes toward Women in Combat," *Sex Roles* 3 (1977): 469–77.

4. Feld, "Arms and the Woman," p. 558.

5. Ibid., p. 559.

6. See, for example, Jeff Tuten, pp. 237–65, this volume; Seth Cropsey, "Women in Combat?" *The Public Interest* 61 (Fall 1980): 58–73; Richard A. Gabriel, "Women in Combat?" *Army* (March 1980): 45, 48–50, 52; William J. Gregor, "Women, Combat, and the Draft: Placing Details in Context" (Paper prepared for presentation to the West Point Senior Conference on Defense Manpower Planning, United States Military Academy, West Point, N.Y., June 5–7, 1980); James Webb, "Women Can't Fight," *The Washingtonian* (November 1979): 144–48, 273, 275, 278, 280, 282.

7. Dennis M. Kowal, "Nature and Causes of Injuries in Women Resulting from an Endurance Training Program," *The American Journal of Sports Medicine* 8, no. 4 (1980): 265–69.

8. Jack H. Willmore, "The Application of Science to Sport: Physiological Pro-

files of Male and Female Athletes," *Canadian Journal of Applied Sports Sciences* 4, no. 2 (1979): 103–15.

9. Frederick F. Andres, Jr., and C. Roger Rees, "Sex Roles in the Swimming Pool: Can Competitive Swimming Programs Reduce Stereotyping in Children?" *Proceedings of the AAHPERD Aquatics Council 3rd Annual National Aquatics Institute* (June 1980).

10. Barbara E. Bernstein, "Effects of Menstruation on Academic Performance among College Women," *Archives of Sexual Behavior* 6 (July 1977): 289–96; Jeanne Brooks, Diane Ruble, and Anne Clark, "College Women's Attitudes and Expectations concerning Menstrual-Related Changes," *Psychosomatic Medicine* 39 (September–October 1977): 288–98; Frances Y. Dunham, "Timing and Sources of Information about, and Attitudes toward, Menstruation among College Women," *Journal of Genetic Psychology* 117 (December 1970): 205–17; Barbara Sommer, "The Effect of Menstruation on Cognitive and Perceptual-Motor Behavior: A Review," *Psychosomatic Medicine* 35 (November 1973): 515–34.

11. For a review of the evidence in a variety of situations, see Nora Scott Kinzer, *Stress in the American Woman* (New York: Doubleday: 1979).

12. Irene H. Frieze et al., *Women and Sex Roles: A Social Psychological Perspective* (New York: W. W. Norton & Co., 1978), pp. 195–203; Robert R. May, "Mood Shifts and the Menstrual Cycle," *Journal of Psychosomatic Research* 20, no. 2 (1976): 125–30; Karen E. Paige, "Women Learn to Sing the Menstrual Blues," *Psychology Today* 7 (September 1973): 41–46; Diane N. Ruble, "Premenstrual Symptoms: A Reinterpretation," *Science* 197 (July 1977): 291–92; Sommer, "Effect of Menstruation."

13. Philip A. Kalisch and Margaret Scobey, "Female Nurses in American Wars: Helplessness Suspended for the Duration" (Paper presented at the meetings of the Inter-University Seminar on Armed Forces and Society, October 1980). *Armed Forces and Society: An Interdisciplinary Journal* (Spring 1982).

14. C. D. Johnson et al., "Women Content in the Army—REFORGER 77 (REFWAC 77)," Alexandria, Va.: U.S. Army Research Institute for the Behavioral and Social Sciences, Special Report S–7 (1978); U.S. Army Research Institute, "Women Content in Units Force Development Test (MAXWAC)," Alexandria, Va.: U.S. Army Research Institute (1977).

15. King, "Women in Combat"; Mattie B. Treadwell, *United States Army in World War II; Special Studies; The Women's Army Corps* (Washington, D.C.: Office of the Chief of Military History, Department of the Army, 1954).

16. Kalisch and Scobey, "Female Nurses in American Wars," p. 6.

17. Ibid., p. 15.

18. See, for example, Anne Eliot Griesse and Richard Stites, this volume pp. 61–84.

19. Peter B. Bloch and Deborah Anderson, *Policewomen on Patrol: Final Report* (Washington, D.C.: Police Foundation, May 1974); Judith Greenwald, Harriet Connolly, and Peter Bloch, *New York City Policewomen on Patrol* (Washington, D.C.: Police Foundation, 1974).

20. For a review of the literature, see Lynn H. Fox, Elizabeth Fennema, and Julia Sherman, *Women and Mathematics: Research Perspectives for Change,*

N.I.E. papers in Education and Work: Number Eight (Washington, D.C.: National
Institute of Education: 1977).

21. Jane M. Armstrong, "Achievement and Participation of Women in Mathematics: An Overview." Report of a two-year study funded by the National Institute
of Education, Report 10-MA-00 (Denver, Colo.: Education Commission of the
States, March 1980); John Ernest, *Mathematics and Sex* (Santa Barbara: University of California, 1976); Lynn H. Fox, "The Effects of Sex Role Socialization on
Mathematics Participation and Achievement," in Fox, Fennema, and Sherman,
Women and Mathematics; Elizabeth Haven, "Factors Associated with the Selection of Advanced Mathematics Courses by Girls in High School" (Ph.D. diss.,
University of Pennsylvania: 1971); Edith H. Luchins, "Women Mathematicians:
A Contemporary Appraisal" (Paper presented at the Annual Meeting of the Amer-
ican Association for the Advancement of Science, Boston, Mass.: 1976).

22. Patricia Lund Casserly, "An Assessment of Factors Affecting Female Participation in Advanced Placement Programs in Mathematics, Chemistry, and Physics." Report to the National Science Foundation (1975); Maita Levine, "Identifi-
cation of Reasons Why Qualified Women Do Not Pursue Mathematical Careers,"
Report to the National Science Foundation (1976); Luchins, "Women Mathematicians"; Donald D. Thompson, "Increasing Women in Science through Reshaping
Role Perception" (Interim Report to the National Science Foundation, 1976).

23. Armstrong, "Achievement and Participation of Women."

24. For a review of the evidence, see David H. Marlowe, "Cohesion, Anticipated Breakdown, and Endurance in Battle: Considerations for Severe and High
Intensity Combat" (Washington, D.C.: Walter Reed Army Institute of Research,
1980).

25. Johnson et al., "Women Content in the Army"; Joel M. Savell and Cecil D.
Johnson, "Predicting Company Performance from Percent Female in Support-
Type Army Units: A Second Report from the 'MAXWAC' Study" (Paper prepared
for presentation at the meeting of the American Psychological Association,
Montreal, Canada, September 1980); E. M. Schreiber and John C. Woelfel,
"Women in Men's Boots: Performance and Adjustment of Women in the Coed
American Army of the 1970s" (Paper presented at the meeting of the American
Sociological Association, Chicago, Ill., 1977); U.S. Army Research Institute,
"Women Content in Units Force Development Test"; John C. Woelfel, "Women
in the Army" (Paper presented at the Southwest Regional Conference of the Inter-
University Seminar on Armed Forces and Society, Dallas, Tex., 1978).

26. Cropsey, "Women in Combat?"; Gabriel, "Women in Combat?"

27. See, for example, Lucian K. Truscott IV, *Dress Gray* (New York: Fawcett
Crest, 1978). The psychological survival mechanisms used by this novel's protag-
onist, a West Point cadet, illustrate how being with women (and thinking about
women) functions as an escape from the world of the Academy.

28. Charles C. Moskos, Jr., "The American Dilemma in Uniform: Race in the
Armed Forces," *The Annals of the American Academy of Political and Social
Science* 406 (March 1973): 94–106.

29. Ibid., p. 96.

30. Yehuda Amir, "Contact Hypothesis in Ethnic Relations," *Psychological*

Bulletin 71, no. 5 (May 1969): 319–42; Rosabeth Moss Kanter, "Some Effects of Proportions on Group Life: Skewed Sex Ratios and Responses to Token Women," *American Journal of Sociology* 82, no. 5 (1977): 965–90.

31. Lois B. DeFleur, "Four Years of Sex-Integration: Changing Attitudes, Beliefs, and Interactions at the U.S. Air Force Academy" (Paper presented at the meetings of the Inter-University Seminar on Armed Forces and Society, Chicago, Ill., October 1980).

32. George H. Quester, "Women in Combat," *International Security* 1, no. 4 (Spring 1977): p. 88.

33. George Gilder, "The Case Against Women in Combat," *New York Times Magazine* (January 28, 1979), 29.

34. Current Population Reports, "Estimates of the Population of the United States and Components of Change: 1974 (with Annual Data from 1930)," Population Estimates and Projections Series P-25, No. 545 (Washington, D.C.: U.S. Government Printing Office, 1975); U.S. Department of Labor, *Handbook of Women Workers,* Women's Bureau Bulletin No. 294 (Washington, D.C.: U.S. Government Printing Office, 1969).

35. Gabriel, "Women in Combat?"; Gilder, "The Case Against Women in Combat."

36. Gabriel, "Women in Combat."

37. DeFleur, "Four Years of Sex-Integration"; Laurie Larwood, Eric Glasser, and Robert McDonald, "Attitudes of Male and Female Cadets toward Military Sex Integration," *Sex Roles* 6, no. 3 (June 1980), 381–90.

38. For discussions of protector roles in society, see Judith H. Stiehm, "Should Women Serve in Combat?" (Paper presented at the Southwest Regional Conference of the Inter-University Seminar on Armed Forces and Society, Dallas, Tex., 1978); Judith Stiehm, "Protectors and Defenders" (Paper presented at the meetings of the Inter-University Seminar on Armed Forces and Society, Chicago, Ill., October 1980).

39. See, for example, Cropsey, "Women in Combat?"; Gabriel, "Women in Combat?"

40. Kalisch and Scobey, "Female Nurses in American Wars."

41. Mady Wechsler Segal and David R. Segal, "Utilization of Women in the United States Military: Domestic and International Considerations" (Paper presented at the annual meeting of the International Studies Association, March 1980) summarize the questions asked and the public responses regarding drafting women; M. C. Devilbiss, "Women and Compulsory Military Service" (Paper presented at the annual meetings of the American Sociological Association, August 1980) includes results on some questions regarding women in combat.

42. See, for example, Devilbiss, "Women and Compulsory Military Service."

43. Gregor, "Women, Combat, and the Draft."

44. Richard A. Gabriel and Paul L. Savage, *Crisis in Command: Mismanagement in the Army* (N.Y.: Hill and Wang, 1978).

45. Bloch and Anderson, *Policewomen on Patrol.*

46. Greenwald, Connolly, and Bloch, *New York City Policewomen on Patrol.*

BIBLIOGRAPHICAL ESSAY

For a summary of the historical background of British, U.S., German and Russian women in World War II, see J. Cassin-Scott, *Women at War 1939–1945* (London: Osprey 1981). The best general introduction to women in the military, although outdated by five years when the present volume goes to print (a fairly long time for this volatile subject), is M. Binkin and S. Bach, *Women and the Military* (Washington, D.C.: The Brookings Institution, 1977), a scholarly and comprehensive overview of the main issues, written just before the major surge of female participation in the U.S. military. N. Goldman has written two thoughtful and suggestive articles: "Women in NATO Armed Forces," *Military Review* (1974): 72–82; and the widely cited "The Utilization of Women in the Armed Forces of Industrialized Nations," *Sociological Symposium* (Spring 1977): 1–23, which is one of the first attempts to relate female military participation with social, industrial, and political peculiarities. On related matters, see J. Klick, "Utilization of Women in the NATO Alliance," *Armed Forces and Society* 4, no. 4 (1978): 673–78. Two good journals for the intelligent reader are *Armed Forces and Society* and *Signs: Journal of Women in Culture and Society*. M. Feld, in his seminal "Arms and the Woman: Some General Considerations," *Armed Forces and Society* 4, no. 4 (1978): 557–68, relates the debate of women in combat to "the symbolism of civic culture and the values through which a state mobilizes its social resources." The same issue of this journal (pp. 695–716) contains a good bibliography by E. Hunter et al., "Women in the Military—An Annotated Bibliography." And see the recent *Weibliche Soldaten: Bibliographie zu einem Reizthema* [Female soldiers: bibliography of a sensitive subject] (Baden-Baden: Nomos Verlagsgesellschaft, 1981), compiled by E. Lippert and T. Rössler.

There is no major historical work on British women in the two world wars. F. Tennyson Jesse's 1917 work, *The Sword of Deborah: First-hand Impressions of the British Women's Army in France* (London: Heinemann, 1918) is very evocative, and A. Marwick's *Women at War 1914–1918* (London: Fontana, 1977) is the best interpretation of that war. E. Bigland's *Britain's Other Army* (London: Nicholson and Watson, 1946) and D. C. Wadge, ed., *Women in Uniform* (London: S. Low Marston, 1947), are interesting treatments of World War II, but a good historical and analytical synthesis still needs to be done. For the contemporary scene, see E. Ewing, *Women in Uniform* (London: Batsford, 1975) and C. Owen, ed., "The Future of Women in the Armed Services," in *Royal United Services Institute for Defence Studies* (RUSI), March 1978.

U. von Gersdorff has tried to encompass the experience of German women in both wars in her *Frauen im Kriegsdienst, 1914–1945* [Women in war service, 1914–1945] (Stuttgart: Duetsche Verlag-Anstalt, 1969). See also the recent work: E. Lippert and T. Rössler, *Mädchen in Waffen? — Gesellschafts-und sozialpolitische Aspekte weiblicher Soldaten in der Bundeswehr* [Young women in arms: social and socio-political aspects of female soliders in the German military] (Munich; Sozialwissenschaftliches Institut der Bundeswehr, 1980). The best work on World War II—and one of the best available works on women at war—is F. Seidler, *Frauen zu den Waffen: Marketenderinnen, Helferinnen, Soldatinnen* [Women to arms: sutlers, volunteers, female soldiers] (Koblenz: Verlag Wehr & Wissen, 1978). The story told there is supplemented in his *Blitzmädchen: die Geschichte der Helferinnen der deutschen Wehrmacht im Zweiten Weltkrieg* ["Blitzgirls": the history of the volunteers of the German Wehrmacht (German Armed Forces) during World War II] (Koblenz: Verlag Wehr & Wissen, 1979). For reviews of both see Jeff M. Tuten in *Armed Forces and Society* 8, no. 1 (Fall 1981). For those who do not read German, two good books are: J. Stephenson, *Women in Nazi Society* (New York: Harper and Row, Barnes and Noble, 1975) for the social and ideological background, and L. Rupp, *Mobilizing Women for War: German and American Propaganda, 1939–1945* (Princeton, N.J.: Princeton University Press, 1978).

There are as yet no comparable studies on the wartime experiences of women in France, Poland, Italy, and most other European countries, but a major monograph on Italian women in the resistance by J. Slaughter is expected in 1982.

The experience of women in Communist societies and in their military activities has captured much attention in recent years—and has partly helped stimulate studies of women in other parts of the world. The Soviet Union, being the most dramatic case has received the most attention. Two important background books, R. Stites, *The Women's Liberation Movement in Russia* (Princeton, N.J.: Princeton University Press, 1978) and G. Lapidus, *Women in Soviet Society* (Berkeley: University of California Press, 1979), help set the historical and the social-political stage for 1941. A fine treatment of the revolution and civil war is R. Johnson's "The Role of Women in the Russian Civil War (1917–1921)," *Conflict* 11, no. 2 (1980): 201–17. The major and indispensable work for World War II is V. Murmantseva, *Sovetskie zhenshchiny v velikoi otechestvennoi voine* [Soviet women in the great patriotic war] (Moscow: Mysl, 1974), with ample documentation. Although slanted, it is extremely detailed and informative on all branches in which women participated. In English see: R. Danysh, section on Soviet Union in "Women in Combat," Staff Support Branch, U.S. Army Center for Military History (unpublished) (Washington, D.C., 1978); J. Cottam "Soviet Women in Combat in World War II," in T. Yedlin, ed, *Women in Eastern Europe and the Soviet Union* (New York: Praeger, 1980), pp. 115–27; and A. Griesse, "The Mobilization of Soviet Women in World War II" (MA thesis, Georgetown University, Washington, D.C., 1980). For the current scene, see H. Scott, "Soviet Women in Uniform," *Air Force Magazine* (March 1976). For comparisons, see R. Stites, "Women and Communist Revolutions" in *Studies in Comparative Communism* (1982). In the same issue there is an article on "Women in the Yugoslav National Liberation Movement," by B. Jancar, the major authority on the subject. Another perspective is to be found in M. Reed, "The Anti-Fascist Front of Women and the Communist Party in Croatia," in the Yedlin volume cited above. For three representative Yugoslav works, see: M. Beoković, *Women Heroes* (Sarajevo: Svjetlost, 1967); R. Bujačhič, et al., *Žene Srbije u NOB* [Serbian women in the national liberation struggle] (Belgrade: Nolit, 1975); and D. Kovačević, *Women of Yugoslavia in the National Liberation War* (Belgrade: Jugoslovenski Pregled, 1977). For Vietnam: J. Werner, "Women in the Vietnamese Revolution," is in *Studies in Comparative Communism* (1982); R. Coughlin, *The Position of Women in Vietnam* (New Haven: Yale University Southeast Asia Studies, 1950) for background; N. Dinh, *No Other Road to Take* (Ithaca, N.Y.: Cornell University SEA Data, Gapaer, No. 102, 1976), a Vietcong woman's memoir and one of the few sources available in English; and *Women of Vietnam* (journal) a North Vietnamese publication, with the expected bias.

The Israeli and the Algerian struggles were two very different kinds of colonial wars. The latter has been very little written about, but see: F. Fanon, *A Dying Colonialism* (New York: Grove Press, 1968); D. Gordon, *Women of Algeria* (Cambridge, Mass.: Harvard University Press, 1968); Algeria. Wizarat al-Akhbar wa-al-Thaqafah. *The Algerian Woman* (Algiers: Ministry of Information and Culture, 1976); and the harrowing *Djamila Bonpacha: The Story of the Torture of a Young Algerian Girl During the Revolution* by S. de Beauvoir (New York: 1962). For the history of Algeria see: C. Ageron, Histoire de l'Algerie Contemporaire, 1830–1973 [History of contemporary Algeria, 1830–1973] (Paris: Presses l'Universitaires de France, 1973). For Palestine-Israel, a good introduction, with documentation, is N. Goldman and K. Wiegand, "The Utilization of Women in Combat: The Case of Israel," in M. Martin and E. McCrate, eds., *The Servants of Arms: Essays in Honor of Morris Janowitz*

(New York: The Free Press, 1982). Among the more useful titles are: A. Maimon, *Women Build a Land* (New York: Herzl Press, 1962); Y. Allon, *The Making of Israel's Army* (London: Vallentine Press, 1970); L. Hazelton, *Israeli Women* (New York: Simon and Schuster, 1977); E. Luttwak and D. Horowitz, *The Israeli Army* (London: Allen Lane, 1975); G. Cohen, *Woman of Violence: Memories of a Young Terrorist, 1943–1948* (New York: Holt, Rinehart and Winston, 1966); V. Dickerson, "The Role of Women in the Defense Force of Israel." Individual Research Project, U.S. Army War College: Alexandria, Va.: 1974); and R. Rabinowitz, "On the Women's Recruitment" in Y. Gelber, *Volunteerism in the Yishiv* (Ph.D. diss., Hebrew University, Jerusalem, Doctoral Dissertation, 1977).

Space does not permit more than the enumeration of a few of the more important titles for the nations treated in Part II of this book. Denmark: K. Fleron, *Kvinder i modstandskampen* [Women in the resistance movement], 2nd ed. (Odense: Sirius Risskov, 1964). Sweden: K. Törnqvist, *Kvinnor i försvaret* [Women in the defense forces] Psykologoskt försvar nr 79 [Psychological defense] (Stockholm: Beredskapsnämnden för psykologiskt försvar, 1977), a report about a public opinion poll on women in the Swedish Defense Forces, carried out at the request of the National Board of Psychological Defense Planning; and Riksförbundet Sveriges Lottakårer [The national organization of Sweden's Lotta Corps], *Svensk Lottarörelse: 1924–1949* [The Swedish Lotta Movement] (Stockholm, 1949). Greece: (no author given), *La femme grécque au combat* [Greek women in combat] (a monograph, privately printed: Athens, 1975); and C. Safilios-Rothschild, "The Options of Greek Men and Women," *Sociological Focus* 5, no. 2 (1972): 71–83. Japan: T. Havens, "Women and War in Japan, 1937–1945," *American Historical Review* 80 (October 1975); *Defense of Japan* (Tokyo: Defense Agency of the Government of Japan, 1979); *The Status of Women in Japan* (Tokyo, 1979).

The American literature is much larger and, of course, more accessible. For one important segment of the historical background, for the U.S. Army, see M. Treadwell, *The Women's Army Corps (U.S. Army in World War II: Special Studies)* (Washington, D.C.: Office of the Chief of Military History, Department of the Army, 1954). This history has been continued by Col. B. Morden, *The Women's Army Corps, 1945–1978* (The U.S. Army Historical Series) (Washington, D.C.: Office of the Chief of Military History, Department of the Army, 1983). The best treatment of women in the U.S. military that deals with the contemporary situation as well as the historical background is *Women in the Military* (Novato, Calif.: Presidio Press, 1982) by J. Holm, retired U.S. Air Force Major General. Among numerous general works on the question of women's role in the U.S. armed forces that have surfaced during recent years, see: N. Goldman, "The Changing Role of Women in the Armed Forces," *American Journal of Sociology* 78 (January 1973): 892–911; U.S. Office of the Assistant Secretary of Defense, *Use of Women in the Military* (Washington, D.C.: Department of Defense, 1977); K. Arbogast, "Women in the Armed Forces: A Rediscovered Resource," in U.S. Air Force Academy, Department of Political Science, J. Endicott and R. Stafford, eds., *American Defense Policy* (Baltimore, Md.: Johns Hopkins University Press, 1977), 489–95; G. Quester, "Women in Combat," *International Security* 1, no. 4 (Spring 1977): 80–91, presents a brief overview of that specific problem. On the major lines of the controversy on women in combat, see these three representative works: R. Gabriel, "Women in Combat: Two Views," *Army Magazine* (March 1980), which sets the problem; G. Gilder, "The Case Against Women in Combat," *New York Times Magazine* (January 28, 1979), which presents the case against; and S. Blank, "Combat is Not for Men Only," *Civil Liberties* (April 1980), which presents the case for. For related and useful data see K. Coffey, *Manpower for Military Mobilization* (Washington, D.C.: American Enterprise Institute for Public Policy Research, 1978). The specific situation of women at the U.S. Air Force Academy is set forth in J. Stiehm, *Bring Me Men and Women* (Berkeley: University of California Press, 1981); for that of women in the U.S. Army, see H. Rogan, *Mixed Company* (New York: Putnam, 1981). On the question of drafting women, a subject closely related to the combat issue, see: M. Devilbiss, "Women and the Draft," in L. Hoffman and M. Anderson, eds., *The Military Draft* (Stanford, Calif.: The Hoover Institution, 1981).

INDEX

ABOUT THE
CONTRIBUTORS

DJAMILA AMRANE was educated at the University of Algiers. She is a Senior Lecturer in the Department of History at the University of Science and Technology in Algiers and she is a Researcher at the National Center of Historical Studies of Algiers. Her doctoral dissertation is on Algerian women in the war of National Liberation.

ANNE R. BLOOM received her Ph.D. from Bryn Mawr College. A consultant psychologist, she is affiliated with the Center for Advanced Studies in Education, The Graduate School and University Center, City University of New York. She is most recently involved in research on women in the Israel Defense Force.

JAMES BROWN is Professor of Political Science, Southern Methodist University. His doctoral degree is from the State University of New York at Buffalo. He has had many articles published on national security policy, and civil-military relations in Greece.

WILLIAM J. DUIKER who received his Ph.D. from Georgetown University is Professor of East Asian History at the Pennsylvania State University. Formerly a foreign service officer with the Department of State, he served at the U.S. Embassy in Saigon in 1964 and 1965. Among his many writings are *The Rise of Nationalism in Vietnam, 1900–1941* (Cornell, 1976) and *The Communist Road to Power in Vietnam* (Westview, 1981). His current area of interest is in revolutionary movements in Asia.

NANCY LORING GOLDMAN is a Research Associate at the University of Chicago, Inter-University Seminar on Armed Forces and Society. In addition to her many publications on women in the military in the United States and other industrialized nations, she is a coeditor of *The Social Psychology of Military Service* (Sage, 1976). She has recently completed a three-year study of women in combat.

ANNE ELIOT GRIESSE received her M.S. in 1980 from Georgetown University in the field of Russian Area Studies, and she has studied Russian language and Soviet culture in Moscow. She is presently employed in Washington, D.C., as a research analyst for the Department of Defense. Her current research projects include a bibliographical study of Soviet women fighter pilots in World War II.

BARBARA JANCAR received her doctorate from Columbia University and is Professor of Political Science and Director, Global Studies Program at State University of New York College at Brockport. Among her many publications are *Women under Communism* (Johns Hopkins University Press, 1978) and *Czechoslovakia and the Absolute Monopoly of Power: A Case Study of Political Power in a Communist Country* (Praeger, 1971). She was the State University of New York exchange Professor with the University of Moscow, March 1980–September 1981.

GEORGE H. QUESTER who received his Ph.D. at Harvard Univesity is Chairman of the Department of Government and Politics at the University of Maryland. His major teaching and research interests lie in military strategy and American foreign policy and he is most recently the author of *Offense and Defense in the International System* (Wiley, 1976). In 1980–1981 he was a Visiting Professor at the National War College, Washington, D.C.

CONSTANTINA SAFILIOS-ROTHSCHILD was born in Greece and received her Ph.D. at the Ohio State University. She is Professor of Human Development at the Pennsylvania State University. Among her many published works are *Women and Social Policy* (Prentice-Hall, 1974) and *Sex Role Socialization and Sex Discrimination: Synthesis and Critique of the Literature* (National Institute of Education, 1979).

MADY WECHSLER SEGAL is an Associate Professor in the Department of Sociology at the University of Maryland and a Research Sociologist in the Department of Military Psychiatry at the Walter Reed Army Institute of Research. She received her Ph.D. from the University of Chicago. She is author of several published articles on the military, including "Women in the Military: Research and Policy Issues," *Youth and Society* 10, no. 2. Her current research is concerned with the integration of women in the U.S. Army and problems of army families.

HENNING SORENSEN was educated at the University of Copenhagen and the University of Arhus. Among his published works are *What Is Economic Democracy? (Hvad er ekonomisk demokrati?)* (København, 1972) and *The Military Profession in Practice and Theory* (Nyt fra Samfundsvidenskaberne, 1981). He is currently involved in research on "the military profession and civil control in Denmark."

RICHARD STITES received his Ph.D. from Harvard University. He is Associate Professor of History, Georgetown University. In addition to the many articles that he has written, he is author of *The Women's Liberation Movement in Russia: Feminism, Nihilism, and Bolshevism, 1860–1930* (Princeton University Press, 1978). He is writing a book on *Utopia and Experiment in the Russian Revolution.*

KURT TÖRNQVIST holds a doctorate in sociology from the University of Lund, Sweden. Since 1964 he has served as Research Director at the National Board of Psychological Defense Planning in Stockholm. He has written many reports on subjects such as attitudes towards society and defense, mass communication, propaganda and psychological warfare.

JEFF M. TUTEN is an operations analyst specializing in mobilization manpower at SRA in Arlington, Virginia. Previously he served for twenty-five years as an infantry officer in the U.S. Army. He received an M.A. degree in history from Radford College. In addition to his other writings on manpower issues, he is coauthor of *Building a Volunteer Army: The Fort Ord Contribution* (Department of Army, 1975).

KARL L. WIEGAND received his Ph.D. from The Ohio State University. For most of his twenty-six-year career in the U.S. Air Force he managed and evaluated behavioral science research; three years were spent as air attaché at the U.S. embassy in Tokyo. He is now a behavioral science consultant in Camp Springs, Maryland. He is coauthor of several works on women in the military and was the major consultant to a three-year research project on women in combat.